AF905460

Research Series on the Chinese Dream and China's Development Path

Project Director
Xie Shouguang, President, Social Sciences Academic Press

Series editors
Li Yang, Vice president, Chinese Academy of Social Sciences, Beijing, China
Li Peilin, Vice president, Chinese Academy of Social Sciences, Beijing, China

Academic Advisors
Cai Fang, Gao Peiyong, Li Lin, Li Qiang, Ma Huaide, Pan Jiahua, Pei Changhong, Qi Ye, Wang Lei, Wang Ming, Zhang Yuyan, Zheng Yongnian, Zhou Hong

Drawing on a large body of empirical studies done over the last two decades, the *Research Series on the Chinese Dream and China's Development Path* seeks to provide its readers with in-depth analyses of the past and present, and forecasts for the future course of China's development. Thanks to the adoption of Socialism with Chinese characteristics, and the implementation of comprehensive reform and opening, China has made tremendous achievements in areas such as political reform, economic development, and social construction, and is making great strides towards the realization of the Chinese dream of national rejuvenation. In addition to presenting a detailed account of many of these achievements, the authors also discuss what lessons other countries can learn from China's experience. This series will be an invaluable companion to every researcher who is trying to gain a deeper understanding of the development model, path and experience unique to China.

More information about this series at http://www.springer.com/series/13571

Yanzhong Wang

Social Security in China: On the Possibility of Equitable Distribution

SSAP

Springer

Yanzhong Wang
The Institute of Ethnology
and Anthropology
Chinese Academy of Social Sciences
Beijing
China

ISSN 2363-6866 ISSN 2363-6874 (electronic)
Research Series on the Chinese Dream and China's Development Path
ISBN 978-981-10-5642-0 ISBN 978-981-10-5643-7 (eBook)
DOI 10.1007/978-981-10-5643-7

Jointly published with Social Sciences Academic Press

Not for sale outside the Mainland of China (Not for sale in Hong Kong SAR, Macau SAR, and Taiwan, and all countries, except the Mainland of China).

Library of Congress Control Number: 2017947448

© Springer Nature Singapore Pte Ltd. and Social Sciences Academic Press 2017
This work is subject to copyright. All rights are reserved by the Publishers, whether the whole or part of the material is concerned, specifically the rights of translation, reprinting, reuse of illustrations, recitation, broadcasting, reproduction on microfilms or in any other physical way, and transmission or information storage and retrieval, electronic adaptation, computer software, or by similar or dissimilar methodology now known or hereafter developed.
The use of general descriptive names, registered names, trademarks, service marks, etc. in this publication does not imply, even in the absence of a specific statement, that such names are exempt from the relevant protective laws and regulations and therefore free for general use.
The publishers, the authors and the editors are safe to assume that the advice and information in this book are believed to be true and accurate at the date of publication. Neither the publishers nor the authors or the editors give a warranty, express or implied, with respect to the material contained herein or for any errors or omissions that may have been made. The publishers remains neutral with regard to jurisdictional claims in published maps and institutional affiliations.

Printed on acid-free paper

This Springer imprint is published by Springer Nature
The registered company is Springer Nature Singapore Pte Ltd.
The registered company address is: 152 Beach Road, #21-01/04 Gateway East, Singapore 189721, Singapore

Series Preface

Since China's reform and opening began in 1978, the country has come a long way on the path of Socialism with Chinese Characteristics, under the leadership of the Communist Party of China. Over thirty years of reform efforts and sustained spectacular economic growth have turned China into the world's second largest economy, and wrought many profound changes in the Chinese society. These historically significant developments have been garnering increasing attention from scholars, governments and the general public alike around the world since the 1990s, when the newest wave of China studies began to gather steam. Some of the hottest topics have included the so-called "China miracle", "Chinese phenomenon", "Chinese experience", "Chinese path" and the "Chinese model". Home-grown researchers have soon followed suit. Already hugely productive, this vibrant field is putting out a large number of books each year, with Social Sciences Academic Press alone having published hundreds of titles on a wide range of subjects.

Because most of these books have been written and published in Chinese, however, readership has been limited outside China—even amongst many who study China—for whom English is still the lingua franca. This language barrier has been an impediment to efforts by academia, business communities and policy-makers in other countries to form a thorough understanding of contemporary China, of what is distinct about China's past and present may mean not only for her future but also for the future of the world. The need to remove such an impediment is both real and urgent, and the *Research Series on the Chinese Dream and China's Development Path* is my answer to the call.

This series features some of the most notable achievements from the last 20 years by scholars in China in a variety of research topics related to reform and opening. They include both theoretical explorations and empirical studies and cover economy, society, politics, law, culture and ecology, the six areas in which reform and opening policies have had the deepest impact and farthest-reaching consequences for the country. Authors for the series have also tried to articulate their visions of the "Chinese Dream" and how the country can realize it in these fields and beyond.

All of the editors and authors for the *Research Series on the Chinese Dream and China's Development Path* are both long-time students of reform and opening and recognized authorities in their respective academic fields. Their credentials and expertise lend credibility to these books, each of which having been subject to a rigorous peer-review process for inclusion in the series. As part of the Reform and Development Program under the State Administration of Press, Publication, Radio, Film and Television of the People's Republic of China, the series is published by Springer, a Germany-based academic publisher of international repute, and distributed overseas. I am confident that it will help fill a lacuna in studies of China in the era of reform and opening.

Xie Shouguang

Acknowledgements

After a relatively short gestation period, the *Research Series on the Chinese Dream and China's Development Path* has started to bear fruits. We have, first and foremost, the books' authors and editors to thank for making this possible. And it was the hard work by many people at Social Sciences Academic Press and Springer, the two collaborating publishers, that made it a reality. We are deeply grateful to all of them.

Mr. Xie Shouguang, president of Social Sciences Academic Press (SSAP), is the mastermind behind the project. In addition to defining the key missions to be accomplished by it and setting down the basic parameters for the project's execution, as the work has unfolded, Mr. Xie has provided critical input pertaining to its every aspect and at every step of the way. Thanks to the deft coordination by Ms. Li Yanling, all the constantly moving parts of the project, especially those on the SSAP side, are securely held together, and as well synchronized as is feasible for a project of this scale. Ms. Gao Jing, unfailingly diligent and meticulous, makes sure every aspect of each Chinese manuscript meets the highest standards for both publishers, something of critical importance to all subsequent steps in the publishing process. That high-quality if also at times stylistically as well as technically challenging scholarly writing in Chinese has turned into decent, readable English that readers see on these pages is largely thanks to Ms. Liang Fan, who oversees translator recruitment and translation quality control.

Ten other members of the SSAP staff have been intimately involved, primarily in the capacity of in-house editor, in the preparation of the Chinese manuscripts. It is time-consuming work that requires attention to details, and each of them has done this, and is continuing to do this with superb skills. They are, in alphabetical order: Mr. Cai Jihui, Ms. Liu Xiaojun, Mr. Ren Wenwu, Ms. Shi Xiaolin, Ms. Song Yuehua, Mr. Tong Genxing, Ms. Wu Dan, Ms. Yao Dongmei, Ms. Yun Wei and Ms. Zhou Qiong. In addition, Xie Shouguang and Li Yanling have also taken part in this work.

Ms. Song Yuehua is the SSAP in-house editor for the current volume.

Our appreciation is also owed to Ms. Li Yan, Mr. Chai Ning, Ms. Wang Lei and Ms. Xu Yi from Springer's Beijing Representative Office. Their strong support for the SSAP team in various aspects of the project helped to make the latter's work that much easier than it would have otherwise been.

We thank Ms. Chen Xiaoshuang for translating this book. The translation and draft polish process benefited greatly from the consistent and professional coordination service by Beijing Moze International Culture Development Co., Ltd. We thank everyone involved for their hard work.

Last, but certainly not least, it must be mentioned that funding for this project comes from the Ministry of Finance of the People's Republic of China. Our profound gratitude, if we can be forgiven for a bit of apophasis, goes without saying.

Social Sciences Academic Press
Springer

Contents

Prologue: Regulating Income Distribution to Promote Equity and Inclusivity

The Social Security System is a governmental policy tool which could regulate income distribution effectively and promote stability and harmony in a society. As an integral part of the modern system of social governance, the Social Security System plays a prominent role in promoting equality and justice, realizing inclusivity and enhancing solidarity and social cohesion amongst members of society. Therefore, no modern society could afford to disregard the development of Social Security System.

The Role of the Social Security System in Regulating Income Distribution in China

The widening income disparity in China, since the initiation of reform and opening-up, has become a pressing issue that has triggered conflict and debate amongst social circles on the direction of the reform of the Chinese economy. The regulation of income distribution and the narrowing of income disparity between the wealthy and the poor have always been important agendas of the Chinese government under market economy. However, not much impressive results have been achieved. Taxation and the Social Security System are the key institutional arrangements to amend and regulate the income distribution during redistribution in the country. In many countries, compared with taxation, the Social Security System is a more effective way in regulating income distribution. China has seen gradual development of the Social Security System, especially the enlargement of the Social Security Fund in the last decade. The role of the Social Security System in levelling the income disparity in China has begun to be realized.

The Subsistence Allowance System exerts direct influence on the income distribution over a population through the allocation of basic allowances and financial stipends to citizens whose annual income fall below the established poverty line. Through this, the issues of income disparity and poverty are addressed in a systematic and targeted manner. In the early days of the People's Republic of China, the "Five Guarantees System" was established in China for the purpose of providing financial and economic aid to the elderly, the disabled, and children under 16 in the countryside who were incapable of work and whose subsistence was deemed insufficient. In the 1990s, the Subsistence Allowance System was established. As of 2011, 75.825 million urban and rural residents enjoyed subsistence security benefits, in addition to the 5.51 million rural residents that were supported by the "Five Guarantees System" and the 1,93,000 urban residents who had no "source of income, capability of work and/or legal guardian". A total of RMB 144.93 billion was disbursed to support low-income urban and rural residents through social security policies such as the "Five Guarantees System". Accordingly, the income of a beneficiary of the Social Security System increased by RMB 1782 on average, which went directly to improving their standard of living.

A fair and equitable Social Security System plays a significant role in narrowing income disparity. The Social Security System covering pension insurance, medical insurance, work-related injury insurance and unemployment insurance amongst other types of Social Insurance is a risk-sharing mechanism and a deferred compensation system that could be an effective way in tackling income disparity, through the utilization of the law of large numbers. In many countries, the expenditure for Social Insurance like those aforementioned accounted for 1/3 and even 1/2 of fiscal expenditures and 1/5 or even 1/3 of GDP. These levels of fiscal expenditures on Social Insurance have a major impact on income distribution in these countries. According to a survey of beneficiaries conducted in China, income from Social Insurance accounted for 14.5% of the per capita income of the respondents and constituted a significant part in the income of urban and rural beneficiaries and the only source of income for some senior citizens. It has been estimated that Social Insurance income has decreased China's Gini Coefficient by 0.04, suggesting that Social Insurance is playing an active role in bridging the income gap. However, within the system there appears to be significant benefit disparity amongst the beneficiaries and over-high proportion of the fund-accumulation system. This presents counter regulatory to the income distribution. Studies suggest that the intervention of the Pension Insurance System has actually widened the income gap between urban and rural residents. The Housing Fund, Enterprise Annuity, Employee Pension and Medical Insurance have also contributed to the overall income disparity.

Social Welfare ensures that low-income residents can have equal access to public services, which in turn theoretically reduce the income disparity. Social Welfare is therefore not only an integral part of the Social Security System, but also a key part of public services. Apart from the benefits received through the Social Security System by disadvantaged members of society, such as old people, children, women, the disabled and entitled groups, Social Welfare also includes public services enjoyed by the general public as well, such as public education and public health services. Social Welfare guarantees low-income groups equitable access to public services, which means the government purchases public goods for them by utilizing public finance as a means of income transfer. The more comprehensive a country's Social Welfare is, the higher the ability of a government to transfer and regulate the income disparity in a population. Of course, it is important to note that experiences and lessons from other countries with high Social Welfare have demonstrated that lack of proper consideration of economic efficiency and capacity makes Social Welfare considerably unsustainable. In the case of China, Social Welfare remains to be highly insufficient, so enormous efforts are still needed for its development.

Realizing Equity, Inclusivity and Effective Social Governance Through a Bigger Role of the Social Security System

In 2015, the 5th Plenary Session of the 18th CPC Central Committee proposed a new development plan for China's economic growth. The plan stipulates the role of Innovation, Coordination, Green Development, Openness and Inclusivity in driving economic growth for the country. This new development plan proposes a new objective and orientation of the Social Security System in China. The goals of Social Security System are to firstly play a role in building a moderately prosperous society and to act as a safeguard against economic turmoil. Secondly, more efforts were needed to deepen the reform to develop a fairer and more sustainable Social Security System, and let it play the role of promoting equity, inclusivity and social governance.

Firstly, the Social Security System must be able to cover all members of society. The rapid development of industrialization and urbanization has substantially improved the living conditions of humankind. However, there are also people that are left behind and are suffering economic hardships. It happens in any society, even the highly developed ones. These disadvantaged sectors of society are unable to alleviate their hardships without external intervention. Social Welfare is an institutional policy that helps alleviate the problem of these aforementioned sectors. Its role is not only to provide for basic subsistence income, but also to provide residents with a sense of security so as to allow them to participate in a social life without distractions. This is a fundamental condition for a society to realize effective governance.

Secondly, the Social Security System needs to provide support for the government to perform social management and offer public services. As state governance systems continuously improve, the boundary between the government, markets, and the society becomes clearer. In most countries, governments have reduced their functions of governance to macroeconomic regulation, market supervision, social management, and public services. Unlike other types of public services, Social Welfare is a system that is difficult to realize proper self-regulation based on market mechanism. Therefore, in most countries, the Social Security System is a legal institution implemented with government mandate and oversight. In these countries, Social Welfare takes up not only a substantial part of government expenditure, but also the largest amount of manpower and material resources.

Thirdly, as an important measure of macroeconomic regulation, the Social Security System should play an active role in guiding consumption and regulating supply. With economic development, many countries have gradually extended the role of Social Welfare from economic security to a tool to improve the quality of life and the value of human capital of its residents. Social security expenditure is expanding in terms of scale and becomes a policy instrument affecting macroeconomic. In the perspective of the government, Social Welfare is a part of fiscal expenditure (or fiscal expenditure in a broad sense), laying restraints on the government's financial resources. For a society, these expenditures are a part of social consumption, laying restraints on production capacity of a society. In the perspective of individuals, Social Welfare is a part of income affecting their decisions on labour supply decisions and consumption patterns and thus becoming a significant variable for national macroeconomic regulation.

Fourthly, the Social Security System should be utilized as a tool to enhance social solidarity and stability. A feature of a modern society is the promotion of independence and self-determination. As a result, Chinese social traditions based on family kinship and regional allegiances for group reliance are gradually weakening. This individualization of the society is being supported by the Social Security System, where mutual assistance and the distribution of responsibilities are emphasized instead of the traditional Chinese social traditions. Though the public have certain interest in national interests, they care more about issues closely related to their own interest, such as retirement pension, health care and employment. Social Security is not only a major issue for the democratic election of a country, but also a basic system bonding individuals.

Lastly, the Social Security System could also show the advantages of the socialist institution with Chinese features. Against the backdrop of globalization, the competition amongst countries is not only reflected in its productivity, but also at the standard of living and a welfare system. Under transnational capital flows, though excessive welfare may become a negative factor for the competitiveness of a country's labour costs, a sound Social Security System may reflect a profound respect for human capital and constitutes a more competitive factor other than just cheap labour. It could be seen through comparison that highly competitive countries tend to be those who enjoy a mature Social Security System, where people enjoy a better quality of life.

The 13th Five-Year Plan (2016–2020) is going to be a critical period for the goal of building a Moderately Prosperous Society, where the Social Security System will play an important role. According to *Suggestions on Making the 13th Five-Year Plan for Economic and Social Development* issued by the CPC Central Committee, during the 13th Five-Year Plan, a more equitable and sustainable Social Security System should be established. The development of the Social Security System will not only focus on the expansion of coverage and the enlargement of the Welfare Fund, but also priority the refinement of the equitability, sustainability and inclusivity of the Social Security System.

The effective functioning of the Social Security System depends heavily on the improvement of the governance of the system itself. The development of the Social Security System should also include the modernization of its governance, where there should be legal support, government supervision, professionalization and wide social participation. The creation of a legal framework for the Social Security System should be accelerated, so as to allow for the designation of administrative functions and the establishment of professional and independent Social Welfare agencies to provide convenient and efficient welfare services. A multiple evaluation system of the social security should be established, which covers the governments, executive agencies, professional agencies and the society. The Social Security System should also encourage public participation in the supervision and evaluation of the system, and actively conduct satisfaction surveys amongst all of its stakeholders.

More external support and reform motivation are needed for continuous improvement of the Social Security System. We should further step up fiscal input in social security. There should be an established mechanism designed to adjust benefits according to the needs of urban and rural, low- and middle-income groups, as well as central and western regions. We should further improve the institutional design, especially the design of the public service and basic security system, mainly focusing on the needs of middle- and low-income population and poverty-stricken population. National coordination should be pursued to realize an urban employee's basic pension insurance system. Provincial coordination should also be realized for the urban employee's basic medical insurance. Other components of the basic Social Insurance System should also be coordinated and enhanced accordingly.

In the implementation of the Social Security System, proper adjustment of the premium rate of benefit should be established. It is also suggested that the option of having a flexible benefit rates should also be explored. The development plan also proposes increased social coordination and the reduction of the contribution ratio of personal accounts in the system, whilst improving the level of benefits targeting low-income groups through establishing a differentiated benefit adjustment mechanism based on the gradual improvement of overall benefits. Furthermore, it has been proposed that further streamlining of the system's bureaucracy should be placed in order to bring about greater equity and efficiency in the operation of the system. It has also been suggested that more effort needs to be channelled towards the development of the Social Security System with a particular focus on the Social Welfare such as education and health care.

To summarize, the Social Security System is a basic economic system and a modern system of social governance for modern countries. With the promotion of industrialization and democratization, its function and influence will eventually expand to various fields of social and economic management and become an integral part of the state's system of governance. Therefore, it should be given more attention to ensuring that the Social Security System is more equitable and sustainable. Additionally, Social Welfare should be based on China's domestic needs and requirements and not just the replication of foreign systems of Social Welfare. As a vehicle for the promotion of social equity and inclusivity, the Social Security System will play a prominent role in building a modern China.[1]

---

[1]This prologue is based on "Bring into Play the Role of Social Security in Regulating Income Distribution" (*People's Daily*, April 3, 2013), with some additional contents.

Chapter 1
The Development of China's Social Welfare System

It was acknowledged in the 17th CPC National Congress that China should channel substantial effort into constructing projects for improving the livelihood of the people by building a harmonious socialist country, which "ensures that all citizens enjoy the right to education, employment, medical care, elderly care, and housing". These projects cover employment, education, medical care, housing, social security, social welfare and social work, which are all contained within the social welfare system in a broad sense. The social welfare system in this report mainly covers social security affairs such as social assistance, labor insurance, social insurance, medical insurance, and social welfare sponsored mainly by the government. For the purpose of discussing the relationship between the social welfare system and urbanization, this report also covers aspects of the social welfare system in a wider sense such as education and housing.

1.1 The Preliminary Establishment of the Chinese Social Welfare System Framework

The establishment and development of the social welfare system in modern China occurred during two periods before and after reform. However, the beginning of the second period was not exactly equivalent to the year 1978 when the reform of the economic system began. The first period mainly consisted of three stages, namely the establishment of a framework (1949–1956), uneven development (1958–1978) and reconstruction (1978–1985). The first stage was a phase in which China's socialist economic system gradually became established, and large-scale industrial construction was conducted under the planned economic system. The building of economic infrastructure and a relatively stable social environment enabled the recovery and development of cities and accelerated urbanization. In 1949, China only had an urban population of 57.65 million, accounting for 10.164% of the total

© Springer Nature Singapore Pte Ltd. and Social Sciences Academic Press 2017
Y. Wang, *Social Security in China: On the Possibility of Equitable Distribution*,
Research Series on the Chinese Dream and China's Development Path,
DOI 10.1007/978-981-10-5643-7_1

national population, which rose to 99.49 million and 15.139% respectively in 1957. However, after the establishment of the household registration system upon the promulgation of the "Regulations of the People's Republic of China on Household Registration" in 1958, the spontaneous migration of rural households to cities for employment and living was no longer permitted, which, in addition to the great fluctuation in economic growth during the "Great Leap Forward" and the "Cultural Revolution", seriously constrained the urbanization of the rural population. During the period between 1958 and 1978 the total urban population (not of rural households) increased from 107.21 million to 172.45 million, with a growth of about 65 million people. However, because these people mainly resulted from the natural growth of the urban population, the urbanization rate during the same period experienced weak growth increasing from 16.125% in 1958 to 17.192% in 1978, with a decline in urbanization over certain periods (1963, 1965–1972, and 1974).

Though the seeds of the welfare system of modern society preceded the process of urbanization driven by industrialization, the process of urbanization was undoubtedly one of the key factors leading to the formation and development of the welfare system of modern society. Land and family played the role of an economic and social safeguard in agricultural society with little fluctuation. However, this is impossible for urban residents, who without land or stable employment and with increasingly smaller family sizes, instead, require a more stable and socialized social security and benefit system to address such social risks as illness, old age and unemployment. In fact, the establishment of a socialized social security and benefit system began the very first day the People's Republic of China (PRC) was founded.

The PRC was confronted with several basic problems in its early days: first, the settlement of wounded and disabled soldiers; second, unemployed urban residents who had been seriously affected by an extended period of war and turmoil; and third, a large number of victims of various natural disasters. The "Common Program of the Chinese People's Political Consultative Conference" promulgated in 1949 stated that "dependents of those who have given their lives for the revolution and of members of the revolutionary forces, who are in need, shall receive preferential treatment from the state and from society. The people's government shall make appropriate arrangements for disabled or retired servicemen who participated in the revolutionary war, providing them with means of livelihood or occupations." This provision, in effect, laid a foundation for China to establish a social security system for servicemen centering on veteran benefit and placement in China. As for the large number of unemployed workers in cities, the government relied mainly on the development of production for job placements as well as providing temporary relief to families living in extreme poverty. In 1950, the Government Administration Council introduced the "Instruction on Relieving Unemployed Workers", and the Ministry of Labor introduced the "Interim Measures for Relieving Unemployed Workers", which served as prototypes for a modern unemployment insurance system to be established in China. In 1951, the Government Administration Council promulgated the "Regulations of the People's Republic of China on Labor Insurance", which, after two revisions in 1953 and 1956, comprehensively established a labor insurance system suitable for urban employees. This system, which resolved the main risks and concerns of urban workers, was one of the most fundamental social systems meeting the demands of urbanization, and therefore became the most important of all social security systems established in the early years of the PRC.[1] Besides the labor insurance system established for enterprise employees, the state gradually established systems such as "medical services at state expenses" and "retirement and resignation" for employees in government departments and public institutions. As to victims of natural disasters spread across rural areas, the PRC established guidelines for disaster relief from the very first day it was founded to take up the responsibility for social relief. In December 1949, the Government Administration Council promulgated the "Instruction on Disaster Relief", and established the Central Disaster Relief Committee to handle disaster relief throughout the country. This responsibility was later succeeded by the Ministry of Internal Affairs (currently the Ministry of Civil Affairs) and has continued to the present as long-term work and basic work for China's social relief system. In addition to the social relief system, China established a "five guarantees system" addressing the elderly, disabled and children under 16 in rural areas, incapable of working and whose subsistence is not guaranteed in the "Constitution on Advanced Agricultural Cooperatives" adopted in 1956. During this period, the central government or relevant departments issued a series of regulatory documents addressing problems such as employment benefits, social welfare services, welfare factories and allowances for those living in straitened circumstances. Over several years' of continued effort, the PRC preliminarily established a basic framework for relieving poverty-stricken urban and rural residents as well as victims of natural disasters, focusing on labor insurance for enterprise employees, supplemented by veteran benefits and placements and state guarantees for public employees.

1.2 Uneven Development of China's Social Welfare Services

In the two decades between 1958 and 1978, China's social security and welfare system was constantly developing and expanding along with a zigzag process of socialist economic construction. In view of the construction of the social insurance system, a major development was initiated with the establishment of the employees' retirement pension system. In 1957 and 1958, the State Council introduced the "Interim Regulations on the Retirement Treatment of Workers and Employees" and the "Interim Regulations on the Resignation Treatment of Workers and Employees" to establish a retirement pension system for enterprise employees and workers. However, as large-scale industrialization was at the heart of its inception, old-age

[1]Zheng Gongcheng et al., *China's Social Security System: Change and Evaluation*, China Renmin University Press, 2002, p. 4.

security was not a serious problem. Due to the ups and downs of the political environment and the economic development at the time, certain new characteristics appeared in the construction of the social security system, particularly reflected in the rapid development of health and education.

The development of healthcare security and healthcare services during this period greatly improved the health of all citizens. By using the establishment of the planned economic system for mass mobilization and vigorously developing the patriotic health campaign, China established an urban-rural triple healthcare service network and an urban-rural healthcare security system consisting of the free healthcare system, the labor healthcare system and the cooperative healthcare service. These covered the overwhelming majority of the population. Meanwhile, the government, through planning and budgeting, strictly controlled the conduct of public hospitals. In addition to drug pricing, a mechanism to balance medical care and drugs was established to ensure that the medical service system "provided basic medical services to all people in the country at a low cost".[2] Despite the failure of a backward economy to relieve China from the shortage of medical services and drugs, the development of medical security and health services greatly improved the health of urban and rural residents, and life expectancy rose from 34 years of age in the early days after the PRC was founded to over 60 years of age.

Meanwhile, the development of education services improved people's level of education. Education occupies an important position in the social welfare system. Despite the historical tradition of valuing education in China, literate and educated people often accounted for a very small portion in the total population. In 1949, 80% of the population of China was illiterate, the enrollment rate of elementary schools and junior middle schools was only 20 and 6% respectively, and there were only 117 thousand students in institutes of higher education.[3] The education of the urban and rural population was continuously improved by vigorously developing education services and with the campaign for wiping out illiteracy. In the second national census, those with college education background amounted to 2.8715 million, 2416 times that of 1949; the number of people receiving elementary and secondary education also enjoyed a huge growth. However, the illiterate population above 13 years of age still accounted for 38% of the total population. The educational cause was subjected to a tremendous blow during the "Cultural Revolution", with a significant decline in the quality of higher education, however elementary and secondary education still saw substantial development. According to the third national census in 1982, the ratio of illiterate and semi-illiterate members of the population was reduced from 38.11% in 1964 to 23.15%, while the number of people who received elementary and secondary education rose substantially.

---

[2]Liu, Xiaomei (2009). The Reform of China's Social Security System: Direction and Comments. In Yoshinori Hiroi and ShenJie (Eds.), *The Social Security System in China and Japan: Comparison and Reference* (p. 55). Beijing: China Labor and Social Security Press.

[3]CPC Party Group of the Ministry of Education: People's Education Builds a Solid Foundation for China: Great Achievements in the Development and Reform of Education in New China over Six Decades, *Qiu Shi*, Vol. 19, 2009.

However, the development of the social security and welfare systems during this period was influenced by frequent abrupt changes in the political environment, the economic plan system and economic and social policies. With regards to China's social welfare system, several institutional changes during this period exerted tremendous and far-reaching effects: First, household registration systems were established. To safeguard the implementation of the national industrialization strategy and prevent the free migration of a huge rural population to cities and towns, the state established the household registration system in urban and rural areas in 1958. This classified the population of China into rural and non-rural households. The establishment of the household registration system artificially divided China's social welfare system and labor market into two blocks, urban and rural, resulting in a typical "binary social" system on the basis of the "binary economy" of a developing country. Second, the social security system became unit-based and closed. During the "Cultural Revolution", the economy and social management became locked in turmoil. In 1968, the Ministry of Internal Affairs, which was in charge of social relief and social welfare, was removed, the Labor Union responsible for labor insurance affairs was paralyzed and the labor department became impaired. As a result, the government had difficulties maintaining the effective operation of the social security system. In February 1969, the Ministry of Finance issued "Opinions on the Reform of Several Systems in the Financial Work of State-Owned Enterprises", which provided that the drawing of labor insurance funds all be suspended in state-owned enterprises, and the labor insurance premiums originally spent as labor insurance funds be converted to enterprises' non-operating expenditures. From then on, the social security system was only able to rely on a number of units and organizations for maintenance, "labor insurance was deprived of the coordination mechanism to turn it into an enterprise or unit security system", while the monopoly of such social affairs by urban enterprises and institutions expanded rapidly. As a result, social security, to a very large extent, turned into "a self-enclosed and unit-based system".[4] In connection with the household registration system and the unit security system were the system of commodity price allowance, the system of public housing and the system of unit welfare for urban residents. The commodity price allowance was for urban residents, while public housing and unit welfare were mainly provided to employees in urban state-owned enterprises and institutions. The lack of adequate price flexibility and supply stimulus led to serious shortage of various goods, especially housing. Social relief thus became very limited, only addressing extremely impoverished people "without economic income, labor capacity or supporters" and disaster-stricken people. Third, China at that time believed unemployment did not exist under the socialist system in place and did not admit the presence of unemployment; therefore no unemployment insurance system was established at that time.

---

[4]Zheng Gongcheng et al., *China's Social Security System: Change and Evaluation*, Renmin University of China Press, 2002, p. 7.

1.3 The Recovery, Adjustment and Pilot Reform of China's Social Welfare Services

During this period, the construction of China's social welfare system underwent three phases: the recovery and adjustment stage (1978–1986), the exploratory reform stage (1986–1993) and the pilot reform stage for the combination of social pooling and individual accounts (1993–1997).

(1) The recovery and adjustment of the social security system. The Third Plenary Session of the Eleventh CPC Central Committee held at the end of 1978 marked the start of a new era of reform and opening-up in China. This year is generally taken as the starting point for the reform of the economic system. However, for the social security system, the Third Plenary Session of the Eleventh CPC Central Committee did not mean the beginning of reform, as the system had largely recovered and reconstruction had taken place for some time by then. In 1978, the State Council promulgated the "Interim Measures of the State Council on Assisting Old, Weak, Sick and Disabled Cadres" and the "Interim Measures of the State Council Concerning the Retirement and Resignation of Workers", which restored the provisions on retirement benefits. During the same year, the Ministry of Civil Affairs and the Ministry of Finance re-issued the "Measures on the Management and Use of Pension and Relief Operating Expenses", which led to the recovery of the pension and relief system; in 1979, the pension standard was raised. However, the significant increase of retiring employees led to an increasingly serious conflict between old and new enterprises with uneven burdens caused by the increase in retirement payments and the direct payment by enterprises. To address the imbalance of social security burdens among state-owned enterprises, a pilot reform on social pooling for retirement and resignation payments for employees of state-owned enterprises was conducted in a number of cities and counties in Guangdong, Jiangsu, Fujian and Liaoning provinces in 1984. The scope of pooling was limited mainly to state-owned enterprises in municipal or county first-level administrative areas. In line with the principle of ratifying expenditures according to revenues on a balanced budget with a small surplus, uniform collection and issuance of old-age pensions and the uniform management of employees' old-age support were implemented. To relieve the problem of too rapid an increase of medical expenses, some enterprises conducted pilot reforms on lump-sum payments of medical expenses with regards to labor insurance medical care. In 1985, the "Proposal of the CPC Central Committee on Formulating the Seventh Five-Year Plan for the National Economy and Social Development" clearly put forward, for the first time, the concept of "social security", and gave the umbrella name of social security system to such systems as social insurance, social welfare, social relief and veteran benefits and placement.

(2) The exploratory reform of the social security system. The main developments of the social security system during this period included: the establishment of an unemployment insurance system. With the gradual deepening of the reform of state-owned enterprises, enterprises urgently needed to establish an independent employment mechanism and had to establish a social security system for employees' withdrawal. In 1986, the State Council promulgated the "Interim Regulations on Unemployment Insurance of Employees in State-owned Enterprises", which introduced the labor contract system and the unemployment insurance system in state-owned enterprises. The applicable scope of unemployment insurance was small, as the unemployment insurance system was implemented only among newly recruited contract workers. During the reform of the old-age pension insurance system, the "Interim Regulations on the Implementation of the Labor Contract System among State-owned Enterprises" issued by the State Council in 1986 stated: an enterprise shall submit 15% of the total wages of workers into the labor contract system as an old-age pension fund for contract workers, and such workers shall also submit 3% of their standard wages as old-age pension premiums. This was the introduction of individual premium payments into China's social insurance system. In 1991, the State Council issued the "Decision on the Reform of the Old-age Insurance System of Enterprise Employees", which stated that social pooling for retirement pay be implemented, with a gradual transition from municipal and county pooling to provincial pooling. Meanwhile, the conception of multi-level old-age support was put forward for "gradually integrating basic old-age insurance with enterprises' supplementary old-age insurance and employees' individual savings old-age insurance". Besides local pooling, some industries also attempted to implement pooling in the old-age insurance industry. By 1993, 11 industries had implemented pooling for the old-age insurance industry. To gradually establish a socialized old-age support system in rural areas, the Ministry of Civil Affairs implemented rural social old-age insurance pilot projects in rural areas in 1986, and promulgated the "Basic Plan for Rural Social Old-age Insurance at County Levels (for trial implementation)" in 1992, which marked the inception of the rural social old-age insurance system. With regards to medical security, some cities conducted various forms of reform on the free medical care system and the labor medical system successively. To overcome the difficulty of a single enterprise paying employees' medical expenses, some cities started to implement social pooling for medical expenses of enterprise employees with serious illnesses, and some places implemented social pooling for the medical expenses of retirees, in an attempt to relieve enterprises from the difficulty of paying medical expenses for employees who suffered from serious illness. On the whole, the reform of the social security system at this stage, which was mainly for the purpose of supporting the reform of state-owned enterprises, was only attempted at a local level, without fundamentally affecting the old system for social security.

(3) Pilot reform for the combination of social pooling and individual accounts. In 1993, the Third Plenary Session of the Fourteenth CPC Central Committee, in the "Decision on Several Issues Concerning the Establishment of the Socialist Market Economic System", acknowledged the social security system to be an important part for the construction of China's socialist market economic framework, marking the transition of the reform of China's social security system from supporting the reform of state-owned enterprises to serving the development of a socialist market economic system. The "Decision on Several Issues Concerning the Establishment of the Socialist Market Economic System" also proposed that an employees' basic old-age insurance system and basic medical insurance system by "integrating social pooling and individual accounts" be established according to China's national conditions, for which a diverse number of pilot reform projects were conducted. In 1995, the State Council launched two reform plans for the local development of pilot projects of a new old-age insurance system. Plan I was inclined towards focusing on individual accounts, while Plan II was inclined towards focusing on social pooling. Each place selected different plans for their respective pilot projects. Some places even managed to invent a Plan III and a Plan IV. As a result, such projects were not uniform, provoking great controversy. With regards to the reform of the medical security system, the State Council selected Zhenjiang, Jiangsu Province and Jiujiang, Jiangxi Province for conducting pilot projects in 1994. The two cities successively formulated and implemented a new mode of medical insurance "combining social pooling and individual accounts," this expanded the scope for the implementation of medical social insurance, established a stable fund raising mechanism, enhanced socialization of medical insurance and brought the rapid increase of medical expenses under control.[5] The coverage of pilot projects gradually expanded. During this period, development was achieved in the construction of other social security projects. In 1994, the Ministry of Labor promulgated the "Provisional Measures for Maternity Insurance of Enterprise Employees", which stated that social pooling shall also be implemented for maternity insurance.[6] In 1996, the Ministry of Labor introduced the "Provisional Measures for Work-related Injury Insurance of Enterprise Employees", with which the work-related injury social insurance system was gradually developed. Some cities established the system of minimum subsistence for urban residents, gradually expanding the coverage from "households of the five guarantees system" to all members of society who lived under the "minimum living standard". During this period, the rural social old-age insurance system also saw rapid developments.

[5]Wang Yanzhong, ShenZhiyu and Du Yingfen, The "Double Jiang" Mode in the Reform of the Medical Insurance System, *China Industrial Economics*, Vol. 7, 1999.

[6]Pan Jintang, The Social Security System for Females in China: Evolution and Evaluation, in Zheng Gongcheng et al., *China's Social Security System: Change and Evaluation*, Renmin University of China Press, 2002, p. 281.

1.4 From Unit Security to Social Security: "Three Lines of Security" and "Two Guarantees"

Since the 1990s, China has been confronted with the increasingly serious problem of unemployment, laid-off workers and urban poverty. Alongside the constant rise of urban employment during this period, the number of traditionally employed persons (urban employees) fell continuously. The number of urban employees was reduced from its largest point in 1995 by 44.16 million to its smallest in 2003, (while a small uptrend began in 2004). The major factor attributing to the sharp reduction of the number of urban employees was the laying off of employees in state-owned enterprises and collective enterprises in the course of restructuring the economic system and adjusting the economic structure. In a short period of over ten years, the number of jobholders in state-owned and collective units was reduced by 77.84 million (the number of employees dropped by 75.34 million). This adjustment of the economic and employment structure is the largest of its kind in the history of mankind. The years of 1997 and 1998 after the outbreak of the economic crisis in Asia were the two years which saw the most drastic adjustment of the economic and employment structures in China, during which 32.39 million jobholders in state-owned and collective units were laid-off (including 31.93 million employees). The way in which to address such a severe peak of unemployment became a formidable challenge facing the Chinese government.

China, in the course of restructuring the economic system and adjusting the economic structure, implemented a certain number of reforms on the traditional unit-based security system. From the 1990s onwards, China began to define the reform of the unit security system and gradually developed a socialized social security system. The "Decision on the Reform of the Old-age Pension System of Enterprise Employees" promulgated in 1991 initiated the reform of the old-age insurance system for employees in state-owned enterprises. From 1993 onwards, some cities gradually established a system of minimum subsistence for urban residents with wider coverage and higher guarantee standards than the "Five Guarantees" relief system. In the "Decision on Several Issues Concerning the Establishment of a Socialist Market Economic System", such reform attempts were defined as establishing a multi-level social security system commensurate with the socialist market economic system, including the social insurance system and the social relief system etc. Centering on the above objectives, the Chinese government conducted pilot reforms on the basic old-age insurance system and the basic medical insurance system for urban employees in the early 1990s, and gradually established the unemployment insurance system ("waiting for work" was changed to "unemployed" in 1994, and it was not until 1999 that the unemployment insurance system was officially established), work-related injury insurance, maternity insurance and the system of minimum subsistence for urban residents were established. However, these newly established social security systems, which were small in scale, could hardly address all of the security needs of such large numbers of laid-off employees from state-owned and collective enterprises at one time. For example, of the 5.53 million registered unemployed people and 8.15 million laid-off employees nationwide in 1996, only 3.31 million people could receive unemployment insurance payments and benefits, accounting for only 24% of all laid-off employees in that year; in 1997, only 3.19 million people could receive unemployment insurance payments and benefits, accounting for only 26% of all the laid-off employees in that year. In 1996 and 1997, the urban residents receiving subsistence allowances totaled only 850,000 and 880,000 respectively, far fewer than the population stricken by poverty (totaling about 20 million). As for weak enterprises with difficulties which did not participate in the basic old-age insurance scheme, their retirees could not receive any or the full amount of old-age pension from the basic old-age insurance system. Thus, the unemployment insurance system, the system of minimum subsistence for urban residents, and the basic old-age insurance system for enterprise employees in their preliminary forms could only partly resolve the severe problems of unemployment, urban poverty as well as the timely and full payment of old-age pensions.

These problems were not only related to the basic life and immediate interests of tens of millions of people, but were also directly related to social stability and to the crucial tasks of economic system transformation and economic structure adjustment in the context of an economic crisis in Asia. Special policies had to be implemented over special periods. The "Three Lines of Security" were launched against these backdrops.

The Three Lines of Security mean the following three systems: basic living allowance for laid-off employees of state-owned enterprises, unemployment insurance and the system of minimum subsistence for urban residents, of which the most unique was the basic living allowance for laid-off employees of state-owned enterprises.

"Laid-off employees" was a special term coined in the 1990s in China. Despite the fact that laid-off employees were found in the early 1990s, it was not until 1997 that China started to publish the number of laid-off employees each year successively from 1997. From 1996 to 2000, the total number of laid-off employees was close to 10 million a year, far exceeding the number of registered unemployed persons. The annual amount of laid-off employees from state-owned enterprises, who constituted the bulk of laid-off employees, also exceeded the number of registered unemployed persons. Therefore, the significance of successfully ensuring the subsistence of laid-off employees from state-owned enterprises was no better than the establishment of an independent unemployment security system. This was a transitional measure with Chinese characteristics. To complete the task of downsizing for enhancing efficiency, the state provided several main preferential policies to laid-off employees from state-owned enterprises. Laid-off employees could receive a basic living allowance and their former enterprises were obliged to buy varied kinds of social insurance for them, and in the case that they were re-employed or self-employed they were entitled to certain preferential policies such as tax reduction or exemption. Preferential treatment regarding industrial and commercial registration, and credit preference was also given. The prerequisite for any laid-off employee to receive the above security was that they should enter the re-employment service center, which was a custodian agency for laid-off employees, funded by public finance, enterprises and society (unemployment insurance), including an annual subsidy of about RMB 10 billion from state revenues. According to policy regulations, laid-off employees should sign an agreement upon entering the "center" and could remain at the "center" for a period of three years at most. This was because the labor relationship with their respective enterprises had to be terminated after three years, and those failing to be re-employed would be transferred to unemployment insurance. Thanks to stable funding, the subsistence of laid-off employees was secured, and the number of people with security accounted for about 95% of the total number of laid-off employees in state-owned enterprises. The re-employment service center was not only responsible for the subsistence of laid-off employees from state-owned enterprises but also actively conducted re-employment training and provided job referral services so that 1/3-1/2 of laid-off employees were re-employed.

In the course of establishing a subsistence security system for laid-off employees, China rapidly improved the unemployment insurance system and the system of minimum subsistence for urban residents as top priorities in the establishment of a socialized social security system. In January 1999, the State Council introduced the "Regulations on Unemployment Insurance", which changed "insurance for those awaiting employment" to "unemployment insurance" and "relief payment for those awaiting employment" to "unemployment insurance benefits"; the coverage of unemployment insurance expanded from state-owned enterprises to various urban enterprises and institutions, the proportion of payment of unemployment insurance premiums was raised (the proportion paid by the employer increased from 1% of the total salary to 2%), an individual payment was added (1% of the individual's salary), and the payment standard and terms of unemployment insurance benefits were provided for. The standard of unemployment insurance benefits was lower than the local minimum wage and higher than the minimum subsistence level of local urban residents, and the period in which one could receive payment was no longer than 24 months. The "Interim Regulations on the Collection of Social Insurance Premiums" promulgated at the same time further defined the coverage and payment obligors of unemployment insurance, to ensure the affordability of unemployment benefits. The promulgation and implementation of the "Regulations on Unemployment Insurance" provided institutional and funding security for laid-off employees "leaving the center".

Meanwhile, to settle the problems regarding livelihood of many poverty-stricken urban residents, such as laid-off workers, people waiting for work, and old people with a long period of retirement, in September 1997, the State Council promulgated the "Circular on Establishing the System of Minimum Subsistence for Urban Residents Throughout the Country", which required that this system be established in all cities and county seats nationwide by the end of 1999. On the basis of summarizing the work experience of various places in establishing the minimum subsistence system, the State Council introduced the "Regulations on the Minimum

Subsistence for Urban Residents" in September 1999, which specified the relief principle of the minimum subsistence system, providing full relief to impoverished people "without income, labor capacity or supporters" according to the minimum subsistence standard and making up for the gap between a family's average per capita income and the local minimum subsistence standard for those urban residents with regular income. To effectively address the difficulties faced by impoverished citizens, the state raised the standard of the minimum subsistence level and fiscal support. By March 2000, 3.01 million impoverished urban residents were covered by the minimum subsistence system, including 2.36 million enterprise employees, unemployed and retired persons (accounting for 78% of the total population covered by security).

In order for the three guarantee systems (basic living allowance for laid-off employees of state-owned enterprises, unemployment insurance and minimum subsistence for urban residents) to function effectively, the State Council launched a series of policies and regulations for establishing and improving the social security system from 1997 to 1999. These systems, together with the Three Lines of Security, became important measures for resisting the impact of the Asian economic crisis in 1997, boosting domestic demand and curbing deflation, and supporting the reform of state-owned enterprises. To make sure that the above regulations and measures played an effective role, the government further defined the policy of "Two Guarantees". This guaranteed that laid-off employees from state-owned enterprises entering the re-employment service center could receive their basic living allowance on time and that the center would pay social insurance premiums on their behalf and also guaranteed that the basic old-age pensions for enterprise retirees in the old-age insurance plan be issued on time and in full.

The policy of "Three Lines of Security" and "Two Guarantees" made a great contribution to China's coping successfully with the unemployment and lay-off peak in the mid and late 1990s. In the year 2000, for example, 3.3 million unemployed people in China received unemployment insurance benefits, about 6.5 million laid-off employees of state-owned enterprises received living allowance, and over 3 million poor urban residents enjoyed the minimum subsistence allowance. These people amounted to over 12 million, accounting for about 6% of the total number of urban citizens in employment. Of them, the number of people receiving unemployment insurance benefits and living allowances for laid-off employees was close to 10 million, exceeding the total number of laid-off and unemployed persons in cities by 60%. Thus, the basic living conditions of the above-mentioned poorer members of society was well guaranteed, social stability was maintained, and economic system restructuring and economic structure adjustments were facilitated. This made a positive contribution to China's coping with the difficult situation of a substantial decline in exports and sluggish economic growth in the aftermath of the Asian economic crisis, resulting in the recovery of high-speed growth of China's economy and to China's preparation for its accession to the WTO.

1.5 Gradually Establishing the Basic Framework of a Modern Social Security System

From 1997 onwards, with the construction of the social security system, China accelerated the formulation and implementation of laws and regulations on social insurance, social assistance, social welfare and rural social security, which marked the transition of the social security reform from pilot reforms to institutional construction. With over ten years of work, the basic framework of a modern social security system was preliminarily established.

With regards to old-age insurance, the State Council introduced the "Decision on Establishing a Uniform Basic Old-age Insurance System for Enterprise Employees" in July 1997, which unified the payment ratios of enterprises and individual employees, unified the scale of individual accounts, and unified the measures for the calculation and payment of basic old-age pensions, marking the start of the unification stage of basic old-age insurance for urban enterprise employees in China. In 2005, the policy for insurance participation and the premium payment of urban self-employed individuals and laborers of flexible employment was unified,[7] the method for calculation and payment of basic old-age pensions was reformed, and the pilot scope of fully funding individual accounts which began in Liaoning Province in 2001 was expanded. Meanwhile, the state actively developed enterprise annuity, promoted the reform of social old-age insurance systems in government departments and public institutions as well as in rural areas, and explored the establishment of an old-age insurance system for rural areas, land-requisitioned farmers and rural migrant workers in cities.

In terms of medical security, the State Council promulgated the "Decision on Establishing a Basic Medical Insurance System for Urban Employees" in 1998, which defined the mode of combining social pooling and individual accounts for basic medical insurance and provided that all employees in urban units should partake in basic medical insurance. To cope with the diverse forms of employment, the coverage of basic medical insurance extended to all employed people in cities in 2003 and 2004. To address the medical security problems of urban residents, choosing not to be employed, pilot projects on the basic medical insurance system for urban residents began in 2007. The pilot implementation of new rural co-operative medical care in the second half of 2003 covered 2679 counties (only 50 counties were not covered), and 810.4 million rural residents (accounting for 91% of the total rural population). Meanwhile, the state sponsored the establishment of medical subsidies for civil servants and subsidies for large-sum medical bills, enterprise supplementary medical insurance and urban and rural medical assistance systems.

---

[7]From 2001, pilot projects on substantiating personal accounts started in Liaoning; by the end of 2006, such pilot projects had been conducted in 11 provinces and regions nationwide, and a personal accounts fund of RMB 48.5 billion had been substantiated. See Basic Conditions of Social Insurance in China, *China Labor Insurance News*, November 30, 2007.

In terms of unemployment security, the State Council promulgated the "Regulations on Unemployment Insurance" in 1999, which marked the gradual transition of China's unemployment security system towards a law-based track. The coverage of unemployment insurance began to expand from state-owned enterprises to all urban enterprises and public institutions including state-owned enterprises, private enterprises and other enterprises. The unemployment insurance system, together with the subsistence security system for laid-off employees and the minimum subsistence system for urban residents established at that time, constituted the "three lines of security" for unemployed people in cities, especially the large number of laid-off workers, and played an active role in addressing the laying-off of a large number of redundant employees in state-owned enterprises during the period of system transformation and structural adjustment.

In terms of work-related injury and maternity insurance, the State Council promulgated the "Regulations on Work-related Injury Insurance" in 2003, which established the basic framework of China's work-related injury insurance system by stating that all types of enterprises, institutions and non-profit organizations must establish a work-related injury insurance system for their employees, that the work-related injury insurance premiums shall be paid by employers and the system of combining work-related injury prevention, work-related injury compensation and work-related injury rehabilitation shall be practiced. During the same period, the participation rate continued to rise and coverage of maternity insurance continued to expand. Especially worth mentioning was the establishment and development of the system of minimum subsistence for urban and rural residents. In 1993, Shanghai took the lead in exploring the establishment of a system of minimum subsistence for urban residents. This Shanghai experiment was promoted nationwide by the Ministry of Civil Affairs in 1995. The State Council issued the "Circular on Establishing the System of Minimum Subsistence for Urban Residents Nationwide" in 1997 and the "Regulations on Minimum Subsistence for Urban Residents" in 1999, which provided that urban residents whose per capita family income was lower than the standard of minimum subsistence may apply for minimum subsistence benefits. Meanwhile, to resolve the problems of residents covered by subsistence security in children's education, medical care, housing and heating etc., China gradually established medical aid, educational aid and housing aid systems.[8] In 2006, the State Council revised the "Regulations on the Support of People Covered by the Five Guarantees System" implemented in 1994, which brought the fund for such support into the fiscal budget. In 2007, the State Council decided to establish the system of minimum subsistence in rural areas nationwide and established a new national strategy of poverty reduction in China's rural areas (the original strategy focused on poverty relief by productive development). From 2003 onwards, China promulgated regulations such as the "Measures for the Management of Aid for Vagrants and Beggars in Cities" (2003) and the "Regulations on the Management of

[8]Tang Jun, Urban and Rural Subsistence Allowance System: History, Status Quo and Future, *Red Flag Manuscript*, Vol. 18, 2005.

Public Emergencies", while the disaster emergency coping mechanism and the disaster relief systems have been gradually improved.

The social security management mechanism has been gradually improved. In August 1998, the State Council issued the "Circular on Relative Issues Concerning the Delegation of Provincial and Industrial Pooling of Basic Old-age Insurance for Enterprise Employees to Local Management", which resolved the long-term conflict resulting from the compartmentalization of industrial pooling and local pooling. The Ministry of Labor and Social Security which was established in 1998[9] is responsible for the centralized management of old-age insurance, medical insurance, unemployment insurance, work-related injury insurance and maternity insurance for urban enterprise employees and rural social old-age insurance. In 1999, the State Council promulgated the "Interim Regulations on the Collection and Payment of Social Insurance Premiums", which provided for the scope of collection and payment, management of collection and payment, supervision, inspection and punishment concerning social insurance premiums, thus gradually improving the social insurance system. The level of old-age insurance pooling continued to rise. By the end of 2006, 13 provinces and municipalities had implemented provincial pooling. To address the pressure from fund payments that might follow a future aging population, the state started to establish a national social security fund of strategic reserves from the year 2000, and had accumulated about RMB 500 billion by the end of 2007.

1.6 Developing a Modern Social Welfare System

At the Seventeenth National Congress of the Communist Party of China held in 2007, the report delivered by Hu Jintao on behalf of the CPC Central Committee clearly put forward the objectives of "ensuring that all citizens enjoy the right to education, employment, healthcare and elderly care, and housing", which were taken as basic requirements in the improvement of people's livelihood and the construction of a harmonious society. Compared with past reforms on the social security system, these objectives had richer connotations, which were tantamount to a new conception for the establishment and development of a modern social welfare system. The social security system is only a preventive measure addressing a survival crisis, while the modern social welfare system is more comprehensive, equitable and sustainable, as it is a more proactive security measure and a people-based strategic measure meeting the requirements of the scientific outlook on development and promoting coordinated development of the economy and society. The establishment of a modern social welfare system not only stresses risk

---

[9]In 2008, the new central government administration combined the Ministry of Personnel and the Ministry of Social Security into the "Ministry of Human Resources and Social Security", for the further unified management of national social security affairs.

prevention but also emphasizes comprehensive security and advocates social co-construction and all-round sharing. Only when a sound education security system is established and compulsory education is not subject to the restriction of family income can the objective of "education for all" be realized for school-age children; only when a sound employment security and unemployment insurance system is established can the objective of "making work pay" be realized; only when a medical security system, an old-age security system, and a housing security system shared by all are established can the objective of "all people enjoying the right to medical care, old-age support and housing" be realized.[10]

Since the Seventeenth CPC National Congress, some new developments have been achieved in the construction of the modern social welfare system upon the existing basic framework of the social security system. First, new steps have been taken in the equalization of the public service system. Compared to an excessive emphasis on "industrialization", "commodification" and "market-orientation" in the fields of social development such as education, health and housing, more emphasis is laid on the equalization of basic public services by realizing indiscriminate nine-year compulsory education in urban and rural areas nationwide, vigorously implementing the fiscal transfer payment system, and improving the capabilities of government departments in less developed regions to provide public services in attempts to provide various equalized basic public services to all of the people in China. Second, the reform of urban-rural household registration systems has deepened, and coordinated urban and rural development was advocated. According to the new national conditions of industrialization and urbanization of China and the new stage of development of the national economy, the development approach of "supporting agriculture with industry and promoting rural development with urban development" has been put forward, with more stress on the support of agriculture and the benefits for farmers so as to promote the more rapid development of the rural social welfare cause. Third, new measures have been adopted in social relief, the construction of rural social security and the reform of medical and health services. Social relief, as a point of progression in coordinating the urban and rural social security systems, was widely developed nationwide in 2007. The next step is to construct a comprehensive relief system. In 2008, the Ministry of Human Resources and Social Security promulgated the "Guiding Opinions on Developing Pilot Projects of New Rural Social Old-age Insurance", and extensively solicited opinions from the general public. In August 2009, the State Council held a working conference on the pilot projects of "national new rural social old-age insurance", which put forward that "new rural insurance" be experimented in 10% of the counties nationwide in 2009 and then the pilot project should be gradually expanded to basically realize full coverage by 2020. Through long periods of multi-party demonstration, China promulgated the implementation plan for the reform of the medical and health system in 2009, which took the improvement of

[10]Wang Mengkui ed., *Establishing a Developing Social Welfare System in China*, China Development Press, 2009.

the medical security system as its key component in the reform plan. By the end of 2009, the number of people covered by basic medical security amounted to 362.95 million; in addition to over 800 million rural residents covered by new rural co-operative medical insurance, nearly 1.2 billion people were covered by the social medical insurance system, accounting for 90% of the national population. Fourth, the construction of the housing security system has accelerated. In light of the problem of the constant rise of prices in commercial residential housing and the small amount and narrow coverage of affordable housing, the Chinese government has stepped up efforts in the construction of low-rent housing while encouraging enterprises to provide dormitories to employees, especially migrant workers. In light of a shrinking market caused by an international financial crisis, the government takes the construction of security housing such as low-rent housing as an important area for expanding investment and mobilizing domestic demand, which plays an important role in solving the housing problem of low-income families.[11]

[11]This chapter is based on some contents of "The Development of the Social Welfare System in China and Its Impact on Urbanization" (*Journal of the Graduate School of the Chinese Academy of Social Sciences*, Vol. 2, 2010) and "Unavoidable 'Three Security Lines' and 'Two Guarantees'" (*China Social Security*, Vol. 11, 2007).

Chapter 2
The Deviation of China's Social Insurance Fund Mode and Its Corrections

The function of the social insurance system as a key part of the modern social security system is reflected in the operation of social insurance funds. The mode of social insurance funds forms the foundation for the social insurance system. To address the pressure of an aging population and to meet the demands of the rapid development of the capital market (especially in international capital flows), along with international momentum for reforming the social security system, intense debates have been triggered on the traditional pay-as-you-go social insurance mode.

2.1 Debates on the Social Insurance Fund Modes

Of the three main worldwide funding modes for social insurance funds (mainly old-age pensions), namely the pay-as-you-go system, the fund accumulation system and the hybrid system or the partial fund accumulation system (see Table 2.1 for their basic characteristics), those which have drawn most attention and provoked controversy are the pay-as-you-go system and the fund accumulation system. Since the successful transition from the pay-as-you-go system to the fund accumulation system in Chile in the 1980s, as well as the rise of the ROI rate of the fund accumulation mode, people have come to prefer the fund accumulation system. It is believed that it is an important pillar for developing the capital market and an effective prescription for overcoming the problems concomitant with an aging population, while helping to increase savings, enhance the fund use rate and promote economic growth.

The main argument is as follows:

(1) the pay-as-you-go system cannot address the heavy burden of an aging population. An aging population, which demands the continuous increase of the social insurance tax rate, may aggravate unemployment and early retirement

© Springer Nature Singapore Pte Ltd. and Social Sciences Academic Press 2017
Y. Wang, *Social Security in China: On the Possibility of Equitable Distribution*,
Research Series on the Chinese Dream and China's Development Path,
DOI 10.1007/978-981-10-5643-7_2

Table 2.1 Comparison of the basic modes of social insurance funds

Fund mode	Fund source and management	Advantages	Disadvantages
Pay-as-you-go	Public, tax, and ratification of expenditures according to revenue	Strong re-distribution function (inter-generational diversion and horizontal transfer), and simple management	With great demands from an aging population, the premium rate has to be adjusted frequently
Fund accumulation	Compulsory, private management, and ratification of expenditures according to revenue	Incentive payment and compulsory savings, promoting capital market and economic growth	The fund is susceptible to the impact of the macro-economy and inflation. It has a poor redistribution function. The investment management is complicated
Hybrid mode	Compulsory source, partial ratification of expenditures according to revenue and partial ratification of revenue according to expenditure	Considering both the re-distribution function and the accumulation function	Management is extremely complicated, and function orientation tends to change

and lead to a reduction in permanent savings and investment. The growth of implicit public pension debts is difficult to sustain.

(2) Fund accumulation may promote economic growth. Old-age pensions are an important force in the capital market. In 1996, gross global assets amounted to about USD 42 trillion, of which about 20% (USD 10-12 trillion) were the pension assets of developed countries (Dawei et al. 2000).
(3) The success of the Chilean model. Chile successfully made the transition from the pay-as-you-go system to the fund accumulation system in the early 1980s. In a period of over 10 years, the country not only made up deficits, but also accumulated a fund of over USD 20 billion. As a result, the difficulty in paying pensions was resolved and fiscal and enterprise burdens were alleviated. The personal contribution rate was also lowered and the pension replacement rate was increased, thus providing a large amount of funds for economic construction.
(4) The accumulation mode is conducive to improving the saving rate and stimulating economic growth. Economic growth is a function of savings. Chile and Switzerland, through compulsory savings plans, increased their respective national savings rate. The savings rate in Switzerland increased from a GDP of 6–8.5%, and Chile's also increased to some extent. Some studies hold that a

pension reform could increase the original aggregate savings rate by about 10–30% (James 1998).
(5) The high ROI of investment funds. Generally speaking, in countries with more open fund management, the ROI of investment funds is higher in the capital market, such as in France, Australia, the United Kingdom, the United States, Ireland and Canada, with notably more outstanding performance in English-speaking countries (see Table 2.2).
(6) Since the 1970s, there has been a wave of reforms of the social security system worldwide, with the purpose of seeking a new relationship between national actions and private actions and strengthening individuals' responsibility for themselves and others.

While analyzing the role of the fund accumulation system, we should note that people have varied opinions regarding the fund accumulation mode. In fact, the fund accumulation system is overrated, thus giving rise to the fallacy of "anything from the fund accumulation system must be good."

The reasons are as follows:

(1) Fund accumulation does not necessarily increase the national savings rate. Cases proving that the accumulation system can enhance the savings rate are found only in Switzerland and Chile, of which the ratio of savings to GDP in Chile dropped from 21% in 1980 to 20% in 1989. As compulsory savings only account for a part of gross national savings, the increase of the compulsory savings rate is not tantamount to the increase of the gross savings rate.
(2) The role of the capital market is overrated. The role of the capital market is growing, but at the expense of huge risks. The Asian Financial Crisis that broke out in 1997 was an obvious case which highlights this point. Stiglitz observes that developing countries should not simply imitate the capital market in developed countries but should face reality, that is, it is very likely, if not inevitable, that their domestic capital market may operate rather poorly (Stiglitz 1989).
(3) The management cost of the fund accumulation mode, especially for private pension funds, is quite high, even significantly higher than the public system. The management cost and commission charges of commercial old-age insurance in the United States account for 35% of insurance premiums, the profit loss caused by the management cost of private funds in the United Kingdom amounts to 5.2% each year, and the management cost of private old-age pensions in Chile accounts for 1.5% of the salary base (see Table 2.3). The International Labor Organization has, after conducting a survey, concluded that it is certainly wrong to consider that the expenditure of administering the public sector is higher than that of the private sector.
(4) Insurance fund modes require a large amount of government subsidies, as is the case with Chile and other countries.
(5) Over-emphasis on fund accumulation, though improving fund efficiency to some extent (but not fully, as no adequate evidence is available so far), also

Table 2.2 Investment portfolio and ROI of old-age insurance funds and gross assets in diverse countries (regions)

Country	Item							
	Bond (%)	Stock (%)	Cash (%)	Real estate (%)	Average ROI (%) (1983–1993)	Gross assets by the end of 1993 (USD 1 billion)		
	Domestic	International	Domestic	International				
Australia	35.87	4.00	36.37	12.05	3.83	7.88	12.1	122.2
Belgium	38.31	11.94	13.93	17.41	7.46	10.95	9.0	5.6
Canada	47.93	0.46	26.85	8.61	8.46	7.49	8.3	162.3
Denmark	67.93	0	18.67	0	6.05	6.35	8.2	14.4
France	62.00	5.00	20.00	0	2.00	11.00	13.0	199.7
Germany	65.05	1.59	9.97	0.91	8.38	12.00	6.5	254.2
Hong Kong	2.10	11.03	34.03	49.05	3.99	0	8.1	6.8
Ireland	33.67	7.14	21.43	27.55	3.06	7.15	11.8	13.8
Japan	53.58	9.00	24.18	5.01	5.01	3.22	6.2	1752.7
The Netherlands	60.60	5.81	7.69	11.31	3.40	11.19	7.5	216.2
New Zealand	25.87	11.19	27.97	23.08	2.80	9.09	10.8	7.9
Norway	74.52	4.70	5.91	1.09	8.70	5.08	8.0	30.6
Singapore	97.35	0	0	0	2.65	0	1.8	32.9
Spain	95.00	0	3.02	0	0	1.98	8.8	13.4
Sweden	92.43	0	4.66	0	0.97	1.94	7.2	61.8
Switzerland	59.00	4.00	9.00	2.00	10.00	16.00	3.5	195.3
The United Kingdom	8.96	3.05	56.01	23.01	3.06	5.91	11.5	726.4
The United States	33.05	0.72	48.52	3.61	11.76	2.34	9.5	2908.0

Source World Bank (1998, p. 79), Lianyou (2000, p. 82)

Table 2.3 A Survey of the International Labor Organization (ILO) on expenditure of social security management

Pay-as-you-go pattern		Fund accumulation pattern		Private pension management cost	
Country	Management cost (%)	Country	Management cost (%)	Country	Management cost (%)
France	1.7	Singapore	0.8	The United	35
Germany	1.5	Malaysia	4.5	States	5.2
The United States	0.8	India	5.4	The United Kingdom Chile	1.5

Source Ministry of Finance (1998, p. 248)

weakens the re-distribution function of the social security system, because only individuals possessing more accumulated funds acquire more gains. This also involves the basic problem of value judgment; that is, how to handle the re-distribution function of social security and how to balance the fairness and efficiency of the social security system.

The debate over the pay-as-you-go mode and the fund accumulation mode is still continuing to provoke controversy in theoretical circles, with no substantial conclusion. Different opinions may be formed from viewing the issue from different perspectives. Gruat, an ILO scholar, believes that despite the claim of a crisis in the World Bank's "Averting the Old Age Crisis: Policies to Protect the Old and Promote Growth", the solution to the crisis proposed in this report not only fails to provide a better guarantee for old-age pension benefits, but also presents larger potential risks than the correctly designed and managed fixed benefit system (Gruat 1998). The World Bank report also acknowledges that without a developed capital market and being unable to establish an effective regulatory authority, it is impracticable for many countries to adopt the solution of fixed pay. In practice, most countries around the world, including developed countries and covering OECD countries, have practiced or still practice the pay-as-you-go mode, with the basis for old-age insurance still being public old-age insurance run by the government. Currently, only 18 countries with great differences in levels of economic development, low socialization and a small scale of economic aggregate, such as Fiji and Ghana adopt the fund accumulation system (Jiangang 1999). However, in light of the disadvantages of the pay-as-you-go mode and the advantages of the fund accumulation system, and inspired by the successful transition of countries such as Chile to implement the fund accumulation system, the World Bank proposed the multi-pillar mode including the fund accumulation system in the early 1990s, which has exerted a degree of influence upon the reform of the social insurance system of many countries (including China).

2.2 Institutional Deviation of the Hybrid Mode of the Social Insurance Fund in China

(i) Institutional design of "completing the whole task in one stroke"

In the course of establishing a socialist market economy, China should reform its traditional social security system. Unlike the transformation of the social insurance system in countries like Chile, the reform of the social insurance system in China is confronted with two basic tasks: First, in coordination with the socialist market economic system, to establish a socialized social security system and complete the institutional transformation from enterprise (unit) insurance to social insurance. That is an important characteristic quite different from the reforms of the social security system having occurred in any other country. Such a transformation is not within the scope of controversy over the pay-as-you-go or the fund accumulation modes. If the pay-as-you-go practice was adopted in the past, this transformation is to meet the demands of increasingly expanding pay-as-you-go practice. The second task is to establish a multi-pillar system including the fund accumulation system so as to follow the trend of economic development and the reform of social security reforms worldwide. The hybrid system (partial fund accumulation system) combining social pooling and personal accounts has been gradually put into practice since the 1990s in China, in the hope that the above two tasks can be accomplished at the same time, that is, the problem of dual system transformation.

After the exploration through pilot reform and theoretical generation conducted since the mid-1980s, the "Decision" of the Third Plenary Session of the Fourteenth Central Committee of the CPC adopted in 1993 put forward that a hybrid system combining social pooling and personal accounts be implemented for the basic old-age insurance and medical care systems for urban employees in China. According to this approach, China has conducted experimental reforms of the hybrid system by different means in different cities and developed several dozen types of reform. In 1997 and 1998, the State Council, through a comparative summary of the reform types in different places, issued the "Decision on Establishing a Uniform Enterprise Employees' Old-Age Insurance System" and the "Decision on Establishing an Urban Employees' Basic Medical Insurance System", which constituted the basic framework of the two major social insurance systems in Chinese urban areas, old-age insurance and medical insurance.

The combination of social pooling and personal accounts is a type of hybrid mode combining pay-as-you-go and fund accumulation, containing characteristics of both modes. The purpose of combining the pay-as-you-go system and the fund accumulation system in the urban social insurance system is, on the one hand, to meet the demands of completing the transformation of the social insurance system so that the current fund can provide basic insurance to retired people without accumulation, and on the other hand, to enable in-service employees to accumulate a certain amount of social insurance funds, especially old-age pensions, during the 20–30 years when economic growth and the demographic structure were optimal in

- Old-age pension payment
  - Old-age pension for "old people"——Calculated and issued according to the original method——Social pooling fund
  - Old-age pension for "in-service persons"
    - Basic old-age pension——Social pooling fund
    - Transitional old-age pension——Social pooling fund
    - Personal account old-age pension——Personal account fund П120
  - Old-age pension for "new persons"
    - Basic old-age pension——Social pooling fund
    - Personal account old-age pension——Personal account fund П120

Fig. 2.1 Diagram of the payment approaches of social old-age pensions in chin

China, so as to alleviate enterprises' fiscal burden and develop the capital market. This institutional design of "completing the whole task in one stroke" has become recognized by most experts, scholars and decision-makers. Compared with the simple pay-as-you-go system or the fund accumulation system, the hybrid system has its own operation mechanism. First, the hybrid system has to guarantee of the payment of retired people ("elderly people"); second, it should provide basic old-age pensions and personal accumulation for in-service personnel ("in-service persons"); third, it should provide basic insurance and complete personal account accumulation for "new persons" (see Fig. 2.1).

The new system increases requirements on value preservation and the appreciation of accumulated funds. To realize the balance of payments is the fundamental principle for the operation of social insurance funds. The partial fund accumulation system requires that social insurance funds realize two "balances of payment"; one balance is to ensure payment to retired people from pooling funds, and the other balance is to realize the long-term dynamic balance of the accumulated fund. This system has to integrate horizontal balance and vertical balance to realize the periodical balance of payment. In the early period, the financing rate is higher than the payment rate so as to realize partial fund accumulation, that is, a reserve fund, in the case that in the advent of the peak period of aging, the peak fund payment demand can be met at a relatively low financing rate, so as to prevent any financial crisis in social insurance funds (see Fig. 2.2).

(ii) Institutional deviation of the hybrid mode of social insurance funds in China

China's social insurance fund hybrid system, to some extent, meets the fund system ideal and the multi-pillar system advocated by the World Bank; however, in practice, these systems are not the same, resulting in a large disparity between the operation mechanism and the operation effect.

First, too much importance is accorded to the role of the fund system. China fails to define the primary and secondary relationship between social pooling and personal accounts in the institutional framework, which means that China is not clear

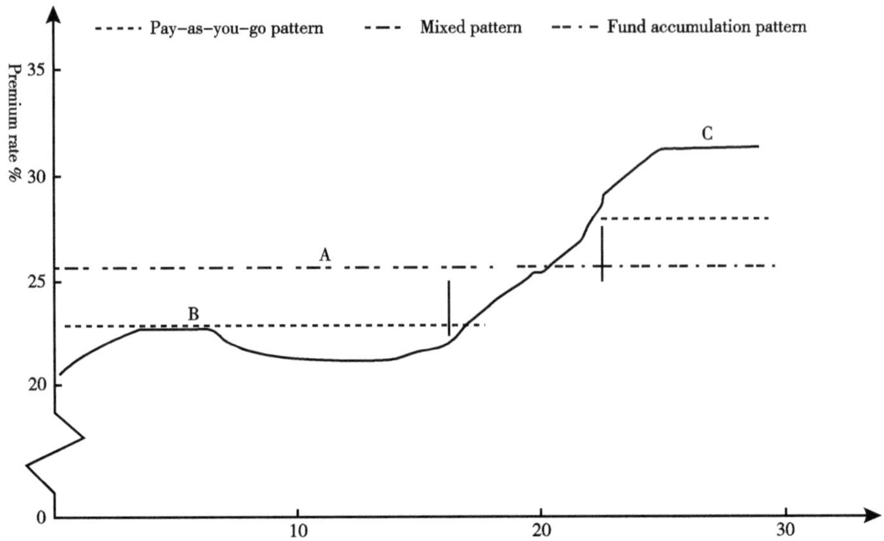

Fig. 2.2 Diagram of variation of premium rates of three financing modes. *Source* Man (1997, p. 169)

with regards to whether the new social insurance system to be established is to be dominated by social pooling (pay-as-you-go) or will be inclined towards developing personal accounts (fund accumulation). In the fund ratio cut of social pooling and personal accounts, no primary and secondary relationship between the two aspects of China's new social insurance system can be discerned. However, as the ratio of personal accounts in China's hybrid mode is larger (see Table 2.4), it can be concluded that the design of China's social insurance fund modes much prefer the fund system commended by the World Bank. However, to complete the "dual system transformation" in the social insurance system, China does not have the practical conditions for realizing the fund system in the short term. Such institutional vagueness is not conducive to the normal operation and sustainable development of the new system.

Second, the design of China's social insurance system has not attached adequate importance to the issue of transitional cost, which affects the effect of personal accounts (the accumulated part of the fund) and is an objective cause for the presence of empty individual accounts. For example, in the design of the old-age insurance system plan, historical debts are under-estimated, and the approach of empty personal accounts going before gradual replenishment is adopted, which leads to empty personal accounts. As future funds are now prepaid, if no solution is worked out, either the institutional design of the mode integrating social pooling and personal accounts will be affected, or a financial crisis will arise. At present, adjustments should be made regarding the old-age insurance system, or the system will be become difficult to sustain.

Table 2.4 Ratio cut of social pooling funds and personal accounts in China's basic old-age insurance and medical insurance

Type of insurance	Social pooling fund		Personal account fund	
	Source of funds	Percentage of the total amount of funds (%)	Source of fund	Percentage of the total amount of funds (%)
Basic old-age insurance	Payment by units (20–16% of the total salary)	13 percentage points of the payment by enterprise, that is, 54.2% of the total amount of insurance funds	The part transferred to personal accounts from enterprise payment (a drop from 7 percentage points to 3 percentage points), personal payment (4–8% of the personal salary base)	11 percentage points, that is, 45.8% of the total amount of insurance funds
Basic medical insurance	Unit payment (16% of total salary)	70% of the enterprise payment (4.2 percentage points), that is, 52.5% of the total amount of insurance funds	The part transferred to personal accounts from enterprise payment (30%), personal payment (2% of the personal salary base)	3.8 percentage points, that is, 47.5% of the total amount of insurance funds

Source Calculated and arranged according to the "Decision on Establishing a Uniform Enterprise Employees' Old-Age Insurance System" (1997) and the "Decision on Establishing an Urban Employees' Basic Medical Insurance System" (1998) of the State Council

Third, China's comprehension of the multi-pillar mode contains deviations. Of the three-pillar system advocated by the World Bank, the first pillar is the pay-as-you-go and public-operated system that ratifies expenditure according to revenue, mainly for providing a social security net for elderly people with a low-income, the second pillar is the compulsory fully-accumulated system that ratifies expenditure according to revenue, with private and competitive fund management, and the third pillar is voluntary savings and annuity providing supplementary retirement income. Though the sources of the second pillar (compulsory personal accounts) are compulsory, its nature is similar to personal savings, its property rights are personal, while its operation and management are conducted by private and competitive fund companies. However, China has not defined the relationship between the two funds or the property right ownership of personal accounts, but practices centralized and interconnected management, thus leaving an institutional loophole for the appropriation of personal accounts by the social pooling fund. Given the difficulty of the social pooling fund to meet the demands of increasing payments, the "gratuitous" appropriation of personal accounts by social pooling accounts has resulted. Not only is it difficult for personal accounts to be fully funded, which become certificated "empty accounts", but fund investment is also unable to be conducted, value cannot be preserved or appreciated, and the accumulation effect of the partial fund accumulation system is lost, all a far cry from the initial objectives of institutional design.

Fourth, the management system for personal accounts (fund accumulation) aspect of China's social insurance fund mode is hindered and not conducive to appreciation on investments. Constrained by many factors such as fund payment pressure and capital market imperfections, the investment channels for the social insurance funds that have been accumulated in China are not smooth, with chaotic management, being barely able to realize value preservation and appreciation. In sum, the hybrid mode of combining social pooling and personal accounts in China, though similar to the fund accumulation system and the multi-pillar system advocated by the World Bank, differs widely from them in terms of operation mechanism and practical conditions. China has confused its system with that advocated by the World Bank, creating many problems in practice.

2.3 Difficulties in the Practice of the Hybrid Mode of Social Pooling and Personal Accounts

The hybrid mode of China's social insurance system attempts to integrate the "fund system" and the "multi-pillar" system. However, the framework of China's new old-age insurance and medical insurance system, which is equipped with the shell of the "fund system" to some extent, does not have the conditions and management mechanism for implementing the fund system; despite its formation as a "multi-pillar" system, it deviates from the "multi-pillar" operational mechanism, thus giving rise to difficulties in fund operation.

(i) The social pooling fund is becoming over-burdened, while old-age insurance personal accounts operate as empty accounts

The expenditure of old-age pensions amounts to the largest amount of expenditure within social security, as all members of society will become old one day, thus requiring an increase in expenditure on old age pensions to meet the pressures of an aging population. At present, though old-age social insurance in China only covers persons employed in urban units, the coverage is considerably widespread (the total number of retired persons in 1999 was 37.3 million, and the total insurance benefits amounted to RMB 336.1 billion). The payment of the old-age insurance fund has turned from "pay-as-you-go" to the hybrid system and historical debts have led to great obstacles when attempting to transform the old-age pension system. Due to the transformation of the old-age security system, a considerable amount of historical debts have had to be paid from the old-age insurance social pooling fund. The expanding expenditure has exerted great pressure on the social insurance pooling fund. Since the implementation of the new old-age insurance system, the social pooling fund has become overburdened, and there is no option but to appropriate funds into individual accounts. As a result, the personal accounts of

Table 2.5 Income and expenditure of China's old-age insurance fund in 1989–1999

Year	Fund income (billion yuan)	Fund expenditure (billion yuan)	Total surplus (billion yuan)
1989	14.67469	11.88292	6.79899
1990	17.88178	14.93363	9.78760
1991	21.57084	17.30714	14.40688
1992	36.5766	32.19145	22.00683
1993	50.35402	47.06303	25.85889
1994	70.74245	66.10902	30.47662
1995	95.00507	84.76087	42.98338
1996	117.17639	103.18689	57.85604
1997	133.791	125.133	68.285
1998	145.9	151.16	61.16
1999	196.5	192.5	73.4

Source The Ministry of Labor (1997, p. 17); the Ministry of Labor and Social Security, and the National Bureau of Statistics (1997, 1998 and 1999)

accumulation accounts cannot be ensured to have adequate funds and can only operate as empty accounts. It was estimated that "empty accounts" in personal accounts have amounted to about 200 billion since 1997. In 1998, the total expenditure of national old-age insurance funds was greater than the total income (see Table 2.5). In this way, not only will personal accounts encounter a tremendous financial crisis, but the social insurance hybrid mode will also face huge institutional risks.

(ii) The nominal social insurance premium is too high, affecting the revenue of social insurance funds

To ensure that the huge fund payment is met, the urban social insurance premium in China has been set very high. With the acceleration of an ageing population, room for further increase of insurance premiums is becoming increasingly narrow. In 1999, urban old-age insurance in China only covered 46.9% of the total number of working people in cities and towns and 55.9% of the number of people who should have been covered by such insurance. Affected by factors such as economic downturns, difficulties encountered by enterprises and insufficient payments, the payment rate of units and individuals that have participated in social insurance has not been satisfactory. For example, the payment rate calculated by Guangdong Province according to the number of insurance participants dropped from 96.9% in 1993 to 91% in 1999. The arrears of social insurance premiums have become more common and the problem is even more serious in economically undeveloped areas. The payment rate in many places is only 70%; arrearages in national basic old-age insurance exceed RMB 36 billion. By regulation, social insurance charges should be deducted from employees' actual salary. But the salary base for premium payments differs widely from the employees' actual salary. In 1999, the average monthly salary base for enterprise old-age insurance in Guangdong Province was

RMB 847, but it was discovered through a survey that the base for old-age insurance premium payments by enterprises only accounted for about 70% of an employees' actual total salary. The World Bank discovered through a survey in 1995 that the actual old-age insurance payment rate of urban employees in China was only about 13% of the total amount of their salary. In that year, the nominal payment rate was above 23.5% (higher than the average rate of about 20% in the world), but the actual payment rate was only 55.3% of the nominal payment rate (World Bank 1998).

The presence of the above problems affected the source of social insurance funding and the stability of income. The average salary of urban in-service employees in 1999 was RMB 8346. Calculated with a coverage of 1.17 billion people and the social insurance premium rate as stipulated by the state (on average about 38–41% of the total salary, with 25–28% for old-age insurance, 8% for medical insurance, 3% for unemployment, and 1% for work-related injury and maternity insurance each), the revenue of urban social insurance in China is enormous, amounting to RMB 539-581.3 billion. If the rate of people participating in the insurance scheme, the fund payment rate and the actual payment rate all surpass 90%, the annual income of the social insurance fund should amount to RMB 377.3–406.9 billion. However, the national income of the social insurance fund only amounted to RMB 220.8 billion in 1999, accounting for only 54%-59% of the due payment, or only 38–41% of the total nominal payment. Due to the excessive discrepancy between the actual amount of collection and actual expenditure in the social insurance fund, China has to stipulate a very high social insurance collection rate, which suppresses an enterprises' initiative for premium payment.

(iii) The social insurance fund is very difficult to manage, with the huge pressure of value preservation and appreciation

The hybrid mode places a set of very high requirements upon fund managers, because it requires the actuarial valuation of the balance of payments of "two funds", the calculation of fund balance at different stages and the management of a large amount of accumulated funds with great risks and high requirements regarding safety. Affected by factors such as institutional design, management systems, management experience and a lack of professionals, the management and value maintenance and appreciation of accumulated funds in the social insurance of China are confronted with increasingly serious problems: On the one hand, the problem of disorderly management and capital loss is so severe that over RMB 10 billion yuan of social insurance funds was illegally appropriated, occupied or embezzled in the mid-1990s (Lianyou 2000). But on the other hand, in righting the wrong, proper limits have been exceeded, without preserving adequate fund investment channels; the fund appreciation rate falls short of inflation or interest rates (see Table 2.6), hardly able to realize the purpose of value maintenance and appreciation.

Table 2.6 Price index, bank interest rate and treasury bill interest rate of 1985–1999

Year	Rise of commodity retailing price (%)	Bank interest rate (%)		Treasury bill interest rate (%)	
		Current	One-year	Annual interest rate	Term (year)
1985	8.8		4.32	9	5
1986	6.0		5.04	10	6
1987	7.3		5.04	10	6
1988	18.5		8.64	10	3
1989	17.8	2.88	11.34	14	3
1990	2.1	2.88	10.08	14	3
1991	2.9	1.8	7.56	10	3
1992	5.4	1.8	7.56	10.5	5
1993	13.0	3.16	10.98	13.96	3
1994	21.7	3.15	10.98	15.86	5
1995	14.8	3.15	10.98	–	–
1996	6.1	1.98	7.47	–	–
1997	0.8	1.71	5.67	9.18	3
1998	−2.6	1.44	4.77	–	–
1999	−30	0.99	2.25	2.89	3

Source Arranged according to "China Statistical Yearbook (2000)" of the State Statistics Bureau

2.4 The Approaches and Measures for Deepening the Reform of the Social Insurance Fund System in China

(i) Stick to the principal status of social pooling and reduce the ratio of personal accounts

The problems arising from the operation of China's social insurance fund are related to the fact that we overburden the institutional design of the "fund system" and the "multi-pillar system". Therefore, to improve the social insurance system with Chinese characteristics, we should accord with the national conditions of China, having a backward capital market, a low level of economic development, and old-age pensions which can only meet the most basic necessities for the survival of retired persons, sticking to the principal status of the public insurance fund system, and weakening the over-dependence on personal accounts and lowering the excessively high expectation of value. The scale of the personal account fund should be determined according to the objective reality, which may start from "small accounts", and based on the principle that personal accounts should be funded by personal payments. If an enterprise also pays, it should be at its own discretion (such as enterprise supplementary insurance) instead of being compulsory. In this way, the independence of personal accounts and the supporting reform of the management system can be guaranteed.

(ii) Stick to the multi-pillar design and improve the fund management system

Though the "multi-pillar" system of the World Bank is more suitable for developed countries with a developed capital market and a healthy management system, the design concept of the "multi-pillar" old-age pension system deserves recognition, because it mobilizes the initiative of various parties to participate in endowment insurance and serves as an active measure addressing the ageing crisis. The traditional urban pension system in China relies too heavily on the guarantee from enterprises, institutions and governments. With the development of the market economy, increasing diversification of property rights, increasing improvement of the capital market, and increasing betterment of the legal system, it is necessary and feasible to establish a pension system with a multi-pillar mode.

Besides the basic old-age insurance and basic medical insurance run by the government, China may also carry forward its cultural tradition of frugality and saving, develop various forms of supplementary insurance, and bring into play the initiative in family security, community help and social charity. It is necessary to point out that to develop a compulsory personal account accumulation system (the second pillar), China must follow the requirements of the market economy and international customary practices to establish a management system in which the social pooling fund is independent from personal accounts. Differing from the social pooling fund, personal accounts cannot be mixed up, as their ownership and right to yields belong to individuals. To implement the fund accumulation mode for personal accounts, scattered and competitive social insurance fund investment companies or foundations should be established. The personal account fund should be handed over to independent and competitive market entities (which may be private), that is, fund management companies, for operation. The government may monitor fund operation through laws, regulations and government control so as to ensure the security of accumulated funds.

(iii) Open up sources of non-conventional insurance funds to address the cost of an institutional transition

An important root cause for the institutional crisis in China's new social insurance system is that the government has failed to establish adequate and sound channels for addressing historical debts through the reform of the social insurance system. Two problems were resolved in the transformation of the old-age pension system in Chile: first, the old-age pension debts under the old system were resolved through the fiscal ("endorsed bond") channel, which created an ideal environment for reform; second, planned investment was conducted for the accumulated fund in personal accounts to realize the value preservation and appreciation of the social insurance fund. The method of West Germany providing East Germany with social insurance financial support after the re-unification of Germany can also be taken for reference. In light of inadequate normal (institutional) sources for the social insurance fund now, non-institutional sources should be opened up through multiple channels so as to resolve historical and implicit debts. We think that fund sources may be expanded in the following ways: first, adjust the fiscal expenditure structure and continue to pay the retirement pension for retirees from state-owned units before 2000; second, sell off some state-owned assets, including some state-owned shares or some state-owned land and public housing etc.; third, issue social security national debts, lottery and introduce special taxes (such as inheritance tax).

(iv) Improve revenue and expenditure control, strengthen investment operation, and realize value preservation and appreciation

Currently, there are many problems with the sources, expenditure management and investment operation of the social insurance fund in China, which should be addressed by resolute and feasible measures. In terms of fund sources, we should strengthen institutional construction to establish a stable and sustainable source foundation for the social insurance fund. (1) Continue to expand its coverage. To reform the original coverage of social insurance, employed persons with permanent urban residential registration should all be included. This is a requirement for the socialization of social insurance and also a necessity to lower the dependency ratio and expand the source foundation for the social insurance fund. (2) Lower the nominal social insurance premium rate, and increase the base salary for the payment of the social insurance fund and the successful collection rate so that the rates are maintained at least above 95%. Meanwhile, measures should be adopted to resolve the problem of a false payment base. The payment base of the social insurance fund should be changed from "total salary" to "total income"; just like the collection of individual income tax, various kinds of "normal income" that employees receive from their respective units should be included into the base for the payment of their social insurance premiums. (3) Implement the tax collection system, strengthen the collection of social insurance fund collection, and gradually convert over to social insurance tax. While fund sources are expanding, we must improve and adjust the expenditure system and structure, thus increasing revenue and reducing expenditure. (1) Effectively lower the retirement pension replacement rate so that basic old-age insurance is based on guaranteeing basic needs. The retirement pension rate should be gradually lowered from above 90% to below 60% or about 50% of the salary for payment (instead of the final salary before retirement), so that basic old-age insurance is based on basic old-age support and room for development is reserved for supplementary old-age insurance. (2) Gradually raise the retirement age, and curb early retirement to alleviate the payment pressure of the old-age insurance fund. (3) Regulate the social insurance fund expenditure adjustment mechanism, and weaken the impact of non-institutional measures on the social insurance fund. The expenditure adjustment of the social insurance fund must be conducted through scientific estimation and through institutionalized and law-based channels, so as to prevent the impact of any temporary decision on the expenditure expectation of the whole social insurance fund. (4) Adjust the expenditure structure and conduct scientific fund management. The basic principle of balance of payments should be adopted for the social insurance pooling fund. "Strike a balance between expenditure and revenues, with a slight surplus". It is not good to have no surplus, but excessive fund accumulation is not good either.

Currently, China exercises strict control over the investment of the social insurance fund, which is a passive preventive measure related to capital market imperfections, few investment channels, big risks in industrial investment, backward operation monitoring measures and the insufficient ability to prevent financial risks. However, considering the long-term sustainable development of the social insurance system and international practices, we must relax control over investment operations of the social insurance fund, and expand investment channels on the basis of rationalizing the institutional design of social insurance and the fund management mechanism, so that the accumulated fund of social insurance can enter the capital market, acquire higher return on investment and realize the value preservation and appreciation of the accumulated fund. (1) Establish a professional investment institution for the social insurance fund, and develop a fund investment monitoring framework. The social insurance investment fund mainly consisting of personal accounts and supplementary insurance must have the transition made solely by professional institutions. Such professional institutions should establish a board of directors, expert wealth management teams and develop fund custodians and an adequate monitoring and control mechanism. A proper entry and exit mechanism should be established for fund institutions to develop a competitive pattern under government oversight. (2) Stick to the principle of gradual improvement and create a good environment. (3) Expand investment areas and innovate investment tools. Currently, the government only allows insurance funds to be deposited in banks and for the purchase of treasury bonds, which cannot be adapted to the requirement of value preservation and the appreciation of social insurance. With the increasing expansion of the scale of personal accounts and supplementary insurance funds, it will be an objective need to relax investment restrictions so that such funds can enter the capital market and create room for the expansion of investment and potential areas for investment.[1]

[1]The contents of this chapter are published in the *Economic Research Journal*, 2001 (2).

Chapter 3
Health Problems and Health Equality in the Transitional Period

Despite achieving significant developments in terms of health services in China, the reform of public services has yet to show relevant results, such as how to establish health services in line with the socialist market economic system. With an overemphasis on market-oriented and industrialized medical care, the efficiency and equity of the health reform have even been subject to decline to some extent. The high cost and lack of accessibility of medical treatment caused by rapidly rising medical expenses has become an economic and social hot topic of general concern. This article mainly addresses the causes and roots of the challenges and problems faced by health services in the course of economic transformation. It provides some opinions and suggestions on how to enhance the efficiency and fairness in the development of the health sector in a socialist market economic system, and how to bring into full play the role of medical care and health security in the construction of a harmonious society.

3.1 Health Security Challenges and Outstanding Problems Caused by Economic Transformation

The main task of Chinese health services under the planned economic system is to find a solution to the "scarcity of doctors and medicine" issue. Thanks to the state's efforts, its sound public health system and the clear guiding principles, China has managed to provide basic health security at a very low level to most urban and rural residents and has created a Chinese health care model despite the relatively low level of economic development and the relative shortage of medical and health resources. With the transformation of the economic operation system and social organization system since reform and opening-up, the traditional health care model based on work units or communities face very big challenges.

© Springer Nature Singapore Pte Ltd. and Social Sciences Academic Press 2017

Y. Wang, *Social Security in China: On the Possibility of Equitable Distribution*, Research Series on the Chinese Dream and China's Development Path,
DOI 10.1007/978-981-10-5643-7_3

In terms of the public health system, China used to mobilize government and mass forces to conduct large-scale patriotic health campaigns and health education campaigns, vigorously clean up the environment of health services. Doing so, it would also step up efforts to control infectious diseases and endemic diseases, and properly implement a "prevention-based" health development strategy. Since reform and opening-up, however, patriotic health campaigns have lost their organizational foundation, and government investment in public health services is hardly enough to maintain the normal operation of health institutions; as a result, grassroots medical and health institutions and even many public health institutions have become commercial or market-based. This affects the functioning of public health and changes the status of the government's "prevention-based" strategy to that of a mere "slogan". The frequent occurrence of public health issues in China exposed the challenges and predicaments facing public health services after the economic transformation.

In terms of the medical and health system, rapid development has been achieved in medical and health institutions under a lenient market-based system. Moreover, the ability to provide medical services has been comprehensively improved since reform and opening-up. Except for a very small number of sparsely populated and poverty-stricken areas with inconvenient transportation, the scarcity of doctors and medicine issue has basically been solved. However, the lack of effective guidance and supervision in the introduction of a market mechanism leaded to distorted services and low efficiency in the medical and health sector and seriously increased the cost of medical and health care. This aggravates the medical burdens of urban and rural residents and gives rise of the serious problem of increasingly non-accessible and expensive medical treatment. In terms of results, since reform and opening-up, the extent of the improvement of the health of Chinese residents does not match the rapid increase of medical expenses. Since the 1990s, in particular, the continuous rapid increase of medical expenses has far exceeded the extent of GDP as well as urban and rural income growth for the same period. The average annual increase of total health expenditures from 1978 to 2003 was 12.09%, nearly three percentage points higher than the average growth rate of GDP in the same period (Dezhi 2005). From 1998 to 2003, the average annual income of urban residents increased by 8.9%, and that of rural residents increased by 2.4%, but medical and health expenditures in urban and rural areas increased by 13.5% and 11.8% respectively. The increase rate of medical service expenditures exceeds the increase of per capita income, and medical and health expenditures now rates third in terms of major expenditures for families after food and education. In 2003, total health expenditures amounted to RMB 658.41 billion, accounting for 5.62% of the GDP, while total health expenditures only accounted for 3.17% of the GDP in 1980. It is noteworthy that the proportion of medical expenditures in urban and rural familial income has rapidly risen to over 10%. A considerable number of urban and rural residents (especially rural residents) have to assume these medical expenses on their own because they lack medical insurance. Rapidly rising medical expenses have become a huge economic burden for urban and rural residents (see Table 3.1).

Table 3.1 Growth of medical expenses in China

Year	1980	1990	1995	2000	2001	2002	2003
Total health expenditures (billion yuan)	14.32	74.74	215.51	458.66	502.59	579	658.41
Proportion in GDP (%)	3.17	4.03①	3.69	5.13	5.16	5.51	5.62
National per capita health expenditures (yuan)	14.51	65.40	177.90	361.90	393.80	450.70	509.50
Urban per capita health expenditures (yuan)		158.50	401.30	813.00	841.20	987.10	1108.90
Rural per capita health expenditures (yuan)		38.80	112.90	314.90	244.80	259.30	274.70
Proportion of urban per capita health expenditures (yuan) in residents' income (%)		10.40	9.40	12.90	12.30	12.10	12.20
Proportion of urban per capita health expenditures (yuan) in residents' consumption expenditure (%)		12.40	11.30	16.30	15.80	16.40	17.00②
Proportion of rural per capita health expenditures (yuan) in residents' income (%)		5.70	7.20	14.00	10.30	10.50	10.50
Proportion of rural per capita health expenditures (yuan) in residents' living consumption expenditure (%)		6.60	8.60	18.90	14.10	14.10	14.10②

Note ① According to the estimate of the World Bank, total health expenditures in China accounted for 3.5% of the GDP in 1990. See *The World Bank Development Report 1993: Investing in Health*, China Financial & Economic Publishing House, 1993. ② According to the household surveys conducted by the State Bureau of Statistics, the proportion of medical and health expenditures in urban and rural residents general living expenditures is obviously smaller than shown in the table. For example, in 2002 and 2003, the proportion of urban residents' medical and health expenditures was 7.13 and 7.31% respectively, and that of rural residents was 7.08 and 7.34% respectively. In 1990 and 1995, the proportion of such expenditures for urban residents was 2.01 and 3.11% respectively; that for rural residents was 5.06 and 4.94% respectively. See *The Statistical Yearbook of China* (2004)

Source of data Ministry of Health: *China's Health Statistic Abstract 2005*, p. 31. For the data on urban and rural residents' income, see *The Statistical Yearbook of China* of relevant years

In contrast with the substantial increase in medical expenses, no significant improvement has been found in the health conditions of urban and rural residents, and some health indexes have even dropped. Urban and rural morbidity has been rising. According to the 2003 national health survey, the two-week morbidity rate for the residents in the regions under survey was 143.0‰ (153.2‰ for urban residents, and 139.5‰ for rural residents), and the prevalence of chronic diseases for residents under survey was 151.1‰ (239.6‰ for urban residents and 120.5‰ for rural residents). Besides, the prevalence of major infectious diseases in recent years (such as SARS) has been rising. From 1995 to 2004, the prevalence of infectious diseases in mandatory reporting rose from 176.24/100,000 people to 235.85/100,000 people, and the death rate rose from 0.34/100,000 people to 0.53/100,000 people. The damages and potential risks of infectious diseases are increasing.

In relation to the above problems, efficiency and equity in dispatching health resources has been declining since the 1990s. The relationship between equity and efficiency has always been one of the core issues of economic research. In the course of modern economic growth, the relationship between equity and efficiency can be generally classified into the following four situations: with the rise of economic efficiency, social equity improves; with the rise of economic efficiency, social equity remains unchanged or even weakens; with the decline of economic efficiency, social equity improves; with the decline of economic efficiency, social equity declines. The first situation is the most desired, but it tends to require quite a long development period. The second and third situations, to some extent, reflect the orientation or focus of economic and social policies in different periods of development, and are also acceptable. The fourth situation is most unacceptable. To overcome "egalitarianism" in the era of planned economy, China has established guidelines for reform and development which both "gives priority to efficiency, and gives consideration to equity".

This policy has played an active role in economic development. However, if applied to an economy where market does not play its role, (especially in the field of social development), and without relevant government function (especially strict market supervision), the result of such a policy would be the decline of equity without any guarantee of enhanced efficiency. The health industry has unfortunately become a typical field in which both efficiency and equity decline. Since 1993, National Health Service surveys have clearly reflected the "market failure" and "government failure" that coexist in the health sector. With rapid increase over twenty-odd years, medical facilities and equipment have improved, while clinic visit rate for urban and rural residents has dropped. The two-week clinic visit rate of urban and rural residents was 19.9 and 16.0% respectively in 1993, which dropped to 11.8 and 13.9% respectively in 2003; their annual hospitalization rate was 5.0 and 3.1% respectively in 1993, which changed to 4.2 and 3.4% respectively in 2003. The average number of patients diagnosed and treated by each doctor and the use rate of sick beds in medical institutions are declining on the whole. A main cause for the decline in the efficiency of medical resources use is the rise of medical costs, which cause a considerable number of people in financial difficulty to give up medical services provided by medical institutions. A 2003 survey showed that the hospital visit rate dropped by 18.4% from that of 1998 (a drop of 27.1% in cities and a drop of 15.4% in rural areas). Of the patients surveyed, 51.1% saw a doctor in medical institutions, 35.7% opted for self-medication, and 13.1% did not take any medical measure. 48.9 of the patients did not visit any clinic (57.0% for cities and 45.8% for rural areas). "Expensive medical treatments" exert more serious impacts on low-income people in urban and rural areas. 38.2% of outpatients not adopting any treatment measure chose to do so because of financial difficulties; of the patients who should have been hospitalized but chose not to, 70.0% blamed financial difficulties. This is a direct reflection of the gradually widening income disparity among urban and rural residents in recent years in the health sector. The increase of economic inequalities is also reflected in the decline of equity in health services. In the global health equity rankings by the World Health Organization, China ranks fourth from the bottom, which, to some extent, reflects the decline of health equity in China.

3.2 The Progress and Perplexity of the "Three Reforms" in China's Health Care System

To address health problems in the course of economic transformation, the Chinese government has adopted a series of policies and measures. In the 1980s, mainly market-based measures were adopted to curb the rise of state-funded medical cost and raise funds for the development of medical and health services. Since the 1990s, especially the mid-1990s, as medical expenses soared more rapidly after the adoption of the market-based system, more and more people found it difficult to receive medical treatment. As a result, the government adopted three institutional reforms centered on accelerating the reform of the medical security system, the medical and health system, and the drug production and circulation system. Other representative policies and regulations launched during this period included: the "Decision of the CPC Central Committee and the State Council on Health Reform and Development" (1997), the "Decision of the State Council on Constructing the Basic Medical Insurance System for Urban Employees" (1998), and the "Guiding Opinions on the Reform of Urban Medicine and Health System by the Economic Restructuring Office of the State Council" (2000), among others.

Since 1998, rapid development has been achieved in the construction of the urban medical security system in China. This is mainly reflected in the expansion of basic medical insurance coverage for urban employees. By the end of 2004, the number of people covered by basic medical insurance was 124.04 million, including 90.45 million in-service employees, and 33.59 million retirees. To relieve the medical burden of poor urban residents in cities, in April 2005, the General Office of the State Council forwarded the Opinions on Pilot Work for the Establishment of the Urban Medical Relief System by the Ministry of Civil Affairs, the Ministry of Health, the Ministry of Labor Security and the Ministry of Finance, to promote pilot work for the medical relief system. In light of rural residents without medical insurance and facing non-accessible and expensive medical treatments, China started pilot work on the new rural cooperative medical system. The central government and local governments employ funds from their fiscal funds, and farmers voluntarily participate in medical insurance based on households as units, thus mainly allowing the treatment of serious illnesses contracted by farmers covered by insurance. By the end of June 2005, 641 counties (cities and districts) conducted pilot work on new rural cooperative medical insurance, including 225 million farmers, of whom 163 million participated in cooperative medical insurance, at a participation rate of 72.6%. Farmers covered by cooperative medical insurance were compensated 119 million person-times of, and expenditures in terms of compensation money amounted to RMB 5.038 billion.[1] Though this went beyond the regulations on employees' basic medical insurance in the "three reforms", it implied the gradual expansion of medical security coverage.

The reform of the medical and health system and of the drug production and circulation system is ongoing. However, it may have engendered more problems and doubts than progress. One issue concerning the reform of China's health system is the direction is should take. Although both theoretical circles and practical work departments all recognize "establishing an urban medical and health system meeting the requirements of the socialist market economy" as the general objective of reform, yet they have a different understanding of the implications of this system. One opinion has it that besides medical and health service institutions assuming public health functions, other institutions should be turned into market-based entities from as in the former planned management system so as to gradually industrialize and marketize the health service sector. In the course of economic reform, this line of thinking has become mainstream in theoretical circles, reflected in the implementation of classified reform in hospitals by relevant government departments as stated in the relevant documents on the health system reform, the implementation of "property right" reform in health centers in some places, and the permission and encouragement of private capital and foreign capital to enter the medical and health service system. At the end of 2003, of the 283 thousand medical institutions registered nationwide (excluding village clinics), state-owned (85 thousand) and collective (49 thousand) institutions accounted for 47.3%; private (136 thousand) and joint venture (60) institutions accounted for 52.7%. Quantitatively, medical institutions not owned by the states and of a collective nature have become the majority. According to the classification by departments such as the Ministry of Health, of the above institutions, non-profit medical institutions (135 thousand) accounted for 47.5%, and profit-making medical institutions (146 thousand) accounted for 52.5%. Most of non-state-owned and collective health institutions, especially profit-making health institutions, tend to behave like ordinary enterprises, that is: oriented by market and profits. Of medical institutions which still retain a state-owned and collective nature or are even classified as non-profit organizations, due to insufficient public investment and competition pressurizing the whole medical market, they have been partly marketized or even mainly target at profit making. The industrialization and market-based tendencies of

[1]The first group of pilot counties (cities and districts) initiated in China in 2003 amounted to 304, which increased to 333 by 2004; by 2005, every prefecture (city) had at least one pilot county. Seethe news report "Pilot work on new rural cooperative medical insurance has scored obvious results" on the Ministry of Health website http://www.moh.gov.cn/index.aspx.

medical and health services since reform and opening-up in China have been very obvious. Another viewpoint is that although state and society cannot and do not have to arrange for all medical services, and although the self-regulatory role of market in medical and health services is not negligible, yet industrialization should not be blindly advocated and marketization should not be over-stressed in health development as well as in medical and health service institutions. The main reasons for such an idea include: ① serious information dis-symmetry exists between the supplier and the purchaser in the medical service market, which is not a perfectly competitive market, and where the market mechanism cannot play an adequate role, let alone effectively allocating health resources; Therefore, playing up the market theory in medical services may lead to serious health inequalities. ② Over-emphasis on market orientation in the medical and health sector will cause both inequality and inefficiency in terms of the administration of medical services, susceptible to double distortion in price and supervision. ③ Commercialization and market orientation in the reform of the health system go against the nature of public enterprise, partial public products property and the requirements of social equality. No government in modern society should leave problems in medical and health services to be solved wholly by market forces.

In over twenty years of reform exploration and theoretical summary, despite the existence of some conflict on the reform of the medical and health sector in China, authorities in charge of health have at least realized that the "excessive dependence on market orientation" in practice is not advisable. It has been proved in practice that the reform of the medical and health system may refer to but cannot simply copy the experiences in the market-oriented reform of ordinary commodity (even drugs). The government must take up responsibilities in the public health system and should reserve and even improve community-based public medical and health institutions with reasonable layout, high accessibility and low cost, so as to meet medical demands of poverty-stricken people (who may be given special medical aid) and the masses. Moreover, appropriate fiscal subsidies and policy support may also be given to fields such as medical technologies research. Of course, there is no society able to bear the tremendous amounts of medical expenses caused by the progress of medical technologies. Medical services other than basic medical needs may be developed gradually by market-oriented and industrialized methods under the guidance of regional medical and health plans. In terms of medical and health institutions, the government and the market can divide the work, and both should play an active role. The government should mainly focus on the public health sector and the basic medical field, and therefore should "focus on basic matters and liberalize medical care"; it should focus on public health, community medical care and preventive health care. However, further exploration is required as to how to implement the above opinions in the specific practices of health development and reform.

Another noteworthy problem is how to realize the complementary support of the "three reforms". Despite certain progress made in simultaneous promotional pilot work of "three reforms", the effect is limited on the whole. The specific reform approach in the health system may require major adjustments. The government's medical cost compensation increase for medical institutions may, to some extent, reduce the medical expenditures of urban and rural residents, yet it is still difficult to control the rise of medical expenditures if the operation mechanism of medical institutions is not fundamentally reformed. In the long run, public funds can hardly be sustained. Meanwhile, there are too many problems in drug production, especially in terms of circulation. Abnormally high drugs prices and excessive waste of medical funds increase drug prices, reduce efficiency and increase the people's burdens. As to how to effectively supervise this field despite a highly-involved market, China has not identified truly effective measures or approaches. Despite the rapid development of medical security, especially in terms of basic medical insurance for urban employees, medical security coverage is less than 50% of the total amount of labor in urban areas. The existence of a large number of people who get medical treatment at their own expenses has become an important symbol of the difficulty of achieving basic effect in the "three reforms".

We should say that despite the progress made in terms of health security for urban and rural residents in China, in comparison with the past, China remains a far cry from the objective of establishing a health security system suitable for the socialist market economy and the current economic development stage while also meeting people's basic health demands. Many theoretical and practical problems should be studied and explored.

3.3 Suggestions on Promoting Health Development, Health Equality and the Construction of a Harmonious Society

(i) To develop health services and promote health equality are a fundamental project for the construction of a harmonious society

The right to health is a basic right granted by the constitution to citizens and also an important part of human rights. The improvement of health conditions directly reflects national and social development and progress. The problem of medical and health care is one of the most fundamental problems which must be addressed for human subsistence and development, as it relates to the people's standards and quality of living as well as to the development objectives and the future of a country and a nation. Since the Central CPC Committee clearly stated the objective of constructing a harmonious socialist society in the resolution of the Fourth Plenary Session of the Sixteenth National Congress, to build a harmonious society has become an important objective for the future development of China. Health services and health equality not only shoulder important missions in the construction of a harmonious society, but also provide an important base for constructing a harmonious society.

Developing health services can promote economic growth. In statistical indexes, health expenditures count as consumption expenditures, while expenditures for public health are deemed to be fiscal burdens, social burdens and family burdens not creating wealth. As the health flexibility coefficient is generally larger than 1,[2] health burdens keep rising. Indeed, for the large number of medium and low-income people whose income grows slowly, the rapid growth of medical cost increasingly exceeds their bearing capacity, and medical cost itself has become a huge barrier constraining their access to medical services. However, in terms of the society as a whole, medical expenditures should be deemed as health investments. For individuals, health investments should become an important part of HR capital investment. Families are reduced or reverted to poverty by diseases because the main labor forces of such families are robbed of their health and thus their main source of income is lost. Therefore, health investment is an inevitable basic expenditure for families and society, as well as an important drive for economic development. An important factor for China's economic development since the founding of the PRC is increased investment in health by the state and society, as well as the constant improvement of the people's health conditions, including the increase of life expectancy, large-scale control of infectious diseases and endemics, the reduction of the number of people who are sick, and the improvement of general health conditions. The World Health Organization also thinks that the expansion of key health services coverage may salvage the lives of millions of people each year, alleviate poverty, stimulate economic development and promote global security.[3]

Health equality plays the role of adjusting income distribution and promoting social equality, harmony and stability. There are various definitions or explanations when it comes to health and equality. Health equality should be taken as an important part and objective for economic and social development, and stress should be laid mainly on people's accessibility to basic medical and health services provided by the state and society, whatever the way, approach or process adopted. From the perspective of result equality, though not every social member has the same ability to pay, yet the right to health as a basic human right should be taken as a public objective, instead of allowing this basic right to be eroded by other forces. If some social members cannot enjoy this basic right for personal or family reasons, the state or society should be obliged to help them obtain basic health security. Maintaining health equality means that the state and society should grant certain help to poor people unable to acquire basic medical security, which is an important responsibility of social security, whereby the role of social security in regulating income distribution, narrowing the wealth gap, and promoting social harmony is

---

[2]According to the estimate of Dezhi (2005), from 1978 to 2003, the average elastic coefficient of per capita health cost versus per capita GDP in China was 1.29.

[3]A WHO Macroeconomics and Health (2002) report held that only USD 14 billion was invested in the intervention of infectious diseases in the most under-developed countries of the world, with which the death of 8 million people could be prevented each year, and 330 million disability adjusted life years (DALYs) could be extended. According to conservative estimate, each DALY got USD 563 and the direct economic benefits of 330 million DALYs amounted to USD 186 billion each year, which amount could be several times higher.

played. Of course, the key to exercising the above functions resides in the realization of health equality.

Health development and health equality are two main pillars safeguarding urban and rural residents' health, and neither are negligible. China has made notable progress in using multiple channels to raise health development funding and in promoting health development since the initiation of reform, but considerable investments in terms of funds, human resources and material resources are still required for the future development of health services, so as to ensure that total health resources keep growing with economic development in order to provide a material basis for securing people's health. Under the socialist market economy, the government should not and cannot be a single entity as it used to be under the planned economic system. Instead, it should draw upon the beneficial experiences in raising health development funding through multiple channels and continue to absorb social, individual and even foreign capital into the health sector. Health investment should be better planned to meet the actual demands and bearing capacity of the level of economic development, instead of being completely market-oriented. In fact, though the insufficiency of social investment channels is a problem facing China's medical and health sector, it is not the main problem, as the worst problem is serious health inequality and efficiency decrease in terms of medical resources use. In particular, improving the efficiency of the use health resources and the equality of health security should become a fundamental project for the construction of a harmonious society.

(ii) The government must fulfill its responsibility for improving health equality

Currently, people have no doubt on the objective of improving health equality. The crux is how to realize the objective of health equality with markets as the main mechanisms for resource allocation. In light of guiding thoughts, the key is that the government should play a guiding role in medical and health services and health security. A review of the history of medical and health services and medical security in all countries of the world, especially developed countries, will find that almost invariably there was a course of development from free market adjustment to centralized social pooling. Because medical and health service security and medical security are fields where "market failure" is relatively prevalent, it is not feasible to rely entirely on free market, and thus the government's role is irreplaceable.

Public health, which means health services provided for all the people and the whole society in a region, is the most fundamental medical and health service to which everyone should be entitled; it implies the social services and public goods with the widest coverage, strongest public interest and best effect, and is also the basis of the entire medical and health security system of a society. As market failure is more serious in the field of public health, without the intervention of the government and society, investment in this field can hardly meet actual demands and serious inequality and overall low efficiency in the use of health resources will ensue. Public health, as public medical care services, has a tremendous external effect, which demands intervention, coordination and integration by a force beyond the market. Preventive public health care and the construction of the medical security system, to some extent, are among the basic unshakable responsibilities of the government.

The government plays a leading role in the three reforms of medical and health care, which are major attempts at establishing a health security system suitable for the socialist market economic system. Constrained by various factors, some progress has been made only in certain aspects, and to carry on the reforms is still a very formidable task. The expansion of medical security coverage requires the powerful promotion of the government; while the deepening of the reforms of the urban employees' basic medical insurance system, the urban residents' medical assistance system, and the new rural cooperative medical system should further resolve the problems affecting the healthy development of the above systems. There is still a longer way to go in the reform of the medical care system, with the crux lying in how micro-operating entities in medical and health services strike a balance between their own interests and social interests, as well as between short-term development and long-term development. This fundamentally requires the government's investment mechanism, as well as reasonable policy guidance, and strict supervision and regulation. In terms of the three reforms, the reform of the field of drug production and circulation allows for the highest degree of marketization, and is also one of the fields with the closest combination of market mechanisms and government regulations. As the reform of the medical and health system has not been fully implemented, and the reform of the drug production and circulation field is entangled in the problem of medical and health care system, many enterprises have not truly become independent entities in the medical industry, lacking the foundation and stamina for healthy development and unable to compete with large-scale enterprises in the world medical circles. As a result, the material and technological support provided for the health of urban and rural residents in China does not meet actual demands.

The government is the formulator and implementer of national and regional health service development plans. The three reforms, which are only periodical reform goals, do not encompass the entire contents of health development and health security. The government's leadership role is indispensable for settling health problems and securing the people's health, as the government has to guide many fields. In some health sectors in which market, society, families and individuals can function more easily and better, the government surely should not over-reach like it did in the period of planned economy, but should shoulder the responsibility for creating an environment, regulating behaviors, conducting supervision and promoting development for them. So to speak, as health issues concern the long-term objective of state and national survival and development, the government of a modern society must play a leading role and shoulder responsibilities in this respect, no matter whether this modern society functions in a planned economy or market economy.

(iii) Several suggestions for promoting health development and health equality

(1) Continue to improve the investment in health services, especially public health services and raise their proportion in terms of total medical expenditures. The absolute amount of fiscal investment in health has been rising year after year in China, and the proportion of government health investment in terms of total health funds has also been growing since 2003; from the perspective of the structure of health funding since the reform, however, the proportion of health expenditures in the government's budget has obviously been declining, while the proportion of individual health expenditures has obviously been rising. Internationally, whether in developed countries or middle-income countries, or even in many low-income countries, government and social health expenditures account for the absolute majority of the total health funds. As it is not enough for health development, especially health equality, to rely on markets alone, as markets have many defects, one of the critical solutions is to step up government investments in health services. The increase of government health investments is not just the proper increase of its absolute value, but should also include a rise of its proportion in terms of total health funding. Only in this way can the relevant financial burdens of the people be alleviated. This is a strong support for the basic medical needs of those patients without sufficient economic bearing capacity, and also the most powerful measure for maintaining health equality. "The issue of whether personal medical and health costs should be borne by individuals or the government makes a big difference. If medical and health costs are mainly borne by the government, poor people can enjoy basic medical and health services, which can help improve the health level of the whole nation and the welfare of the whole society fundamentally." (Shaoguang 2003). Given the fast increase of payment for medical care, in accordance with international experience as well as China's national conditions, we should strive to approximately double the proportion of government health expenditures in total health expenditures during the 11th Five-Year Plan period. In the meantime, the proportion of governmental, social and individual health expenditure in the national total is expected to be around one third respectively. With the adjustment of the structure of health expenditures, the public nature of health services and the equality of health security will be obviously improved.
(2) Deepen the reform of the medical and health system so that the main bodies in medical and health service providers recover their nature as public institutions instead of being industrial or business entities. In the course of reforming the health system, though the property rights of health resources are mainly publicly owned or state-owned, yet the absolute majority of medical and health institutions, including a substantive number of state-owned and collective institutions, are subject to major transformations due to insufficient fiscal investments and the "industrialization" slogan, the latter which so excessively pursues commercialization and market profits that their nature of public institutions is lost—obviously a major behavioral distortion. Medical and health service institutions as public institutions, and especially medical professionals

as employees of public institutions, should reverse their tendency to excessively pursue commercial interests so that the main bodies of medical and health service providers restore their nature as public institution and discard the industrial or business nature. To realize this point under the market economy, we should gradually separate revenue and expenditure in the business projects of medical and health service institutions and fundamentally cut off their income channels by adopting a market-based approach towards their service items.

(3) Strengthen supervision over the drug production and circulation industry and the behaviors of medical and health service providers, as well as increase the entry threshold and fines for non-compliance. In fact, the best constraint for some medical services exceeding basic medical demands is the personal payment system. Under such a condition, some market-based medical and health service institutions should be allowed or even encouraged to develop. China has a large population with complicated medical demands, so the development of the drug and health industry is indispensable. Meanwhile, a large number of health service institutions should also conduct cost accounting with reference to market prices. All these cannot be separated from the development of the medical market. However, as a typical market of incomplete competition with information asymmetry, and in addition to the fact that medical and health services are life-and-death matters, all countries should conduct very strict regulation over this market. The behaviors of both service agencies and relevant personnel should be strictly regulated.

(4) Strive to improve efficiency in terms of the usage of medical and health resources. The fiscal budget and society cannot bear the sole expansion of the total amount of health investments without the improvement of efficiency in the use of health. We should establish full-time institutions and expert consultation committees for "deepening the reform of the health sector", strengthen the leadership of the health reform, and study the overall approach and development plans for the health reform under the new situation. We should make regional health plans meet the reality in China and truly guide and supervise health facilities and staff. We should integrate health resources, strengthen the uniform management of the public health system, and break the isolation and blockade between traditional healthcare institutions and in the whole system. We should deepen and effectively promote the reform of the drug production and circulation system and the medical and health service system, strengthen the supervision of the entities in drug production and circulation and medical and health services, rigorously conduct health supervision and law enforcement, and strictly prosecute any violator. We should shoulder the responsibility of planning for the allocation of health resources and expand the main or leading role of government investment in rural health and urban community work by means of moderately cutting government investment in urban healthcare. We should improve the social and public interest and the welfare nature of rural health services, especially national public health services, by increasing government investment in rural health services, particularly rural

health services in West China, and guide medical resources in changing their focus from "treatments neglecting prevention" to preventive health care. We should actively explore the reform of the public health investment system and gradually turn from investment in medical and health service institutions towards the provision or purchase of public health services for urban and rural residents, providing compensation funds according to the effect of medical services and encouraging medical and health service institutions to be oriented not towards profit but towards the safeguarding of residents' health. To truly change the system of combining medical treatment and medicine, we should ensure that the fiscal compensations for public health institutions meet basic demands so that public health institutions and medical service entities prioritize the provision and the development of basic medical services. The central government should increase transfer payment for public health in West China and rural health services to effectively solve the "scarcity of doctors and medicine" in these places. We should mobilize the transfer of medical professionals towards West China, step up the training of health technical personnel and improve health services.

(5) We should improve the mandatory implementation of the medical security system, and especially the medical assistance system, in order to provide the most basic medical and health services to poor people in our society. Under the conditions of the market economy, the establishment of a sound medical security system is one of the primary measures for the government to interfere with the medical and health sector, besides direct fiscal investment. Meanwhile, this is also a key measure for improving health equality. While securing and promoting public health services and new cooperative medical care, the government should focus on social pooling for serious diseases and continue to explore different types of rural medical security systems. For all farmers, serious diseases are the main health threat. Therefore, it is appropriate for new cooperative medical care to focus on serious disease insurance, as such a practice can effectively prevent a most serious phenomenon, that is: impoverishment, or backsliding to poverty due to illness. However, on the other hand, "serious illness insurance" under the prerequisite of voluntary insurance coverage will inevitably lower coverage rate, and the higher the minimum payment line, the narrower the scope of income. New rural cooperative medical care should explore the security mode of balancing both serious and minor diseases on the basis of insuring serious illness. In the management of serious illness insurance funds, the mode of operation management in commercial insurance companies may be introduced to ensure the effective use of the funds. This is in fact a sort of semi-commercial and semi-social security medical insurance. Similar practices can be found at home and abroad. In the light of the narrow coverage of urban basic medical insurance and new rural cooperative medical insurance, we should step up the establishment of an urban-rural medical assistance system. Medical assistance is one part of the medical security system and an important content of the entire social security system, as well as an effective measure for providing welfare medical security to poor people, and

plays an important role in freeing them from being impoverished or backsliding to poverty ergo illness. Medical assistance plans should be implemented for rural poor people within a region or a district. Medical assistance plans may be integrated with the whole social security system. For example, the scope of targets for implementing medical assistance could be determined by using the standard of the rural subsistence security system. In this way, not only could poor people be truly relieved but also the plan would be conveniently implemented as well as organizational costs reduced. On the whole, in the construction of the medical security system, not only should the government play a leading role, but also a multi-level and multi-type medical security system should be established according to farmers' actual demands and bearing capacity, and on the basis of respecting farmers' wishes.

(6) We should mobilize the public, especially public service organizations, to participate in patriotic health campaigns and effectively address urgent health problems in the course of economic and social transformations, such as health services for the migrant population, treatment of large-scale public health events, control of new modern infectious diseases, and increasingly serious mental health problems. In the establishment of a medical security system, we should closely combine medical security and public health, focusing on preventive health care so as to maximize the benefits of limited medical and health resources. With the state's strengthening of public health investment and improvement of the medical security system, medical and health services should be based on grassroots community services, efforts should be made to improve the training quality and professional skills of grassroots medical personnel, effectively solve the problem of people blindly crowding big hospitals and not going to community health centers, and truly implement the strategy of prevention first. Meanwhile, we should increase funding, investment and efforts to prevent new main infectious diseases and properly cope with emergency public health incidents. In light of the health problems of the migrant population, we should adopt a new mechanism with the objective of gradually including them into the management and services of their communities. We should mobilize social forces and citizens to participate in the construction of public health. As the absolute majority of public health problems are closely related to residents' awareness and behavior, through public participation, not only can public health resources be expanded but also more effective health education can be conducted in the course of their participation to promote the construction of the health environment and the changes of citizens' health-related behaviors.[4]

---

[4]This article is published in *China Industrial Economics*, Vol. 12, 2005.

Chapter 4
Establishing a Basic Rural Medical Security System

Since 1998, the establishment of an urban employees' basic medical insurance system has been considered one of the key reform projects in China, for which significant progress has been achieved. However, still no clear approaches or policies address the medical security problems of farmers, who make up of the absolute majority of the population. Due to profound changes in the social and economic structure, the cooperative medical system has been subject to overall decline since the 1980s, causing about 90% of the rural population to be without any medical security and to pay medical expenses out of their own pockets. Although the state put forward the task of restoring and reconstructing cooperative medical services in the 1990s, yet for various reasons this decision has yet to bear any fruits. The slow growth of farmers' income cannot keep up with the rapid increase of medical costs. Numerous poor farmers are plunged into such a predicament as they find themselves without resources to obtain medical treatments and purchase drugs. In recent years, the health of a significant number of farmers has even been deteriorating. A large number of farmers have been reduced or reversed to poverty due to illness, which not only directly imperils the life of these poor families but also affects the results of China's poverty alleviation strategy. Farmers' health problems have become major problems that cannot be ignored.

4.1 The Feasibility of Establishing a New Rural Medical Security System

Despite the awareness of the importance and necessity of establishing a medical security system in China's rural areas, people have yet to reach consensus on whether a rural medical security system meeting national conditions can be established at the present stage. The issue is whether China has sufficient financial resources and reliable institutions for the establishment of rural medical security.

© Springer Nature Singapore Pte Ltd. and Social Sciences Academic Press 2017
Y. Wang, *Social Security in China: On the Possibility of Equitable Distribution*,
Research Series on the Chinese Dream and China's Development Path,
DOI 10.1007/978-981-10-5643-7_4

Those opposing rural medical security hold that as limited financial resources have rendered it very difficult for China to establish an urban medical security system, it would be impossible to establish a rural medical security system based on the state's financial resources; meanwhile, due to the reform of government institutions, government organs and personnel have been streamlined, and grassroots governments do not have institutions on which rural medical security needs to rely upon. Besides, China's traditional rural cooperative medical system existed under the conditions of planned economy; profound changes have taken place in China's urban and rural economic and social structure, rendering it impossible to establish a cooperative medical system according to traditional ways. There is no experience to draw upon for the establishment of a new rural medical security system suitable for the socialist market economic system.

The above opinion, so to speak, reflects that to comprehensively establish a rural medical security system in China at the current time is no easy matter, but rather one beset with difficulties. However, such difficulties can be overcome if real importance is given to farmers' health issues and effective measures adopted. Therefore, we need not ask ourselves whether we can establish rural medical security, but rather whether we want to or not. In our opinion, we are not only able to develop rural medical security; in China's new situation, doing so is necessary.

First, by developing the rural economy and increasing farmers' income, the financial resources for establishing rural medical security have been accumulated. Medical security requires funds, and a higher level of security requires more funds. In over twenty years since the initiation of reform and opening-up, farmers' per capita net income has increased tenfold from less than RMB 200 to over RMB 2200. If farmers could bear the expenditure of cooperative medical security in the time of planned economy with very low income, they could also bear the establishment of rural medical security to some extent, according to their current income. In terms of the government's financial resources, recent years have seen rapid increase of tax revenues in China; national tax revenues amounted to RMB 1.266 trillion in 2000. Therefore, the government should be able to inject some funds in rural medical security. Of course, due to the decline of the grassroots collective economy and the implementation of the system of tax distribution, in most regions of China, public finances below the county level, especially township finances, are in difficulty, which is the objective reality. However, this is only an issue of fiscal structure; in terms of economic power, China should now have more financial resources to establish rural medical security than twenty years ago.

Second, the issue concerning the establishment of institutions for the development of rural medical security can also be overcome. Cooperative medical care during the period of planned economy mainly relied on people's communities and production brigade organizations which grasped political and economic resources etc. Since reform and opening-up, although township governments and villagers' autonomous organizations' control of economic resources and their intervention in economic activities have been substantially weakened, these organizations still exist. Meanwhile, the number of rural doctors has increased and their professional qualifications have largely improved in comparison with the time before reform.

Table 4.1 Composition of China's medical security system in 1998, *Unit* percentage

Survey index	Urban and rural total	Urban	Rural				
		Total	Total	Class I	Class II	Class III	Class IV
Free medical care	4.95	16.01	1.16	1.07	0.76	1.98	0.26
Labor protection medical care	6.22	22.91	0.51	1.40	0.54	0.15	0.03
Semi-labor protection medical care	1.62	5.78	0.20	0.64	0.10	0.07	0.05
Medical insurance	1.88	3.27	1.41	2.39	1.63	1.16	0.12
Social pooling medical care	0.39	1.42	0.05	0.15	0.03	0.01	0.00
Cooperative medical care	5.54	2.74	6.50	22.21	3.24	1.62	1.83
Out-of-pocket medical care	76.40	44.13	87.44	71.79	93.17	94.77	81.49
Other forms	2.98	3.73	2.73	0.34	0.52	0.23	16.22

Source Initial Report on the Main Results of the Second National Health Service Survey in 1998

More than that, great development has also been achieved in other types of social organizations, such as rural financial institutions. If we expand our vision, we would find that there do exist institutions establishing the rural medical security; If we raise them from the village level to the county level (which is the direction of development), we will have richer organizational resources, as a county (municipal) unit enjoys relatively independent organizations resources of various types, such as a medical security system and a financial insurance system.

Finally, as for the lack of experience in establishing rural medical security under the new situation, the practice experiences of relevant regions have fully proven that a multi-level and multi-type rural medical security system can be established. Although there no longer exists a nationwide cooperative medical system, cooperative medical care is still maintained in South Jiangsu and Shanghai, while a variety of rural medical security initiatives have been taken and newly developed, such as rural labor insurance medical care, cooperative medical insurance and social pooling for serious illness. The results of the "Second National Health Service Survey" held by the Ministry of Health in 1998 showed that nationwide 61.50% of rural residents participated in cooperative medical care, and about 6.11% participated in some other type of medical security (see the following Table 4.1). This demonstrates that although it is difficult to restore the traditional cooperative medical care system in the rural areas,[1] yet it is necessary and feasible to develop a multi-type and multi-level medical security system in rural areas, where there is a huge space for development.

[1]For relevant analysis, see the author's article "A Report on the Rural Medical Security System", in Chen Jiagui ed. (2001), *The Development of Social Security in China: a Report*, Social Sciences Academic Press.

4.2 Suggestions and Measures for Establishing a New Rural Medical Security System

(i) Principles for establishing a new rural medical security system

To establish a basic medical security system for farmers in the new situation of socialist market economy, we should stick to the following basic principles: First, we should stick to the principle of state support. A mechanism in which the state and farmers make joint investments and share risks should be established, so that the limited fund investments by the state can guide farmers in their participation in the medical security system. Meanwhile, we should lay emphasis on a mechanism of diversified investments, and substantiate farmers' medical security fund by using the donations from community economies, enterprises, charity institutions, foreign-funded institutions and individuals. In terms of state investments, the majority may be diverted from state health service funds and some from tax revenues. Second, measures can be adjusted to local conditions. China has a vast territory with great disparity in economic and social development; as this cannot be changed on the short term, we cannot and should not adopt a "sweeping approach" or "unified pattern" for the nationwide establishment of farmers' medical security. We should allow all regions to start from their own reality and actively explore a multi-form and multi-level medical insurance system, especially a cooperative medical insurance system addressing the local characteristics of rural areas. Third, we should stick to the principle of socialization. We should promote the participation of farmers through national legislation (instead of just relying on "voluntary participation") based on county-level regions (instead of villages or townships), which would help expand the scale of medical security funds and enhance the ability to resist risks. Meanwhile, we may draw upon the form of personal accounts in urban employees' medical care to establish farmers' family medical security accounts, promote farmers' fund saving and lessen the risks of illness. Fourth, we should stick to the principle of insuring against serious illness. Farmers' illness threats mainly come from serious illness, a risk which they cannot bear. However, due to limited state investments, it is impossible to establish comprehensive and advanced medical security; therefore, such limited funds may only be applied to most urgent needs, that is: the most serious illnesses which pose the biggest threats to farmers. As the state has established the "basic medical insurance" system for urban employees, it should also establish the "essential serious illness security" system for farmers.

(ii) State attention and support are the basis and prerequisite for establishing farmers' medical security

With the disintegration of collective economy, the absolute majority of rural grassroots community organizations has lost or lacks the ability to collectively invest in farmers' medical security, which is a fundamental cause for the decline of community-based cooperative medical care. Since the initiation of reform in the tax-sharing system, financial resources have been concentrated in upper level governments, while grassroots governments have weaker funding to the point that a significant number of township governments operate in debt, while many counties and cities maintain payroll finance or "subsidized" finance. Reforming grassroots government agencies and combining townships could indeed reduce administrative expenditures, but leaves the issue of increasing financial resources for grassroots community authorities unaddressed. A root cause is that the state employs its main financial resources to solve large and medium state-owned enterprises issues, and it practices the "one country two systems" policy for urban and rural areas, which includes seriously urban-biased policymaking in terms of education, health, electricity, roads, credits, water conservancy, post and telecommunications and other infrastructure.[2] Rural resources are being abused while investment in these areas is inadequate, leading to financial difficulties for township enterprises, small and medium enterprises, and farmers' household economies, as well as to shrinking county economies. A substantial number of grassroots governments are weighed down with education expenditures, employees' salaries and retirement pensions, etc. The state may lack determination to solve the issue of farmers' medical security, but grassroots governments not only unable to address farmers' medical security but also have no such a wish or motive.

Currently, the state has included the establishment of a socialized urban employees' basic medical insurance system as one of the five key reform projects, which shows that the state has assumed the burdensome responsibility of urban employees' basic medical insurance. This is a basic reflection of state functions and also an inevitable requirement for establishing a fair society. Based on the objective reality of the great urban-rural disparity in China, it is impossible to completely unify the urban-rural medical security system within a short period, and the urban-rural gap in the scope and level of medical security will persist for a long time. However, such factual disparity cannot excuse the state from shirking its responsibility for securing farmers' health. In a way, farmers whose income is lower need more support and protection from the state in medical security than urban employees. Our health policy should not merely focus on enhancing the health of a few healthy people, but should enable those without health security to have access to the most essential health security. Meanwhile, medical security, particularly public health care, is typically considered as a social "public goods", and should be made available to the whole society instead of its access being limited to urban residents. This is an objective requirement for establishing a complete market economy system and also a public investment producing maximum benefits for the whole society. Additionally, to establish a medical security system for all people, especially farmers, is a necessary development in order to maintain the healthy

[2]The Research Team of the Academy of Macroeconomic Research, SDPC (2001), Problems of Rural Tax Reform: A Study, Review of Economic Research, 2001 (24).

operation of the basic medical insurance system for urban employees. With rapid industrialization and urbanization in China, the rural population has been migrating to cities and towns (the ratio of urban population has exceeded 36% according to the 2000 census data). If farmers' medical security issue is not soon settled, the impact on the urban medical security system will be tremendous, and the stable operation of the urban medical security system will be affected.

(iii) The establishment of farmers' basic medical security should focus on security for serious illness

New approaches are required for the settlement of farmers' medical security problems under the conditions of the market economy. In light of the extreme complexity of the medical security system and difficulty in managing medical consumption, we cannot do for farmers' medical care as was done for solving the issue of urban employees' medical insurance. Our foothold is to establish and resolve farmers' most essential medical security, especially security for risks of major illness which farmers can hardly bear. On the whole, farmers' medical security relies mainly on self-protection based on families, because of low productivity and also because of the large proportion for which farmers account nationally. In this regard, the situation cannot be compare with that of developed countries in the West. However, we cannot leave all the burdens of medical security to self-protection based on farmers' families, because farmers' families have limited bearing capacities. For ordinary and minor ailments, families can manage to bear medical costs. As for major and serious illnesses, low-income farmers absolutely cannot afford treatment. It should be noted that currently rural families are becoming smaller, thus farmers' income increases slowly, while various taxes are constantly rising, posing excessive burdens. From 1994 to 1999, farmers' per capita income increase rate (12.16%) was lower than the increase rate of their burdens, which actually reduced their families' self-protection abilities, especially the ability to resist serious illnesses.

Therefore, to alleviate farmers' burdens, as well as reduce management difficulties and the cost of the medical security system, we advocate that we should first establish farmers' serious illness insurance based on counties (or townships) in rural areas. The sources of funds for farmers' serious illness security would mainly be comprised of funds contributed by farmer households and fiscal subsidies. To establish a farmers' serious illness security fund, the ratio of contributions may be adapted to actual local conditions. Compared with traditional cooperative medical care, farmers' serious illness security—which has such advantages as a high level of social pooling, strong resistance against risks, low level of fund raising, as well as facility in fund raising, management and settlement—is a basic rural medical security system adapted to new situations. Of course, in regions with better conditions (such as suburban villages in South Jiangsu, Shanghai, and medium and large cities), more comprehensive medical security (including outpatient services) may be developed on the basis of farmers' serious illness insurance.

(iv) Several measures for establishing the rural medical security system

(1) We should enhance the awareness of the government as well as that of the whole society on the issue of rural medical security. We have noted that whether the farmers' medical security system can be established mainly depends on awareness levels. Only when awareness is enhanced will great importance be attached to this issue, and thus will feasible measures be actively explored and adopted to be implement in the system. We stress the major responsibilities of the state in resolving farmers' medical security problems, not just because the state should more proactively adopt measures in terms of the institutional design of and fiscal investment for farmers' medical security, but more importantly because we wish to arouse the close attention of the government and that of the whole society. The state is obliged to settle farmers' medical security problems, which is also an inevitable path to modernization.

(2) We should adjust the government's medical and health investment structure to focus on supporting disadvantaged groups and patients. With the reform of the health system and especially the emergence of a large number of private hospitals, the state's focus on health investment should gradually shift from health service providers to medical service consumers; that is because the current problem is not the "scarcity of doctors and medicine", but rather that people in most regions lack even the most essential medical security. State support may promote the growth of medical consumption, drive the development of the medical industry, and increase employment opportunities so that people can enjoy better medical services and living standard. Except for remote areas and some medical institutions and public health institutions which the state must control, medical institutions' access restriction may be lifted so that medical institutions can raise funds in market and become independent market players who assume sole responsibility for their own profits or losses. This can not only promote medical service institutions such as hospitals to improve their service quality and better their service attitude but also reduce state investments, which can be diverted to the establishment of medical security for the people. As a whole, the state's total investments in medical and health services would not increase significantly, but the effect would become more significant and fairer.

(3) Reasonably distribute health resources and effectively reduce medical costs. "Shortage" (poor facility capacity) and "redundancy" (disorderly scattering of service professionals and service centers, and loss of control over scale) coexist due to seriously unreasonable allocation of medical and health resources in China, which lead to the rise of medical costs. To control the rise of medical costs, we should focus on controlling the expansion of the scope of medical services and the rise of internal costs. Based on the scope of regional health care, we should strictly enforce the examination and approval of new medical institutions, control the expansion of the current scope, remerge unreasonably overlapping institutions, and adjust and rationalize service functions. In light of the disorderly situation in the medicine and medical market, to strengthen the supervision of pharmaceutical production, sales link and medical institutions is

an important step in order to control the rise of medical costs and alleviating farmers' burdens. The reform and supervision of urban and rural medical markets should be conducted simultaneously to plug up loopholes and improve efficiency.

(4) Strengthen public health work and improve the public health system. Preventive healthcare is for everybody and it has the nature of low cost, good efficiency and significant effect. "In line with the principle of cost-effectiveness and fairness, preventive healthcare can obviously reduce risks of illness, disability and death, improve life quality, effectively protect social productivity, and promote social and economic development," and thus should remain a priority in terms of rural healthcare work, with strengthened input in funding, personnel and facilities. Significant achievements have been made in public health (mainly marked by epidemic prevention, health supervision and patriotic health campaigns), maternal and children's health care, and medical preventive health systems. However, the three systems overlap and are separated so that their limited resources cannot be effectively utilized. We should, while keeping in view the implementation of regional health planning and the adjustment of medical service institutions, and basing ourselves on the current situation of township health centers and village health stations with integrated management, establish a health care system of "one network with multiple uses". Based on the nature of provided services (public health care and preventive care or general operating business, health care for poverty relief or ordinary treatment, etc.), we should reasonably solve the issue of the compensatory mechanism for public health and preventive care, and enable public preventive care to have stable funding, as well as ensure the normal development of preventive health care.

(5) Establish a medical assistance system and strengthen health care for poverty relief. The rural medical security system with Chinese characteristics should also include a medical assistance system. The role of the government is not just "to add flowers to the brocade", but more importantly to "provide fuel in snowy weather" by including poverty relief through health care for poverty-stricken areas and people as one of the key contents for promoting rural health care. This is necessary in order to realize the objective of "making health available to everyone" and to develop production and prevent people from "being reduced or reversed to poverty" because of illness. The poverty relief plans implemented in China focus on economic poverty relief. Economic poverty relief and health poverty relief should be integrated. With the support of the central government and developed regions, we should first solve the health care facility construction and "scarcity of doctors and medicine" issues in poverty-stricken areas, and allocate a part of the state's special fund for poverty relief and relevant support funds to specially address the medical poverty relief in poor regions. As for rural poor people in different regions and areas, medical assistance plans should be implemented. Medical assistance plans are part of the medical security system, which is an important part of the whole social security system. We should incorporate health poverty relief into social

security, especially the social assistance system, and integrate medical assistance plans into the whole social security system. For example, the scope of targets for medical assistance may be determined by using the standard of the rural subsistence security system. In this way, we can truly assist poor people, while reducing organizational cost so that such a practice becomes convenient and feasible.[3]

[3]This article is published in Research on Economics and Management, Vol. 3, 2001.

Chapter 5
Analysis of Factors Affecting Rural Residents' Satisfaction with Medical Services

5.1 Introduction

With the development of the rural economic society, rural residents have growing demands in terms of medical services, and the quality of medical services provided to rural residents has been drawing more and more attention. Medical service satisfaction is an important index for evaluating the quality of medical services, and it can, to some extent, reflect the people's potential medical demands. Satisfaction generally comprises a series of indexes. Yiren and Pengde (2005), through questionnaire surveys of patients in a certain hospital in Nanjing, classify patients' satisfaction indexes into five dimensions by using the factor analysis method, that is: medical effect, medical professionals' technique and capability, medical professionals' attitude, medical environment, and medical support and expenditure. In recent years, especially since the implementation of the new rural cooperative medical care system (Hereinafter referred to as New Rural Co-op), many scholars have, on the basis of field surveys, studied the medical service satisfaction of rural residents as well as the factors affecting satisfaction. A survey conducted by Liming et al. (2009) on 245 farmer households in three provinces shows that the satisfaction of farmers who subscribe to the New Rural Co-op on medical services is relatively high, but their satisfaction concerns more the "volume" of supply than the "quality" thereof. Wang et al. (2006) has found out through research that farmers' overall satisfaction with the implementation of the New Rural Co-op program is related to their age, policy awareness, medical service expenditures, satisfaction on reimbursement, and their expected coinsurance rate. Liu et al. (2008) have found out through research on the New Rural Co-op that farmers' age, marital status, education background, occupation, self-rated health conditions and self-rated happiness in life have a significant impact on their satisfaction with the New Rural Co-op, while gender has no significant impact. Zhou and Shi (2009) have found out through research that the satisfaction with the New Rural Co-op reimbursement system shows a significant positive correlation with the New Rural Co-op

© Springer Nature Singapore Pte Ltd. and Social Sciences Academic Press 2017
Y. Wang, *Social Security in China: On the Possibility of Equitable Distribution*,
Research Series on the Chinese Dream and China's Development Path,
DOI 10.1007/978-981-10-5643-7_5

reimbursement ratio and procedures, and a significant negative correlation with whether farmers subscribe to other health insurances, their family's yearly medical expenditures, and personal expectation on the amount raised.

In light of past studies, besides the quality of medical services per se, the personal traits of medical service users and their economic, social and cultural background are also important factors affecting their satisfaction with medical services. However, different factors affect satisfaction with medical services differently, with some directly affecting satisfaction with medical services while others coming into play via an intermediate variable. However, in extant literature, many studies analyze all factors as factors directly affecting satisfaction with medical services, instead of differentiating the direct factors and the indirect factors affecting satisfaction with medical services; therefore, it is very difficult for them to analyze how different factors affect satisfaction with medical services.

Studies on satisfaction with medical services cannot be separated from the rating of medical services by rural residents, who are the direct consumers of medical services. How do rural residents comment on the current medical services? How many are satisfied, and how many are not? What factors affect their satisfaction with medical services? This article will use the data of a questionnaire survey by a task force of the Chinese Academy of Social Sciences (CASS) on "the study of the demand for medical services by medium and low-income people in China and innovation of service modes" conducted in 2009, and adopt the path analysis method to analyze factors affecting rural residents' satisfaction with medical services and how each factor affects such satisfaction.

5.2 Course of Survey and Framework of Research

(i) Course of survey

The data used in this article are the initial data concerning rural areas concluded by the task force of the Chinese Academy of Social Sciences (CASS) on "the study of the demand for medical services by medium and low-income people in China and innovation of service modes" conducted in 2009. This survey mainly addressed medium and low-income rural and urban residents in China. Limited by funding, human resources and time, representative regions were sampled, including six urban areas and four rural areas (ten areas in total) in seven provinces (municipalities) in Northeast China, North China, Northwest China, Southeast China, Southwest China and Central China. The four rural regions were respectively Miyun County, Beijing, Xinzheng City, Henan, Yuzhong City, Gansu, and Kaiyuan City, Yunnan. These regions cover different levels of income in rural areas while including three geographical units in the eastern, central and western parts of China.

This survey adopted the method of visiting homes with questionnaires. The survey was conducted from July to October, 2009. During the course of the survey, strictly trained interviewers asked questions and filled out questionnaires by themselves, and gave explanations to questions raised by interviewees. Over one hour was spent on filling out each questionnaire on average, and the project principal checked each questionnaire, and even re-visited interviewees one by one to ensure the accuracy and validity of the data. Finally, this survey acquired the information of 903 rural residents and their families (including some local residents whose household register was not rural), among whom there were 441 rural households which met medium and low-income standards, and 462 (relatively) high-income rural households. As this survey did not adopt the method of random sampling nationwide, the results of the research were deficient to deduce the overall situation, but it was hoped that they could illustrate rural residents' satisfaction with medical services nationwide to some extent.

(ii) Framework of research

This research held that rural residents' rating on medical institutions, medical professionals, drugs and the medical insurance system directly affected their satisfaction with medical services, whereas their social and demographic characteristics such as age, gender, region and educational background, as well as family income, family members' health status, diagnosis and treatment methods after taking ill, use of medical services, accessibility of medical resources, ratio of medical and health care expenditure, and time interval of medical expense reimbursement, etc., mainly affected their satisfaction with medical services through the above four factors. Therefore, this study takes these four factors (such as rating of medical institutions) as intermediate variables, and factors such as social and demographic characteristics as initial variables, and adopts a path analysis to disclose the courses of initial variables and intermediate variables affecting satisfaction with medical services (see Fig. 5.1 for the framework of analysis).

The dependent variables are interval variables, which are measured by the method of direct value assignment to answers, with 1 ~ 5 points assigned to answers ranging from "very dissatisfied" to "very satisfied" (the highest point being 5). The intermediate variables are all interval variables, which are measured through a series of indexes. The rating for medical institutions consists of variables

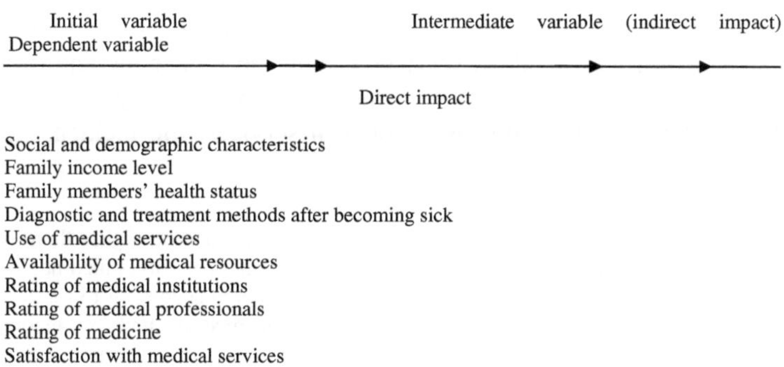

Fig. 5.1 Framework of Research

such as quantity of institutions, medical environment, convenience and medical equipment; the rating for medical professionals consists of variables such as technical accomplishments, explanation of state of an illness and service attitudes of medical professionals; the rating for drugs consists variables such as types, quality and prices of drugs; the rating for the medical insurance system consists of variables such as the level of contribution, convenience in reimbursement, amount of reimbursement and catalog of reimbursed drugs.

Besides the interviewees' personal, social and demographic characteristics, initial variables mainly appeal to the family characteristics of interviewees, mainly out of the consideration that in one family, whenever a member is taken ill, the other members will generally be involved in the care of the sick one; therefore, to some extent, families are basic units using medical services. Initial variables mainly include: ① Social and demographic characteristics, including interviewees' age, gender (male or female), national geographical location (east, central or west), education background and occupation; ② Family income level (low, medium or high)[1]; ③ Family members' illness status, including the main types of diseases caught by family members in the previous years (chronic diseases, acute diseases or other diseases) and the incidence of disease; ④ Treatment and diagnosis methods adopted after family members are taken ill, including not adopting any measure, self-diagnosis and treatment as well as seeing a doctor in a medical institution; ⑤ Use of medical services, including the medical institutions mainly used (grassroots medical institutions, pharmacies, town health centers and county hospitals) and drug use frequency in the previous year; ⑥ The proportion of medical and health expenditures, referring to the ratio of year-round medical and health care expenditures against total expenditures; ⑦ Accessibility of medical resources, including the distance to the nearest big hospital and the distance to the nearest village clinic; ⑧ Time interval of reimbursement of medical expenses, including spot reimbursement and off-the-spot reimbursement.

The following hypothesis is proposed in this article based on experiences and available literature: ① Satisfaction with medical institutions, medical professionals and drugs exerts more impact on satisfaction with medical services than satisfaction with the medical insurance system. ② Gender has no impact on satisfaction with medical services. ③ Age, location, occupation and education background have a significant impact on satisfaction with medical services. ④ Family income levels indirectly affect satisfaction with medical services in that the higher income rural residents have, the lower their satisfaction with medical services is. ⑤ Types of diseases are not related with satisfaction with medical services; the incidence of

[1]The task force, in the beginning, defined "medium and low income" as income higher than the local minimum subsistence level, and lower than 50% of the local rural net per capita income, and classified "medium and low income" into medium income and low income according to research needs. Medium income refers to the income level above 50% of the medium and low-income standard (that is, 25% of the per capita income of the previous year), while low income refers to the income level below 50% of the medium and low-income standard. The families under survey whose income is above "medium and low income" standard are called high-income families.

diseases is related with satisfaction with medical services in that the higher incidence of diseases rural residents have, the lower their satisfaction with medical services is. ⑥ The conditions of medical institutions used exert a direct impact on satisfaction with medical services in that the higher level of medical institutions rural residents use, the higher their satisfaction with medical services is; the frequency of drug use has no impact on satisfaction with medical services. ⑦ The accessibility of medical resources indirectly affects satisfaction with medical services mainly by affecting satisfaction with medical institutions. ⑧ The ratio of medical and health care expenditures against total expenditures directly affects satisfaction with medical services. ⑨ The time interval of medical expense reimbursement indirectly affects satisfaction with medical services by affecting satisfaction with the medical insurance system.

5.3 Results of Research and Analysis

(i) Statistical description of variables

(1) Basic description of rural residents' satisfaction with medical services

In light of the survey results, rural residents currently are not highly satisfied with medical services. The average score is 3.46 points, between "so so" and "fairly satisfactory"; 35.3% of the interviewees choose "so so"; 43.3% of them choose "fairly satisfied"; 12.7% of them choose "dissatisfied", that is, giving a score less than 3 points; while only 8.3% of them choose "very satisfied".

(2) Statistic description of intermediate variables

Table 5.1 indicates that the average rating for medical institutions is 13.54 points, of which rural residents have higher rating on the convenience of getting medical care than on the quantity, environment and equipment of medical institutions; the average rating for medical professionals is 9.94 points, of which rural residents have higher rating over the service attitudes of medical professionals than on their medical skills and explanation of diseases; the average rating for drugs is 9.13

Table 5.1 Statistical description of intermediate variables

	Total score	Average value	Minimum value	Maximum value	Standard deviation
Rating for medical institutions	20	13.54	5	20	2.32
Rating for medical professionals	15	9.94	3	15	1.92
Rating for drugs	15	9.13	4	13	1.44
Rating for the medical insurance system	20	11.50	4	20	2.43

points, of which rural residents have the highest rating on types of drugs and the lowest rating on prices of drugs; the average rating for the medical insurance system is 11.50 points, of which rural residents have the lowest rating on the scope of reimbursement. On the whole, rural residents' ratings on the medical insurance system differ the most, whereas their ratings on drugs differ the less.

(3) Statistic description of initial variables

Tables 5.2 and 5.3 indicate that of the 903 interviewees, mid-aged people are dominant, and their average age is 45; in terms of gender, females outnumber males; in terms of geographical location, people from the western region are most numerous; in terms of education background, most have only received primary school education or below; in terms of occupation, most work in the field of agriculture (mostly farmers). The family income level of most interviewees is above the middle level in local rural areas; the diseases afflicting their family members are mostly acute diseases, and most adopt the measure of "seeing a doctor in a medical institution" after a disease is contracted, opting mostly for rural grassroots medical institutions; the distance to the grassroots medical institution closest to the interviewees is 2.69 km on average; the medical expenses can be reimbursed directly (directly deducted from the New Rural Co-op fund) after the interviewees and their family members see a doctor.

(ii) Multivariate regression analysis of intermediate variables on rural residents' satisfaction with medical services

According to the framework of analysis, intermediate variables are used first to conduct a multivariate regression analysis of satisfaction with medical services. The explanatory power of the model is 26%, with relatively satisfying goodness-of-fit. According to the results of the analysis, with the exception of the rating of the medical insurance system, the rating of medical institutions, the rating of medical professionals and the rating of drugs have all passed the significance test. The rating with the biggest impact is that of medical professionals, with a standardized regression coefficient of 0.355, followed by the rating of medical institutions, with a standardized regression coefficient of 0.14 (see Table 5.4). Therefore, in the subsequent path analysis, the rating of the medical insurance system will not be incorporated into the regression model.

(iii) Multivariate regression analysis of the impact of initial variables on intermediate variables and dependent variables

The multivariate regression analysis method adopted in this article is the optimal scaling regression analysis method, which allows independent variables to be classified variables and gives each class an appropriate quantitative rating. Based on the framework of models expected to be fit, this method analyzes the changing degrees of impact of different classified variables on dependent variables and adopts certain nonlinear transformations to reiterate original classified variables, so as to find the best quantitative rating for them and then fit an optimal equation.

Table 5.2 Statistical description of initial variables (1)

Variable		Assignment	Number of samples	Effective percentage
Gender	Male	1	425	52.93
	Female	2	477	47.07
Location	East	1	250	27.68
	Central	2	199	22.04
	West	3	454	50.28
Education background	Primary school and below	1	392	43.61
	Junior middle school	2	301	33.48
	Senior middle school and above	3	206	22.91
Occupation	Agricultural management personnel	1	48	5.34
	The self-employed	2	40	4.45
	Rural migrant workers	3	17	1.89
	Agricultural practitioners (farmers)	4	794	88.32
Family income level	Low income	1	137	15.17
	Middle income	2	304	33.67
	High income	3	462	51.16
Main types of diseases that family members had in the previous year	Chronic diseases	1	108	12.27
	Other diseases	2	164	18.64
	Acute diseases	3	608	69.09
Main method of diagnosis and treatmentadopted after a family member is taken ill	Not adopting any measure	1	21	2.47
	Self-diagnosis and treatment	2	206	24.21
	See a doctor in a medical institution	3	624	73.32
Medical institutions mainly used in the previous year	Township health centers	1	161	21.70
	Rural grassroots medical institutions	2	401	54.04
	County hospitals	3	71	9.57
	Pharmacies	4	109	14.69

(continued)

Table 5.2 (continued)

Variable		Assignment	Number of samples	Effective percentage
Time interval for reimbursement of medical expenses	Spot reimbursement	1	386	70.57
	Off-the-spot reimbursement	2	161	29.43

Note In this table, the sums of samples of each group of classified data are not inter-equivalent and are not necessarily equivalent to the number of effective samples (903), which is caused by the large amount of sample missing value. However, in order not to lose the information of missing cases, this article preserves case records with missing value and incorporates samples with missing value into the regression model in optimal scaling regression

Table 5.3 Statistical description of initial variables (2)

Variable	Average value	Minimum value	Maximum value	Standard deviation
Age	45.35	16	84	13.89
The distance to the large hospital closest to the interviewee's home (km)	45.85	1	260	40.73
The distance to the community health center (village clinic) closest to the interviewee's home (km)	2.69	0	24	3.04
Frequency at which family members were taken ill in the previous year	2.36	0	11	1.37
Frequency at which drugs were use in the whole family in the previous year	135.55	0	3285	336.05
Ratio of medical and health care expenditure against total expenditures (%)	26.97	0	705.88	48.84

Table 5.4 Multivariate regression analysis of the direct impact of intermediate variables on satisfaction with medical services

	Unstandardized regression coefficient	Standardized regression coefficient
Rating of medical institutions	0.052	0.140***
Rating of medical professionals	0.161	0.355***
Rating of drugs	0.049	0.081*
Rating of the medical insurance system	0.021	0.059
Constant term	0.465	
F	68.278***	
R^2	0.256	

Note *** and * show the significance level of 0.1% and 5% respectively

In light of the multivariate regression analysis of initial variables to intermediate variables and dependent variables, the four regression models all have a relatively good fit. Table 5.5 indicates that the explanatory power of the initial variables to several intermediate variables are all above 15%, of which the one with the strongest

Table 5.5 Multivariate regression analysis of the impact of initial variables on intermediate variables and dependent variables (standardized regression coefficient)

Initial variables	Intermediate variables			Dependent variables
	Rating of medical institutions	Rating of medical professionals	Rating of drugs	Satisfaction with medical services
Age	0.166*	0.198**	−0.001	0.271***
Gender	−0.028	0.027	−0.039	−0.100
Location	0.345***	0.303***	0.260***	0.273***
Education background	−0.143*	−0.094	0.036	−0.045
Occupation	0.213***	−0.243***	0.217***	0.172***
Family income level	−0.058	−0.119*	−0.024	−0.159***
The distance to the large hospital closest to the interviewee's home (km)	−0.129	−0.080	−0.138	−0.109
The distance to the village clinic closest to the interviewee's home (km)	−0.015	0.012	0.129*	−0.018
Main types of diseases contacted by family members in the previous year	−0.150**	0.112*	0.165***	−0.077
Number of times family members were taken ill in the previous year	0.038	−0.135*	−0.042	0.019
Main method of diagnosis and treatment adopted after a family member is taken ill	0.102*	0.143**	0.064	0.069
Main medical institutions used in the previous year	−0.056	0.070	−0.172***	−0.082
Frequency of drug use by the whole family in the previous year	0.011	−0.015	−0.086	0.003
Proportion of medical and health care expenditure in the previous year	−0.085	−0.076	0.067	−0.076
Time interval for medical expense reimbursement	0.075	0.054	0.044	−0.003
F	1.931**	1.486*	1.584*	1.671*
R^2	0.182	0.150	0.154	0.164

Note ***, ** and * respectively indicate the significance level of 0.1%, 1% and 5%

explanatory power is that initial variables against the rating of medical institutions; the direct explanatory degree of the initial variables to dependent variables is 16%, obviously lower than the explanatory power of intermediate variables to dependent variables. This shows that directly applying initial variables to explain dependent variables is subject to very big defects, as initial variables affect dependent variables mainly through intermediate variables, which also illustrates that the above preset framework of research is reasonable. In light of the regression results, the initial variables significantly affecting the rating of medical institutions are age, location, education background, occupation, main types of diseases contracted by family members in the previous year, and main method of diagnosis and treatment adopted after a family member is taken ill; initial variables significantly affecting the rating of medical professionals are age, location, education background, occupation, main types of diseases contracted by family members in the previous year, and main method of diagnosis and treatment adopted after a family member is taken ill; initial variables with significant impact on drug ratings are location, occupation, distance to the closest village clinic, main types of diseases contracted by family members in the previous year, and main medical institutions visited in the previous year. Initial variables with significant and direct impact on satisfaction with medical services are age, location, occupation and family income level.

(iv) Path analysis of the impact on satisfaction with medical services

Table 5.6 indicates the course in which initial variables impact dependent variables, of which indirect impact = the standardized regression coefficient of an initial variable to an intermediate variable × the standardized regression coefficient of the intermediate variable to dependent variables; total impact = indirect impact + direct impact; in accordance with Table 5.5, the standardized regression coefficients with $p > 0.05$ are not included in the table.

The results of path analysis show that location exerts the greatest impact on satisfaction with medical services (according to the absolute value of the path coefficient), with its coefficient reaching 0.450; age comes next, with a coefficient of 0.365; family income level ranks the third, with a coefficient of −0.211. Gender, distance to the closest large hospital, frequency of drug use by the whole family in the previous year, proportion of medical or health care expenditure in the previous year and time interval for medical expense reimbursement have no impact on rural residents' satisfaction with medical services.

Next, let's further analyze the impact of various factors on satisfaction with medical services.

(1) Age exerts a positive impact on satisfaction with medical services, that is, rural residents' satisfaction with medical services increases with their age. For one thing, current medical services can meet the demands of elderly people but fail to meet young people's demands; for another, elderly people probably have lower requirements for medical services than young people.

Table 5.6 Path analysis of initial variables on satisfaction with medical services

	Total impact	Indirect impact			Direct impact
		Rating of medical institutions	Rating of medical professionals	Rating of drugs	
Age	0.365	0.023	0.071	–	0.271
Gender	–	–	–	–	–
Location	0.450	0.048	0.108	0.021	0.273
Education background	−0.020	−0.020	–	–	–
Occupation	0.134	0.030	−0.086	0.018	0.172
Family income level	−0.201	–	−0.042	–	−0.159
Distance to the closest large hospital	–	–	–	–	–
Distance to the closest village clinic	0.010	–	–	0.010	–
Main types of disease family members contracted in the previous year	0.032	−0.021	0.040	0.013	–
Frequency at which family members were taken ill in the previous year	−0.048	–	−0.048	–	–
Main method of diagnosis and treatment adopted after a family member is taken ill	0.065	0.014	0.051	–	–
Main medical institutions used in the previous year	−0.014	–	–	−0.014	–
Frequency of drug use by the whole family in the previous year	–	–	–	–	–
Ration of medical and health care expenditure in the previous year	–	–	–	–	–
Time interval for medical expense reimbursement	–	–	–	–	–

(2) In terms of location, the satisfaction with medical services of rural residents in western regions is higher than that in central regions, while the satisfaction with medical services in eastern regions is the lowest.
(3) Educational background exerts a negative impact on satisfaction with medical services; that is, the better rural residents' educational background is, the lower their satisfaction with medical services is. Educational background affects rural residents' satisfaction with medical services mainly by affecting their rating of medical institutions. This is probably because residents with better educational background have very high expectations on medical services, which in turn reduces their satisfaction.

(4) In terms of occupation, agricultural management personnel are the least satisfied with medical services, while farmers are the most satisfied. This is probably because people engaged in different occupations have different expectations when it comes to medical services. Farmers, who did not have such medical security before the implementation of the New Rural Co-op feel quite satisfied with the availability of medical security, which is an important reason for their enhanced satisfaction with medical services.
(5) Family income level exerts a negative impact on satisfaction with medical services; that is, the higher rural residents' family income level is, the lower their satisfaction with medical services is. This is mainly because high-income families have higher demands in terms of medical services, while a certain gap exists between such demands and the current service level, thus affecting their satisfaction with medical services.
(6) Distance to the closest village clinic has a positive impact on their satisfaction with medical services; that is, the farther rural residents live from their village clinic, the higher their satisfaction with medical services is. This is mainly because the farther rural residents live from their village clinic; the less likely they are to visit it, thus the fewer problems they discover, which in turn increases their satisfaction.
(7) Frequency at which family members contracted diseases in the previous year has a negative impact on their satisfaction with medical services; that is, the more often family members are taken ill, the lower their satisfaction with medical service is.
(8) In terms of main types of diseases contracted by family members in the previous year, rural residents' families whose members mainly contact acute diseases have a higher satisfaction with medical services than those whose members mainly suffer from chronic diseases and other diseases. This is probably because acute diseases under survey are mainly influenza, for which there are very mature drugs and medical techniques, thus improving patients' satisfaction.
(9) In terms of the main treatment and diagnosis methods adopted after family members are taken ill, rural residents who see a doctor in a medical institution after having been taken ill have a higher satisfaction with medical services than those resorting to self-diagnosis and treatment (buying drugs themselves or self-recuperation). This is probably related to the medical institutions attended. Rural residents choosing self-diagnosis and treatment generally visit pharmacies. In this research, rural residents who often attend pharmacies have a lower satisfaction with medical services that those visiting other types of medical institutions.
(10) In terms of main medical institutions used in the previous year, rural residents using township health centers have the highest satisfaction with medical services, while those using pharmacies have the lowest satisfaction with medical services. This is mainly because township health centers are designated medical institutions for the New Rural Co-op, where medical facilities and doctors' skills are better than grassroots medical institutions and pharmacies; also, such health centers are closer to county hospitals and are less costly, thereby rural residents are more satisfied with them.

5.4 Conclusion and Policy Implications

This article attempts to analyze the factors currently affecting rural residents' satisfaction with medical services by mean of the path analysis method and referring to the survey data of 903 rural households in China. The results of this analysis indicate that currently rural residents have a low satisfaction with medical services. Such intermediate variables as the rating of medical institutions, rating of medical professionals and rating of drugs directly affect rural residents' satisfaction with medical services; in terms of initial variables, the age, location, occupation and family income level of rural residents directly affect their satisfaction with medical services while educational background, main types of diseases family members suffer from, and diagnosis and treatment methods after being taken ill indirectly affect their satisfaction with medical services.

Therefore, to improve rural residents' satisfaction with medical services, efforts should be made in the following aspects: first, in terms of provision of medical services, rural residents' medical service demands should be met mainly by medical institutions, medical professionals and drugs; second, ways for diversified medical services to meet the medical service demands of rural residents of different ages, income level and education background should be explored. With the development of the rural economy and society, rural residents' disparity in income and educational background become more and more significant. This leads to the diversification of their demands in terms of medical services. The past "sweeping approach" to rural medical services can no longer meet the requirements of the development of rural medical services. As a result, we need to be more insightful in terms of rural residents' medical demands and diversify rural medical service products on the basis of providing basic medical services, thus satisfying the diverse medical demands of the rural residents and improving their satisfaction with medical services.[2]

[2]This article, written in collaboration with Jiang Cuiping, is published in *Chinese Rural Economy*, 2010 (8).

Chapter 6
Analysis of Social Security Expenditures by the Chinese Government

Since reform and opening-up, the Chinese government has been constantly increasing fiscal investments in social security. Significant results were achieved, which in turn play an important role in providing for people's basic life needs, maintaining social stability and promoting economic development. However, there is still a sizable gap between fiscal investments in social security and people's demands for social security. Not only is the total amount of fiscal expenditures insufficient, but also the structure of expenditures is unreasonable, and fiscal expenditures in social security does not play a satisfactory role in adjusting income distribution.

6.1 Introduction

Social security—an important system for alleviating poverty, ensuring people's livelihood, promoting economic and social development, and maintaining social stability, social fairness and justice—is also a key area of modern government expenditures and a main part of public expenditures. Due to differences in developmental stages and developmental modes, the total volume, structure, scope, key points and operation mechanism of different countries' social security expenditure vary. Great disparity can also found in one country's different periods in terms of social security expenditures. By studying the changes in the development of the status of social security expenditures, we can discern the importance attached by the government to the construction of social security. This reflects the stages and levels of economic and social development of a country or a region and deepens our understanding of a country's path and mode of development.

Different countries' concept of a social security system differs widely. Welfare states in Europe generalize social security as social protection expenditures or social expenditures, while in the United States social security mainly refers to various poverty-relief expenditures and security expenditures under the direct charge of

© Springer Nature Singapore Pte Ltd. and Social Sciences Academic Press 2017

Y. Wang, *Social Security in China: On the Possibility of Equitable Distribution*,
Research Series on the Chinese Dream and China's Development Path,
DOI 10.1007/978-981-10-5643-7_6

government finances. In China, social security is a huge concept covering social assistance, social insurance and social welfare, but often excludes affordable housing, basic health services and education services. This article classifies the fiscal expenditures of the Chinese government for social security into three types. The first type refers to retirement pensions in traditional public institutions, social welfare and relief expenditures, and social security subsidy expenditures (hereinafter referred to as Caliber I); this is the caliber currently used for statistics of fiscal social security expenditure. The second type includes social insurance, social welfare, social care and social assistance expenditures, for which funding is mainly comprised of state fiscal expenditures and various social insurance funds not included in fiscal management (hereinafter referred to as Caliber II). The third type is social security expenditures in the broad sense, including government expenditures in education, medical care and health (hereinafter referred to as Caliber III); this is similar to some countries' social expenditures.

Since reform and opening-up, China has been deepening its understanding of the social security system and its functions in the course of building a socialist market economic system. In the 1980s, some pilot reform projects were conducted mainly for the purpose of serving the reform of state-owned enterprises (SOEs). However, on the whole, security provided by state-owned enterprises and government departments and public institutions to their employees constituted the main part of social security. State finances only provided subsistence security for the strictly defined population in absolute poverty, and provided limited social welfare to targets entitled to preferential policies. In 1992, China's expenditures in social special care, welfare and relief amounted to RMB 6.645 billion, accounting for 1.78% of fiscal expenditure and 0.25% of GDP.[1] From the 1990s to the early 21st century, centering on building the socialist market economy system and on the basis of reform experimentations, China gradually established the basic institutional framework for modern social security. Though the individual contribution and multi-agent responsibility sharing mechanism was introduced in the social insurance system, yet with the constant expansion of social security and improvement of security levels, the government expenditures directed at social security kept increasing. In 2002, the Chinese government spent RMB 37.297 billion on social special care, welfare and relief; in addition to the retirement pensions of public institutions, the national fiscal expenditures in social security, in the narrow sense, amounted to RMB 263.622 billion, accounting for 11.95% of the total fiscal expenditures of the year; meanwhile, the expenditures from social insurance funds in the same year was RMB 347.15 billion. Increasing expenditures from social insurance funds have become an important part of social security expenditures.

After the Sixteenth CPC National Congress, the Party and the government attached more importance to the development of social security and increased government expenditures in social security. In the second half of 2003, China started pilot projects as part of the new rural cooperative medical system. By 2008,

[1]Calculated on the basis of relevant data of *China's Fiscal Statistic Yearbook 1993*.

this system had covered 90% of the rural residents in China. In 2007, the State Council suggested that an urban residents' basic medical insurance system be established. By the end of 2009, this system had covered over 1/2 of urban residents. Rural residents' minimum subsistence system had covered all rural areas nationwide by the end of 2007. In 2008, the State Council studied and deployed pilot work for new rural social old-age insurance. In 2009, pilot projects were conducted in over 300 counties nationwide. The scope of related fiscal expenditures also kept expanding. By the end of 2008, fiscal expenditures in social special care welfare and relief amounted to RMB 680.429 billion, accounting for 10.96% of fiscal expenditures of the same year; though the proportion was basically the same as that of 2002, the absolute scope was not at the same level. Revenues and expenditures in terms of social insurance funds increased more rapidly. In 2008, expenditures in five social insurance funds was RMB 992.51 billion (the revenues being RMB 1.36961 trillion), with an accumulated surplus of RMB 1.5176 trillion.[2] While developing social insurance and increasing government social security expenditures, the Chinese government attached more importance to the development of social services such as education and health. The funding for nine-year compulsory education in rural areas was entirely included in .fiscal security. In 2009, it was decided to conduct a new round of drug and health system reform in preparation for a RMB 850 billion increase in fiscal investments within three years. To cope with the world financial crisis, constructing low-rent housing and reconstructing urban and rural buildings in a state of disrepair became important fields in terms of large-scale treasury bond investments. In 2008, China planned to invest RMB 900 billion to construct affordable housing in three years, part of which was from fiscal funds. In 2009, the central finances arranged for a fund of RMB 55.1 billion specially establishing to subsidize affordable housing; in 2010, RMB 63.2 billion was arranged. Housing security, like education and health, has become a content of social security in the broad sense that cannot be ignored in China. In 2008, state finances invested RMB 1.176725 trillion in education and health services.[3]

6.2 Constant Increase in Social Security Expenditures by the Chinese Government

On the whole, since reform and opening-up began, fiscal expenditures of the Chinese government in social security have been constantly increasing. In absolute terms, special care and social welfare, relief expenditures, retirement pensions of public institutions, and expenditures in social security assistance (fiscal

---

[2]Related data are based on *Statistical Bulletin on the Development of Human Resources and Social Security Services* in past years.

[3]Related data are based on *Financial Statistics Yearbook* in 2008.

expenditures in social security in the narrow sense) increased by 401.26 times from RMB 1.891 billion in 1978 to RMB 760.668 billion in 2009 (Caliber I). On the basis of fiscal expenditures in social security in the narrow sense, the scope of expenditures in provenance from social insurance funds (minus fiscal subsidies) (Caliber II) also rapidly increased by 7.2 times, from RMB 221.098 billion in 1998 to RMB 1.813295 trillion in 2009. If consideration is given to the fact that the Party and the state have taken public service equalization as an important objective for constructing a socialist harmonious society, social security expenditures should include fund security and basic public services. Including state financial expenditures in education and health, we can see that the state's total expenditures in social security will be further increased. Fiscal social security in the narrow sense, social insurance expenditures, and fiscal education and health investments, added together (Caliber III), increased from RMB 452.734 billion in 1998 to RMB 3.256368 trillion in 2009, with quite a significant overall scale.[4]

In terms of the proportion of fiscal expenditures in social security against total fiscal expenditure, Caliber I expenditures in 1978 accounted for 1.65% of total fiscal expenditures, which rose to 9.97% in 2009; Caliber II expenditures accounted for 17.81% of total fiscal expenditures in 1998, which rose to 20.88% in 2009; Caliber III expenditures accounted for 11.53% of total fiscal expenditures in 1978, which rose to 37.51% in 2009. The proportion of expenditures of various calibers against total governmental fiscal expenditures increased the fastest in 1998, mainly resulting from the increase in subsidy expenditures for social insurance funds centering on the reform of state-owned enterprises; the proportion was the highest in 2002 (mainly resulting from the substantial increase of subsidy expenditures for social insurance funds by state finances), while the proportion after 2003 was relatively stable. In light of the proportion of social security expenditures in the GDP, Caliber I expenditures in 1978 accounted for 0.52% of GDP, which rose to 2.23% in 2009; Caliber II expenditures in 1998 accounted for 2.62% of GDP, which rose to 5.33% in 2009; Caliber III expenditures in 1978 accounted for 3.55% of GDP, which rose to 9.56% in 2009. In terms of the proportion in fiscal revenues, Caliber I expenditures accounted for 1.67% in 1978, which rose to 11.1% in 2009; Caliber II expenditures accounted for 22.39% in 1978, which rose to 26.46% in 2009; Caliber III expenditures accounted for 45.84% in 1998, which rose to 47.53% in 2009. In light of the proportion in the sum of fiscal revenues and social insurance fund revenues, there was no significant change, with Caliber II having been maintained at around 20%, and Caliber III between 35 and 40% (see Table 6.1). It should be noted that the proportion of fiscal expenditures in social security dropped somehow in 2008 and 2009, mainly as a result of other investments aimed at coping with the financial crisis.

Obvious periodical characteristics have been found in China's social security fiscal expenditures since reform and opening-up. In the early period of reform and

[4]Calculated by the author according to relevant statistics, not including housing security due to the difficulty of acquiring data.

Table 6.1 Social security expenditure of the Chinese government

Unit billion yuan; %

Year	Caliber I	Caliber II	Caliber III	Proportion in total fiscal expenditures			Proportion in GDP		
				Caliber I	Caliber II	Caliber III	Caliber I	Caliber II	Caliber III
1978	1.891		12.94	1.65		11.53	0.52		3.55
1986	3.558		43.253	1.61		19.62	0.35		4.21
1992	6.645		91.677	1.78		24.50	0.25		3.41
1994	9.514		145.62	1.64		25.14	0.20		3.02
1996	12.803		200.535	1.61		25.26	0.18		2.82
1998	59.563	221.098	452.734	5.52	17.81	36.47	0.71	2.62	5.36
2000	151.757	360.452	649.356	9.55	20.05	36.13	1.53	3.63	6.54
2002	263.622	559.043	960.493	11.95	22.36	38.41	2.19	4.65	7.98
2004	311.608	722.371	1236.839	10.94	22.16	37.95	1.95	4.52	7.74
2006	436.178	995.023	1689.814	10.79	21.63	36.73	2.06	5.18	7.97
2008	680.429	1509.851	2686.576	10.87	21.30	37.90	2.26	5.02	8.94
2009	760.668	1813.295	3256.468	9.97	20.88	37.51	2.23	5.33	9.56

Unit %

Year	Proportion in total fiscal revenues			Proportion in the sum of fiscal revenues and social insurance fund revenues	
	Caliber I	Caliber II	Caliber III	Caliber II	Caliber III
1978	1.67				
1986	1.68				
1992	1.91				
1994	1.82				
1996	1.73				

(continued)

Table 6.1 (continued)

Unit %

Year	Proportion in total fiscal revenues			Proportion in the sum of fiscal revenues and social insurance fund revenues	
	Caliber I	Caliber II	Caliber III	Caliber II	Caliber III
1998	6.03	22.39	45.84	19.23	39.37
2000	11.33	26.91	48.48	22.47	40.48
2002	13.95	29.57	50.81	24.36	41.85
2004	11.80	27.37	46.86	22.45	38.44
2006	11.25	25.67	43.60	20.99	35.65
2008	11.09	24.62	43.81	20.12	35.81
2009	11.10	26.46	47.53	21.43	38.48

Note Caliber I includes special care and social welfare, relief expenditures, retirement pensions of administrative institutions, and expenditures in social security assistance; Caliber II is expenditures of social insurance funds (minus fiscal subsidies) plus Caliber I, and the denominator for calculating the proportion of Caliber II (total fiscal expenditures) includes social insurance fund expenditures minus fiscal subsidies. Caliber III is education and health expenditures plus Caliber I; it should be noted that the proportion of social security fiscal expenditures in 2002 was relatively big as a result of the substantial increase in state fiscal subsidies for social insurance funds

Source of data based on relevant data in *Chinese Financial Statistics Yearbook*, *China Statistics Yearbook*, and *China Health Statistics Yearbook* of past years; the data in social insurance fund expenditures from 1998 to 2008 are from *China Financial Statistics Yearbook 2008*; the data of 2009 are from the Report on the Final Accounting of Expenditure that year; due to different statistical calibers in different years, there are some differences in the data of some years opening-up, the absolute value of social security fiscal expenditures and its proportion in total fiscal expenditures were both low. With the acceleration of reform and opening-up as well as economic and social development, social security fiscal expenditures increased year after year. Since the start of the 21st century, China has been attaching more importance to the development of services for people's livelihood; the framework of the social security system has been gradually developed and improved; and the increase in the scale of social security fiscal expenditures has been further accelerated. Meanwhile, due to the rapid increase of economic and fiscal revenues of the state during this period, the proportion of social security expenditure by the government has been relatively stable. However, with the increase of future social security demands, expenditures in education, medical and health care, and housing, in particular, should be further increased.

6.3 Gradual Expansion of Social Insurance Fund Revenues and Expenditures

China has not taken social insurance funds as a budgetary management item. With the deepening of the SOE reform and the development of the socialist market economic system, the traditional unit security system has been gradually turned into the new social insurance system, and social insurance funds have become an important part in total social security funding. China's current social insurance system mainly includes two types. Type I is old-age insurance, medical insurance, unemployment insurance, work-related injury insurance and maternity insurance for regularly employed urban employees; type II consists of the new rural cooperative medical care system (New Rural Co-op), urban residents' basic medical insurance and the new rural old-age insurance (NROAI) under pilot test, as well as the to-be-launched urban residents' basic old-age insurance system. Different from social services such as social relief and medical and education services which mainly rely on state fiscal investments, the social insurance system has established a mechanism with tripartite investments—the employer, the participating individual and government finances—in which the three forces play different roles in different types of social insurance. With the development of employees' social insurance starting from the 1990s, urban and rural residents' basic old-age insurance and the basic medical insurance system have been gradually established, the coverage of social insurance has been expanding in China (see Table 6.2), and the scale of revenues and expenditures of social insurance funds has been expanding (see Table 6.3). Table 6.4 shows the proportion of government social security expenditures, including expenditures of five social insurance funds, in the revenues of social insurance funds and fiscal revenues of the year; in 2000, the proportion of government social security expenditures, including the expenditures of five social insurance funds, in the revenues of social insurance funds and fiscal revenues was 40.48%, which dropped to 38.48% in 2009 (the drop was related to the accumulation of social insurance funds).

Table 6.2 Number of people participating in social insurance in China. *Unit* million people

Year	Employees' basic old-age insurance	Employees' basic medical insurance	Unemployment insurance	Work-related injury insurance	Maternity insurance	New rural cooperation medical care	Urban residents' medical insurance	New rural old-age insurance
1995	109.79	7.459	82.38	26.148	15.002			
1998	112.031	18.787	79.279	37.813	27.767			
2000	136.174	37.869	103.263	43.503	30.016			
2002	147.366	94.012	101.816	44.056	34.882			
2004	163.529	124.036	105.839	68.452	43.838	80.00		
2006	187.663	157.318	111.866	102.685	64.589	410.00		
2008	201.369	199.956	123.998	137.872	92.541	815.00	118.26	55.95
2009	235.50	219.37	127.15	148.96	108.76	833.00	182.10	86.91

Source of data The data for 1989-2008 are from *China Labor Statistics Yearbook 2009*; the data of new rural cooperation medical care are from *China Health Statistics Yearbook 2009*; the data of new rural social old-age insurance are from *Statistical Bulletin on Labor Security* of past years. The data of 2009 are from relevant statistical bulletins of 2009

Table 6.3 Revenues, expenditures and balance of China's employees' social insurance funds. *Unit* billion yuan

Year		1989	1995	1998	2000	2002	2004	2006	2008	2009
Old-age insurance	Revenues	14.67	95.01	145.9	227.85	317.15	425.84	630.98	974.02	1149.1
	Expenditures	11.88	84.76	151.16	211.55	284.29	350.21	489.67	738.96	889.4
	Accumulated balance	6.8	42.98	58.78	94.71	160.8	297.5	548.89	993.1	1252.6
Medical insurance	Revenues		0.97	6.06	17.0	60.78	114.05	174.71	288.55	367.2
	Expenditures		0.73	5.33	12.45	40.94	86.22	127.67	201.97	279.7
	Accumulated balance		0.31	2.0	10.98	45.07	95.79	175.24	330.36	427.6
Unemployment insurance	Revenues	0.68	3.53	7.26	16.04	21.56	29.1	40.24	58.51	58.0
	Expenditures	0.2	1.89	5.61	12.34	18.66	21.1	19.8	25.35	36.7
	Accumulated balance	1.36	6.84	13.34	19.59	25.38	38.6	72.48	131.01	152.4
Work-related injury insurance	Revenues		0.81	2.12	2.48	3.2	5.83	12.18	21.67	24.0
	Expenditures		0.18	0.9	1.38	1.99	3.33	6.85	12.69	15.6
	Accumulated balance		1.27	3.95	5.79	8.11	11.86	192.9	33.5	40.4
Maternity insurance	Revenues		0.29	0.98	1.12	2.18	3.21	6.21	11.37	13.2
	Expenditures		0.16	0.68	0.83	1.28	1.88	3.75	7.15	8.8
	Accumulated balance		0.27	1.03	1.68	2.97	5.59	9.69	16.82	21.20
Sum of five items	Revenues	15.36	100.6	162.31	264.49	404.87	578.03	864.32	1369.61	1611.6
	Expenditures	12.09	87.71	163.69	238.56	347.15	462.74	647.74	992.51	1230.3
	Accumulated balance	8.16	51.68	79.11	132.75	242.34	449.34	825.59	1517.6	1894.2

Note The balance of revenues and expenditures of urban employees' basic medical insurance funds in 2007 and 2009 included urban residents' basic medical insurance. Source of data: the data of 1989–2007 are from *China Fiscal Statistics Yearbook 2008*; the data of 2008 are from *China Labor Statistics Yearbook 2009*; the data of 2009 are from *Statistical Bulletin of Human Resources and Social Security 2009*

Table 6.4 Government social security expenditure including social insurance expenditure. *Unit* trillion yuan; %

Year	2000	2001	2002	2003	2004	2005	2006	2007	2008	2009
The sum of expenditures on five types of insurance and government fiscal expenditures on social security (A)	0.6494	0.783	0.9605	1.0647	1.2368	1.4606	1.6898	2.1172	2.6866	3.2564
The sum of revenues of five types of insurance and fiscal revenues (B)	1.604	1.9488	2.2952	2.6598	3.2177	3.8625	4.7403	6.2134	7.5026	8.4634
A/B	40.5	40.2	41.9	40.0	38.4	37.8	35.7	34.1	35.8	38.5

6.4 Structure and Characteristics of the Chinese Government Social Security Expenditures

The structure of the social security fiscal expenditures in China is mainly characterized by the following points:

First, the increase of social security expenditures in the narrow sense obviously outpaces that of the investments in education and health services. In terms of the structure of fiscal expenditures, the proportion of fiscal expenditures in social security in the narrow sense is relatively small, while investments in education and health are the focus of government public expenditures. In 1994, education and health investments accounted for 23.5% of fiscal expenditures. Since then, the absolute amount of education and health expenditures in government fiscal expenditures increased still, but its proportion dropped substantially, which has maintained basically around 18% ~ 19% since the start of the 21st century. During this period, the Chinese government vigorously developed social insurance and social security, and the amount of fiscal investments in social security in the narrow sense and its proportion in fiscal expenditures increased gradually (see Table 6.5). In 2006, the proportion of social welfare benefits, retirement pensions of public institutions, and fiscal subsidies for social security accounted for 10.8% of fiscal expenditures of the same year. Fiscal subsidies for social security accounted for 5.25%, which became the biggest expenditure in social security fiscal expenditures in the broad sense after education expenditures. As the social insurance system was just established then and was also faced with fund risks, subsidy expenditures on social insurance funds became a focus of subsidy expenditures on social security. Fiscal subsidy expenditures on social insurance funds increased by 81.4 times from RMB 2.155 billion in 1998 to RMB 177.67 billion in 2009, and the fiscal subsidies for social insurance funds amounted to RMB 1.09158 trillion from 1998 to 2009.[5]

Second, the increase of social security fiscal expenditures in China has promoted the transformation of the social insurance system from a pay-as-you-go system to the partial fund accumulation system. In terms of social security, in the earlier stage of reform and opening-up, the pay-as-you-go mode was mainly practiced, characterized by ratifying revenues according to expenditures on a balanced budget with a small surplus. In the course of establishing a modern social security system, China has established an institutional mode combining "social pooling and personal accounts" for employees' basic old-age insurance and basic medical insurance. Besides, personal accounts (such as enterprise annuity and housing provident fund) or family accounts (New Rural Co-op and NROAI) systems have also been introduced to other social insurance systems in China. As a result, China's social insurance system has become a partial fund accumulation system. To cope with the demands of a future aging population, the National Council for Social Security Fund was established in 2000 to manage social security funds allocated from state

---

[5]Related data are based on *China Fiscal Statistics Yearbook* of past years.

Table 6.5 Structure of Social Security Fiscal Expenditures in China. *Unit* billion yuan; %

Year	Education expenditures		Medical and health care expenditures		Expenditures on special care, social welfare and relief		Retirement pensions of public institutions		Expenditures on social security subsidies	
	Absolute value	Proportion	Absolute value	Proportion	Absolute value	Proportion	Absolute value	Proportion	Absolute value	Proportion
1978	7.505	6.69	3.544	3.16	1.891	1.69	–	–	–	–
1982	13.761	11.19	6.899	5.61	2.143	1.74	–	–	–	–
1986	27.472	12.46	12.223	5.54	3.558	1.61	–	–	–	–
1990	46.245	15.00	18.728	6.07	5.504	1.78	–	–	–	–
1994	101.878	17.59	34.228	5.91	9.514	1.64	–	–	–	–
1998	172.63	15.99	59.006	5.46	17.126	1.59	27.436	2.54	15.001	1.39
2000	217.952	13.72	70.952	4.47	21.303	1.34	47.857	3.01	82.597	5.20
2002	310.599	14.08	90.851	4.12	37.297	1.69	78.884	3.58	147.441	6.69
2004	385.11	13.52	129.358	4.54	56.346	1.98	102.812	3.61	152.45	5.35
2006	516.905	12.79	177.886	4.40	90.768	2.25	133.02	3.29	212.39	5.25
2008	901.021	14.39	275.704	4.40	104.192	1.66	181.249	2.90	248.465	3.97
2009	1043.754	13.68	399.419	5.23	97.683	1.28	209.295	2.74	275.748	3.61

Note The proportions in the table refer to the proportions in fiscal expenditures; due to changes in government fiscal revenues and expenditures items in 2007, expenditures on special care, social welfare and relief, retirement pensions of public institutions, and social security expenditures were combined as "social security and employment expenditures". *Source of data China Fiscal Statistics Yearbook* and Report on the Final Accounting of State Revenues and Expenditure of past years finances and raised by other channels, also responsible for partly managing social insurance accumulated funds. From the year 2000 to the end of 2009, the net fiscal allocation to national social security funds amounted to RMB 380.256 billion.[6] By the end of the year 2009, the cumulative balance of national social insurance funds was RMB 1.5721 trillion; the accumulated amount of national social insurance funds reached RMB 776.62 billion; the cumulative balance of enterprise annuities was RMB 253.3 billion; the cumulative balance of new rural cooperative medical care funds was RMB 18.51 billion; and the cumulative balance of rural social old-age insurance funds was RMB 68.1 billion. The sum of cumulative balance of the above items amounted to RMB 2.68863 trillion in 2009, accounting for 7.9% of GDP (see Table 6.6). If we consider the accumulation of housing provident funds, this sum and proportion is even bigger. The management and investment of funds have become an important task and a difficult problem in the course of developing the social security system.

Third, the increase of social security fiscal expenditures expanded the coverage of minimum subsistence security. Since reform and opening-up, urban and rural residents' incomes have been rising and their living standards have been improving. In 2008, the Engel coefficient for rural families in China was 43.7%, having dropped by 24.0 percentage points from 67.7% in 1978. The Engel coefficient for urban families in China dropped to below 40% by 2000.[7] The Engel coefficient for rural families in China dropped to below 50% by 2000. The absolute poverty incidence in rural areas kept dropping. In 1978, the absolute poverty incidence in rural areas was 30.7%, which dropped to 4.2% by 2008. Nevertheless, there are still a large number of poor people in China. In quite a long period of time, China only offered minimum subsistence security to extremely poor people unable to subsist (such as households of the five guarantees system). In the course of the SOE reform, a large number of laid-off workers became part of new poverty-stricken groups whose problems could not be resolved by the traditional social relief system. From the mid-1990s, regions such as Shanghai started to establish a minimum subsistence security system for poverty-stricken people. By the end of the 1990s, the government had started to implement the policy of "realizing universal coverage for all eligible residents", constantly increasing fiscal investments in the minimum subsistence security system. The rural subsistence security system had basically covered all the rural areas nationwide by 2007. In 2009, 23.477 million urban residents and 47.593 million rural residents received minimum subsistence allowances from the government.[8]

Fourth, the increase in social security fiscal expenditures in China, to some extent, affects both basic subsistence security and developed security. The

---

[6]Source of data: Website of the National Council for Social Security Fund (http://ww1ssf1gov1cn/zjcj/dzqk/201005/t20100510-26851html).

[7]National Bureau of Statistics of the People's Republic of China: Urban and Rural Residents' Lives Are Improved from Poverty to Prosperity". See the website of the National Bureau of Statistics (http://www1stats1gov1cn/tjfx/ztfx/qzxzgcl60zn/t20090910-4025858491html).

[8]Source of data: *Statistical Bulletin on the Development Civil Undertakings* in China of past years.

Table 6.6 Cumulative balance of national social insurance funds from 1989 to 2008. *Unit* billion yuan; %

Year	Five social insurance funds	National social security funds	Enterprise annuity	NRCMCS funds	Rural social old-age insurance funds	Accumulated total	The proportion of accumulate total in GDP
1990	11.73					11.73	0.6
1995	51.68					51.68	0.9
1998	79.11					79.11	0.9
2000	132.75					132.75	1.3
2002	242.34	124.19				366.53	3.0
2004	449.34	171.14		1.12	28.5	650.1	4.1
2006	825.59	282.77	91.0	5.78	35.4	1240.54	5.9
2008	1517.6	562.37	191.1	12.23	49.9	2333.2	7.8
2009	1572.1	776.62	253.3	18.51	68.1	2688.63	7.9

Source of data The data of the five social insurance funds are taken from the Data Center of the DRCNET, including urban basic old-age insurance, basic medical insurance, unemployment insurance, work-related injury insurance and maternity insurance; the data of national social insurance funds are taken from the annual reports of the National Council for Social Security Fund; the data of enterprise annuities and rural social old-age insurance are taken from *Labor Statistical Bulletin* of past years; the New Rural Co-op data are based on *Green Book on Social Security* in China 2010, and the data for 2009 ended by September traditional social security system has a narrow coverage with a low level of security, mainly addressing the issue of the subsistence of extremely poor people. With the gradual improvement of the social security system and the increase of state fiscal investments, while stepping up investments in education and health, there is, to some extent, a will to allocate more fiscal investments of social security in China to both basic subsistence security and developmental security projects. Though fiscal expenditures in terms of employment subsidies amounted to RMB 114.168 billion for the period from 1998 to 2007, the fiscal investments in terms of social security for developmental projects were insufficient; during the ten-plus years of economic transformation in which the focus was particularly set on ensuring basic subsistence, the government's fiscal investments in education and health services increased slightly. The proportions of education expenditures and medical and health care expenditures saw no improvements and even dropped somehow, directly leading to problems such as "expensive medical services" and "schooling difficulties". That is an important reason why China has no other choice but to further increase investments in education and health services now.

6.5 Fiscal Expenditures of Social Security in China: Problems and Countermeasures

(i) Main problems in China's social security fiscal expenditures

First, the total amount of social security fiscal investments is insufficient. Since reform and opening-up, the total amount of social security fiscal expenditures in China has been increasing. However, the current investments are insufficient to meet the growing social security demands of urban and rural residents. Compared with the social security expenditures of some other countries, China still lags behind in terms of social security fiscal expenditures (see Table 6.7).

Second, social security fails to play a satisfactory role in adjusting the distribution of residents' income. From 1981 to 2009, farmers' per capita net income increased by 22.1 times, while the disposable income of urban families increased by 36.1 times, so that the income disparity of urban and rural residents became more and more serious. Old-age insurance, an important item in the overall social insurance and social security system, instead of playing the role of narrowing the gap between different groups and ensuring different groups to fairly share old-age insurance benefits security, widens, to some extent, the gap between different groups. In 1990, the ratio of per capita monthly pension for urban enterprise employees, employees in public institutions and civil servants was 1:1.06:1.10, which showed that the benefits they received were basically the same; by 2005, the monthly per capita pension of public institutions increased to 1.89 times that of urban enterprise employees; meanwhile civil servants' monthly per capita pension expanded to 2.06 times that of enterprise employees'[1].

Table 6.7 Proportion of social security expenditure in GDP in some OECD countries. *Unit %*

Year	1960	1980	1985	1990	1995	1998	2001	2005
Canada	–	14.3	17.4	18.6	19.6	18.4	17.8	16.5
France	13.4	21.1	26.6	26.6	29.2	29	28.5	29.2
Germany	20.5	23	23.6	22.8	27.5	27.4	27.4	26.7
Japan	5.8	10.2	11	11.2	13.5	14.5	16.9	18.6
Mexico	–	–	1.8	3.8	8.1	8.8	11.8	7.4
Sweden	12.8	28.8	30	30.8	33	30.4	28.9	29.4
Turkey	–	4.3	4.2	7.6	7.5	11.1	–	13.7
The United Kingdom	13.9	17.9	21.1	19.5	23	21.5	21.8	21.3
The United States	10.3	13.3	13.0	13.4	15.5	14.5	14.8	15.9

Note The data in the table are based on related data of OECD. The data for Japan in 1960 is replaced by the data in 1970; the per capita GDP of the United Kingdom, Sweden, the United States, France and Germany in 1960 was USD 1,363, USD 1,641, USD 2,783, USD 1,297, and USD 1,345 respectively. China's per capita GDP in 2004 was USD 1,532. *Source of data* Task force of the Division of Social Security of the Ministry of Finance: International Comparison of Social Security Expenditure, *Public Finance Research*, 2007, Vol., 10, pp. 36–42; *International Statistics Yearbook*; OECD database

Third, the focus of social security fiscal investments is not clear, which does not well address the adjustment of income distribution. Currently, a large part of fiscal investments in social security is used to subsidize social insurance funds and complement national social security funds. On one hand, due to imperfections in the design of the social insurance system, the benefits brought by social insurance subsidies to high-income people are more than those to low-income people, creating a "rob the poor to support the rich" situation, thus exacerbating income disparity; on the other hand, although a large amount of funds is accumulated, it is, however, not well used, leading to difficult problems in the management and investment of accumulated funds, promoting fund security, as well as maintaining and increasing fund value. Other projects in urgent need of fiscal investments, such as medical and health care services, do not have sufficient investments. In recent years, the proportion of government budgetary expenditures in total health expenditures has been dropping. In 2008, government expenditures on medical and health care only accounted for 4.4% of yearly total fiscal expenditures. The proportion of education expenditures in government fiscal expenditures has been stumbling and even dropping to some extent. By 2006, fiscal expenditures in education in the Chinese government just surpassed 3% of GDP. The proportion of government education expenditures in total education expenditures is declining. Besides, investments in security housing should also be strengthened. By the end of 2006, only RMB 4 billion of public finance was used in the construction of low-rent housing, which increased to RMB 72.6 billion in 2009. However, as far as the demands of the many low and medium-income people are concerned, it is just like a drop in the bucket, while huge amounts of housing provident funds have not even been brought into full play.

Fourth, the proportion of central and local fiscal expenditures is not reasonable. Compared with the fiscal revenues of central and local governments, the proportion of fiscal expenditures in social security is out of balance, with the proportion of local government expenditures far exceeding that of central government. In light of central and local governments' social security expenditures in 2008, the central government's expenditures on social security and employment (social security expenditures in the narrow sense) only accounted for 40.3% of the fiscal expenditures of the whole country, 30% of medical and health care expenditures, and 17.8% of education expenditures. In light of fiscal revenues, in 2008, the fiscal revenues of the central government accounted for 53.3% of the total fiscal revenues, while local fiscal revenues accounted for only 46.7%.[9]

(ii) Suggestions on strengthening and improving social security fiscal expenditures in China

First, we should further increase fiscal investments in social security and improve the level of social security. In the future, we should further increase fiscal investments in social security and gradually explore the establishment of a long-acting mechanism for social security fiscal investments. While improving the public finance mechanism, we should establish and improve social security budgets. Currently, social security in China is mainly subsistence security, with a low level and narrow scope of security. To further improve the equity and sustainability of economic and social development in China, we should establish a developed social welfare system for the benefits of all people. It is estimated that by 2012 we will realize the objective of basically establishing a new social welfare system for the benefit of all people and the full coverage of the social security system, which will require a fiscal investment of about RMB 2.6 trillion. By 2020, we should basically realize the full coverage of all people, which will require a fiscal investment of about RMB 5.74 trillion (He et al. 2009). Increases fiscal investments in social security should be managed in accord with the actual conditions of economic and social development, and social investments and personal contributions should be mobilized to develop social security.

Second, we should optimize the structure of fiscal expenditures in social security and improve the performance of such expenditures. Investments in subsistence security are the most fundamental investments, but they accounts for a relatively small proportion in fiscal expenditures, and other security projects may be developed and improved to reduce the amount of poor people and minimum subsistence security demands. Government medical and health care expenditures should be raised to 6% of fiscal expenditures as soon as possible, and should continue to be raised step by step. By 2020, we should strive for that figure to reach 8% ~ 10% of

[9]Source of data: National fiscal revenues and expenditure final account report of China 2008; the total fiscal revenues and expenditure data are from *China Statistics Yearbook 2009*.

fiscal expenditures. In terms of education investments, the proportion of state fiscal education expenditures should account for 4% of GDP by 2012 (Zhu 2008), and by 2020 the proportion should reach over 5%, and the proportion in fiscal expenditure should reach 20%. In terms of housing security, considering the tremendous demands for low-rent housing by low-income families, fiscal investments in this regard should be increased urgently; by 2012, the investments in housing security should reach about RMB 260 billion, and by 2020 about RMB 700 billion. In terms of old-age security, according to the demands of old-age security and considering the accelerated growth of the aging population, by 2012, the fiscal expenditures in terms of old-age security should reach about RMB 800 billion, and by 2020 about RMB 1.4 trillion (He et al. 2009); the focus of recent investments is old people without security in urban and rural areas as well as rural residents. In the course of adjusting the structure of fiscal expenditures in social security, we should not only ensure the equitable fiscal expenditures, but also improve the efficiency of fiscal expenditures. We should establish a performance assessment system of social security fiscal expenditures in order to improve the political, economic and social performance of social security fiscal expenditures (Lin 2007).

Third, we should improve the governmental responsibility sharing mechanism of social security fiscal investments at different levels. To strengthen fiscal investments in social security, the central government should not take the whole responsibility, while the burdens of local governments should not be aggravated. Instead, responsibilities should be reasonably allocated between the central government and local governments. We should, on the basis of clarifying the responsibilities for social security between the central government and local governments, define the responsibilities of governments at various levels in terms of fiscal investments in different social security items. In China, due to the constraint of the economic development level and the government's control over financial powers, the central government delegates more expenditure responsibilities to local governments so that local governments have to take up the main responsibility for expenditures in the absolute majority of expenditure items, which is a direct cause for the fact that fiscal expenditures of the central government only accounts for 30% of national fiscal expenditure (Kou and Zhou 2007). We should further increase social security fiscal expenditures by the central government and try to balance local governments' fiscal expenditures through transfer payment.

Fourth, we should improve the function of social security fiscal expenditures in income distribution adjustment and narrow the gap among different residents. To improve the function of social security in adjusting income distribution, we should make efforts in various aspects. On one hand, we should try to maintain social equity and justice through the social security system by improving the institutional design of social security; on the other hand, we should allow social security fiscal expenditures to play their role in adjusting income distribution and narrowing wealth disparity. The function of social security in adjusting income distribution can be realized by adjusting the investment structure and directions and clarifying the key projects, regions and groups of people for fiscal investments. Fiscal investments should be channeled towards urban and rural low and medium-income people, meet their social security demands, and improve their income level; and meanwhile they should also be channeled towards rural areas and the central and western parts of China.[10]

[10]This article is published in *Finance and Trade Economics*, 2011, Vol. 1, written in collaboratin with Long Yuqi.

Chapter 7
Several Major Issues in the Reform and Development of China's Social Security System: Comments and Suggestions on China's Social Security Report

Of the many research results on social security, China's Social Security Report (hereinafter referred to as The Report) stands out as one of the achievements in the first phase of "China Economic Research and Consultation Projects" for its selection of key issues and strong lineup of researchers. Besides internationally famous experts on social security such as Nicholas Barr, the participants included Chinese experts such as Li Jian'ge, Gao Xiqing, Zheng Silin, Xiang Huaicheng, Zhou Xiaochuan, Liu Zhongli, Wu Jinglian, Lou Jiwei, Guo Shuqing, Yu Yongding, HouYongzhi, Li Shaoguang and Zheng Beingwen. Resulting from several years' study, The Report is quite original in that it draws on the latest international experiences as reference, examines China's national conditions, compares and analyzes the advantages and disadvantages of different modes of old-age insurance, and suggests that the "Non-financial (Notional) Defined Contribution" (NDC) system which is practiced in some European countries be implemented in China, in attempts to straighten out the thinking for the reform of China's social security system and resolve problems such as the pension fund financial crisis. This report also gives a series of policy suggestions for establishing a uniform social security management system, raising retirement age, allocating state-owned assets, expanding coverage, improving the capital market, and promoting social equity. It is a report analyzing China's reform on its social security system from a very broad perspective, and also a very deep report about China's reform on its social security system. In light of my own understanding, I would like to put forward some of my opinions focusing on the key points of this report.

7.1 The NDC Issue

The NDC system put forward in China's Social Security Report is the central concept of the whole report, and also has the strongest impact of all other suggestions because it addresses the issue of selecting a system and mode for China's

© Springer Nature Singapore Pte Ltd. and Social Sciences Academic Press 2017

Y. Wang, *Social Security in China: On the Possibility of Equitable Distribution*,
Research Series on the Chinese Dream and China's Development Path,
DOI 10.1007/978-981-10-5643-7_7

urban employees' basic old-age insurance. Since the establishment of the basic old-age insurance system combining social pooling and personal accounts in China, the issue on the scale of personal accounts, the issue of the management system, the issue of notional accounts and the issue of investment, among other issues, have become focuses of controversy and difficult obstacles in the process of establishing of a new system. Although ten years of exploration have passed, a system integrating social pooling and personal accounts with healthy operation and meeting China's basic national conditions has yet to be found. This has been a major factor impeding the government from making breakthrough in China's urban employees' basic old-age insurance system. The Report suggests the adoption of the NDC system to resolve the institutional dilemma, as it is indeed a great breakthrough and a new development from the World Bank's suggestions on China's implementation of the "three-pillar" mode.

The Report suggests that the main arguments for China's adoption of the NDC system include: ① the NDC system maintains the role of personal accounts but actually does not allow for real fund accumulation, nor does it require this generation to contribute to the richer next generation, thus avoiding unreasonable inter-generational income re-distribution. ② The NDC system is operated by the public old-age pension administrative department, and is not subject to the constraint of the inadequate financial capability or management capability of any private sector while it is able to avoid the fluctuation of assets value in the capital market within a short term; as a result, insurants are subject to less risk, which is especially important when the banking and financial market system is still at the developmental stage. ③ The NDC pension system currently does not require any rise in contribution or any increase of central fiscal subsidies. ④ As China has a very high savings rate, and its capital market is not sound, it is not necessary to fully fund "notional personal accounts" into a form of complete fund accumulation, while maintaining that notional personal accounts can provide a basis for a future transition to accumulation personal accounts. We should say that the above reasons are sufficient and highly persuasive.

The conclusion from the above reasons is that China does not have to fully fund personal accounts and may maintain the current basic mode of "mixed account management" of social pooling and personal accounts. From the perspective of feasibility, this is perhaps a realistic choice for reforming the current basic old-age insurance system. However, if the absolute majority of provinces in China still carry on the practice of not fully funding personal accounts, they are actually adopting the NDC mode. The presentation of the NDC system will provide a theoretical explanation or "extrication" for the viewpoint that it is not necessary to fully fund personal accounts in the current period. From the perspective of report drafters, the proposal of the concept of NDC may free the system from the empty account entanglement problem arising in the recent decade, while maintaining the personal account system design put forward as a reform measure. As the "personal accounts" of basic old-age pension are maintained, its scale would not shrink so much as to finally lose the significance of the "personal account" system. This is a compromise with which personal accounts are actively maintained but do not have to be "fully funded". Although this concept will help to transform fixed income into fixed contribution, clarify that the social insurance premium that each person submits is related to their future welfare income (Feldstein 2009), clear up the misunderstanding that accounts have are constituted of a single type of full accumulation system, and maintain the position of large scale personal accounts in the basic old-age insurance system given the fact that it is basically impossible to fully fund big accounts in China. However, as far as I am concerned, from the perspective of improving China's old-age insurance system and operation mechanism, the NDC system, instead of a deep reform of the institutional mode combining social pooling and personal accounts (it is by nature still a pay-as-you-go system), delays the solution of the problem concerning the "full funding" of personal accounts. In the issue of the personal account system, some basic notions should be clarified.

(i) In terms of institutional design, should it consider this system as part of the basic old-age insurance system or as a new supplementary system? Should we stick to mandatory participation or opt for voluntary participation by those eligible? Should it be turned into a system universally enjoyed by all workers participating in the basic old-age insurance system or a system mainly covering people whose employment or income is more stable? Since designing the personal account system, China has actually taken it as an organic part of the basic old-age insurance system and insisted that it be universal and mandatory. As a result, it is inevitable that personal account funds be managed along with social pooling funds instead of being independently managed. Consequently personal accounts cannot become a full fund accumulation system in the true sense, but only in the notional sense, thus not significantly different from the NDC other than in name. Currently, though some provinces are conducting pilot projects on fully funding personal accounts, yet it is still difficult to completely separate personal accounts from social pooling funds due to institutional design, and little progress has been made in this regard; the proportion of fully-funded personal accounts is increasingly dropping, and in practice, it is increasingly difficult to manage personal accounts in parallel with social pooling funds. The practice of fully funding personal accounts illustrates that if personal accounts are fully funded, the scale of funding cannot be big (as it is unnecessary and impossible) and only small-scale funding can be conducted at an appropriate ratio (the ratio of personal accounts that are fully funded is only 2.5% in Sweden, accounting for 13.5% of total old-age pension contribution). Meanwhile, once personal accounts are fully funded, they should be managed as per the full fund accumulation system, instead of being tied up with social pooling funds. In light of the fact that personal accounts can only cover a small proportion and noting that it is difficult to cover all workers participating in the basic old-age insurance system, we can see that the personal account system is a subordinate and supplementary system in the whole old-age insurance system, and thus should not be designed as a basic system on par with the pay-as-you-go social pooling system. Pay-as-you-go has been and remains still the main mode in terms of basic old-age insurance system worldwide, especially with great international powers. The large population and the huge scale of old-age security funds in big powers determine that the market mechanism cannot be fully relied upon to establish old-age security funds for the personal account system, as that would cause risks of enormous inflation for accumulated old-age pension funds and weaken the re-distribution function of old-age insurance funds. Besides, maintaining huge personal accounts and high premium collection rates for the issuance of current old-age pensions is not conducive to the expansion of the coverage of the basic old-age insurance system. To maintain the universality of personal accounts, this system can be made mandatory to some extent, but this should be mainly be reflected by tax preferential policies. Moreover, it is impossible to cover all workers.

(ii) In terms of the fund management system, the management of personal account funds still lacks a clear institutional guarantee. Given that personal accounts are not fully funded, such funds are jointly managed along with social pooling funds. The problem as to whether they should be managed independently or on a market basis is not very prominent. However, once personal accounts are fully funded according to the fund accumulation system, the management and investment problems about personal account funds will surface, and a commensurate management system will have to be established. We maintain that given that personal accounts are gradually fully funded, a management system relatively independent from social pooling funds should be established. Personal account funds should be pooled and managed on a provincial basis, to be entrusted to qualified investment institutions for investment. National centralized management over such funds is not appropriate. To some extent, the management of personal account funds could be inspired of that of enterprise annuity and occupational annuity funds, or be appropriately combined with them.

(iii) If personal accounts are fully funded, it is worth asking what the appropriate size should be. On the whole, in light of the impact of such factors as the huge historical debt gap in China's old-age pensions, a capital market that is not sound enough and a relatively high overall savings rate, the size of personal accounts after being fully funded should not be too large. Currently, except for Liaoning, which funds personal accounts at 8%, all the remaining pilot provinces generally fund personal accounts at 5 or 3% (equivalent to 11–18% of the current total contribution rate of old-age insurance). We may deem practice as more persuasive than theories and policies, as a too high ratio will make it too difficult and risky to fully fund personal accounts, while a too low ratio will lose practical significance. It is appropriate for each province to establish personal accounts at a ratio of 3–5%.

In sum, in light of the NDC system suggestion put forward in The Report, we think that the direction of further reform in China's basic old-age insurance personal account system is a transformation into a supplementary system with a moderate scale. This system may be mandatory to some extent or comprise tax reductions or exemptions, but most importantly should address regularly employed personnel. To avoid the impact of the financial market, personal account funds may be appropriately concentrated in provincial personal account management centers, but should be managed uniformly nationwide. Old-age pension funds in the full fund accumulation system should stick to market-based investments and operations, and insurants should have certain decision-making authority in terms of investments in their respective account funds.

II. The Problem with the Expansion of Old-age Insurance Coverage and the Framework of the Old-age Insurance System

It is exactly correct for The Report to put forward the suggestion of expanding old-age security "coverage". This suggestion is unequivocally summarized in the report of the 17th CPC National Congress as "all people should are entitled to old-age care", which illustrates that this has become a consensus both in theoretical circles and at the policymaking level. This is of great significance for the promotion of the construction of China's old-age pension system.

No schedule has been set up to expand the coverage of the old-age pension system. Currently, besides government departments and public institutions, almost all people regularly employed in the city have been included into the employees' basic old-age insurance system. In principle, government departments and public institutions should also accelerate the socialized reform of old-age pensions, so as to accelerate the construction of a uniform labor market system. The reform of public institutions' old-age insurance system has been ongoing since 2009, with specific schemes being identical with enterprise employees' basic old-age insurance. Besides, the construction of various types of rural social old-age insurance systems has been ongoing in various places. More typically, Beijing has established a rural basic old-age insurance system based on 10% of annual income, and meanwhile established an old-age allowance system with which urban and rural old people above 60 years old without any pension benefits can receive a fiscal subsidy of RMB 200 each month, thus realizing full coverage. Theoretical circles have proposed the development strategy of "three types of insurance and one allowance" for China's old-age security system. Specifically, the public employees' basic old-age pension system, the employees' basic old-age insurance system, the farmers' basic old-age insurance system and the urban-rural residents' old-age allowance system should be co-established in order to set up old-age security system covering all the people without any loophole so that everybody enjoy the right to old-age care. (Gongcheng 2008).

Old-age security is classified into two types: contributory social insurance and non-contributory social benefits. For the latter, China only had social assistance of non-contributory social benefits (the subsistence security system) in the past, and was lacking an old-age allowance system that each person could enjoy. For a very long period, China's social insurance system could hardly cover all jobholders, and old people above 60 years old without any pension benefits amounted to 50–60 million, of whom most were rural old people. To alleviate old-age poverty, China should establish a minimum income security system for old people, which should cover both urban and rural areas. Of course, at the starting stage, security benefits may be maintained at a low standard, while the age of entitlement may be higher than the retirement age as is regarded appropriate.

Regarding jobholders, the contributory social insurance system is undoubtedly a main part of the old-age security system. Multiple types co-exist in the current old-age insurance system, including: the retirement pension system of government departments and public institutions, the employees' basic old-age insurance system, the flexible jobholders' old-age insurance system, as well as the migrant workers' old-age insurance system and the rural social old-age insurance system in some places, among others. There is a great diversity of systems at a low level of social pooling. Provincial pooling has not been realized in most places and localized management is conducted for funds, thus making it difficult to transfer social insurance across different regions. This situation is not conducive to the flow and transfer of laborers and retirees.

The Report develops conceives the expansion the urban social insurance system and the improvement pooling levels, but does not define ways to realize these objectives. In fact, we still lack a complete and clear approach for the overall design of China's old-age insurance system. From the perspective of social insurance legislation, various types of jobholders whose income reaches a certain standard in China should be covered by the basic old-age insurance system. The crux is whether to establish one system, one mode, or multiple systems, multiple modes, or a national uniform basic system (basic old-age pension system) supplemented by several other relevant systems. The answer to this question will determine China's approach to establishing a basic old-age insurance system for job holders. The United States started to establish a national uniform basic system (basic old-age pension system) in 1935, providing basic old-age security for all insurants, while establishing a flexible occupational annuity system. This is of reference value for China. In light of such factors as the large population, urban-rural disparity and path-dependent reform modes in China, I suggest that China basically stick to the institutional framework of multiple systems and multiple modes, and establish different systems for public servants, enterprise employees, flexible workers, individual industrialists and businesspeople, and rural employees (especially agricultural workers). However, a basic old-age pension system which is roughly identical nationwide should be established for all insurants, so that when they reach relevant conditions such as the statutory retirement age, basic or fundamental old-age pension with a roughly balanced substitution rate and reaching on the whole above the basic subsistence level is provided to these people. That is to say, a diversified and multi-level basic old-age insurance system with uniform basic old-age pension should be established for urban job-holders. The foundation of this system includes two points: first, establishing an old-age allowance system for urban and rural old people without retirement pensions, and providing a certain amount of old-age pensions (fiscal allowances) to all old people at various levels; second, gradually establishing a national uniform basic old-age pension system for urban and rural laborers, especially non-rural job-holders. As per the requirements of raising the level of pooling, basic old-age pensions should be pooled nationwide, and be directly managed by a department in the charge of the central government.

To establish a diversified and multi-level basic old-age insurance system for basic old-age pensions cannot be separated from the reform of the basic old-age insurance of public servants. Currently, government departments and public institutions still function according to the retirement pension system which does not require the payment of old-age insurance premiums and so must be reformed as it cannot be adapted to the current situation. The reform of old-age pensions for all public servants, people working with public institutions, and employees in public institutions whose salary originates mainly in public finances, that is, civil servants provided for by public finance, should be considered and planned for as a whole for comprehensive reform and coordinated promotion. As state employees, they are entitled to basic old-age insurance, assume the obligations for premium payment, as well as touch the basic old-age pension and the balanced "occupational annuity" security relevant to their occupation and with certain incentive functions.

III. The Problem with the Development and Mode Selection of Rural Social Security

While developing urban social security, China did not neglect the development of rural social security. However, the development of China's rural social security obviously lags behind due to great urban-rural disparity and regional disparity. The rural subsistence security system was not established nationwide until 2007, which is about ten years later than the establishment of the urban subsistence security system; pilot projects started in 2003 for rural new cooperative medical care, which realized basic coverage by 2008, that is 5–10 years later than the urban employees' basic medical insurance system. The "personal account-based" rural social old-age insurance established in line with the principle of "being mainly based on personal contribution, supplemented by collective subsidies and supported by government policies" started early (1991) and developed rapidly, but has become basically stagnant since the 1997 Asian economic crisis. It is not until the latest few years that some coastal developed provinces started pilot work on the construction of a new rural social old-age insurance system. No uniform system has been developed by the state. See Table 7.1 for the development of rural social old-age insurance from 2002 to 2008.

There are two main rural social old-age security policies at the state level. One is the old-age security policy for rural families practicing birth control. Since 2004, rural couples adhering to the birth control policy and who had only one child (or two daughters) have been entitled to a monthly subsidy no lower than RMB 600 as reward until their death. The subsidies are jointly paid by the Central Government and local governments (Information Office of the State Council, The People's Republic of China 2004). The other is the comprehensive social security system for farmers who have lost land. In line with the principle of "exchanging land for security", farmers whose land has been requisitioned can generally join the urban social security system, but at a security standard lower than urban employees. By the end of

Table 7.1 Development of rural social old-age insurance

Year	2002	2003	2004	2005	2006	2007	2008
Number of insurants (million people)	54.62	54.28	53.78	54.42	53.74	51.71	55.95
Funds accumulated (billion yuan)	23.3	25.9	28.5	31.0	35.5	39.2	49.9
Number of people receiving old-age pensions (million people)	/	1.98	2.05	3.02	3.54	4.12	5.12
Amount of old-age pensions paid (billion yuan)	/	1.5	/	2.1	3.0	4.0	5.7

Source Statistical Bulletin on the Development of Labor and Social Security Services (2002–2008)

2008, social security for land-requisitioned farmers was provided in 1201 counties and cities in 27 provinces nationwide, and 13.24 million land-requisitioned farmers had been included into the basic subsistence or old-age security system.

The Chinese government has promised to establish a social security system ensuring that "every old person is taken care of" and covering both urban and rural areas, as well as to guarantee that "everyone is entitled to social security". The construction of the rural social old-age insurance system is one of the key and most difficult points, of which one difficulty is the selection of modality. As to the institutional mode of rural social old-age insurance, theoretical circles have mainly put forward the following ideas:

- Establishing the "universal old-age allowance system" on the basis of the subsistence security system. That is to say, rural people reaching a certain age, regardless of their employment history or income, should be able to receive a guaranteed monthly old-age pension based on national public finances.
- "The personal account full fund accumulation system". The funds contributed by farmers all enter their personal accounts and fund accumulation is practiced.
- "Be included in urban social insurance". Fiscal subsidies are used to emulate employers' contribution to include farmers into urban social insurance.
- "Basic old-age pension + personal accounts". Basic old-age pension consists in the inclusive old-age pension supported by public finances, while personal accounts are old-age pension of full fund accumulation from personal contribution.
- "Material objects in exchange for security". Material objects that farmers have such as agricultural products, land and equities are transformed into insurance premiums, for which practical and feasible social old-age insurance systems have been respectively designed. The insurance mode in rural areas of Beijing (i.e., "basic old-age pension + personal accounts") is receiving more and more attention and recognition.

Based on China's current economic and social developments and future developmental trends, I think the developmental mode of combining insurance and welfare should be maintained for rural social security in China. In this way, some old people, low-income groups and poverty-stricken people can obtain subsistence despite their inability to pay premiums, while middle-income people engage in obligatory contributions, and high-income people in rural areas can enjoy a higher level of security benefits according to the contributions they make. As a result, not only can all the farmers enjoy appropriate social security benefits but also no excessive burden is imposed on national public finances; this developmental mode not only allows for the combination of rights and obligations, but also for the realization of the developmental objective of "all people sharing" and the promotion of the sustainable development of the rural social security system. We should flexibly combine insurance and welfare according to the diverse farmer groups and their income differences. A welfare-focused institutional mode should be implemented for specific regions and people, while an insurance-focused institutional mode should be implemented for other regions and people. The welfare-based social security institutional mode should be implemented for old people in rural regions, low-income people and poverty-stricken people, whereas subsistence security and old-age allowances should be developed and the social assistance system improved in the way that it will be mainly funded by national public finances. Regarding people living in rural regions with relatively high income and a certain capability to pay premiums, such as employees in township enterprises, people with off-farm employment, and migrant workers, their social insurance system should be integrated with urban social security with consideration to the diversity in rural economic development. In terms of fund-raising methods, we suggest that rural social insurance funds be raised by premium payment, as they help better clarify rights and obligations and are also a main source of funds for social insurance in China. Funds for welfare projects are mainly borne by national public finances. Although the central government and local governments share responsibilities, the central public finances taking up the main responsibilities. We should step up transfer payment from the central public finances with priority given to central and western regions and regions inhabited by ethnic minorities, especially remote mountain areas, poverty-stricken areas, old revolutionary areas, areas suffering from resource depletion, areas with harsh natural conditions and counties of ethnic minorities, while appropriately considering some distressed areas in the east. As for distressed areas in the eastern region, provincial public finances should further raise the ratio of special subsidies, principally for financially distressed counties and cities within the province. In light of the rapidly aging population, on one hand, we should accelerate the development of rural social security; on the other hand, we should be far-sighted, make scientific decisions and prudently design the rural social security system, instead of setting up too high security standards.

As for the social security of migrant rural workers in cities, some people in theoretical circles maintain that an independent system be established, which I think not very appropriate. In principle, they should be included in the urban social security system. As their employment is not stable and their income low, migrant workers' social security system should be designed on the basis of reality. First, we should resolve the problems of work-related injuries and major disease security, which should be directly included into the urban social insurance system. The basic requirements for migrant workers' old-age insurance system are low premiums, wide coverage, as well as connectivity and transferability. We should formulate and implement as soon as possible the measures for the transfer and continuation of migrant workers' old-age insurance relations. We should encourage governments in places where conditions permit to involve migrant workers with stable jobs into the urban employees' basic old-age insurance system. It should be defined whether they participate in the employees' basic old-age insurance system or the rural laborers' basic old-age insurance system according to their respective work arrangements. All resident rural workers with stable employment in cities, regardless of their household registers, should participate in the local employees' basic old-age insurance system. Migrant workers with no stable employment should have the right to independently select the type of basic old-age insurance system they wish to participate in.

IV. The Problem with the Management System of Old-age Security Funds

The sources of funds for the two major old-age security systems in China—that is, contributory social insurance and non-contributory social welfare (subsistence security system and old-age allowance system)—differ. The funds for non-contributory social welfare are directly taken from public finances, directly collected by taxation departments, and directly disbursed according to financial resources and the needs of the security system. It is a fiscal security system supported by taxation, and the management of such security funds is generally not involved in the self-sustainability of expenses.

Three systems coexist currently in the contributory social system. First, in the case of regionally managed social insurance pooling funds, except for a few provinces which practice centralized provincial management, social pooling at the provincial level has not been realized. The main practice is to manage social pooling at the county level and prefecture city level. Second, in the case of the personal account system, personal accounts are basically not fully funded; in pilot provinces which have fully funded personal accounts, provincial special financial accounts are mainly used for management. Third, in the case of enterprise annuities, the number of enterprises and employees with annuities nationwide is not large, and the scale of funds collected is limited (about RMB 90 billion in 2008). The trust management mode is generally selected for enterprise annuities, and an expert committee formed by the enterprise annuity management department selects a qualified financial institution for investment. Similar to expanding commercial insurance, the funds of enterprise annuities are managed through the market.

Of the above two major types of old-age security systems, the first type and the third system in the second type are two extreme types, in which no significant difference or controversy is found between the management and operation systems at home and abroad, and for which it is not necessary to reform the fund management mode. What causes serious disputes still is the selection of the management system for social pooling funds and the personal account funds under the urban employees' basic old-age insurance system. As the main part in China's old-age security system, the urban employees' basic old-age insurance fund management system is a key to deepening the reform of China's old-age security system. With the issue of personal accounts being studied in the previous part, here we will mainly discuss the management system for employees' basic old-age insurance social pooling funds.

Currently, two systems coexist for the collection of employees' basic old-age insurance funds, with the human resource and social security departments and local taxation departments collecting respectively about half. This peculiar dual collection system was developed ten years ago when it was difficult to collect social insurance premiums against the backdrops of the economic crisis; it was recognized by the State Council through the promulgation of the "Regulations on the Collection of Social Insurance Funds" in 2000. In 2007, the two departments competed for the power to collect social insurance premiums. As neither party would give in, the final result was to maintain the dual collection system, which has been in operation for nearly ten years now.

The Report suggests that old-age insurance premiums should be collected by the taxation department, and that the definition of income for old-age insurance premium payment should be the same as that of the base for income tax. This proposal intends to transform the "dual collection system" that has been operating in China for ten years into a unitary collection system and thus link old-age insurance premium to income tax rather than to the total salary issued by a unit or the employees' individual salary. This proposal, if successfully implemented, should be able to help straighten out the old-age security fund collection system and base. However, The Report shuns the disputes on the "dual collection system" in China's social insurance funds, without giving sufficient reasons for transforming the "dual collection system" into a collection system by the taxation department, the feasibility of which is dubious, without mentioning that such a transformation could hardly dispels the misgivings of the human resource and social security department, nor does it address the resistance against the reform of the social insurance collection system. In fact, social insurance premium collection systems vary in different countries worldwide; there is no fixed and uniform mode.[1] However, with consideration given to convenience, the collection of one tax or fund fees is generally completed by one department. It is more common for taxes to be collected by the taxation department and fees collected by the social security department.

---

[1]The study of Researcher Zhou Hong from the Chinese Academy of Social Sciences proves that the tax collection mode, the social security department collection mode and tax and fees hybrid collection mode are found for social insurance in various countries worldwide.

Currently, one of the focuses in the disputes on the "dual collection system" in China is whether social insurance funds are "fees" or tax. Under general conditions, social insurance funds should be special purposes "fees"; collection rates and payment benefits are determined by scientific estimates to ensure the balance of collection and payment. From this perspective, it is right for the social security department to collect social insurance funds. However, as for "social pooling funds" in social old-age insurance, the boundary between "fees" and "tax" is not very clear; in particular, with the constant rise of social pooling in old-age insurance, social pooling funds in social old-age insurance is slowly evolving from "fees" to "tax". In this light, it is reasonable for the taxation department to collect social pooling funds for social old-age insurance. Therefore, whether the nature of social pooling funds in social old-age insurance is defined as "fees" or "tax" is an important basis for whether they should be collected by the taxation department or the social security department.

Before the establishment of social old-age insurance, various enterprises and employers issued retirement pensions for their retirees from their own income. With the establishment of the social old-age insurance system, old-age pensions for retirees are issued from social old-age insurance funds. In 1997, it was decided to classify old-age insurance funds into social pooling funds and personal account funds, to establish localized management for employees' old-age pensions (provincial pooling), and to gradually raise the pooling level of old-age insurance funds. Retirement pensions were transformed into old-age pensions so that unit-based security was transformed into social security. Pooling at the departmental, industrial and district and county government levels were all redirected to the prefecture and even province level, which meant that old-age insurance funds came to have more rigid constraints and gradually turned into social security funds as defined by state policies or laws. Currently, the pooling level of old-age insurance is not high enough, and different regions show different contribution ratios and management methods. If it was determined that national pooling be practiced for social pooling funds of old-age insurance in China (with basic old-age pensions being issued), and the rates and the management system be centralized, they would not be any different from the national "social security tax", and it would be justified for the taxation department to collect fees nationwide. Therefore, determining which department should collect social insurance funds seemingly depends on the nature of the collected funds more than any other factor.

Besides fund collection and the rationalization of the old-age security fund management system, two other problems must be solved: first, the establishment of a national uniform old-age pension management system; second, the establishment of scientific and reasonable issuance adjustment mechanism for old-age pension benefits. These two problems have both been mentioned in The Report, for which principles were proposed. The establishment of a national uniform old-age pension management system under the direct charge of the central government is an important measure for resolving such problems as low pooling levels for old-age insurance funds, great differences in premium payment between different regions, difficulties in adjusting local surplus funds, and regulating the issuance of old-age pension benefits. I think we should push forward the development of this system, and in particular national uniform laws and regulations, such as the "Social Insurance Law", should be promulgated and implemented as soon as possible. However, this system should not be too complex, and we should mainly manage the collection, supervision and issuance of old-age insurance social pooling funds under centralized national management. As to non-large scaleold-age insurance personal account funds, it is suggested that the National Council for Social Security Funds be entrusted with the management of these funds, or that provincial personal account funds management committees manage them respectively so that they can be separated from the funds managed by the government and become market-based funds under strict supervision conditions. As for the old-age pension benefit adjustment mechanism, in-depth discussions cannot be held due to its complicated nature. If national pooling is practiced for basic old-age pensions, such retirement pensions should be of a pay-as-you-go nature, and the issuance standards should be raised as appropriate. The basic old-age pension replacement rate of insured employees reaching retirement conditions will at least reach above 40% of their salary before retirement; as for the insured whose statutory retirement age and contribution years are raised and prolonged as appropriate, their replacement rate may be raised accordingly, but should not exceed 50%. Attention should be paid to the principle that "certain differences may exist in benefit standards between various regions, but such differences should not prevent the transfer of old-age pensions and mobility of laborers nationwide" as proposed in The Report.

In sum, if national pooling is practiced for the future basic old-age pension system, a department under the central government should be assigned to its uniform management. As for the basic old-age pensions of all of the eligible insured people, the state should be responsible for its uniform management, as well as for fund raising and benefit issuance. The transfer and renewal of social insurance among various regions will not be as difficult as it is now. As for personal account funds, due to their shrinking in scale, it is proposed that they be combined with occupational annuities, for which decentralized management and investment should be conducted on a provincial basis; market-based investment institutions are employed for their operation and remunerated from the amount of payment and return on investment. As the return on investment is personal, the transfer and continuation problem of social insurance relations in personal accounts would barely exist.

V. The Problem with Managing the Debt of Old-age Security Funds and State-owned Share Transfer and Holding

A problem that can hardly be bypassed in the course of reforming China's old-age security system is the problem of explicit and implicit old-age security fund debts. The explicit debts are caused by the fact that old-age insurance funds currently collected, especially social pooling funds, are inadequate to pay retired people's pensions; the implicit debts refer to the deficits in the personal accounts of "in-service persons" and "new persons" not fully funded (which have to be paid once these people reach retirement age). Moreover, there are potential deficits in the balance of payments resulting from expanding old-age security expenditures (such as old-age allowances and subsistence security expenditures) and from the expansion of the old-age security system as well as that of the rapidly aging population.

The issue of the actual social pooling funds debts and the implicit debts in personal accounts is mainly resolved by improving the old-age security system so that old-age security funds gradually become self-sustainable. Various measures discussed now, to some extent, also serve this objective. In accordance with China's aging population and the changes in its demographic and labor structure, The Report makes the suggestion of raising the "age for receiving old-age pensions". The main reasons given include the rapid rise of the burden rate of non-laboring population over the laboring population (from 1:1.3 in 1980 to 1:3 in 2002 to 1:2 in 2030); as well as international lessons and experiences (the actual retirement age in developing countries is young, while the retirement age in developed countries has been raised to over 65) showing that the retirement age for workers is low in China, and even so there exists a serious issue of early retirement. With the actual retirement age lower than the statutory retirement age, the retiring population not only exerts pressure on the payment of current old-age security funds but also aggravates old-age security debts, which is not good for the long-term equilibrium of social security funds. Therefore, The Report proposes that "regardless of gender, the minimum age for receiving full pension from social pooling should be gradually raised to 65, the practices of encouraging or forcing early retirement should be stopped, and old-age pension benefits should be reduced pro rata for those with inadequate employment years." This proposal is forward-looking and insightful. The opinions put forward in The Report merit the attention of the social security administrative department, which should carefully study the appropriate time and specific methods for implementing these proposals (the implementation may be delayed several years in light of the pressure of the employment peak). I approve of the opinion on gradually raising the retirement age, but consideration should be given to the characteristics and demands of different occupations; the boundary between retiring from the labor market and receiving "statutory old-age pensions" should be defined; and the problem of early retirement should be resolved. Employing the appropriate measures, the statutory retirement age should be gradually raised to the level of developed countries in order to overcome the pressure of early payment of old-age security funds.

Old-age security expenditures resulting from the expanding coverage of the old-age security system are generally yet limitedly supported by tax and public finances, and such subsidies will gradually be withdrawn in the future and thus will not pose a big problem. Currently, the fiscal department allocates subsidies amounting to several tens of billions RMB for social insurance, especially old-age insurance funds, so as to offset the deficits in old-age pensions. In the short term, the normal operation of the old-age insurance system may be maintained in terms of fiscal subsidies and social insurance funds with expanding coverage. Of course, with the establishment of social security budgets, the deficits in social security funds of the current year may have institutional solutions. The social security debts posing the most serious problem are the expanding deficits in personal accounts and the balance of payment risk from the aging population. As we have already discussed about the personal accounts, how to cope with the risk of the aging population will be focused on as follows.

To cope with the above debts of old-age security funds, the Chinese government established the National Council for Social Security Fund in 2000, which is responsible for raising and operating national social security funds. Through nearly ten years' accumulation, the national social security funds have amounted to RMB 562.37 billion, a small amount in scale with consideration given to the huge social security fund debts. The enormous state-owned assets, state-controlled enterprises and state-holding enterprises in China provide the national social security fund with the material base for raising funds from state-owned enterprises and state-owned assets; the key point is to find the method and approach suitable for the transfer of state-owned assets and shares into the national social security funds. Due to the difficulty to cash state-owned assets, it is now very difficult to directly transfer state-owned assets to the national social security funds for management and operation. A more realistic approach is for national public finance to inject funds and transfer funds from listed state-owned enterprises to national social security funds. National public finances inject some funds each year but on a limited scale; the key funds are from the transfer of state-owned shares. The Chinese government decided in 2003 to transfer some state-owned assets, especially some state-owned shares of listed companies and non-listed shareholding companies to replenish national social security funds. The idea several years earlier was to transfer funds after cashing state-owned shares by selling through the capital market to the national social security funds. As the overall scale of China's capital market is limited, and because it is difficult for China to bear the pressure of selling a large amount of state-owned shares within a short period, it is very difficult to sell and cash state-owned shares. This may bring violent fluctuations in the capital market. It is difficult to have the national social security fund play an effective role by selling state-owned shares.

The proposal in The Report is to change "selling state-owned shares" to "transfer state-owned shares to substantiate social security funds". Social security funds should hold these shares for a long period and pay old-age pensions by bonuses. As strategic shareholders, they can maintain their owners' rights, including bonuses at a reasonable level through company supervision, voting rights and a seat at the Board of Directors, etc. Social security funds must hold shares for a long period, have well-defined responsibilities and independent management authority, and regularly publicize audited account details. To transfer state-owned shares to substantiate social security funds may prevent the loss of state-owned assets similarly to what occurred in Russia. Meanwhile, as long-term strategic shareholders, old-age pension funds may play an important role in supervising corporate operation and improving governance structure. This proposal is very valuable in that it is highly persuasive, pertinent and operable.

In June 2009, upon the approval of the State Council, the Ministry of Finance, the State-owned Assets Supervision and Administration Commission, the China

Security Regulatory Commission and the National Council for Social Security Fund jointly promulgated and implemented the "Implementation Measures for the Transfer of Some State-owned Shares from the Domestic Securities Market to the National Social Security Fund". According to the "Implementing Measures", after the implementation of the policy of separating the new from the old in the share-trading reform, a joint stock limited company with state-owned shares which makes IPOs and gets listed in the domestic securities market shall, unless it is otherwise provided for by the State Council, transfer some of its state-owned shares to the NCSSF, namely 10% of the actual number of the IPO stocks. If the number of shares held by the state-owned shareholder is less than the number of shares which should be transferred, the transfer shall be made on the basis of the number of the shares actually held by it. For state-owned shares of domestically listed companies transferred to social security funds, social security funds will take up the obligations of the original state-owned shareholders in the lock-up period. As for shares transferred by companies which have IPO and are listed after the implementation of the policy of separating the new from the old in the share-trading reform and before the promulgation of these measures, the lock-up period shall be prolonged for three years. After state-owned shares are transferred to social security funds, social security funds have the rights to earnings and disposals with regards to the transferred shares, but shall not interfere with the daily management of the listed companies operations. According to the implementing measures for the transfer of state-owned shares, altogether 131 listed companies were involved, thus 8.394 billion shares should have been transferred, with a market capitalization of about RMB 63.933 billion, which should have amounted to RMB 83.56 billion by the end of transfer, cumulating in a 30% increase. The transfer of state-owned shares this time coincided with the proposal of The Report, which shows the foresight and practicability of the proposal. The transfer of state-owned shares, to some extent, can alleviate the pressure of selling state-owned shares that has been troubling the Chinese stock market for a long time, and help substantiate social security funds. It is also an important measure for improving the social security system and benefiting all people. Of course, the transfer of state-owned shares to substantiate social security funds is only one of the possible measures for resolving the issue of long-term debts of social security funds. There is still a large amount of difficult work and thinking to do, such as how to raise savings social security funds through multiple channels based on demands and reality, and realize value preservation and increase during a long period of time. This is a major preemptive strategy that China must take in order to cope with its aging population.[2]

---

[2]This chapter is published in *China Industrial Economics*, 2009 (8).

Chapter 8
A Study on the Income Redistribution Effect of Social Security in China: A Case Study on Social Insurance

Social security is an important tool for regulating income distribution. Some scholars have studied the role of income redistribution of social security in China, and have come to different and even conflicting conclusions due to different sources of data, time of investigation, and research perspectives. In 2012, a task force of the Chinese Academy of Social Sciences conducted an urban and rural household questionnaire survey using an experience stratification method and non-strict random sampling in six provinces, namely: Sichuan, Heilongjiang, Hunan, Shanxi, Jiangsu and Hainan. 3417 effective questionnaires were recovered to conduct macro theoretical analysis and empirical analysis on the income redistribution effect of social security.

8.1 Problem Introduction and Literature Review

The expanding income gap has become a major problem drawing extensive concerns from various social circles in China. In the mid-1980s, China's Gini coefficient stood at 0.16, which rose to 0.44 in 2000 and to about 0.49 in 2008.[1] The reasons for the expansion and exacerbation of the income gap are multifold; some are reasonable, while many others are unreasonable; some are about primary distribution, while others are about redistribution. Some experts hold that a very important reason for the expanding income gap among residents is the unhealthy and unfair social security system.[2] Social security is an important tool for the redistribution of residents' income, which important role in income distribution

[1]Li Shi and Yang Sui (2009), The Impact of China's Urban Subsistence Security Policy on Income Distribution and Poverty, *Chinese Journal of Population Science*, 2009 (5).
[2]ZhengGongcheng (2010), Social Security: Basic Institutional Guarantee for Regulating Income Distribution, *Chinese Cadres Tribune*, 2010 (6).

© Springer Nature Singapore Pte Ltd. and Social Sciences Academic Press 2017
Y. Wang, *Social Security in China: On the Possibility of Equitable Distribution*,
Research Series on the Chinese Dream and China's Development Path,
DOI 10.1007/978-981-10-5643-7_8

among residents is fully reflected in both international and domestic social security and income distribution practices.

In light of past studies, the redistribution effect of social security has been verified in many countries. David Jesuit and Vincent Mahler, through a comparative study of fiscal redistribution based on the LIS datain 13 developed countries from 1980 to 2000, discovered that national social security outperforms taxation in regulating the income distribution gap. In Sweden, a welfare state, the role played by social security in income distribution accounts for over 80%, while that of taxation only for about 10%.[3] Social security contributed to over 40% in the drop of the Gini coefficient in the United States.[4] Japan's social security system plays a key role in regulating the income distribution gap, and the Gini coefficient after the regulation of social security is about 0.02–0.07 lower than the Gini coefficient before redistribution, with the redistribution rate reaching over 4%.[5] In 2004, after redistribution, the Gini coefficient in the United Kingdom dropped from 0.52 to 0.38, at a rate of 36.8%, to which various direct social security measures made the biggest contributions, alone reducing the Gini coefficient by 15%.[6] When reviewing the OECD data, we discover that in 2010 the Gini coefficient underwent very obvious changes in some countries after the regulation of taxation and transfer payment. The Gini coefficient after the regulation of taxation and transfer payment (mainly social security) dropped by 0.2 on average, while the drop of the Gini coefficient in Austria, Belgium, Finland, France, Germany and Slovenia was over this average.

China's social security is a comprehensive system including social insurance, social welfare and social assistance. In recent years, some experts and scholars have studied the topic of social security and income distribution from different perspectives. Due to their different grasp of national conditions, different sources of data, different research perspectives and different research methods, they have come to different conclusions, causing disagreements, disputes and even conflicts over the specific role of social security in regulating income distribution in China.

Many scholars think that the effect of social security on income distribution regulation is not satisfactory. A "contrary regulation" effect on income distribution can even be observed, showing an important regression effect.[7] Some scholars think

---

[3]David Jesuit and Vincent Mahler (2004), "*State Redistribution in Comparative Perspective: A Cross-National Analysis of the Developed Countries*". Luxembourg Income Study Working Paper.

[4]Ervik, R. (1998), "The Redistributive Aim of Social Policy: A Comparative Analysis of Taxes, Tax Expenditure Transfers and Direct Transfers in Eight Countries". LIS Working Paper, 1998 (184).

[5]Liu Leshan (2008), Overseas Fiscal Measures for Regulating Income Gap and Their Implications, paper delivered at the 18th Annual Conference of the Chinese Society of Laws of Economics.

[6]J.IgnacioConde-Ruiz and Paola Profeta (2007), "*The redistributive design of social security systems, The Economic Journal*", 117(April), 686–712.

[7]Xiang Ling (2007), Several Problems Concerning the Redistribution Regression Effect in the Old-age Insurance System, *Fujian Forum (Humanities and Social Sciences Edition)*, 2007 (1).

that the transfer payment of social security widens income gap between rural residents and urban residents, and that after the transfer payment of social security, the gap between low-income households and medium-income households become wider than before transfer payment, as for that between medium high-income households and high-income households.[8] With a social security system of separate practices in rural and urban areas, social security has further aggravated urban-rural inequality. The per capita social security transferred income of urban residents in 2000 was 10.04 times that of rural residents; the same ratio was 15.45 in 2003 and 13.37 in 2005; if all the welfare "implicitly subsidized" to urban employees is taken into account, the actual income gap of urban-rural residents will expand 5–6 times.[9] The benefits of China's basic old-age and medical insurance for residents of medium and high income far exceed those of residents of low income, thus expanding the income gap.[10] Under the 2005 reform scheme, people above 40 in 2002 had obvious tendency of reverse income transfer.[11] Compared with the original old-age insurance system, the new old-age insurance system obviously weakens the intra-generational redistribution effect and may give rise to serious intergenerational inequalities.[12] In terms of income redistribution, China's current medical security system lacks a regulatory mechanism and fails to bring into play its regulating function for income redistribution. Under the "low insurance premiums and high coinsurance rate" mode, inequalities exist among those receiving benefits from the cooperative medical services.

Many other scholars think that despite the many problems and inadequacies in the institutional design of China's social security, other types of securities such as China's subsistence security, old-age security, medical security, unemployment security and education security all play a positive role in regulating income distribution in China. A research based in Baoji, Shaanxi Province has found that the transfer income from social security has reduced the Gini coefficient between urban and rural residents' by 4.53%; furthermore, the Gini coefficient for urban residents has dropped by 22.76%, while income gap among rural residents has dropped by 1.82%.[13] The current arrangements in China's social old-age insurance system play

---

[8]Wang Maofu and XieYongcai (2012), A Study about Negative Regulation of Income Distribution by Social Security, *Studies on Mao Zedong and Deng Xiaoping's Theories*, 2012 (6).

[9]Gu Cheng and Li Junyi (2004), Expansion of the Gap between Urban and Rural Income Distribution and the Integration of China's Social Security System, *Journal of the Dongbei University of Finance and Economics*, 2004 (4).

[10]Wang Xiaolu and Fan Gang (2005), The Trend of Income Gap in China and Analysis of Influence Factors, *Economic Research Journal*, 2005(10).

[11]He Lixin (2007), The Effect of Income Distribution by the Reform of the Urban Old-age Insurance System in China, *Economic Research Journal*, 2007 (3).

[12]PengHaoran and ShenShuguang (2007), A Comparative Study of the Income Redistribution Effect of China's Old-age Insurance System before and after the Reform, *Statistical Research*, 2007 (2).

[13]GaoWenshu (2012), The Effect of Social Security on Regulating Income Distribution Gap: an Empirical Study Based on the Data of a Survey over Residents in Baoji, Shaanxi, *Social Security Studies*, 2012 (4).

an obvious role of income redistribution.[14] Old-age pension property has exerted a major redistribution effect on property distribution in families of enterprise employees in China's urban areas by reducing the Gini coefficient of family property distribution by 8% points and reducing family property distribution inequalities by 20%.[15] After the institution of compensations for new rural cooperative medical services, inequalities have been alleviated to some extent.[16] Compensations for new rural cooperative medical services are more inclined towards sick people, and those with low income receive higher compensations than those with high income. The subsistence security system can improve the living conditions of some low-income people, and play a certain effective role in alleviating urban poverty; therefore, the subsistence security system constrains, to some extent, the income gap within cities and within rural areas.[17]

Thus, we can conclude that China's research on the role of social security in income redistribution is not very mature, and major disputes and conflicts exist as to how to evaluate the role of the social security system in regulating income gap. Some studies only discuss the role of China's social security in income distribution theoretically or by employing simple statistic data, or even jump to qualitative judgment and conclusion on the role of social security in income distribution by subjective observations. Quantitative studies on the role of social security in income distribution are lacking, and an investigation basis is lacking for subjective evaluation on the role of social security in income redistribution. Thus different research conclusions have been drawn as a result of different sources of data, different survey time and different research perspectives. The income redistribution effect of the entire social security system is different from that of different single social security project, thus leading into some contradictory results. This situation is not ideal for the accurate understanding and grasp of the role of social security in income distribution in China, which is so complicated that hardly any absolute standard can be employed for measurement. Therefore, we should give full consideration to real national economic and social conditions as well as residents' value judgment; as we objectively measure the effect of social security in income redistribution, we should fully examine the subjective evaluation by the public.

Based on current research, this study wishes to examine the important role of social security in residents' income distribution; employ the data of questionnaire surveys to conduct quantitative analysis of the current role of social security in

[14]Wang Xiaojun and Kang Bowei (2009), Analysis of the Effect of China's Social Old-age Insurance System on Income Redistribution, *Statistical Research*, 2009 (11).

[15]Yang Zhenlin and Wang Yake (2007), An Empirical Analysis of the Redistribution Effect of China's Enterprise Old-age Insurance System, *China Soft Science*, 2007 (4).

[16]Ren Ran and Jin Feng (2007), A Study on the Health Service Accessibility and Medical Service Burdens after the Implementation of New Rural Cooperative Medical Care, *China Health Economics*, 2007 (1).

[17]Chen Jiandong, Yang Wen and Feng Ying (2001), An Empirical Study on the Income Distribution Effect of Subsistence Security and Individual Income Tax, *Reform of Economic System*, 2001 (1).

income distribution; and analyze the practical evaluation of different residents on the role of social security in income distribution by taking social insurance as an example, in an attempt to comprehensively analyze and grasp the role of social security in income redistribution in China from both subjective and objective perspectives. The task force of the Chinese Academy of Social Sciences conducted urban and rural household questionnaire surveys using an experience stratification method and non-strict random sampling in six provinces, namely: Sichuan, Heilongjiang, Hunan, Shanxi, Jiangsu and Hainan. 3417 effective questionnaires were recovered. The questionnaire's content concerning the role of social security in income redistribution mainly included items such as the basic conditions of interviewees, their current social security (including social insurance, social welfare and social assistance), and their subjective evaluation, relevant problems and suggestions on social security, as well as its role in income distribution. This article consists mainly of five parts: first, problem introduction and literature review; second, examination of the role of China's social security in income redistribution; third, an objective measurement of the role of social security (social insurance) in income redistribution; fourth, subjective evaluation of the role of social security in income redistribution; fifth, conclusion and suggestions.

8.2 China Attaches Great Importance to the Effective Role of Social Security in Income Re-Distribution

(i) China attaches great importance to the role of social security in income redistribution

Since the start of the 21st century, the CPC Central Committee and the State Council have been attaching great importance to the excessive income gap by actively taking various measures to narrow income gap and promote social equality and justice. Since the 18th CPC National Congress, China has been according more importance to resolving the excessive income gap and deepening the reform of the income distribution system and the social security system in the course of comprehensively deepening reform, and attaching more importance to the role of social security in income redistribution. The 18th CPC National Congress, the Third and the Fifth Plenary Sessions of the 18th CPC Central Committee have all put forward that we should further step up efforts in redistribution regulations and improve the redistribution regulatory mechanism which is mainly based on taxation, social security and transfer payment.

The nature of social security is to maintain social equality and justice, as its function is to distribute and redistribute people's income. With the constant economic and social development in China, people have increasing demands in terms of social security. Various social security systems have been established and improved, the coverage of social security has been constantly expanding, and the fund scale of social security has been expanding. Social security takes up an important position in the distribution pattern of people's income, and its important role in regulating residents' income distribution has become increasingly prominent.

In recent years, China has been gradually establishing and improving various social security systems. In terms of old-age security, the rural residents' and the urban residents' old-age insurance systems have been established successively, and efforts have been channeled to promote the integration of the urban-rural residents' old-age insurance system and construct a multi-level old-age insurance system; while attention is paid to fund security, more and more importance has been accorded to old-age service security. It is especially noteworthy that in 2015, the central government decided to implement the reform on the old-age insurance system in government departments and public institutions, which is conducive to alleviating the "benefit gap" and promoting social equality. In terms of medical security, outpatient social pooling for urban residents' basic medical insurance has been basically established; exploration is being made on the establishment of a major disease insurance system; and the urban-rural medical insurance systems are being gradually integrated. Important steps have been taken in the establishment of unemployment, work-related injury and maternity insurance systems. In terms of subsistence security, the number of people covered tends to be stable, a dynamic regulatory mechanism for urban and rural subsistence security standards has been established, and supervision and service for subsistence security have been improving.

With the establishment and improvement of various social security systems, a social security system covering urban and rural residents has been basically developed, and full institutional coverage has been realized. The medical insurance system, which has taken the lead to cover all the people in China, has developed the largest medical security network in the world. By September 2015, the number of people covered by basic old-age insurance, basic medical insurance, unemployment insurance, work-related injury insurance, and maternity insurance was respectively 852 million, 658 million, 171 million, 211 million, and 178 million. In terms of social assistance, the number of urban residents covered by subsistence security has been maintained at about 20 million, the number of rural residents covered by subsistence security has been maintained at about 53 million, and the number of old people provided for by the Five Guarantee System has been maintained at about 5 million.[18] With the constant improvement of the social insurance system and its expanding coverage, the scale of income and social security expenses has been expanding. By the end of 2014, the income of the five social insurance funds (urban and rural residents' basic old-age insurance, medical insurance, unemployment insurance, industrial injury insurance, and maternity insurance) amounted to RMB 3.9828 trillion, a RMB 457.5 billion increase from 2013 at a rate of 13.0%. Fund

[18]Source of data: *Statistical Bulletin on the Development of Social Services in China 2014*.

expenditures amounted to RMB 3.3003 trillion, a RMB 508.6 billion increase from 2013 at a rate of 18.2%.[19]

With China's increasing fiscal investments in social security, the benefits of social security have obviously improved, and the income redistribution effect of social security is becoming increasingly obvious. China has consecutively raised old-age pensions for enterprise retirees 11 times. As a result, the basic old-age pension for enterprise retirees has risen from a monthly average of RMB 647 in 2004 to over RMB 2000. The consecutive substantial increase of the basic old-age pension has played an active role in improving enterprise retirees' living standards and promoting social equality. The minimum standard for the basic old-age pension of national urban and rural residents' basic old-age insurance has been improved to a monthly pay of RMB 70 for each person. In terms of medical insurance, in 2014, 1.52 billion person-time urban employees received medical services, and 420 million person-time urban residents received medical services. The reimbursement ratio of inpatient medical expenditures within the coverage of employees' basic medical insurance and urban residents' basic medical insurance policies reached above 80% and around 70% respectively. The highest limit of payment from funds was improved to six times that of the local employees' average annual salary and local residents' annual per capital disposable income, which, to some extent, alleviated the problem of overpriced medical treatment. In terms of unemployment, work-related injury, and maternity insurance, the number of people receiving benefits and the amount of benefits have also been substantially improved. Subsistence security levels have been stably improved. In terms of rural poverty relief, in 2011, the state defined the new rural poverty relief standard as RMB 2300 for farmers' per capita net income. Increasingly more poor people have been covered by poverty relief efforts, and come to share the results of reform and development in China.

(ii) The expenditure scale of social security in China and its role in income redistribution

After the 1990s, with the establishment and improvement of various social security systems in China, the coverage of social security gradually expanded, security levels gradually improved, and the social security system became an important tool for China to regulate laborers' and national income distribution, with a more obvious impact on income distribution. In terms of the social security expenditure ratio in fiscal expenditures, since 2000, the social security ratio in the narrow caliber (caliber I) has been maintained at above 10%, the social security ratio in the medium caliber (caliber II) at above 20%, and the social security ratio in the wide caliber (caliber III) including the expenditure of education and health at above 36%, reaching 40% in 2012. In terms of the social security expenditure ratio in GDP, since 2000, the social security expenditure in the narrow caliber has been basically maintained at above

---

[19]Source of data: *Statistical Bulletin on the Development of Human Resources and Social Security Services in China* of past years.

2%, reaching 2.4% in 2012; with the rapid development of China's social insurance system, social security expenditures in the medium caliber has been increasing quicker, with the ratio from 2.6% of GDP in 1998 to 6% of GDP in 2012; the social security expenditure ratio in the wide caliber increased from 5.4% of GDP in 1998 to 11.4% of GDP in 2012 (see Table 8.1). Of course, various factors should be considered in terms of the impact of social security income on income distribution. Only with a sound institutional design and a scientific operation mechanism can the goal of income distribution through social security be effectively achieved, the "negative regulation" of income distribution by social security avoided, and the "positive regulation" by social security truly realized.

With the improvement of the social security system and the rise of the ratio of social security fund income and expenditure in national economy, social security systems such as subsistence security, old-age security, medical security, unemployment security and education security have come to play an active role in income distribution in China. Different social security items have different mechanisms for and effects on income redistribution. As social insurance funds are collected according to income in primary distribution, and are paid according to the risk level in secondary distribution, the lower the income is, the higher the replacement rate of social insurance is; therefore, social insurance has a very strong income regulation function. According to our survey, with the establishment and improvement of the social insurance system in China, more and more people have become beneficiaries of social insurance, and social insurance benefits have become an important part in individual and family income. In 2011, all individual social insurance benefits accounted for 14.5% of individuals' annual income; the ratio of social insurance benefits in retirees' income was even higher, being 43%. Social assistance is the state's subsistence security provided for people without or with low income due to disasters or poverty; the recipients do not have to pay premiums, payment is mainly made in cash or in kind by national public finances. Such assistance is distributed according to subsistence needs without requiring the beneficiaries' reciprocity in rights and obligations, thereby with a more direct and obvious redistribution effect. Social welfare consists in subsidies and services mainly addressed to specific weak people such as children, old people and the disabled; these are all funded by national public finances and social donations, and distributed according to the needs of these specific people, thus also having a significant function in terms of narrowing income gap.[20]

In practice, social security may not only promote income redistribution and narrow the income gap, but may also give rise to negative regulation and widen income gap. The positive or negative role of social security in income redistribution depends on relevant factors such as institutional mode, coverage, institutional design, institutional transition, and management services. We should bring into full play the positive regulation role of social security in income redistribution, as well

[20]As to the analysis of the specific mechanisms of different social security items for income redistribution, please refer to our other works.

Table 8.1 Social security expenditure in China (*unit* billion yuan; %)

Year	Caliber I	Caliber II	Caliber III	Ratio in total fiscal expenditure			Ratio in GDP		
				Caliber I	Caliber II	Caliber III	Caliber I	Caliber II	Caliber III
1978	1.89	–	12.94	1.7	–	11.5	0.5	–	3.6
1992	6.65	–	91.68	1.8	–	24.5	0.3	–	3.4
1996	12.8	–	200.54	1.6	–	25.3	0.2	–	2.8
1998	59.56	221.10	452.73	5.5	17.8	36.5	0.7	2.6	5.4
2000	151.76	360.45	649.36	9.6	20.1	36.1	1.5	3.6	6.5
2002	263.62	559.04	960.49	12.0	22.4	38.4	2.2	4.7	8.0
2004	311.61	722.37	1236.84	10.9	22.2	38.0	2.0	4.5	7.7
2006	436.18	995.03	1689.81	10.8	21.6	36.7	2.1	5.2	8.0
2008	680.43	1509.85	2686.58	10.9	21.3	37.9	2.3	5.0	8.9
2010	913.06	2163.93	3827.35	10.2	21.1	37.4	2.3	5.4	9.5
2012	1258.55	3093.92	5942.64	10.0	20.9	40.1	2.4	6.0	11.4

Note Caliber I includes the expenditures related to special care and social welfare and relief, retirement payment of administrative and public institutions, and expenditures in terms of social security subsidies; Caliber II is the addition of social insurance fund expenditures other than fiscal subsidies to Caliber I, and the denominator (total fiscal expenditures) for calculating the ratio of Caliber II includes social insurance fund expenditures except for fiscal subsidies. Caliber III is the addition of education and health expenditures to the basis of Caliber II; it should be noted that the ratio of social security fiscal expenditures in 2002 was big, which was related to the substantial increase in national fiscal expenditures in terms of social insurance fund subsidies. Source of data: based on the relevant data in *China's Fiscal Statistics Yearbook*, *China's Statistics Yearbook*, and *China's Health Statistics Yearbook* in past years; the source of data for the expenditure of social insurance funds from 1998 to 2008: *China's Fiscal Yearbook 2008*; the source of data for 2010: The National Fiscal Expenditure Final Report; the source of data for 2012: Final Account Data of National Fiscal Expenditure 2012, Statistical Bulletin of National Economic and Social Development 2012, and Statistical Bulletin on Human Resources and Social Security 2012; due to different statistical calibers in different years, the data of some years deviate to some extent as prevent and avoid its negative regulatory role. On the whole, China adopts the insurance-based social security mode and generally employs the mode of "combining social pooling and personal accounts". The introduction of personal accounts and the many problems arising in the course of implementation have further weakened the overall role of social security in terms of income redistribution in China.

8.3 Evaluation of the Re-Distribution Effect of China's Social Insurance Revenues

(i) The income redistribution mechanisms of different social insurance items

The social insurance system is the most important part of the whole social security system. The mechanism for the social insurance system in regulating income distribution is complicated, and consideration should be given to such aspects as fund-raising mode, fund source, responsibility allocation, fund-raising level, benefit determination mode, and benefit adjustment mechanism. Also, different social insurance items also vary in their regulation mechanism for income distribution.

The old-age insurance system is the center of the social insurance system. The regulation of income distribution by the old-age insurance system is mainly reflected in two aspects: the fund-raising mode and the benefit determination mode. The pay-as-you-go fund-raising mode and the defined-benefit mode, through the social pooling and payment of old-age insurance funds, play a major role in income distribution; the fund accumulation mode and the contribution-defined mode are mainly income regulation systems employed within an individual's lifetime, from his/her youth (working period) to his/her old age (non-working period). It should be noted that the pay-as-you-go system and the benefit-defined system do not correspond one-to-one, while the fund accumulation system and the contribution-defined system also do not correspond exactly. The old-age insurance systems in many countries tend to be a mixture of different fund-raising modes and benefit-defining modes, and their role in determining income distribution is even more complicated.

The medical insurance system is also an important system in social insurance. It is not only is related to individuals' health, but also regulates income distribution to some extent. The measurement of the role of the medical insurance system in income distribution should be made in the light of the different types of medical insurance system, as well as that of the fund-raising mechanism and benefit compensation mechanism selected. The modes of the medical insurance system include the national (all-inclusive) medical insurance mode, the social medical insurance mode, the commercial medical insurance mode, the cooperative medical insurance mode and the savings medical insurance mode. Due to differences in the fund-raising mechanism and compensation modes, different modes of medical insurance play different roles in the regulation of income distribution.

Compared with the old-age insurance and medical insurance systems, the unemployment system, work-related injury system and maternity insurance system, though relatively small in coverage and fund scale, can regulate income distribution to some extent. Unemployment insurance mainly regulates income distribution by way of fund raising and benefit payment. Different types of unemployment insurance system (including compulsory unemployment insurance, voluntary unemployment subsidies and unemployment assistance, etc.) have different effect in regulating income distribution. Compared with other social insurance systems and social security systems, the unemployment insurance system can better help to directly or indirectly regulate primary distribution. Work-related injury insurance, which does not require personal contributions and provides relevant compensation for anyone subjected to work-related injury, especially helps those of medium and low income and poor people alleviate medical burdens and thus plays a significant role in regulating income distribution. The maternity insurance system, by providing relevant economic support and services for women before and after giving birth, also regulates income distribution to some extent.

(ii) Measurement of the effect of social insurance on income redistribution

To further analyze the effect of social security on income redistribution, this study made a detailed analysis on the social security income gap regulations by using the survey data in 2012. In terms of the basic information of interviewees, males accounted for 47.2%, and females accounted for 52.8%, with an even gender ratio; age was mainly between 18 and 60, accounting for 84.3% of the surveyed population; CPC party members accounted for 17.9%; in terms of religious beliefs, 93.8% of the interviewees had no religious belief; in terms of household register types, those with rural household registers accounted for 53%, and those with non-rural household register accounted for 47%, with a basically balanced ratio; in terms of educational background, those who without any schooling accounted for 4.8%, those with primary school education accounted for 18.1%, those with junior middle school education accounted for 30.7%, those with senior middle school education accounted for 15.1%, those with technical high school/vocational high school/technical secondary school education accounted for 6.4%, those with junior college education accounted for 11.7%, and those with a bachelor's degree and above accounted for 13.2%; in terms of occupation, white-collars accounted for 20.7%, blue-collars accounted for 53.1%, retirees accounted for 12.7%, and other people (students, people awaiting employment and unemployed people) accounted for 13.5%; in terms of employers, those employed by publicly-owned units accounted for 20.7%, those employed by privately-owned units accounted for 24.4%, farmers accounted for 39.5%, and other people accounted for 15.3%. Through comparison, samples are characteristically close to the data of the sixth national census, in which males accounted for 51.27%, and females accounted for 48.73%; the population aged 0–14 accounted for 16.60%, the population aged 15–59 accounted for 70.14%, and the population aged at and above 60 accounted for 13.26%; the urban population accounted for 49.68%; the rural population accounted for 50.32%; of the population above 6 years old (1,242,546,122 people), those without any schooling accounted for 5%, those with primary school education accounted for 28.7%, those with junior middle school education accounted for 41.7%, those with senior middle school education accounted for 15%, those with junior college education accounted for 5.5%, those with a bachelor's degree accounted for 3.7%, and those with an academic degree above the master's accounted for 0.3%. On the whole, the samples are evenly distributed and representative of China's overall conditions.

In this survey, the average annual income of families covered by subsistence security is RMB 15,690.25, and the average subsistence social security they receive is RMB 5564.16, with an average subsistence security replacement rate of 24.36%; in 2010, the subsistence demand was RMB 10,926.48, while the subsistence compensation rate reached 45.10%. In terms of the income of residents covered by social insurance, the per capita benefits from the social insurance system account for 14.5% of the annual income. The average social benefits and income ratio of the non-rural population is 18.0%, and that of the rural population is 12.1%. Therefore, we can conclude that social security income has become an important source of income for Chinese residents, especially those with low income.

As the ratio of the population samples receiving social assistance and social welfare is very small and the role of social assistance and social welfare in regulating income gap is direct and obvious, this article mainly analyzes the effect of social security on income redistribution taking social insurance as an example. In terms of measurement methods, the Gini coefficient of residents' income before and after social insurance is for reflecting the impact of the income transferred from social insurance (see Tables 8.2 and 8.3). The transferred income of social insurance here mainly refers to pure social insurance income after the deduction of various social insurance contributions and expenditures, which has a relatively good measurement value. Constrained by space, the detailed revenues and expenditures of various types of social insurance will not be repeated here, as they can be found in another book we have edited.[21]

The Gini coefficient is an international index for measuring income gap, and the changes in the Gini coefficient in 2012 survey samples before and after the transfer of annual social insurance income into total annual income can reflect the regulation of income gap by the social insurance system. The social insurance annual income in this article is the sum of = all types of social income of each sampled interviewee in 2012, that is, the sum of annual income from urban employee's basic old-age insurance, urban employee's basic medical insurance, urban resident's social old-age insurance, urban resident's basic medical insurance, new rural cooperative medical insurance, new rural social old-age insurance, unemployment insurance, work-related injury insurance, and maternity insurance.[22]

[21]See Wang Yanzhong ed. (2013), *A Survey of Income Redistribution by Social Security in China*, Social Science Academic Press.

[22]To be consistent with the total annual income, social income expenditures are not deducted from social insurance revenues in this article. In the survey, social insurance contribution, as part of personal expenditures, is not deducted from personal annual income.

Table 8.2 The impact of the income transferred from social insurance on the Gini coefficient in 2012

	Income before the transfer of social insurance		Income after the transfer of social insurance		Extent of Gini coefficient reduction (%)
	Mean value	Gini coefficient	Mean value	Gini coefficient	
All samples	28,761.55	0.547	30,261.19	0.512	6.40
Non-rural household register	36,648.70	0.525	39,407.54	0.462	12
Rural household register	21,160.02	0.546	21,448.43	0.536	1.80
– Farmers	12,490.17	0.461	12,706.17	0.447	3.00
– Migrant workers	38,463.44	0.570	38,608.82	0.569	0.10

Table 8.3 The impact of the transfer of various types of social insurance on the Gini coefficient

Social insurance item	After the transfer of social insurance income		Reduction of the Gini coefficient (%)
	Mean value	Gini coefficient	
Old-age insurance	30,020.45	0.515	5.88
– Urban employee's old-age insurance	29,926.68	0.518	5.30
– Urban resident's old-age insurance	28,810.56	0.545	0.24
– Rural resident's social old-age insurance	28,806.31	0.545	0.32
Medical insurance	28,984.25	0.544	0.49
– Urban employee's medical insurance	28,914.51	0.546	0.20
– Urban resident's medical insurance	28,771.65	0.547	0.02
– New rural cooperative medical insurance	28,821.19	0.545	0.27
Maternity, work-related injury and unemployment insurance	28,779.58	0.547	0.04

On the whole, before the transfer of social insurance, the Gini coefficient of the annual income of all the samples is 0.547, which turns into 0.512 after the transfer of social insurance. Therefore, the transferred income from social insurance plays an obvious role in terms of income redistribution, seeing as the Gini coefficient is reduced by 6.4% after the transfer of social insurance.

Among residents holding urban household registers, the Gini coefficient is 0.525 before the transfer of social insurance income, and turns into 0.462 after the transfer of social insurance; the social insurance income reduces urban residents' Gini coefficient by 12%. Among residents holding rural household registers, the Gini coefficient is 0.546 before the transfer of social insurance income, and turns into 0.536 after the transfer of social insurance; the social insurance income reduces rural residents' Gini coefficient by 1.8%. Thus, although social insurance plays a positive role in regulating income redistribution among urban residents and rural residents, the effect of the urban social insurance system on regulating income distribution significantly outperforms the rural social insurance system. Meanwhile, among residents holding rural household registers, the effect of social insurance on narrowing income gap is mainly reflected in the gap between farmers engaged in agricultural production and migrant workers working in cities. The Gini coefficient in terms of individual income among farmers engaged in agricultural production stands at 0.447, while that of migrant workers is 0.569. Between urban residents and rural residents, social insurance has a "reverse regulation" effect in that before the transfer of social insurance, the income of residents holding non-rural household registers is 1.7 times than that of residents holding rural household register, while after the transfer of social insurance, the income of residents holding non-rural household registers is 1.8 times that of residents holding rural household registers, meaning that the gap is not narrowed, but further expanded.

In terms of the impact of various types of social insurance on income redistribution, old-age insurance exerts the greatest impact, followed by medical insurance, while maternity insurance, work-related insurance and unemployment insurance, due to their narrow coverage, only play a limited role in redistribution. After the transfer of old-age insurance income, the Gini coefficient is reduced by 5.88%; after the transfer of medical insurance income, the Gini coefficient is reduced by 0.49%; maternity insurance, work-related insurance and unemployment insurance, together, only reduce the Gini coefficient by 0.04%. The income redistribution effect of different old-age insurance and medical insurance also differs. Urban employee's old-age insurance reduces the Gini coefficient by 5.3%, urban resident's old-age insurance reduces the Gini coefficient by 0.24%, and rural social old-age insurance reduces the Gini coefficient by 0.32%. In comparison with urban employee's old-age insurance, urban resident's old-age insurance and rural social old-age insurance were established not long ago, with low benefits, so that their role in income redistribution is limited. Meanwhile, it is the benefit gap between urban old-age insurance and rural old-age insurance that leads to the adverse old-age insurance regulation of income distribution and the whole social insurance system between urban and rural residents. New rural cooperative medical insurance reduces the Gini coefficient by 0.27%, while urban employee's medical insurance and urban resident's medical insurance reduce the Gini coefficient by 0.2 and 0.02% respectively. Though the redistribution effect of medical insurance is limited, it plays a positive regulation role between urban and rural areas, and the establishment and implementation of the new cooperative medical insurance system, to a limited extent, has narrowed the income gap between urban and rural areas.

In sum, as to the coexistence of positive and negative social insurance regulations for internal income distribution in rural and urban areas and income distribution between rural and urban areas, there is an obvious stratification. On the whole, urban residents and rural residents belong to the same or to a similar class stratum within their place of residence, but the class difference between rural and urban residents is obvious. Despite the fact that people have the same opportunity to be covered by social insurance, more urban residents belong to advantageous classes, with discourse power for social security and a stronger sense of the need to safeguard their rights to social security, thereby acquiring more social security resources; while rural residents tend to passively receive security, and due to their limited capability and other reasons, they lack the opportunity to participate in the preparation of social security policies, thus can hardly safeguard their own rights and interests. This situation tends to expand the social security benefits gap between urban and rural residents.

8.4 Subjective Comments on the Re-Distribution Effect of China's Social Insurance Revenues

We process to the evaluation on the income redistribution effect of the social insurance system mainly on the basis of two aspects: the public's satisfaction with the social insurance system and its fairness.

(i) Satisfaction evaluation

The concept of public satisfaction originates from that of customer satisfaction in the field of marketing. Tang (2012) proposes that public satisfaction is the public's recognition of the gap between their expectations of the effect before consuming any public goods or services, and their actual experiences after consumption. Social insurance in China covers old-age insurance, medical insurance, work-related injury insurance, unemployment insurance and maternity insurance. Different systems vary substantially in terms of time of establishment, sources of funds, security targets, fiscal investment, contribution level, and benefit level; it is inevitable for the public to have varying satisfaction with various systems. By analyzing the survey data, we can see that the overall satisfaction with the social insurance system is not very high, as only 3.5 and 40.5% of the interviewees are very satisfied or satisfied with the system respectively. The low satisfaction fully illustrates the substantive gap between the public's expectations of the system's effect and their actual experiences. The satisfaction with work-related injury insurance, unemployment insurance and maternity insurance is even lower. The proportions of interviewees very satisfied and satisfied with work-related injury insurance are 1.2 and 29.6% respectively; the figures for unemployment insurance are 1.7 and 23.8% respectively, and those for maternity insurance are 1.8 and 28.2% respectively. The satisfaction gap among different types of insurance in the old-age insurance and medical insurance system is wide, with rural residents being more satisfied with

Table 8.4 Evaluation of satisfaction with the social insurance system

	Evaluation of satisfaction with the system				
	Very satisfied	Satisfied	So-so	Dissatisfied	Very dissatisfied
Overall evaluation of the system	3.5	40.5	34.7	18.7	2.5
Urban employee's old-age insurance	1.7	26.1	42.9	24.2	5.1
Urban resident's old-age insurance	2.7	25.2	47.1	23.0	2.1
Rural resident's old-age insurance	7.1	52.9	26.6	12.1	1.3
Urban employee's medical insurance	1.5	26.2	44.2	23.8	4.3
Urban resident's medical insurance	2.6	26.3	47.3	21.5	2.4
Rural residents' medical insurance	8.0	56.0	22.9	11.7	1.4
Work-related injury insurance	1.2	29.6	45.3	20.7	3.2
Unemployment insurance	1.7	23.8	49.9	20.2	4.4
Maternity insurance	1.8	28.2	48.9	17.8	3.3

old-age and medical insurance. 7.1 and 52.9% of the interviewees are very satisfied and satisfied with rural resident's old-age insurance respectively, while 8.0 and 56.0% of the interviewees are very satisfied and satisfied with rural residents' medical insurance. These figures, obviously higher than other types of insurance, show that farmers are more satisfied with the insurance systems (see Table 8.4).

(ii) Fairness evaluation

Fairness is one of the objectives pursued by social policies. Fairness may be classified into objective and subjective fairness (Zou 2012). In this article, fairness refers to the public's subjective evaluation of the fairness of the social insurance system. From the survey data, it can be concluded that the fairness evaluation of the social insurance system is not high on the whole, as only 4.6 and 35.9% of the interviewees think it very fair and fair respectively, which shows that there are big problems with the design of China's social insurance system in terms of fairness and operation effect. The serious fragmentation and segmentation of the system, as well as the lack of overall consideration and top-level design, lead to the failure of the system to bring into full play its role in regulating income distribution. Rural residents have given higher fairness evaluations of old-age insurance and medical insurance. With regards to the farmers' old-age insurance system, the ratios of interviewees who consider it very fair and fair are 8.7 and 45.2% respectively; in the case of the farmers' medical insurance, the ratios of interviewees who consider it very fair and fair are 9.1 and 49.3% respectively (see Table 8.5). These results

Table 8.5 Evaluation of fairness of the social insurance system

	Evaluation of fairness of the system				
	Very fair	Fair	So-so	Unfair	Very unfair
Overall evaluation of the system	4.6	35.9	36.9	19.4	3.2
Urban employee's old-age insurance	3.1	26.9	36.2	27.4	6.4
Urban resident's old-age insurance	2.9	27.4	42.4	22.2	5.1
Rural resident's old-age insurance	8.7	45.2	31.0	13.3	1.9
Urban employee's medical insurance	2.7	26.5	41.2	24.6	5.0
Urban resident's medical insurance	2.2	27.4	46.7	20.1	3.6
Rural residents' medical insurance	9.1	49.3	28.1	11.9	1.6
Work-related injury insurance	3.4	24.6	48.1	19.4	4.6
Unemployment insurance	2.5	22.9	48.9	19.8	5.8
Maternity insurance	3.4	28.3	48.3	15.3	4.7

show that though farmers do not receive high benefits from the social insurance system, and although there is a big gap between them and urban employees, yet they do not have a strong sense of unfairness about the current system.

The existence of this phenomenon does not negate the existence of unfairness in social insurance, but only shows the different class consciousness and right awareness as well as the different expectations about social security among different classes in urban and rural areas. In practice, this point cannot be taken to conceal the fairness of social insurance. However, we cannot look at problems statically. With the change of urban and rural class structures, change in class awareness and rise of demand, disadvantaged people will change their attitude towards the fairness of social insurance.

(iii) Factors affecting the evaluation of the effect of social insurance on income redistribution

(1) Variable setup

First, the dependent variable of this study is the public's evaluation of the effect of the social insurance system in alleviating income gap. In the questionnaire, there are five options: "very big", "big", "so-so", "low" and "very low". This article studies the factors affecting the public's evaluation of income gap, and therefore it is very necessary to appropriately handle dependent variables and combine them into binary variables. In analysis, "very big", "big" and "so-so" are combined into "good effect", with a value assignment of "1"; "low" and "very low" are combined into "poor effect", with a value assignment of "0". Second, the author has selected three levels (the personal level, focusing on individual interviewees, the social level, and the system level, each level containing three variables) according to the author'sanalysis of relevant literature and understanding of this problem (see Table 8.6 for the meaning, value assignment and descriptive statistic analytic results of each variable).

Table 8.6 Variable setup and their statistical descriptions

Variable		Meaning of variable	Value assignment of variable	Mean value	Standard deviation
Individual	X1	Gender	Male = 1; female = 2	1.53	0.50
	X2	Age	15 ~ 89	47.9	13.62
	X3	Political affiliation	CPC party member = 1; Others = 0	0.18	0.39
	X4	Religious belief	Having religious belief = 1; having no religious belief = 0	0.06	0.24
	X5	Education background	No schooling = 1; primary school = 2; junior middle school = 3; senior middle school or occupational secondary school = 4; technical secondary school = 5; junior college = 6; bachelor's degree = 7; postgraduate degree = 8	3.90	1.83
Social	X6	Household register	Agricultural household register = 1; non-agricultural household register = 2	1.47	0.50
	x7	Location factor	West China = 1; Central China = 2; East China = 3	2.11	0.67
System	X8	Level of contribution	Too high = 1; high = 2; appropriate = 3; low = 4; too low = 5	2.88	0.69
	X9	Level of benefits	Too high = 1; high = 2; appropriate = 3; low = 4; too low = 5	3.43	0.72

(2) Model selection

Suppose that the probability that the public i thinks that the social insurance system has a "good effect" on alleviating the income gap is p (y = 1|X) = pi, and 1—pi means the probability that the public thinks that the social insurance system has "no good effect" on alleviating the income gap. They are both nonlinear functions formed by the dependent variable vector X:

$$
\begin{aligned}
p_i &= \frac{1}{1+e^{-\left(\alpha+\sum_{i=1}^{m}\beta_i x_i\right)}} = \frac{e^{\alpha+\sum_{i=1}^{m}\beta_i x_i}}{1+e^{\alpha+\sum_{i=1}^{m}\beta_i x_i}}, \\
1-p_i &= 1-\frac{e^{\alpha+\sum_{i=1}^{m}\beta_i x_i}}{1+e^{\alpha+\sum_{i=1}^{m}\beta_i x_i}} = \frac{1}{1+e^{\alpha+\sum_{i=1}^{m}\beta_i x_i}}
\end{aligned}
\tag{8.1}
$$

The ratio of the probability that the public thinks that the social insurance system has a "good effect" on alleviating the income gap against the probability that the public thinks that the social insurance system has "no good effect" on alleviating income gap, pi/1—pi, is called the odds of experiencing an event (shortened as Odds) which must be of a positive value (because 0 < pi < 1) without an upper bound. Logarithmic transformation is conducted for Odds to get the linear representation of the logistic regression model:

$$\mathrm{Ln}\left(\frac{\mathrm{p_i}}{1-\mathrm{p_i}}\right) = \alpha + \sum_{i=1}^{m} \beta_i x_i \tag{8.2}$$

In formulas (8.1) and (8.2), α is a constant term, m is the number of independent variables, and βi is the coefficient of independent variables, reflecting the direction and degree of the influence of independent variables on the public's attitude towards the social insurance system.

(3) Results of examination by the regression equation

To examine how the nine independent variables of the above three levels affect the public's attitude towards the effect of the social insurance system on alleviating income gap and the degree of influence, independent variables meeting the level of significance are added to the model one by one; through three selection steps, independent variables X9, X7 and X3 are entered into the model one by one to get two logistic regression models:

$$\text{Logit P} = 4.188 + 0.437\text{X3} - 0.531\text{X7} - 0.772\text{X9}$$

In which the p value of the regression coefficient significance examination of X1, X2, X4, X5, X6 and X8 is bigger than the significance level 0.05, and thus these independent variables are removed from the model. From the significance examination by a regression equation (Table 8.7), it can be found that the probability P value corresponding to the observed value of the likelihood ratio chi-square is less than the significance level 0.05. Therefore, the linear relationship between all the

Table 8.7 Significance check of the regression equation (gradual selection strategy)

		Chi-square	Degree of freedom	Significance
Step 1	Step	64.729	1	0.000
	Module	64.729	1	0.000
	Model	64.729	1	0.000
Step 2	Step	18.936	1	0.000
	Module	83.665	2	0.000
	Model	83.665	2	0.000
Step 3	Step	5.894	1	0.015
	Module	89.559	3	0.000
	Model	89.559	3	0.000

Table 8.8 Partial regression coefficient check

		B	S.E.	Wald	df	Sig.	Exp(B)
Step 1 (a)	X9	−0.774	0.100	59.922	1	0.000	0.461
	Constant	3.147	0.345	83.196	1	0.000	23.265
Step 2 (b)	X9	−0.777	0.101	59.603	1	0.000	0.460
	X7	−0.528	0.123	18.432	1	0.000	0.590
	Constant	4.270	0.444	92.441	1	0.000	71.521
Step 3 (c)	X9	−0.772	0.101	58.556	1	0.000	0.462
	X7	−0.531	0.123	18.667	1	0.000	0.588
	X3	0.437	0.183	5.680	1	0.017	1.548
	Constant	4.188	0.445	88.598	1	0.000	65.916

explaining variables and Logit P is significant, which shows that it is reasonable to adopt this model. In light of the partial regression coefficients (Table 8.8), the partial regression coefficients of the equality have all passed the significance check. Therefore, the linear relationship between independent variables X3, X7 and X9 and dependent variables is significant.

Through the above analysis, we can get the final form of the model:

$$P = \frac{1}{1 + \exp[4.188 + 0.437X_3 - 0.531X_7 - 0.772X_9]}$$

To sum up, the factors affecting the public's evaluation of the effect of the social insurance system on alleviating the income gap mainly include: the political affiliation on the public's personal level, the location factor on the social level and the benefit level on the system level. Other variables, such as gender, age, religious belief, educational background, type of household register, type of place of residence, and level of contribution, have no significant impact.

Influence of factors on the personal level. Political affiliation, at a statistic level of 5%, has a significant positive influence on the public's evaluation of the effect of the social insurance system on alleviating the income gap; that is to say, CPC party members think that the social insurance system has an obvious effect on alleviating income gap (EXP (β) = 1.548). The results of descriptive statistics also support this conclusion. Of CPC party members, 48.5% think that the system has a good effect on alleviating the income gap, while only 34.1% of those who are not CPC party members think that the system has a good effect on alleviating the income gap. The possible explanation is that CPC party members, through their regular party member study activities, have a better understanding of the party's guidelines and policies and of the state's social insurance system, and thus have a more positive subjective evaluation of the effect of system implementation. Therefore, in future system development and improvement, we should strengthen state policies propaganda so that the masses can have a full understanding of the original intention, course of implementation and possible predicaments of policy implementation.

Then the objective performance of policy development will be fully recognized by the people.

Influence of factors on the social level. The location factor has a significant negative impact on the public's evaluation of the effect of the social insurance system on alleviating the income gap; that is, those in Central China and West China have better evaluation of the effect of the social insurance system on alleviating the income gap than those in the developed regions in East China. The statistic results of the survey show that 41% of those surveyed in Central China and West China think that the social insurance system has a good effect on alleviating the income gap, while this ratio is 36.6% in East China. A possible explanation is that Central China and West China are less developed regions; the public's overall income is lower than that in East China, and therefore social insurance income accounts for a higher ratio in citizens' personal income, with a better effect on narrowing the income gap than in East China. The location difference in system evaluation fully illustrates the imbalance in the development of the social security system in China, which, closely related to the regional imbalance of economic development in China, obviously fails to conform to the value of "fairness, justice and sharing" in the development of the social security system in China. In the future, we should pay more attention to the fairness of basic security projects and gradually strike a basic balance between the regional allocations of government public investments.

Influence of factors on the system level. The statistical level with a 1% benefit level has a significant negative impact on the public's evaluation of the effect of the social insurance system on alleviating the income gap; with higher benefits from the social insurance system, the system has better effect on alleviating the income gap. The public's subjective evaluation also verifies the effect of the social insurance system on regulating income distribution, and the effect of regulation has positive correlation with the level of benefits. Therefore, to improve the benefits level of the system has obvious effect on alleviating the income gap. With the stable increase of government fiscal investments, the effect of the social insurance system on alleviating the income gap will become more and more obvious, and meanwhile, the principle of moderation of fiscal investments should also be reasonably grasped to avoid any fiscal problem resulting from "welfare rigidity" in the future.

8.5 Survey Conclusion and Policy Suggestions

Since the initiation of reform and opening-up, major progress has been achieved in the development of the social security system in China, and the system has promoted the reform of the economic system, maintained social stability and safeguarded people's basic livelihood, thus alleviating the expansion of the income gap and regulating income distribution to some extent. The interviewees do not have a high evaluation of the role of the social security system in narrowing residents' income gap, and their negative evaluation even exceeds their positive evaluation with regard to some social security items, which, from one perspective, illustrates that there is still a certain discrepancy between the social security system in China and the public's psychological expectations.

The effect of China's social security system on income distribution is not satisfactory for many reasons. First, policy propaganda and coverage is inadequate. The understanding of social security is an important factor affecting urban and rural residents' participation in social security (mainly social insurance). Some people do not quite understand the social insurance system, especially those with medium and low incomes and lower educational backgrounds, as well as rural residents. For various reasons, quite a number of people do not participate in social insurance. Some poor people have not been included into subsistence security, and a large amount of people have not enjoyed their due social welfare. Second, the development of social security is out of balance. Social assistance and social welfare for poor and under-privileged people are not adequately developed, while the limited fiscal investments are inclined towards social insurance, resulting in inadequate investments in social welfare and social assistance, which naturally affects the overall effect of social security on income redistribution. Over a long period of time, China's social security system mainly addressed urban residents, without mentioning the backward development of rural social security, which all in all are not ideal conditions for social security to effect its role in narrowing the income gap between urban and rural residents. Due to occupational advantages, public employees acquire higher social security benefits, while people of low income, no regular employment or flexible employment do not have satisfactory social security. Third, the design of the social security system is not good enough. Many current social security items are specifically "tailored" for some people, thus segmented and unable to be shared by all, thereinafter affecting the fairness of the social security system. In terms of fund raising, the unreasonable responsibility sharing mechanism is not conducive to the regulation of income distribution, and the inadequate government fiscal investment mechanism is also not good for income redistribution. In terms of benefits, the benefits of current social security are mainly based on the contribution-defined mode, and benefits are largely correlated with contributions, which is not ideal for improving the income of poor people.

Therefore, in the future course of deepening reform, promoting reasonable income distribution among residents, and improving the social security system in China, we must attach greater importance to and conscientiously resolve the problems above. First, we should strengthen propaganda and guidance related to social security policies, and actively expand the coverage of social security. In particular, we should allow the under-privileged people, the low-income people and the poor people to gain better access to social security and make social security the risk resolving mechanism and subsistence security mechanism for these people. The expansion of social security coverage has entered a key stage, and the targets for key support include rural residents, migrant workers, residents in former revolutionary bases, and people with flexible employment. Quite a number of such people do not have a very clear understanding of social insurance, and relevant government departments should strengthen propaganda and guidance to reduce their concerns about participating in insurance. Second, we should break down the barriers of household registries as well as promote urban-rural social pooling and the system integration of social security. We should take the urban-rural social pooling of residents' old-age insurance system as a breakthrough point, and promote the development of urban-rural social pooling for the medical insurance system, the subsistence security system and the social assistance system. In the future, we should improve the unity of basic social security; strengthen system integration, and narrow gaps among different groups of people. Third, we should strengthen the fairness of the basic social security system. People have low overall satisfaction with the social insurance system and low overall evaluation of the effect of the system for alleviating the income gap, which fully illustrates that the unfair benefits of China's social insurance system have been challenging people's critical tolerance. People attach more importance to the fairness and justice of the basic social security system, and the fairness of basic social security should be further strengthened in the future. Fourth, we should improve fiscal investments in social security as well as the transfer payment mechanism. While maintaining a balanced aggregate of social security fiscal funds, we should improve the fiscal investment mechanism, define the key directions and fields of fiscal investment, strengthen the development of social assistance and of the social welfare system, and strengthen rural social security and fiscal transfer payments for Central China and West China. Fifth, we should improve the design of the social insurance system. In terms of fund raising, we should give particular support to people of medium and low incomes and poor people, and appropriately lower the contribution rate of their basic social insurance. We should increase the ratio of social pooling and appropriately reduce the contribution ratio of personal accounts. We should explore a "progressive" contribution method. Those with higher incomes should have a higher contribution rate. We should establish an effective interactive mechanism for the fund-raising mechanism and the benefit compensation mechanism, and bring into better play their role in regulating income distribution. For example, with old-age insurance, we may establish a "regressive" benefit sharing mechanism related to benefit sharing and benefit balance, and explore the establishment of a balanced minimum benefit guarantee mechanism.

In terms of specific social security items, we should focus on promoting the development of old-age security, medical security and the social assistance system in the future, so as to further effect the role of social security in income redistribution in China. In terms of old-age security, we should follow the principle of "everybody participates, everybody contributes and everybody shares" in order to promote the development of an equitable and sustainable old-age security system; we should establish a reasonable responsibility sharing mechanism, realize national pooling of the basic old-age insurance system and establish a scientific benefit adjustment mechanism; we should continue to improve the modes of the old-age insurance system, and optimize the design of the old-age insurance system; we should strengthen and improve investments in old-age insurance funds, and improve the risk-resistance capability of social insurance funds; we should improve the multi-level old-age insurance system, and gradually establish a basic old-age service and care system for old people of advanced age. In terms of medical security, we should accelerate the integration of urban-rural residents' medical insurance policies and management; we should improve the personal account system, gradually incorporate the funds in personal accounts into outpatient pooling, and improve the scope and ratio of reimbursement for outpatient services of insured people; we should improve the negotiation mechanism for the terms of payment of health care costs, and strengthen the whole-process supervision and the internal constraints of medical services; we should comprehensively implement the urban-rural residents' serious disease insurance system, and develop a diversified medical security system. In terms of social assistance, we should better effect its poverty alleviation and income regulation functions, and coordinate the development of the social assistance system; we should coordinate the development of subsistence social assistance and development social assistance; we should coordinate fund assistance, material assistance and service assistance, and bring into play the role of the social assistance system for comprehensive support; we should realize the organic connection of social assistance with social insurance and poverty-relief and development policies, and bring into play the function of social assistance as general support.

Of course, we do not advocate the "equalization" of social security, and try to prevent hyper-correction. We should appropriately reflect the "appropriate" differences of benefits and contributions in fields that stress the personal responsibilities of workers and social members. Due to long-term interest accumulation and the complexity of influential factors, the role of social security in income redistribution cannot be fulfilled in one single step. We should absolutely not pursue the "overnight accomplishment" of such a task, but rather should closely refer to and adapt to the current economic and social backgrounds in China, actively and properly promote the reform of the social security system, properly handle the interest relationship of different groups, and stimulate economic and social vitality while promoting the equitable development of the social security system.[23]

[23]This article, written in collaboration with Long Yuqi, Jiang Cuiping and Xuqiang, is published in *Economic Research Journal*, 2016 (2).

Chapter 9
Establishing a More Equitable and Sustainable Social Security System

The "Suggestions on Preparing the Thirteenth Five-Year Plan for National Economic and Social Development" of the CPC Central Committee clearly points out that a more equitable and sustainable social security system should be established during the Period of the thirteenth Five-Year Plan. The Suggestions not only directly reflects the new outlook on development—that is: innovation, coordination, green, opening-up and sharing—but also will surely guide the healthy development of the social security system with clear targets in the new period.

9.1 Social Security Lays an Important Institutional Foundation for All People to Share the Results of Reform and Development

Social security, a social policy handling social risks and resolving social problems in order to protect and improve the basic living standard of social members, is an important equalizer of basic public services. The nature of social security is to maintain social equity and thus promote a stable social development. The social security system not only helps workers and social members guard against personal risks but also helps distribute and re-distribute national revenues, and is thus a very important guarantee that all people may share the results of development. Since reform and opening-up, especially during the period of the twelfth Five-Year Plan, rapid development has been achieved in terms of China's social security system, which has not only realized full coverage but also has been playing an increasingly important role in the coordinated development of economy and society.

© Springer Nature Singapore Pte Ltd. and Social Sciences Academic Press 2017
Y. Wang, *Social Security in China: On the Possibility of Equitable Distribution*,
Research Series on the Chinese Dream and China's Development Path,
DOI 10.1007/978-981-10-5643-7_9

(i) The social security system keeps improving and has basically realized full coverage

During the period of the twelfth Five-Year Plan, China gradually established and improved various social security systems on the basis of the original reform on social security. In terms of old-age insurance, in June 2011, the State Council issued the "Guiding Opinions on Conducting Pilot Projects in Urban Residents' Social Old-age Insurance" to explore the establishment of an urban residents' old-age insurance system; in February 2014, the State Council issued the "Opinions on Establishing a Uniform Urban-Rural Residents' Basic Old-age Insurance System", covering all eligible urban and rural residents; meanwhile, the Ministry of Human Resources and Social Security also improved the "Interim Measures for Linking-up the Urban-Rural Old-age Insurance System" to actively promote the connection, integration and integrative development of urban and rural residents' old-age insurance systems, clarify policies on enterprise annuities, occupational annuities and personal income tax, as well as accelerate the construction of supplementary old-age insurance systems. In terms of medical security, outpatient pooling for urban residents' basic medical insurance has been basically established. In August 2012, six ministries and commissions including the NDRC jointly issued the "Guiding Opinions on Developing 'Serious Disease Insurance' for Urban and Rural Residents" to explore the establishment of an insurance system for serious, special and major diseases. Important steps have also been taken in the establishment of unemployment, work-related injury and maternity insurance systems. Explorations are being made to use unemployment insurance funds to prevent unemployment and promote employment; active efforts are being made in terms of work-related injury rehabilitation and work-related injury prevention, as well as to expand pilot projects on work-related injury prevention. The coverage and expenditure scope of maternity insurance have been constantly expanding, and residents' maternity medical expenses are being gradually included into the urban residents' medical insurance and the new rural cooperative medical system's scope of reimbursement. In terms of subsistence security, in March and May 2011, ministries and commissions such as the NDRC, the MOCA and the MOF issued the "Circular on Establishing a Linkage Mechanism Connecting Social Assistance and Security Standard with Price Rise" and the "Guiding Opinions on Further Regulating the Preparation and Adjustment of Subsistence Security for Urban and Rural Residents", which marked the official establishment of a dynamic adjustment mechanism for urban and rural subsistence security standards; in September 2012, the State Council issued the "Opinions on Further Strengthening and Improving Subsistence Security", which further standardize the urban and rural subsistence security. In terms of old-age services, in 2011, the General Office of the State Council issued the "Plan for the Construction of a Social Old-age Service System (2011–2015)"; in 2013, the State Council issued "Several Opinions on Accelerating the Development of the Old-age Service Industry" to promote the rapid development of the old-age service industry. In terms of charity services, in 2011, the MOCA issued the "Guidelines on the Development of the Charity Services in

China (2011–2015)"; in 2014, the State Council issued the "Guiding Opinions on Promoting the Healthy Development of Charity Services", which put forward objectives and policy measures for promoting the healthy development of charity services. In terms of supplementary security, in 2014, the State Council issued "Several Opinions on Accelerating the Development of the Modern Insurance Service Industry", which clearly mention that "commercial insurance should be developed into an important pillar for the social security system", which especially mentioned that the supplementary role of commercial insurance for basic old-age and medical insurance should be brought into full play. In 2014, the Office of the Ministry of Human Resources and Social Security issued the "Opinions on the Further Filing of Enterprise Annuity Schemes", to actively promote the development of the enterprise annuity system. Active development has also been achieved in terms of the construction of other types of social security systems. The revised "Regulations on Work-related Insurance" took effect on January 1, 2011. The revised "Regulations on Pension and Preferential Treatment on Servicemen" officially took effect on August 1, 2011. By 2015, all provincial governments nationwide had issued new opinions on the implementation of urban and rural residents' insurance, whereas urban and rural residents' basic old-age insurance systems had been basically unified. Meanwhile, the central government decided to reform the old-age insurance system for government departments and public institutions, which should be implemented simultaneously nationwide in line with the principle of "one unity (the basic old-age insurance system integrating social pooling and personal accounts is implemented for urban employees in government departments, public institutions and enterprises etc.), and five simultaneous measures". This reform, which has integrated the old-age insurance system for government departments, public institutions and enterprises, is conducive to alleviating the "benefit gap", promoting social equity and harmony, promoting the reform of government departments and public institutions as well as the development of a mechanism of reasonable personnel mobility, and has been widely recognized by all social circles.

(ii) The gradual increase of social insurance coverage and the constant expansion of social insurance funds

The later period of the Twelfth Five-Year Plan saw rapid expansion of social security coverage in China. With the establishment and improvement of various social systems, a social security system covering urban and rural residents has been basically developed, and full coverage had been realized. With the establishment and improvement of the urban employees' basic medical insurance system, the new rural cooperative medical system, and the urban residents' medical insurance system, the medical insurance system has taken the lead to cover all people in China by developing the largest medical security network in the world. In light of the number of people covered by the five items of social insurance, the number of people covered by basic old-age insurance increased from 235 million in 2009 to 820 million in 2013; the number of people covered by urban basic medical insurance increased from 401 million in 2009 to 571 million in 2013; the number of people

Table 9.1 Status of social assistance. *Unit* million people

Index	2009	2010	2011	2012	2013	2014	August 2015
Urban residents covered by subsistence security	23.456	23.105	22.768	21.435	20.642	18.770	17.685
Rural residents covered by subsistence security	47.600	52.140	53.057	53.445	53.880	52.072	50.056
Rural residents supported by "Five Guarantees"	5.534	5.563	5.51	5.456	5.372	5.291	5.209

Source of data Statistical Bulletin on the Development of Social Services in 2014, and statistical data on the website of the MOCA

covered by unemployment insurance increased from 127 million in 2009 to 164 million in 2013; the number of people covered by work-related injury insurance increased from 149 million in 2009 to 199 million in 2013; and the number of people covered by maternity insurance increased from 109 million in 2009 to 164 million in 2013. By the end of 2013, 2489 counties (cities and districts) nationwide had developed new rural cooperative medical care, covering 802 million people at a coverage rate of 98.7%.[1] In terms of social assistance, the number of urban residents covered by subsistence security has been maintained around 20 million, the number of rural residents covered by subsistence security around 53 million, and the number of old people supported by the "Five Guarantees" around 5 million (see Table 9.1). By June 2014, the number of people covered by basic old-age insurance nationwide had reached 824 million, and the coverage of the three basic medical insurance systems, namely employees' medical insurance, urban residents' medical insurance and new rural cooperative medical care, exceeded 95%, accomplishing the Twelfth Five-Year Plan's objective in advance. By September 2015, the number of people covered by basic old-age insurance, basic medical insurance, unemployment insurance, work-related injury insurance and maternity insurance nationwide was respectively 852 million, 658 million, 171 million, 211 million, and 178 million, having increased by 9.39 million, 60.17 million, 0.86 million, 4.27 million and 7.42 million respectively from the end of 2014. In light of the number of people covered, China has established the largest social insurance and social security network in the world.

With the development of the social security system, especially with the constant improvement and expanding coverage of the contribution-based social insurance

[1]Source of data: *Statistical Bulletin on the Development of Health and Family Planning Services in 2013*, and the website of the Commission of Health and Family Planning.

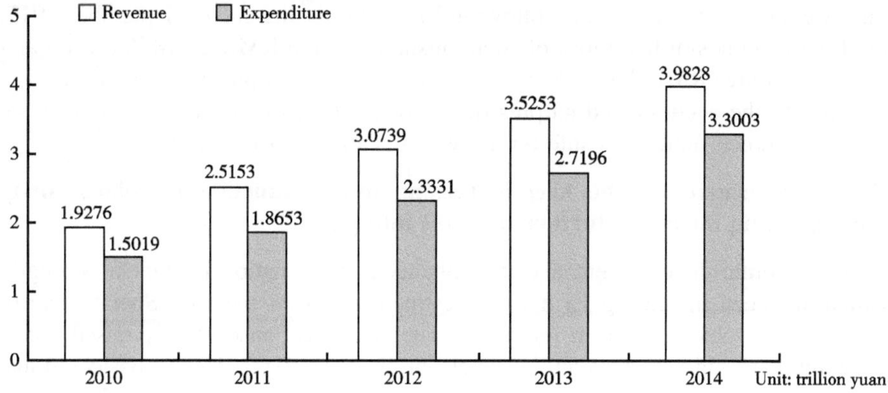

Fig. 9.1 Social insurance fund revenues and expenditures of in the recent five years. *Unit* trillion yuan

system, the scale of revenues and expenditures of social insurance funds has also been expanding. The fund revenues of the five types of social insurance (excluding new rural social old-age insurance) rose from RMB 1.6116 trillion in 2009 to RMB 3.5253 trillion in 2013; and fund expenditures rose from RMB 1.2303 trillion in 2009 to RMB 2.7916 trillion in 2013. Specifically, the fund revenues of basic old-age insurance in 2013 were RMB 2.4733 trillion, having increased by 13.3% from the previous year; fund expenditures of basic old-age insurance in 2013 were RMB 1.9819 trillion, having increased by 18.6% from 2012. The total revenues of urban basic medical insurance funds in 2013 were RMB 824.8 billion, and total expenditures were RMB 680.1 billion, having increased by 18.9 and 22.7% respectively from 2012. In 2013, the fund revenues of unemployment insurance were RMB 128.9 billion, having increased by 13.2% from 2012; the expenditures were RMB 53.2 billion, having increased by 18.0% from 2012. In 2013, the fund revenues of work-related injury insurance funds were RMB 61.5 billion, and fund expenditures were RMB 48.2 billion, having increased by 16.7 and 18.7% respectively from 2012. In 2013, the fund revenues of maternity insurance were RMB 36.8 billion, and fund expenditures were RMB 28.3 billion, having increased by 21.1 and 28.9% respectively from 2012.[2] By 2014, the annual surplus of urban employees' basic old-age insurance, basic medical insurance, work-related injury insurance and maternity insurance was RMB 587.5 billion, and the accumulated surplus was RMB 4.3765 trillion. By the end of 2014, the total fund revenues of the five types of social insurance (including urban and rural residents' basic old-age insurance) amounted to RMB 3.9828 trillion, having increased by RMB 457.5 billion from 2013 at an increase rate of 13.0%. Fund expenditures amounted to RMB 3.3003 trillion, having increased by RMB 508.6 billion from 2013 at an

[2]Source of data: *Statistical Bulletin on the Development of Human Resources and Social Security Services in 2013.*

increase rate of 18.2% (see the following Fig. 9.1). By the end of September 2015, the fund revenues of five types of social insurance were RMB 3.31866 trillion and the expenditures RMB 2.81905 trillion, with a 10–20% surplus after break-even; in addition to the accumulated surplus of RMB 5.7366 trillion, the operation of the social insurance funds was safe on the whole, capable of resisting risks.[3]

(iii) Social security benefits keep increasing and the function of social security for regulating income is further brought into play

With economic development and the enhancement of national financial strength, China has been increasing its fiscal investment in social security. Social security benefits have obviously been improved. The state has consecutively raised enterprise retirees' old-age pension 11 times; on January 1st 2015 the basic old-age pension of enterprise retirees was raised by 10%. By the end of 2014, 230 million people received old-age pensions, including 85.93 million retirees and 143 million urban and rural senior citizens. After 11 years of consecutive adjustments, the basic old-age pension of enterprise retirees has increased twofold from a monthly pay of RMB 647 in 2004 to over RMB 2000 now. The consecutive large-scale adjustments of basic old-age pension have been playing an active role in improving enterprise retirees' life and promoting social equity. The standard minimum basic old-age insurance benefits for all urban and rural residents nationwide has risen to RMB 70 each month for each person; that is a 15-yuan increase from the original base of RMB 55 per person each month, increased benefits being counted from July 1st 2014.[4] In terms of medical insurance, in 2014, urban employees received 1.52 billion person-times of medical insurance benefits, urban residents received 420 million person-times of medical insurance benefits, and the reimbursement ratio of inpatient medical expenses covered by the policies of employees' basic medical insurance and urban residents' basic medical insurance reached over 80% and about 70% respectively; the maximum amount of payment from funds was raised to 6 times that of the annual average salary of local employees and that of the per capita annual disposable income of local residents respectively, which, to some extent, alleviated the problem of expensive medical treatment. In terms of unemployment, work-related injury and maternity insurance, the number of people entitled to benefits and the level of benefits were substantially improved. The level of subsistence security has been stably rising. The average standard for subsistence security of urban residents rose from RMB 251.2/person/month in 2010 to RMB 373/person/month in 2013; the monthly per capita subsidy for urban residents covered by subsistence security nationwide rose from RMB 189 in 2010 to RMB 293 in August 2015. The average standard for rural subsistence security rose from RMB 117.0/person/month in 2010 to RMB 202.8/person/month in 2013; the per

[3]Website of the Ministry of Human Resources and Social Security, *The Development of Human Resources and Social Security Work in Q3 of 2015 and Arrangements of Work for the Next Step*, October 27, 2015.

[4]Source of data: "Another 100% Rise in Enterprise Retirees' Basic Old-age Pension after 11 Consecutive Rises", http://finance.people.com.cn/GB/n/2015/0116/c1004-26396343.html.

capita subsidy for rural residents with subsistence security rose from RMB 74/person/month in 2010 to RMB 135/person/month in August 2015. In terms of poverty relief in rural areas, in 2011, the state determined that the new rural poverty relief standard should be RMB 2300, equivalent to farmers' per capita net income, as well as on par with the international standard absolute poverty line, so that more and more poor people are included into the scope of poverty relief to share the results of reform and development in China.

With the constant improvement of the social security system and the rise of the ratio of the revenues and expenditures of social security funds in the national economy, the social security system including subsistence security, old-age security, medical security, unemployment security and education security has been playing an active role in income distribution in China. In 2012, social security revenues accounted for 14.5% of urban and rural residents' income, and over half (the biggest portion) of senior urban residents' income came from social old-age pension. The transferred income from social security reduced the Gini coefficient of urban and rural residents' income by 4.53%, including a 22.76% drop of the Gini coefficient between urban residents, and a 1.82% drop between rural residents'. The old-age pension property has a significant property redistribution effect in the families of urban enterprise employees, as it reduces the Gini coefficient of family property distribution by 8% points, and also reduces the inequality of family property distribution by 20%. The compensation of new rural cooperative medical care is more inclined towards the sick, and people with lower income receive higher compensations than those with higher income. The subsistence security policy can improve the living conditions of some low-income people and help relieve urban poverty. In Gansu and Yunnan, the effect of subsistence security policies is more obvious in that the Gini coefficient in these regions was reduced by 1.23 and 1% after the adoption of subsistence security, and the average income ratio of the 10% people with the highest income as well as that of the 10% people with the lowest income was reduced by 3.2% after the adoption of subsistence security. The subsistence security system indeed restrains the income gap within urban areas and within rural areas.

(iv) The lawful governance of social security has been obviously improved as more attention is paid to the development of legislation and management capability

The Fourth Plenary Session of the 18th CPC Central Committee gave more attention to the strategy of "rule-of-law" as well as to the development of the executive power of systems, which provides an important basis for the law-based development of social security. The development of a legal system is an important guarantee for the scientific and sustainable development of social security. During the period of the twelfth Five-Year Plan, China attached great importance to the construction of a legal system for social security and positive progress has been achieved. The most outstanding achievement was the NPC Standing Committee's adoption of the Social Insurance Law of the People's Republic of China in October 2010, which took effect on July 2011. This is an important mark for the legal system of the social security system in China, laying a legal basis for the development of social insurance services in China. The "Social Insurance Law" provides norms for basic old-age insurance, basic medical insurance, work-related injury insurance, unemployment insurance, maternity insurance, collection and contribution of social insurance premiums, social insurance funds, and social insurance handling. The "Military Service Insurance Law" adopted at the 26th meeting of the 11th NPC Standing Committee on April 27th 2012 provides for military injury and death insurance, decommissioning old-age insurance, decommissioning medical insurance and the establishment, payment and transfer of insurance for servicemen's spouses in the army who are not employed. In February 2014, the "Interim Measures on Social Assistance" promulgated by the State Council defined the management system, fund guarantee and content system of social assistance, promoted the integration and improvement of social assistance systems, and rendered the social assistance systems scientific and normal. Moreover, positive progress has been made in the "Regulations on Urban Housing Security" and the "Measures on Maternity Insurance". In 2014, the State Council promulgated the "Regulations on the Personnel Management of Public Institutions", and the Ministry of Human Resources and Social Security along with the Commission of Health and Family Planning promulgated a number of laws and regulations, such as the "Administrative Measures on the Appraisal of Work Capacity of Employees Injured in Work", which provide a better defined legal basis and operational norms for the regulation of personnel management in public institutions, guaranteeing the legal rights and interests of personnel working in public institutions, and strengthening social security in fields such as work capacity appraisal management. By holding various types of law popularization and business backbone training activities, the degree of lawful governance in the field of social security has been constantly improving.

To sum up, in terms of the developments of social security in China during the period of the twelfth Five-Year Plan, we have observed the following outstanding characteristics. First, more stress is laid on the top-level design and coordinated promotion of social security, with efforts focused on strengthening theoretical study and policy design of social security development strategies, overcoming the deficiencies resulting from earlier emergency coping reforms, and the constant optimizing of various social security systems. Second, the objectives of the development of social security are more defined, striving for the equitable and sustainable development of social security, conducting policy improvement for social security problems issues related to equity and sustainability, striving to enhance the equity and sustainability of social security, while stressing the role of social security in the promotion of income redistribution and maintenance of social equality and justice. Third, we've been actively promoting the urban-rural coordinated development of social security, the integration of social security systems, realize the integration of urban and rural residents' old-age insurance, and strive to realize the coordinated development of urban and rural residents' medical insurance and subsistence security. Fourth, we've been actively promoting the development of the lawful governance of social security; with the promulgation and implementation of social security laws such as the "Social Insurance Law" and the "Military Service Insurance Law", important steps have been taken in the legal system for social security in China, which will surely promote the scientific development of social security in China. Fifth, more importance is being attached to the coordinated development of social security systems; while stressing economic security, more and more importance is given to service security; while stressing basic security, more and more importance is given to the development of supplementary security; while the social insurance system has been improved, more and more importance is given to the development of social welfare and the social assistance system. Sixth, more and more importance is gradually being given to the effective combination of government and market. The government is always the dominant player in terms of social security, as well as an important bearer of responsibilities; while stressing the government's role, the reform of social security attaches more and more importance to market and social forces, in attempts to jointly improve social security equity and efficiency.

9.2 The Social Security System Is Still Confronted with Tremendous Equity and Sustainability Challenges

The Third Plenary Session of the 18th CPC Central Committee decided to establish a more equitable and sustainable social security system. The "Proposal on Preparing the thirteenth Five-Year Plan for National Economic and Social Development" of the Fifth Plenary Session of the 18th CPC Central Committee reiterated this objective, which means that in the development of the social security system in the period of the thirteenth Five-Year Plan, we should not only attach importance to extensive developments, such as the expansion of coverage and the expansion of fund scale, but also give priority to the equity and sustainability issues of the social security system.

The social security system is intended to be a social system promoting social equality, preventing social risks and maintaining social stability. However, the realization of the above objectives depends on the constant improvement of this system. For example, as one function of social security is to regulate income distribution, social security may not only promote income redistribution and narrow the income gap, but may as well induce negative regulation and widen the income gap. The negative or positive role of social security in income redistribution depends on the relevant factors of influence such as system mode, coverage, system design, system transition and management services. We should give full play the positive regulation role of social security for income redistribution and prevent negative regulation. Meanwhile, the development of the social security system is conducted against the macro background of drastic economic and social transformation in China. The change of the social stratification structure and the reform of the social security system are conducted almost simultaneously in China, with the two related to and influencing each other. Different social classes' economic and social status as well as group awareness varies greatly, and the standards for judging social equity are even more varied. It is very difficult to reach a consensus in terms of the reform and development of the social security system, which makes it more difficult to reform the social security system. During the reform and construction of the social security system in the new period, we face the following formidable challenges in terms of the further establishing a more equitable social security system: ensure that each class and each group (such as farmers and migrant workers) can equitably and conveniently acquire reasonable social security resources; ensure that more and more people enjoy increasing benefits; narrow the gap of social security benefits among different groups; and improve the sense of acquisition of an increasing number of people, if not that of all residents.

Another major challenge related to the above challenges is improving China's security system, especially in terms of the sustainability issue of social insurance systems such as basic old-age insurance. On the one hand, with the tendency of the Chinese population to age at a very rapid speed, to resolve the basic security problems of a huge number of old-age people who fail to become rich before they become old is the huge responsibility of each family, as well as that of the whole society and various levels of governments. In 2015, the population over 60 exceeded 200 million in China (accounting for 15% of the total population in China), and 230 million people were receiving old-age pensions (accounting for 17% of the total population). Old people above 60 will double in the future two decades, and at their peak they will account for about 1/3 of the total population. Currently, only employee's basic old-age pensions can secure basic life needs after retirement, while the role of basic old-age pensions for urban and rural residents is very limited. If basic old-age pensions of urban and rural senior residents were raised to 50% of the current retired employees' basic old-age pensions, old-age pension expenditures alone would double, far exceeding the payment capacity of current old-age security and even of the whole social security system. Keeping the growth of old-age pensions basically abreast with the growth of the national economy and urban and rural residents' income while providing basic security for the basic life and service of old people at their population peak has presented very urgent and formidable pressure and challenges to the construction of the social security system in China. To further stress the sustainability of the social security system at this moment is of very great strategic significance in terms of guiding the construction of the social security system in the future five years or more. On the other hand, effectively strengthening the management capability of the social security system, improving the efficient and reasonable use of social security funds, improving the value preservation and increase of accumulated funds, and strengthening social security funds risk control and monitoring are all important tasks for the construction of the current social security system. Since the start of the 21st century, there has been some small surplus after the balance of revenues and expenditures in the funds for the five types of social insurance (including urban and rural residents' basic old-age insurance) nationwide, which amounted to RMB 5.23

trillion as of 2014. If the national social security funds and each year's fiscal social security allocations are taken into account, the social security funds are of a tremendous scale and have increasing management chains and links. Managing such funds, especially accumulated surplus funds, is an enormous challenge for China's social security management team. As social security funds are the "survival money" of the people, we must ensure their security and must not allow even the smallest error, let alone any unwarranted diversion. A stricter fund management system and information disclosure system should be established to further effectively strengthen the preventive mechanism against the evasion of social security funds. However, strict regulation does not mean that the accumulated surplus funds should be allowed to "fall asleep". To address the depreciation risks imposed by inflation and falling interest rates, we must deepen the reform of the fund investment system and mechanism, and conduct diversified investments with a more flexible mechanism (provided that the security of funds is ensured) so as to realize the preservation and increase of accumulated funds value. In 2005, the central government introduced Regulations on Investment Operations for the Basic Old-age Insurance Fund. The new reform measures are good for expanding fund sources and enhancing the supporting capacity of old-age security funds, thus rendering social security funds less vulnerable to risks, which is of great significance in terms of the sustainable development of the old-age insurance system and the stability of the social security system. The crux is how to implement the above conceptions and reform measures and achieve good results. This is not only a challenge in terms of professional fund management for the social security department, but even more so in regards to the construction of relevant departments as well as that of the whole national security system.

9.3 Vigorously Constructing an Equitable and Sustainable Old-Age Security System

Old-age security, as the center of the social security system, is the basic security that must be established for an aging society as well as the foundation for the basic public service system. During the period of the thirteenth Five-Year Plan, the reform and development of the old-age insurance system in China remains a formidable task. We should continue to deepen reform by actively adapting to the rapidly aging population and the new economic and social development norms. In line with the principle of "everybody participates, everybody contributes and everybody shares", we should render the basically established basic old-age insurance system more fixed and mature, and at the same time, in light of the further rise of demands for old-age services, we should integrate various forces, such as government, society, market and family, in order to take new steps in terms of old-age life services security. As per the suggestions in the third Five-Year Plan, we should focus on work in the following aspects:

(i) Deepen the reform of the basic old-age insurance system and improve the employees' old-age insurance personal account system

The combination of social pooling and personal accounts constitute the institutional mode of basic old-age insurance in China, which is a product of international experiences and Chinese national conditions. To introduce personal accounts is an important measure in the reform of China's old-age insurance system. In practice, this mode is constantly being reformed and improved. Personal accounts are an important part of China's basic old-age insurance system, playing an important role in balancing equity and efficiency, securing the interests of those covered by old-age insurance, and enhancing the incentives of the old-age insurance system. Currently, personal accounts still present several practical problems to solve, such as orientation, the "empty accounts", management, scale, as well as pension granting method, which affect the interests of insurants. In the future, we should rationally understand the significance and orientation of personal accounts, and continue to reform and improve the personal account system. Provided that the equity of the system is not influenced, we may appropriately adjust the scale of personal accounts, and improve the pension granting method of personal accounts by adjusting the number of months according to per capita life expectancy. We should enhance the flexibility of personal account accumulation, improve the mechanism allowing for more benefits based on contributions, mobilize individual contributions, and enhance the incentive, efficiency and sustainability of the old-age insurance system. The establishment of the personal account system is good for defining individuals' contribution obligations; in the future, we should establish and improve the contribution-related benefit granting mechanism in line with the principle of combining rights and obligations. We should strengthen the management and investment of personal accounts, improve the of personal account management and investment system, promote the value preservation and increase of personal accounts of old-age insurance, and effectively maintain the rights and interest of insurants to their personal accounts.

(ii) Realize national pooling and establish a reasonable adjustment mechanism for employees' basic old-age pensions

China's basic old-age insurance benefits include two parts, basic pension and personal account pension, of which the pay-as-you-go system relates to basic pension. Social pooling for basic old-age insurance in China is of low level, and has been mostly practiced at the prefecture and municipal pooling for a long period; currently, provincial pooling has been basically realized. Nevertheless, social pooling levels for old-age insurance in China are still very low, while the management of the old-age insurance system is subject to local segmentation; this situation is not conducive to the integration of old-age insurance resources nor the improvement of the management services of old-age insurance, nor that of personnel trans-regional migration, nor that of the management and investment of old-age insurance funds, nor to that of the equity and efficiency of the old-age insurance system. Therefore, it is imperative that we further improve the social pooling level of the basic old-age insurance system; in particular, we should realize national pooling for basic old-age pensions sooner rather than later. To realize national pooling for employees' basic old-age pensions, we should have all-round considerations and arrangements for the nation as a whole, strengthen the mutual assistance of the basic old-age insurance system, and consider the financing, payment, management and supervision activities related to basic old-age pensions. National pooling for employees' basic old-age pensions requires the establishment of an old-age insurance financing mechanism commensurate with said pensions as well as the establishment and improvement of basic old-age insurance budgeting. We should regulate old-age insurance revenues and expenditures, and centralize the base, contribution rate and collection for basic old-age insurance. We should unify the expenditures of basic old-age pensions and balance old-age burden differences across different regions. We should establish a reasonable responsibility sharing mechanism and define the relationship between the central government and local governments as well as the relationship between local governments. In the future, we should continue to promote the realization of the national pooling of the whole basic old-age insurance system on the basis of national pooling for employees' basic old-age pensions.

Reasonable benefits are inevitably required for insurants to be able to share the results of development as well as for the sustainable development of the system. We should establish a basic old-age insurance benefit regulation mechanism in line with the principles of equity, sharing and sustainability. In recent years, China has raised old-age pension benefits for several years in a row so as to secure the basic life of retirees and enable them to enjoy the results of reform and development. However, there are still has many issues with the adjustment of old-age pension benefits in China, as the basis for adjustment is not clearly defined, the adjustment actions are not standardized in that mainly temporary policy documents are relied upon to promote benefit adjustment, and no scientific old-age pension benefit adjustment mechanism has been developed, which is not conducive to maintaining retirees' old-age rights and interests. In the future, we should establish and improve a basic old-age pension benefit adjustment mechanism on the basis of regulating and improving the old-age pension benefit granting method. In light of international experiences, we have observed that there are mainly three practices in the adjustment of overseas old-age pension benefits: adjustment according to the salary increase of in-service personnel, adjustment according to price level, and adjustment in light of salary increase and price level. The adjustment of basic old-age pension benefits in China should not be based on salary increase or price increase alone, but should take into account equity and efficiency by comprehensively considering factors such as financial sustainability, life expectancy, regional economic development, salary level, and price level, in order to establish a scientific benefit adjustment index and realize index-based, normalized and scientific benefit adjustments.

(iii) Strengthen and improve investment of old-age insurance funds and reduce the vulnerability of social insurance funds

To strengthen the scientific management and investment of old-age insurance funds and to realize the value preservation and increase of old-age insurance funds are the important tasks of the reform and development of the old-age insurance system in the future. We should establish a scientific and highly effective old-age insurance fund investment system and make investment in old-age insurance funds more professional, independent, diversified, social and law-based. We should further improve the management system of old-age insurance and realize the independent financing, management and investment for old-age insurance funds. We should develop a number of professional fund investment institutions, as well as realize moderate and orderly competition, reduce investment cost and improve return on investment. We should strictly regulate the old-age insurance funds access threshold for investment institutions. We should attempt to establish a minimum income guarantee mechanism for old-age insurance investment funds. The diversification of old-age insurance fund investment requires further expansion of investment channels, the improvement of investment portfolio strategies, the active and steady promotion of the entry of old-age insurance funds into the capital market, and the strengthening of old-age insurance funds' investments in major domestic public projects. We should strengthen investment in old-age insurance funds, improve returns on investment, and require the improvement of supervision over investment in old-age insurance funds and the establishment of a risk control mechanism. We should establish an information disclosure mechanism for the investment of old-age insurance funds, realize supervision over various stakeholders' whole participation course in old-age insurance fund investment, prevent old-age insurance funds investment risks and timely settle problems in the course of fund investment.

With the constant acceleration of population aging, China will face tremendous pressure in terms of old-age care; when the aging population peaks, in particular, the old-age insurance system will have to face the pressure of revenues falling short of expenditures. Also, in the course of the transition of the old-age insurance system, system transition debts are forming due to improper treatment of the rights and interest of some "in-service persons", and this issue should be resolved by raising funds through effective channels to cope with the payment demands when said "in-service persons" retire. Therefore, improving the old-age insurance funding mechanism and expanding the funding channels for old-age insurance are inevitable requirements for the reform of the old-age insurance system against the backdrops of the aging population. To transfer state-owned capital to substantiate old-age insurance funds and social insurance funds is an important measure for strengthening old-age insurance funding and deal with old-age insurance debts. Due to the public nature of state-owned capital, income should belong to the state and benefit all the people as it is property shared by all. In the future, the reform of the old-age insurance system, the reform of state-owned enterprises and the reform of the financial and taxation system should be taken into consideration as a whole, in order to gradually improve the ratio of state-owned capital gains to be submitted to public finance, and thus substantiate old-age insurance funds in the form of fiscal expenditures, or support old-age insurance funds by selling state-owned shares. Since reform and opening-up, China's state-owned enterprises have been constantly developing and expanding, and a tremendous amount of state-owned capital has been developed, which creates conditions for substantiating old-age insurance funds and social insurance. In the future, we should prepare specific measures for state-owned capital to substantiate old-age insurance funds and define the procedure, amount and proportion of state-owned capital transfer, as well as specific management issues and relevant supporting work after such transfer.

(iv) Progressively postpone the retirement age and improve the basic old-age pension pickup incentive and constraint mechanism

The definition of the retirement age is an important consideration of China's retirement system, which is also an important parameter for China's old-age insurance system. With the rapidly accelerating aging of the population and the obvious prolongation of life expectancy in China, the problem of retirement age has become an important concern in the various social circles in recent years. Currently, the retirement age in China basically copies the practices of the early days of the People's Republic of China, and thus is seriously out of balance in consideration with current life expectancy. The connection between the definition of retirement age and the old-age care system is not flexible, and the retirement age has become an important condition for receiving old-age pensions, which exerts pressure on the payment of old-age insurance funds against the backdrops of an aging population. To postpone the retirement age is inevitable in terms of the future economic and social development in China, so as to help cope with the disappearance of the "population bonus", make full use of human resources, and improve the old-age insurance system. To postpone the retirement age is an important task related to the interests of various stakeholders, so it should be actively and steadily promoted with the correct strategies and measures while considering all parties' interests and the overall situation of economic and social development. We should postpone the retirement age gradually, instead of suddenly. There are different approaches and methods for postponing the retirement age, and one feasible method is to "advance gradually with women preceding men". In the near future, the retirement age of both men and women should be set at 60 years old. On this basis, the retirement age of men and women will be postponed jointly and gradually. The method of "being slow at first and accelerating later" or "postponing at an even pace" may be adopted to postpone the retirement age in 20–30 years. We should fully consider the interests of different groups against the overall interest framework of national economy and society, taking into accounts the employment wishes and development demands of some people as well as the retirement wishes, health rights and interests, and social security rights and interests of some other people.

As the reform of the retirement age and old-age pension covers a wide range, relevant schemes should be publicized as early as possible in order to enhance the rights of relevant personnel to know and participate. The determination of the scheme will require quite a long period if we are to realize a steady transition. With the postponement of the statutory retirement age, detailed schemes may be prepared according to different industries, different types of work and different labors, so as to establish a flexible retirement system to some extent, and integrate the compulsory retirement system and the voluntary retirement system. While defining minimum retirement age, standard retirement age and latest retirement age, some people should be allowed to choose early retirement, but may receive old-age pensions only after they reach the standard retirement age. People with qualifications and such an intention should be encouraged to voluntarily postpone their retirement age. Besides, a dynamic adjustment mechanism connecting retirement age and life expectancy may be established through explorations. An old-age pension claim system connecting pension benefits with length of service and payment years should be established to strengthen incentives and constraints of pensions over the retirement system.

(v) Improve the multi-level old-age insurance system, and gradually establish a system of basic services and care for people of advanced age

The old-age security system is significantly diversified, including not only the basic old-age insurance system but also the supplementary old-age insurance system and the personal savings old-age insurance system, in addition to family old-age security, social charity and community services, etc. This kind of diversification may reduce the government's fiscal pressure in the old-age security system, and also help improve different people's diversified old-age insurance demands as well as their old-age security benefits, while ensuring the equity and efficiency of the old-age insurance system. The establishment and improvement of a diversified old-age insurance system is an important objective for the reform and development of China's old-age insurance system, which has been mentioned in many important documents. However, constrained by various factors, China's basic old-age insurance system has not been finalized; the contribution rate stipulated in the basic old-age insurance system is too high, affecting the development of old-age insurance system of other levels. Therefore, many important tasks have to be undertaken to improve a diversified old-age insurance system. We should properly handle the relationship between basic old-age insurance and supplementary old-age insurance, define the functional orientation of the two types of insurance, actively develop occupational annuities, enterprise annuities and commercial old-age insurance, so as to develop a multi-level old-age insurance system in which basic security and supplementary security support and complement each other. We should properly handle the relationship between the government and the market. The government should encourage and often use the market mechanism to develop the supplementary old-age insurance system and further improve the tax policy support of supplementary insurance in order to create a fine environment for the development of a multi-level old-age insurance system.

In light of the objective reality of population aging, and particularly the objective reality of an aging population with too few children, we should establish a basic care system for people of advanced age. We should vigorously develop a home-based community old-age care and service system and provide necessary basic care and services to incapacitated old people by developing social work teams. The method of government purchasing family care service experimented in some regions of Jiangsu merits our attention; regions with fitting conditions may try the old-age care insurance system to better combine basic old-age insurance benefits with old-age care and overcome the lack of care caused by family downsizing. We should establish the social service index system as soon as possible so as to promote the healthy development of old-age care and basic public services.

9.4 The Deepened Reform of Medical Insurance Promotes the Construction of "Healthy China"

Remarkable achievements have been made in the new round of medical care and health system reform implemented since 2009 in China. However, in face of the tremendous pressure on the health system exerted by the aging population, mal-adjustment still exists in many aspects of the current medical care and health system. The steady and rapid rise of health costs imposes a tremendous burden on national public finances, social insurance funds and residents' income. Leveraging the medical insurance system plays a fundamental guiding role in deepening the reform of the medical care and health system during the period of the thirteenth Five-Year Plan and promoting the construction of a healthy China.

(i) Integrate urban and rural residents' medical insurance policies and gradually implement the policy for retired employees to pay medical insurance premiums

Rural residents and urban residents in most regions of China are covered by the new rural cooperative medical care system and the urban residents' basic medical insurance system respectively. The new rural cooperative medical system is often managed by the health and family planning department, while the urban residents' basic medical insurance is managed by the human resources and social security department. In fact, the two systems are similar in many aspects, such as payers, funding method, reimbursement method, financial balance method, and management method. With the acceleration of urbanization in various regions of China, the current separate participation of urban and rural residents' in insurance and their compartmentalized handling and management will further constrain the orderly movement of rural laborers and the urbanization process. This results in over expensive handling and management costs for local governments and affects the sharing of information about insurance coverage. Against the backdrops of accelerating urbanization and the deepening of the reform of the government's administrative system, we must: accelerate the integration of urban and rural residents' medical insurance policies, handling and management; actively explore the connection and integration of the urban and rural residents' medical insurance policies and urban employees' basic medical insurance system; improve the management efficiency of medical insurance funds; eliminate repeated insurance coverage by systems and promote the free movement of laborers across rural and urban areas and across regions.

In the course of integrating the urban residents' basic medical insurance system with the new rural cooperative medical care system, the medical insurance system covering urban and rural old-age residents should extend to the employees' basic medical insurance system. Currently, urban employees whose payment years have reached the standard defined by the state when they reach statutory retirement age do not have to pay premiums for their basic medical insurance after retirement, while they enjoy basic medical insurance benefits as per state regulations.[5] However, rural residents and urban residents have to go on paying for medical insurance. The difference of this contribution mechanism tends to exert a negative impact on the fairness of the medical insurance system and the sustainability of system fund operations. From 2010 to 2014, the ratio of retired urban employees covered by insurance in the total number of urban employees covered by insurance was respectively 25, 24.9, 25, 25.3 and 25.6%, presenting a gradually increasing trend year by year; however, the ratio of retired urban employees covered by basic medical insurance in the total number of urban employees insurance was respectively 13.7, 13.3, 12.3, 12.2 and 12.1%, presenting a gradually decreasing trend year by year.[6] The two data groups show that with the constant increase of urban retirees, the shares of medical resources that retirees have to occupy in the entire urban employees' medical insurance will also keep increasing. The ratio of old people's medical expenses in their living expenses is far higher than that of middle-aged laborers. Therefore, to study the policy for retired employees to pay medical insurance premiums is not only an internal requirement for the finalization and optimization of medical insurance, but also an important measure for the horizontal fairness among insurants, the safety of the system, and financial sustainability. We may revise the relevant articles in the "Social Insurance Law" and gradually explore the measures for retired employees to pay premiums for basic medical insurance on the basis of pilot projects. During the transition period, special government fiscal subsidies may be stepped up so as to guide individuals' participation in insurance, and resolve the issue of individuals unable to pay premium and

[5]Note: according to the provisions in the "Social Insurance Law of the People's Republic of China", individuals participating in basic medical insurance for employees whose cumulative premium payment period reaches the period stipulated by the State at the time they reach the statutory retirement age will no longer pay basic medical insurance premiums after they retire and may then enjoy basic medical insurance benefits in accordance with the provisions of the State; if cumulative premium payment has not reached the period stipulated by the State, he/she may continue to pay premiums until reaching the period stipulated by the State.

[6]Note: Arranged and calculated on the basis of the data in *China Statistics Yearbook 2011–2014* and the *Statistical Bulletin of the Development of Human Resource and Social Security Services in 2014*.

allow them to participate in the basic medical system by allocating state-owned assets gains as well as employing other methods.

(ii) Improve personal accounts in basic medical insurance and deepen the reform of medical insurance payment method

In the early period after the establishment of the social security system, the personal account system was set up in the basic medical insurance system in China. However, with the passage of time, the functions of the personal medical account system have been gradually adjusted. No personal account have been set up in urban residents' basic medical insurance; since 2008, pilot projects of outpatient social pooling have been carried out in most regions' new rural cooperative medical care system. Currently, personal accounts have been set up only in the initial period urban employees' basic medical insurance system, and a large amount of fund deposit has been accumulated, which, to some extent, constrains patients' afflicted by chronic diseases and serious illnesses in terms of the amount to be reimbursed for outpatient services, and leads to poor use and efficiency of medical insurance funds. The thirteenth Five-Year Plan clearly promotes the improvement of the personal account system, and the gradual inclusion of personal account fund into outpatient service pooling, which will not only improve the reimbursement scope and ratio of insurants who receive outpatient services but also enhance the financial sustainability of medical insurance.

The medical insurance handling institutions of most countries and regions in the world are confronted with the problem of inadequate financial sustainability, with much appeal to the control of medical insurance costs. As the population keeps on aging, this problem has been receiving even more attention from various social circles. In face of the rapid increase of medical costs, the cost control function of medical security should be brought into better play. Traditional medical security is mainly to bring into play the function of compensation (reimbursement) after the administration of medical services, while there is a lack of will to get involved in the reform of medical organization, medical mode and medical cost. Currently, the payment of medical expenses is directly settled by medical insurance handling institutions and medical service provision institutions, and consists in a medical cost post-payment system paid mainly according to items, with cost control limited effect.[7] As the main sources of total medical cost and an organized group purchase mechanism, medical insurance funds should function better as a guide for controlling the excessive increase of medical cost. The post-payment system based on items should be reformed, diversified and compound medical insurance payment methods (such as payment according to persons, types of disease and total pre-payments) should be actively promoted, and the negotiation mechanism for the terms of payment of medical insurance costs should be improved to strengthen the

[7]Note: The post-payment system means that a patient, after the occurrence of expenses, goes to a handling institution for reimbursement or applies for reduction in a medical institution, and the amount of reimbursement or reduction is calculated according to the actual amount incurred.

whole-course supervision and internal constraints of medical service behaviors. We should deepen the reform of the medical service system focusing on the reform of public hospitals and constrain the profit-seeking trend in public hospitals.

(iii) Comprehensively implement the urban and rural residents' serious illness insurance system and develop a diversified medical security system

The serious illness insurance system consists in the development and extension of the combined functions of the new rural cooperative medical care system and the urban residents' medical insurance system. Serious illnesses are one of the important reasons reducing and reverting urban and rural families to poverty. Due to poor production and living environment and low basic public health services, the very low ratio of actual reimbursement of various basic medical insurance systems, and the very limited coverage of the medical assistance system,rural farmers' families and West China's urban and rural families, in particular, are unlikely to be able to resist being impoverished by serious and major diseases. Therefore, there is a very strong realistic need for the construction of a diversified medical security system to address these expensive medical expenses. In August 2015, the State Council issued the "Opinions on Establishing the Urban and Rural Residents' Serious Illness Medical Insurance System", which suggested that a sound serious illness insurance system be established in 2–3 years, and should be closely connected with such systems as medical assistance so as to jointly play the role of basic security, effectively prevent catastrophic medical expenses and significantly improve the fairness of urban and rural residents' medical insurances.[8] Currently, the framework of the serious illness insurance system has been established in most Chinese provinces, but with narrow coverage, small funding scale and limited functions. We should grasp the opportunity to implement the thirteenth Five-Year Plan to further improve the operation mechanism and management mechanism of the serious illness medical insurance system, and better leverage the active role of commercial insurance institutions in providing more management support for the operations of the serious illness insurance system.

The basic medical insurance and serious illness medical insurance system, to some extent, are still within the scope of basic medical security guided by the government. Though the policy-based compensation ratio of basic social medical insurance stands 70% or even higher, yet the actual compensation ratio is only reaches about 50%, which means that the absolute majority of insurants have to bear a large proportion of medical care cost. While improving the current medical insurance system, we should further improve measures such as taxation preference to encourage enterprises to establish supplementary security, support individuals' purchase of supplementary medical insurance and commercial health insurance, create a social atmosphere and legal environment in which commercial insurance

[8]General Office of the State Council, "Opinions on Establishing the Urban and Rural Residents' Serious Illness Medical Insurance System", official website of the State Council, at http://www.gov.cn/zhengce/content/2015-08/02/content_10041.htm, accessed on November 4, 2015.

institutions actively underwrite residents' health insurance in an orderly manner, and actively use the advantages of the market in addressing risks to resolve urban and rural residents' risks of being impoverished by illness. The development of commercial medical insurance is not only a useful supplement to basic medical security but can also reduce governmental costs in terms of handling and providing relevant management technologies and experiences. An important task in the period of the thirteenth Five-Year Plan is to improve the management and operation efficiency of the basic medical insurance system and provide better services to people covered by insurance. On one hand, we should further develop grassroots medical insurance handling teams at county and township levels; on the other hand, we may expand the method of government purchase of social services and fully leverage the advantages of commercial insurance institutions with good qualification in medical insurance handling. In recent years, rapid development has been achieved in both state-owned commercial insurance institutions and non-public-owned commercial insurance institutions, which has laid a solid foundation for their participation in the handling of basic social medical insurance. We should further improve the mechanism and method for government purchase of services from commercial insurance institutions to make them play a larger role.

(iv) Deepen the reform of the medical insurance management mechanism and strengthen the management and handling capability of medical insurance

Currently, the five social insurance systems for urban employees are managed in a scattered manner; the internal relationship between basic medical insurance and maternity insurance is artificially cut apart, and further exploration should be made to establish a new system for integrating the two. Maternity insurance benefits include maternity medical expenses and maternity subsidies, etc. By the end of 2014, altogether 170.39 million people were covered by maternity insurance nationwide; and 6.13 million person-times enjoyed maternity insurance benefits that year. Different from urban employees, whose maternity medical expenses have to be compensated through the maternity insurance system, women covered by the new rural cooperative medical system and the urban residents' basic medical insurance system may directly get reimbursement from the medical insurance system. By drawing on the management experience of urban and rural residents' maternity insurance, we should explore a new system combining urban employees' maternity insurance and basic medical insurance during the period of the thirteenth Five-Year Plan. The combination of the two systems may reduce the workload of social insurance handling institutions in terms of the collection of maternity insurance premiums and the supervision of fund revenues and expenditures, reduce the operating cost of handling institutions, improve social insurance handling management, and reduce application costs for urban employees' compensation of maternity medical expenses. Currently, China's maternity insurance funds comprise a big surplus. The combination of the two funds may enhance financial sustainability and improve the equity of urban employees and urban and rural residents in terms of maternity security.

Currently, the urban and rural residents' basic medical insurance system follows the principle of localized management, with a relatively low level of social pooling.

The level of pooling and the size of a region directly decide the amount of reimbursement and the cost of medical expense reimbursement for the hospitalization of insurants. We should explore the gradual raise of the level of medical insurance pooling, gradually transit to prefecture-level (municipal) pooling in places with mature conditions, strengthen the interconnection of information systems, realize IT-based management for the long-distance settlement of medical expenses within a province, and gradually promote the exploration of long-distance medical treatment across provinces; in particular, for retired employees inpatient medical expenses, direct settlement will be gradually adopted for convenient and high-efficient services. The main reform measures are: the basic medical system should be gradually raised to provincial pooling; the medical insurance information management systems of various provinces should be integrated and a national medical insurance information sharing platform should be set up to provide powerful technical guarantee for the direct settlement of long-distance medical expenses across regions. We should strengthen supervision over medical insurance funds, and increase penalties for institutions and personnel who commit any insurance fraud so as to ensure fund security.

9.5 Bring into Better Play the Anti-poverty Function of the Social Relief System

Social assistance is an important part of China's social security system, and plays a critical role in terms of subsistence security for poor people and those subject to any accident. The period of the thirteenth Five-Year Plan is a decisive period for China to complete the process of building a comprehensive moderately well-off society. To channel efforts in poverty alleviation, and help poor people and regions throw off poverty, are strategic objectives defined for the thirteenth Five-Year Plan, while relieving rural poor people from poverty is also the most difficult task in the comprehensive construction of a moderately well-off society. On one hand, we should vigorously find ways to alleviate poverty, accurately support the poor and relieve them from poverty, take measures addressing individual and local needs, and improve the effect of poverty relief. On the other hand, we should implement the subsistence security policy and connect such policy with poverty relief policies for residents without labor capacity, and ensure all poor people are covered to better bring into play the functions of social security, especially that of social assistance systems such as subsistence security.

(i) Do a good job in social assistance for survival, and promote social assistance for development

To secure basic survival is the core objective of traditional social assistance. For a long period of time, social assistance in China consisted in providing subsistence security for urban and rural residents to help them overcome difficulties and maintain subsistence. The function of social assistance in securing subsistence cannot be negated, rather it should be especially stressed and improved at the initial stage of development of social assistance; however, with the improvement of economic and social development and the increasing demand of urban and rural residents, the effect of subsistence assistance is limited, even subject to vicious circles and causing an "assistance trap", which makes it difficult to realize the true objective of social assistance. Therefore, while improving the "subsistence security" function of social assistance, we should also improve its assistance methods and adjust its assistance benefits levels so that the function of "promoting development" comes to be highlighted as it secures subsistence. Personal development will raise income levels, thus realizing a virtuous circle. With the gradual improvement of the social security system, urban and rural residents' living standards keep improving, the absolutely poverty-stricken population has been substantially reduced; however, the problem of relative poverty is becoming more and more serious. Social assistance cannot stop at survival assistance in the traditional sense; the scope and level of social assistance should be gradually improved. To upgrade survival assistance to development assistance is also required in the period of economic transition in China to improve human capital and expand domestic demands. With economic development shifting to a new normal, we should transform the traditional mode of economic growth and drive economic growth by improving human capital and expanding domestic consumption. The investment in human capital in a country should not rely on ordinary education and training alone, but should focus on developing special groups of people including the poor.[9] Against the backdrops of new Chinese economic development norms, we should actively promote investment in human capital and foster the sources of power promoting economic growth. Developing social assistance can help improve the poorer population's human capital, cut down the inter-generational cycle of poverty, and help improve the consumption capacity of poor families, thus expanding domestic demands.

Besides developing traditional survival assistance and improving social assistance benefits, we should attach more importance to employment assistance, education assistance and medical assistance, and thus improve the health conditions and labor capacity of assistance recipients, enhance their human capital, and upgrade their life quality. Development assistance not only involves the upgrading and improvement of the contents of assistance but also the reform of assistance measures. We should improve the past traditional assistance target identification measures, exit mechanism and benefit payment mechanism. In the identification of assistance targets, we should change the passive practices of the past and establish a pro-active identification mechanism to "assist all those that should be assisted in an

[9]Guan Xinping (2014), Towards a More Proactive Social Assistance System: On the Direction of Reform of China's Social Assistance System in the New Situation, *China Public Administration*, 2014 (7), pp. 16–20.

accurate manner". We should not only "assist all those that should be assisted" but also "should withdraw assistance from all those for whom assistance is unnecessary" to prevent assistance dependencies and traps. The assistance benefits should be paid according to demands, instead of being fixed payments. For assistance targets that are marginal and can easily overcome poverty, in particular, we should enable them to actively withdraw from the team of assistance recipients by enhancing the incentive of the social assistance system.

(ii) Promote fund assistance, material assistance and service assistance coordinately and leverage the role of the social assistance system as comprehensive support

Based on different demands of social assistance targets, social assistance includes such items as fund assistance, material assistance and service assistance. With the improvement of the social assistance system and the level of assistance, we should actively promote the development of service assistance. The targets of social assistance are often poor and weak people, such as old people and the disabled, who not only need fund support and material provision but also are in urgent need of services. To promote service assistance on the basis of fund assistance and material assistance is an effective way to improve the effect of social assistance. The development of service assistance can help improve the health conditions and living standards of assistance targets. Poverty is often related to illness and poor health, which lead to a vicious circle. Service assistance can help strengthen disease prevention and treatment for poor people and help the disabled to recover as much as possible of their health and labor capacity. Service assistance can also provide convenience for the life of assistance recipients and improve their living standards. The specific contents and methods of service assistance should be decided according to the recipients' different needs. Social assistance services mainly include diversified and individualized services such as life assistance, psychological counseling, emotional aid, resource connection, ability enhancement and social integration; all of these may be classified into three types: daily care services, ability development services and support and integration services.[10] Due to the special and professional nature of social assistance services, we should train a large amount of social assistance service professionals, improve the professionalism of social assistance services and improve the effect of social assistance services. We should integrate the service resources of social assistance, and vigorously develop social work, volunteer services and community services, so as to provide different people with different types of social assistance services. We may make full use of private social assistance service resources through government purchases. Assistance services may be purchased from social organizations. The mechanism for government purchase of social assistance services should be improved.

[10]Lin Mingang (2015), Reflection on Government Purchase of Social Assistance Services, *Administration Reform*, 2015 (8), pp. 24–27.

(iii) Coordinately consider the life assistance and employment development of targets of subsistence security with labor capacity, and realize the organic connection of social assistance with social insurance, poverty relief and development policies

The coordinated development of life assistance and employment assistance is an important reflection of the coordinated development of survival assistance and development assistance. Social assistance implementation, especially in regards to demand evaluation and method adoption, should fully consider the actual conditions of families and individual recipients, while integrating the two based on the former. The life difficulties and labor capability of assistance recipients should be accurately evaluated. While actively securing the survival needs of poverty-stricken families, various measures should be taken to encourage and constrain assistance recipients with labor capacity to take an active part in work and acquire income and means of subsistence through work. On one hand, such measures can help prevent assistance recipients from becoming assistance-dependent, improve the use efficiency of subsistence security and social assistance resources, reduce the institutional burden, and enhance the equity and efficiency of the social assistance system. On the other hand, these measures can help assistance recipients gain self-respect, self-reliance and self-improvement as well as improve their living standards. We should appropriately classify them in classes such as: no labor capacity and conditions, partial labor capacity and conditions and full labor capacity and conditions; moreover we should adopt a differentiated subsistence security system, and maximize the effect of the subsistence assistance system. As for people with full labor capacity, we should not let them sit back and wait for assistance, but should help them dismiss their dependence on assistance and maintain their subsistence and that of their families through work and employment, and help them get jobs by job introduction, training and education. Even if they fail to get a job, they should fulfill their work obligations through voluntary work or earn their assistance through work. For those with partial labor capacity, we should comprehensively use life assistance and employment assistance to help them work properly. To promote assistance recipients with labor capacity to take an active part in work, we should adjust the current subsistence security system, and should particularly reform the current benefit examination and approval mechanism to enhance benefit grant incentives. The level of subsistence security should be appropriately improved to create conditions for assistance recipients to get employment. The connection between subsistence security benefits and employment income may be appropriately relaxed to improve the incentive for people receiving subsistence security to work.

Social assistance should be reformed and developed on the basis of the overall framework of social security and improvement of people's livelihood, so as to realize the coordinated development of social assistance, social insurance, social welfare and poverty relief, and bring into full play the comprehensive functions of the social security system. Social assistance and other items of social security all play an important role in fighting poverty. Social assistance should focus on poverty governance and poverty reduction. Traditional social assistance mainly consists in post-event assistance and passive assistance, mainly for securing the recipients' subsistence. Social assistance focuses on the prevention of poverty. Various measures should be taken for fighting poverty, with equal attention being given to prevention and governance. While securing the subsistence of poor families, we should actively support families receiving assistance to participate in social insurance such as old-age insurance and medical insurance to strengthen the defense against poverty. The continuous progress of social assistance entails its shift from subsistence-oriented to development-oriented for people's higher enthusiasm and proactivity in it. The government should introduce proper institutional and policy support to facilitate social insurance participation for able-bodied social assistance recipients through employment or by fiscal subsidies so that they can better overcome poverty and improve their life quality.

Social assistance and poverty relief are direct measures fighting poverty, and the coordinated development of the two can help improve their effectiveness. With regard to the connection of subsistence security and poverty relief, in particular, we should follow the idea of accurate security and realize accurate assistance and poverty relief. We should follow the idea of development-based assistance and development-based poverty relief and improve the "hematopoietic" role of subsistence security and poverty relief. In the course of poverty relief, we should actively strengthen occupational skills training for poor people with labor capacity, enhance the labor skills and employment competitiveness of assistance recipients, and fully tap in the human capital and labor capacity of targets of subsistence security to relieve poor people from poverty.

(iv) Explore the regional coordinated development mechanism for the social assistance system and help diversified recipients of social assistance overcome poverty

For a long period of time, China's social assistance system has had a low level of coordination and been subject to such problems as urban and rural segmentation and regional segmentation, which, to some extent, impedes population mobility, goes against the equitable development of social assistance, and is liable to widen urban and rural gap and regional gap with regard to social assistance. The need for coordinated urban and rural development has become a consensus for the future development of the social security system in China, and progress has been made in the coordinated urban and rural development of social assistance. With the deepening of the reform of the household registry system, in particular, the coordinated urban and rural development of social assistance will be further promoted. In contrast, the regional segmentation and regional gap of social assistance have not received adequate attention, which is not ideal for population cross-regional migration and integrated regional development. Therefore, while actively promoting the coordinated urban and rural development of social assistance, we should also promote the regional coordinated development of social assistance to cope with population migration and promote social equity. We should stick to the idea of coordinated and shared development, and improve the practice of localized management, so as to meet the social assistance needs of relevant local people. We suggest that a national uniform social assistance system and basically uniform classified security standards be established with provinces as units according to the actual conditions of income and living expenditures as well as the assistance needs of urban and rural residents; moreover, we suggest that the implementation mechanism and actions of social assistance be regulated, a social assistance standard system be established, and the diversified social assistance needs of various groups of people in a region be secured in line with the principle of equity. We should establish a regional pooling and coordination mechanism for social assistance and strengthen inter-regional cooperation on social assistance, so as to ensure the seamless full coverage of social assistance when population mobility is realized, to promote the social assistance targets within a region to acquire roughly equal security benefits, and enhance the unity and equity of social assistance. The practice of enjoying social assistance benefits based on household registry should be reformed; the household registry factor should be weakened, a residents' residence permit system should be established, and actual living and residential needs should be taken as important basis for enjoying social assistance benefits.

(v) The basic role of different social assistance entities such as government, market and society should be well leveraged

The government is always the most important entity of responsibility for social assistance. The leading role of the government in social assistance is mainly reflected in coordinated planning, system development, fiscal investment, talent training, organization and coordination. We should establish a uniform and sound social assistance system under the leadership of the government, while actively promoting the legislation of social assistance, stepping up the training of professionals for social assistance management and services, and coordinating the relief efforts of different assistance entities. Special stress should be laid on the government's responsibility for social assistance fiscal expenditures, the power of office and the financial power should be reasonably divided, and a social assistance responsibility sharing system between the central government and local governments should be established to allow governments at different levels to better play their respective role in the social assistance system. We should define the responsibility of provincial governments for fiscal expenditures, establish an inter-regional coordination mechanism for local governments, and prevent expenditure loopholes and repeated expenditures. We should further strengthen the responsibility of the central government for social assistance expenditures, establish and improve a scientific central fiscal transfer expenditure mechanism, and integrate the use of various types of social assistance funds. The government's leading role does not mean that the government should take care of everything; we should actively cultivate market and social resources and realize social assistance through government service purchases. Social assistance should not entirely depend on the state and the government, but the market mechanism and social resources should be made full use of in terms of resource collection and service purchase. The "Interim Measures on Social Assistance" have clearly provided that the state should encourage social forces such as employers and individuals to participate in social assistance by donation, establishing sponsorship projects, creating service organizations and providing volunteer services. In the future, we should vigorously cultivate private resources for social assistance, strengthen the "socialization" of social assistance, professionalize social assistance and thereby realize a "strong government" and "strong society" in terms of social assistance. In light of international experiences, the gradual transition from state responsibility to "state + market" responsibility and "state + market + society" responsibility is an important trend in the social welfare reform of developed countries.[11] In the future development of social assistance in China, while stressing the leading role and basic responsibility of the government, we should establish a responsibility sharing mechanism, actively employ market and social forces, and fully mobilize individuals' initiative.[12]

[11]Han Keqing (2015), The Reform and Development of China's Social Assistance System, *Teaching and Research*, 2015 (2), 29–35.

[12]This article was published in *The Journal of Liaoning University*, 2016 (1).

Postscript

This book is a collection of special topic articles arranged upon the invitation of Ms. Song Yuehua of the Social Sciences Academic Press. Due to press limitations, this collection only includes ten articles, most of which detail the representative results of my researches, as well as record my reflections and main viewpoints in the field of social security and medical security. It should be noted that all these articles have been published either in newspapers or periodicals. Content or viewpoints have not been alterated in any way, except for the abridgment of some chapters and the adjustment of some titles. As the articles collected in this book span over nearly two decades, the overlap of some content is inevitable. Some articles co-authored in collaboration with my doctoral students are also collected here as required by the theme. Here, I would like to express my sincere gratitude to the Social Sciences Academic Press for its invitation, the newspapers and journals that allowed me to re-publish these articles, and the students who have joined me in the writing of these articles, Long Yuqi, Jiang Cuiping, XuQiang, etc.

January 22, 2016 Wang Yanzhong

© Springer Nature Singapore Pte Ltd. and Social Sciences Academic Press 2017

Y. Wang, *Social Security in China: On the Possibility of Equitable Distribution*,
Research Series on the Chinese Dream and China's Development Path,
DOI 10.1007/978-981-10-5643-7

References

Chen, Jiagui, and Wang, Yanzhong. 2004. *The Development of Social Security in China: a Report* (2001–2004) [M]. Beijing: Social Sciences Academic Press.
Chen, Jiagui, and Yanzhong Wang. 2007. *The Development of Social Security in China: a Report (2007) [R]*. Beijing: Social Sciences Academic Press.
Chen, Jiagui, and Wang, Yanzhong. 2010. *Green Book on Social Security in China 2010*. Social Sciences Academic Press.
Chen, Jiandong, Yang, Wen and Feng, Ying. 2011. The Income Distribution Effect of Subsistence Security and Individual Income Tax: An Empirical Study. *Reform of the Economic System* (1).
China Development Research Foundation. 2009. *Establish a Development-Based Social Welfare System Shared by All People*. Beijing: China Development Press.
CPC Central Committee. 2015. The Suggestions of the CPC Central Committee on Preparing the Thirteenth Five-Year Plan for National Economic and Social Development
Dong, Yiren, and Tao, Pengde. 2005. Statistical Analysis of Factors Affecting Patients' Satisfaction. *Journal of Applied Statistics and Management* (1).
Fan, Liming, E., Xie, and Yin, Lin. 2009. Farmers' Participation in New Rural Cooperative Medical Care and Analysis of Their Satisfaction. *The Journal of Shandong University* (1).
Feldstein, Paul J. 1998. *Health Care Economics*. Beijing: Economic Science Press.
Gao, Wenshu. 2012. The Effect of Social Security on Regulating Income Distribution Gap: An Empirical Study Based on the Data of a Survey over Residents in Baoji, Shaanxi. *Social Security Studies* (4).
Gao, Linyu. 2011. The Relationship between Social Security and Income Distribution Gap in Developed Countries and Its Implication for China. *Local Public Finance* (7).
Gruat, J.V. 1998. Trends in Social Security System Development, Presentation Paper on Social Security Funds Management at International Seminar, Beijing.
Gu, Cheng, and Li, Junyi. 2004. Expansion of the Gap between Urban and Rural Income Distribution and the Integration of China's Social Security System. *The Journal of the Dongbei University of Finance and Economics* (4).
Guan, Xinping. 2014. Towards a More Proactive Social Assistance System: On the Direction of Reform of China's Social Assistance System in the New Situation. *China Public Administration* (7).
Guo, Yang. 2008. A Study of the Old-age Benefit Gap between Enterprises and Government Departments and Public Institutions in China. *Gansu Social Sciences* (6).
Han, Dawei, Fang Li, and Jiaheng Wu. 2000. *The Old-age Pension System: International Comparison*. Reform Approach and Development Measures: Economic Science Press.
Han, Keqing. 2015. The Social Assistance System in China: Reform and Development. *Teaching and Research* (2).
He, Lixin. 2007. The Effect of Income Distribution by the Reform of the Urban Old-age Insurance System in China. *Economic Research Journal* (3).

© Springer Nature Singapore Pte Ltd. and Social Sciences Academic Press 2017
Y. Wang, *Social Security in China: On the Possibility of Equitable Distribution*,
Research Series on the Chinese Dream and China's Development Path,
DOI 10.1007/978-981-10-5643-7

He, Ping, Li, Shi and Wang, Yanzhong. 2009. Study of Public Financial Support of the Development-Based Social Welfare System in China. *Public Finance Research* (6).
James, E. 1998. New System for Old-Age Security: Theory, Practice, and Empirical Evidence, Presentation Paper on Social Security Funds Management at International Seminar, Beijing.
Jin, Caihong. 2005. A Study of the Income Redistribution Mechanism of China's Medical Security System. *Reform of Economic System* (6).
Kou, Tiejun, and Zhou, Bo. 2007. International Experience and Implication with Regard to Responsibility Division of Government Expenditure: A Comparative Analysis Based on the Government Expenditure Structure of Developed Countries and Developing Countries. *Public Finance Research* (4).
Li, Lianyou. 2000. *Theory on the Operation of Social Insurance Funds*. Southwestern University of Finance and Economics Press.
Li, Shaoguang. 2000. *The Old-age Pension System and the Capital Market*. China Development Press.
Li, Shi, and Yang, Sui. 2009. The Impact of China's Urban Subsistence Security Policy on Income Distribution and Poverty. *Chinese Journal of Population Science* (5).
Lin, Mingang, 2015. Reflection on Government Purchase of Social Assistance Services. *Administration Reform* (8).
Lin, Yuming. 2007. Government Performance in Social Security and the Evaluation Index System. *The Journal of the South-Central University for Nationalities (Humanities and Social Sciences)* (1).
Liu, Jin'an, Sun, Hui, Xu, Lingzhong, Tang, Cheng, Yang, Zhenhui, Cao, Xiuling, and Song, Xiaofei. 2008. Satisfaction with New Rural Cooperative Medical Care and Analysis of Influencing Factors. *Chinese Journal of Public Health* (2).
Liu, Leshan. 2008. Overseas Fiscal Measures for Regulating Income Gap and Their Implications, paper delivered at the 18th Annual Conference of the Chinese Society of Laws of Economics.
Long, Yuqi. 2013. Theoretical Speculation on the Role of Social Security in Income Redistribution. *Theory Monthly* (11).
Ma, Junsheng et al. 2005. Reflection on Improving China's Medical Insurance Fund Supervision System. *Chinese Health Economics* (10).
Martin, Feldstein. 2009. Reflection on Social Insurance. *Comparative Economic & Social Systems* (4).
Mu, Huaizhong. 2003. *National Wealth and Redistribution of Social Security*. China Labor and Social Security Publishing House.
Peng, Haoran, and Shen, Shuguang. 2007. A Comparative Study of the Income Redistribution Effect of China's Old-age Insurance System before and after the Reform. *Statistical Research* (2).
Qing, Lianbin. 2009. Four Distributions of National Wealth. *People's Forum* (19).
Ren, Ran, and Jin, Feng. 2007. A Study on the Health Service Accessibility and Medical Service Burdens after the Implementation of New Rural Cooperative Medical Care. *China Health Economics* (1).
Shen, Yan. 2012. On the Realization Mechanism of Social Security for Regulating Income Distribution. *The Journal of Hubei Normal College* (5).
Shi, Jianxiang. 2003. *On the Development Mode of Medical Insurance in China*. Beijing: China Price Press.
Statistical Bulletin on the Development of Labor and Social Security Services. 2002–2008. Co-issued by Ministry of Human Resources and Social Security of the People's Republic of China and National Bureau of Statistics of the People's Republic of China
Stiglitz, J.E. 1989. Financial Marker & Development. *Oxford Economic Policy Review* (4).
Tan, Xiaoting, and Zhong, Funing. 2010. The Effect of Income Distribution of Different Modes of Compensation in New Rural Cooperative Medical Care: Empirical Analysis Based on 1500 Rural Households of 30 Counties in Jiangsu and Anhui. *Chinese Rural Economics* (3).

Tang, Xingzhi. 2012. Analysis and Reflection on Public Satisfaction with Community Health Services: Empirical Analysis of Research Data of An Area in Beijing. *Dongyue Tribune* (8).

Tao, Jikun. 2008. Social Security System and Urban-Rural Income Gap. *Lanzhou Academic Journal* (12).

Tao, Jikun. 2010. A Comparative Analysis of the Regulation of Distribution Gap by Social Security System in Western Countries. *Contemporary Economic Research* (9).

The Beijing Cairncross Economic Research Foundation. 2004. China's Social Security Report [R]. Internal document.

The General Office of the State Council. 2015. *The Opinions of the General Office of the State Council on Comprehensively Implementing Serious Disease Insurance for Urban and Rural Residents*.

The Information Office of the State Council of the People's Republic of China. 2004. China's Social Security Status and Policies (White Paper) [R].

The Ministry of Finance and the American Lincoln International Group. 1998. *The Reform of the Social Security System and Its Fund Management: A Global Common Topic*. Modern Publishing House.

The Ministry of Labor and Social Security and the National Bureau of Statistics. 1998–2000. *Statistical Bulletin on the Development of Labor and Social Security Services* (1997, 1998 and 1999).

The Social Insurance Administration of the Ministry of Labor ed. 1997. *China Social Insurance Yearbook 1997*. China Personnel Publishing House.

Wang, Hong et al. 2005. The Benefit Equity of Rural Cooperative Medical Care in China. *Chinese Health Economics* (2).

Wang, Hongman, Gu, Danan, Du, Yuanju, Deng, Xixian, and Wang, Hongyan. 2006. Analysis of Factors Affecting the Participation in, Satisfaction with and Sustainability of New Rural Cooperative Medical Care. *Chinese Journal of Population Science* (5).

Wang, Jiangang. 1999. *Balance of Social Old-age Insurance*. Economic Management Press.

Wang, Maofu, and Xie, Yongcai. 2012. A Study about Negative Regulation of Income Distribution by Social Security. *Studies on Mao Zedong and Deng Xiaoping's Theories* (6).

Wang, Shaoguang. 2003. Public Health in China: Crisis and Turning Point [A], Wu Jinglian, *Comparison Vol. 7* [C]. Beijing: CITIC Publishing House.

Wang, Xiaojun, and Kang, Bowei. 2009. Analysis of the Effect of China's Social Old-age Insurance System on Income Redistribution. *Statistical Research* (11).

Wang, Xiaolu, and Fan, Gang. 2005. The Trend of Income Gap in China and Analysis of Influence Factors. *Economic Research Journal* (10).

Wang, Yanzhong. 2001. A Tentative Discussion of the State's Role in Rural Health Care. *Strategy and Management* (3).

Wang, Yanzhong. 2004. *Labor and Social Security Problems in China*. Economic Management Press.

Wang, Yanzhong. 2012. *The Development of Social Security in China: a Report*. Beijing: Social Sciences Academic Press.

Wang, Yanzhong. 2013. *A Survey of Income Redistribution by Social Security in China*. Social Science Academic Press.

Wang, Yanzhong, and Long, Yuqi. 2010. The Role of People's Livelihood Improvement in Coping with the Financial Crisis, *Studies of the History of the Communist Party of China*. (6).

Wang, Yanzhong, and Long, Yuqi. 2013. Social Security and Income Redistribution: Problems, Experience and Improvement Mechanism. *Academic Research* (4).

Wang, Yanzhong (ed.). 2015. *The Report on the Development of Social Security in China: Social Security during the Period of the Thirteenth Five-Year Plan*. Beijing: Social Sciences Academic Press.

WHO Macroeconomics and Health Committee. 2002. *Macroeconomics and Health*. Beijing: People's Health Press, World Health Organization.

Wolinsky, 1999. *Health Sociology*. Beijing: Social Science Academic Press.

World Bank. 1994. *Averting the Old Crisis: Policies to Protect the Old and Promote Growth.* Washington D.C: Oxford University Press.

World Bank. 1998. *Old-age Security: Reform of China's Old-age Pension System.* China Financial & Economic Publishing House.

Wu, Min and Zhong, Jingjing. 2009. Special Report: State-owned Shares Transferred to Social Insurance Funds [N]. *Beijing News*, June 20, 2009, at http://news.163.com/09/0620/01/5C7CCBGH001124J.html .

Xiang, Ling. 2007. Several Problems Concerning the Redistribution Regression Effect in the Old-age Insurance System. *Fujian Forum* (Humanities and Social Sciences Edition) (1).

Yang, Jun. 2011. Analysis of the Effect of Income Redistribution of Social Pooling Old-age Insurance System. *Social Security Studies* (1).

Yang, Zhenlin, and Wang, Yake. 2007. An Empirical Analysis of the Redistribution Effect of China's Enterprise Old-age Insurance System. *China Soft Science* (4).

Yu, Dezhi. 2005. Analysis of Health Expenditure Growth. *China Health Economics* (3).

Zhao, Man. 1997. *The Analysis of the Structure and Operation of the Social Security System.* China Planning Press.

Zheng, Gongcheng. 2008. *China's Social Security: Reform and Development Strategies.* Beijing: People's Press.

Zheng, Gongcheng. 2010. On Income Distribution and Social Security. *Heilongjiang Social Sciences* (5); Zheng, Gongcheng. 2010. Social Security: Basic Institutional Guarantee for Regulating Income Distribution. *Chinese Cadres Tribune* (6); Zheng, Gongcheng. 2008. *Three Decades of Social Security in China.* Beijing: People's Press.

Zhou, Xuliang, and Shi, Shaobin. 2009. Analysis of Satisfaction with the Reimbursement System of New Rural Cooperative Medical Care. *Collected Essays on Finance and Economics* (6).

Zhu, Qing. 2008. Focus on People's Livelihood: Direction and Approach of the Adjustment of Fiscal Expenditure Structure. *Finance & Trade Economics* (7).

Zou, Xiang. 2012. Improving the Equity of the Old-age Insurance System in China. *China Social Security* (7).

MIX
Papier aus verantwortungsvollen Quellen
Paper from responsible sources
FSC® C105338

If you have any concerns about our products,
you can contact us on
ProductSafety@springernature.com

In case Publisher is established outside the EU,
the EU authorized representative is:
Springer Nature Customer Service Center GmbH
Europaplatz 3, 69115 Heidelberg, Germany

Printed by Libri Plureos GmbH
in Hamburg, Germany

Aquatic Ecology Series

Volume 9

Series Editors
Ulrich Sommer, GEOMAR Helmholtz Centre for Ocean Research, KIEL, Germany
Ingrid Chorus, Berlin, Germany

Aquatic ecology is an extraordinarily broad and interesting field. It investigates the interplay between aquatic organisms and their physical, chemical, and biological environment. Aquatic ecology encompasses all freshwater and marine ecosystems, including streams, rivers, lakes, wetlands, coastal environments, and the vast expanses of the open ocean. Aquatic ecology studies a wide diversity of different organisms, ranging from tiny bacteria to large whales, facing a myriad of different processes such as biogeochemical cycles, genetic differentiation, and climate change. Fundamental research in aquatic ecology adds new discoveries almost every day. Applied research makes major contributions to biotechnology, fisheries, water management, nature conservation, and environmental policy. Reassessments and syntheses in aquatic ecology are stimulating to the discipline as a whole, as well as enormously useful to students and researchers in ecological sciences.

A series of succinct monographs and specialized evaluations in aquatic ecology has been developed. Subjects covered are topical (e.g., coastal hydrodynamics, microbial loops, alpine lakes) rather than broad and superficial.

The treatments must be comprehensive and state-of-the-art, whether the topic is at the biochemical, mathematical, population, community, or ecosystem level. The objectives are to advance the topics by the development of arguments, with documented support, that generate new insights, concepts, theories to stimulate thought, ideas, directions, controversies. The books are intended for mature as well as emerging scientists to stimulate intellectual leadership in the topics treated.

If you have questions regarding our book series or would like to submit a proposal to Aquatic Ecology, please contact the Publisher Éva Lőrinczi (eva.loerinczi@springer.com).

Lora A. Harris • Jessica Cohn • Scott W. Nixon

Ramet Rules

Individual Based Modelling of Clonal Plants

Springer

Lora A. Harris
Chesapeake Biological Laboratory
University of Maryland Center for Environmental Science (UMCES)
Solomons, MD, USA

Jessica Cohn
Massachusetts Division of Ecological Restoration
Boston, MA, USA

Scott W. Nixon
Graduate School of Oceanography
University of Rhode Island
Narragansett, RI, USA

ISSN 1573-4595 ISSN 2543-005X (electronic)
Aquatic Ecology Series
ISBN 978-94-024-2364-8 ISBN 978-94-024-2365-5 (eBook)
https://doi.org/10.1007/978-94-024-2365-5

© Springer Nature B.V. 2026

This work is subject to copyright. All rights are solely and exclusively licensed by the Publisher, whether the whole or part of the material is concerned, specifically the rights of translation, reprinting, reuse of illustrations, recitation, broadcasting, reproduction on microfilms or in any other physical way, and transmission or information storage and retrieval, electronic adaptation, computer software, or by similar or dissimilar methodology now known or hereafter developed.
The use of general descriptive names, registered names, trademarks, service marks, etc. in this publication does not imply, even in the absence of a specific statement, that such names are exempt from the relevant protective laws and regulations and therefore free for general use.
The publisher, the authors and the editors are safe to assume that the advice and information in this book are believed to be true and accurate at the date of publication. Neither the publisher nor the authors or the editors give a warranty, expressed or implied, with respect to the material contained herein or for any errors or omissions that may have been made. The publisher remains neutral with regard to jurisdictional claims in published maps and institutional affiliations.

This Springer imprint is published by the registered company Springer Nature B.V.
The registered company address is: Van Godewijckstraat 30, 3311 GX Dordrecht, The Netherlands

If disposing of this product, please recycle the paper.

To
Joanne, Scott G., Jasper, and Stella
You have been the encouraging whisper in my ear, hand on my back, and ground beneath my feet

Foreword

Ramet Rules is an ambitious and deeply informed modeling guide that presents an innovative yet grounded approach to simulating the dynamics of *Zostera marina* meadows. Rather than functioning solely as a theoretical treatise, the book is structured as a detailed, step-by-step guide to the development and application of the Virtual Eelgrass Meadow (VEM) model. This model integrates process-based physiological modeling, clonal plant ecology, and spatially explicit individual-based modeling (IBM). One of the book's greatest strengths is its balance between ecological fidelity and practical application: the model framework is designed not only to test hypotheses but also to directly support restoration planning in real-world contexts.

What also sets this book apart is its dual commitment to ecological realism and computational efficiency. The model uses empirically derived rules to simulate complex, emergent behaviors such as ramet competition, spatial expansion, and density-dependent growth. This approach ensures that the VEM is both theoretically robust and computationally manageable. The book's explicit discussion of Levins' (1966) framework (balancing generality, realism, and precision) is particularly refreshing, offering philosophical depth that is rare in applied modeling texts. The botanical framing of *Ramet Rules* is both accurate and conceptually rich. *Z. marina* is depicted not as a passive habitat-forming species but as a dynamic clonal organism capable of strategic, plastic responses to fine-scale environmental heterogeneity. This nuance is often lost in broader ecological models that treat seagrasses as static background variables.

This book will be of interest to restoration practitioners, graduate students in ecological modeling, and researchers seeking to apply seagrass ecology concepts in a predictive modeling context. It provides a solid foundation for future work aimed at integrating biological detail into spatial models and may serve as a reference point for continued model development.

University of North Carolina Wilmington
Wilmington, NC, USA

Jessie C. Jarvis

Preface

This book has been decades in the making. The Virtual Eelgrass Meadow was the subject of my (Lora Harris) dissertation in collaboration with Scott Nixon, and then expanded to include Jessica Cohn's (née Foley) seed and seedling descriptions while she pursued her master's degree as my advisee (included throughout where Foley 2017 is cited). Those efforts to finalize and perfect the model followed Scott's early death, and somehow led to a terrible case of writer's block. It has only been at this stage of my mature career that I see Scott Nixon's body of work as a full-throated rejection of the perfectionism that delayed this publication. Scott loved to publish in obscure journals and conference proceedings so that his language could flow, and he could rapidly publish the ideas that drove his worldview and career. I expect he would be flabbergasted and relieved to finally see this text in print!

Ramet Rules seeks to peer behind the modeling curtain while also focusing in on some critical questions around seagrasses. I hope that my efforts to update and expand the model and literature review since the days of my dissertation provide an opportunity to dive into exactly how a model is crafted. Having the luxury of a book format also expands our capacity to query and test some of our fundamental assumptions about *Zostera marina* and the challenge of understanding, conserving, and restoring clonal plants.

One of the fundamental topics I hope readers will identify in our writing is the tricky balance of both building on the legacy of models that have come before and bringing critical new eyes to approaches and formulations that may no longer serve the science or questions that are being asked. When Scott Nixon and I were discussing a book proposal for *Ramet Rules*, he expressed his hope that at one end of his career might sit his book with Jonathan Kremer describing a model for Narraganset Bay and, at the other, this *Ramet Rules* text. While I grieve not providing Scott with this book-end before his death, I know that the bold steps forward in modeling philosophy and seagrass formulations in particular were exactly the kind of progress he had hoped might occur over the timespan connecting these two efforts. That span of progress is because of all of the modeling that precedes this book, the incredible work of my estuarine colleagues around the world, and our dogged focus on science that can inform efforts to conserve and restore these critical plants. Scott's thinking in this book is the emphasis on as much realism as possible, and a drive for extensive grounding in literature to honor and respect the empiricists who contribute so much to any modeling exercise.

Jessica and I hope you will see the joy and love of botany that we brought to the Virtual Eelgrass Model. This really began with the work of the late Dr. Joanne Bintz as a student in Scott's lab, who was one of my early peer mentors, and who carried out extensive experiments in the lagoon mesocosm facility at the University of Rhode Island. I remember Joanne bringing in a section of eelgrass from her tanks that she had carefully dug out of the sediment, with rhizomes and ramets connected into a beautiful network. We marveled at the precise spacing and branching, the sublime green of the meristem. Later, when I discovered William Setchell's drawings of *Zostera marina* published nearly 100 years ago, I easily embraced the botanical perspective that shaped so much of that early eelgrass literature. The Virtual Eelgrass Meadow is a direct response to connecting the dots of clonal plant growth within a simulation: the astounding "of course!" realization that all aquatic vascular plants are clonal, the reality that rhizomes essentially move across the sediment, and the intricate connection between leaf growth and clonal expansion.

I embrace the ethos of writing as a form of thinking, and I hope the reader will find something useful in this model description. It is certainly not exhaustive of all of the clonal plant, seagrass, or eelgrass literature. I expect there are different, new, or improved formulations, parameterizations, or model rules that might be considered. There are aspects of model implementation in the software that will continue to benefit from improvements. And! I do think the steps outlined here illustrate one way of crafting a model, and they might offer others a pathway into model conceptualization and formulation. Of course, I hope that researchers and modelers will use this text to explore their own candidate organisms. When using this book in a classroom setting, there are also exercises that can be simply developed following the logic and approaches outlined herein. I have created a section at the end of each of the first four chapters clearly identifying those steps and suggesting prompts to encourage model development.

In the chapters ahead, we build on a literature review and our approach to clonal plant ecology (Chap. 1) to construct a model that we call the Virtual Eelgrass Meadow (VEM). This model first simulates biomass specific growth rates in response to environmental conditions (Chap. 2), and then outlines programming rules driven by empirically derived formulations and parameters that direct this growth to above- and below-ground growth, using the cyclic pattern of plastochrone and leaf growth timing (Chap. 3). With these basics in hand, Chap. 4 can turn toward botanical conditions in the eelgrass meadow itself, directing additional rules around sexual reproduction and seed germination, vegetative lateral branching (both timing and branch angle), and death of a ramet. These processes are implemented in a 2-D space to simulate meadow expansion, and a critical integrated feedback loop that connects shading by neighbors to ramet scale light availability to simulate how dense canopies can limit light availability. Finally, we take time in Chap. 5 to explore the VEM in an example hypothesis testing format. This includes testing hypotheses regarding maximum power, the complex impacts of temperature on both growth and reproduction, exploration of resource allocation hypotheses, and a testing of restoration protocols using seeds.

Solomons, MD, USA Lora A. Harris

Acknowledgments

I am reminded in writing these acknowledgments that good work is best done in the company of friends. My first editor, Martine van Bezooijen, was so encouraging and also sadly passed away before this book's publication. I have benefited from the patience of subsequent editors Judith Terpos, Eva Loerinczi, and Srinivasan Manavalan. In this year of finalizing the book, my laboratory group has been especially supportive as I spent time away writing; thank you Cindy Ross, Will Dorsey, Kaitlin Beasley-Polko, Chelsea Ihnacik, Scott Shatto, and Julia Smeltzer. Coral Davenport was pursuing her own writing related challenge in 2025, and I have so valued that comradery and our loyal friendship.

This book was largely written in three historic homes: a whaling captain's 1842 Greek Revival in New Bedford, a guest house and one of the original laboratories of the Tvärminne Zoological Station in Finland, and a 1672 precolonial home in West River called Sudley House. These spaces provided the peace and freedom from distraction for me to think and write. My husband, Scott Galczynski, has been an unwavering source of support, and our shared values of hard work and pursuit of creativity-rooted careers have sustained these efforts and our marriage. My son, Jasper, was born on the eve of this book and is launched to college near its publication. Seeing him combine both care for the world and an ease with systems thinking reminds me that raising children alongside a career that gives me latitude for an intellectual life has enriched my experience and effectiveness as a mother and scientist. And Stella, my surprise gift of a daughter, has always grounded me along with her brother. I am especially thankful for evenings spent reading *Anne of Green Gables* together as a welcome break from model runs and writing.

Advisory work with Drs. Kalle Matso, Jud Kenworthy, Michael van den Heuvel, and Simon Courtenay in the Great Bay inspired finishing this project and brought me up to speed on the literature. Along with Jud, Fred Short and Mark Fonseca generously granted permissions for use of their figures. Dr. Jessie Jarvis provided a review that greatly improved the book and was also a valuable advisor to Jessica Cohn during implementation of the reproductive portion of the VEM. I am also thankful to Dr. Tom Miller, who saw me through shapeshifting my career and recognizing this book for what it is, against a backdrop of many other products of my research. Maryland Sea Grant and a Finland Fulbright Scholar award at the Tvärminne Zoological Station both provided funding to support time to work on the model. Following Scott Nixon's death, Drs. Walter Boynton and Jeremy Testa have steadfastly supported the completion of this manuscript. Walter has been a cheerleader since the very beginning, and Jeremy has teased with frequent admonitions and quotes from Voltaire about perfection. I do hope this book is good enough for them.

Perhaps the key to overcoming my perfectionism has been the wisdom shared with me by Drs. Julia Parrish and Fredrika Moser about navigating the work of doing science within the culture of academia; that advice could fill an entirely different book! Their down-to-earth advice, practical strategies, and listening ears have reminded me that at the heart of *Ramet Rules* is the true enjoyment and satisfaction I find in thinking and writing about science and watery life, and how wonderful it is to be able to share that with each of you.

Competing Interests The authors have no competing interests to declare that are relevant to the content of this manuscript.

Contents

Chapter 1
Seagrass Ecology and the Clonal Plant Perspective

1.1 Introduction

Widespread interest in maintaining and managing seagrass habitat has arisen from the much cited paradigm of seagrass meadows as essential habitat for shallow water fish and invertebrates, as well as their functions in stabilizing sediments, enhancing water quality, and providing various ecosystem services that benefit both the environment and human populations (do Amaral Camara Lima et al. 2023; Nordlund et al. 2016, 2018). However, patterns of seagrass decline, frequently as a consequence of deteriorating water quality, have been observed on a global scale and have motivated a wide array of monitoring, conservation, and restoration programs. Dunic et al. (2021) documented a 19.1% decline in seagrass meadow area since 1880.

Throughout the Northeastern United States, extensive decline (concurrent with global losses) of eelgrass (*Zostera marina* L.) over the past century has been attributed to wasting disease (Short and Mathieson 1985), deterioration in water quality from nitrogen loading (Hauxwell et al. 2003), and rising water temperatures (Plaisted et al. 2022). While the effects of wasting disease on seagrasses have been especially well documented for *Zostera marina*, decreasing light availability and associated poor water quality have been implicated for losses of other temperate and tropical species of seagrasses, often as a result of nutrient enrichment, adjacent land development, and population increases (Lotze et al. 2006; Touchette and Burkholder 2007). Fortunately, as a result of regulatory activity, wastewater treatment and land-use management have improved coastal water quality in many areas, and many other efforts are underway to enact management objectives targeting nutrient pollution with the goal of re-creating water quality conducive to seagrass growth. These efforts have led to several commentaries regarding the feasibility of restoration in estuarine and coastal systems that have experienced long-term eutrophication (Nixon 2009; van Katwijk et al. 2016). In particular, Duarte et al. (2009) caution that shifting climate and biogeochemical baselines may result in restoration trajectories that do not correspond to linear, direct reversals of system function. Instead,

© Springer Nature B.V. 2026

L. A. Harris et al., *Ramet Rules*, Aquatic Ecology Series 9,
https://doi.org/10.1007/978-94-024-2365-5_1

estuarine ecosystems in their review also exhibited regime shifts and system hysteresis that made desired results such as seagrass restoration unsuccessful. This concept has been propagated throughout our seagrass literature including a proposed framework for seagrass ecosystem resilience (Unsworth et al. 2015), incorporating feedbacks into seagrass related management (Maxwell et al. 2017), and pursuit of early warning signals to predict a regime shift (Rindi et al. 2024). Given these potential complications for estuarine and coastal restoration, those concerned with seagrasses may naturally be interested in understanding whether a given area is amenable to natural recolonization or restoration following nutrient reduction, sediment controls, or other watershed-based management actions.

Restoration ecology evolved from efforts by Aldo Leopold to restore prairie grasslands during the Dustbowl of the 1930s. In the course of these early efforts to combine both agriculture and ecology, it became clear that restoration must necessarily rest on knowledge gained from basic research and the synthesis of available knowledge. Over time, terrestrial restoration endeavors have proved that attempting to reassemble and ensure functionality in a restored system is one of the most rigorous methods of testing and developing ecological understanding. Restoration of seagrasses in this century has translated this tradition into subtidal marine ecosystems, with clear evidence that this approach is a possible path forward for seagrass ecosystems (Paling et al. 2009; Orth et al. 2020). Restoration efforts have also illuminated the complexity of understanding the influence of site conditions, restoration techniques, and life history stage on likely success (or failure) for a given project (Unsworth and Rees 2025; van Katwijk et al. 2016; Orth and Heck 2023). It is clear that seagrass restoration could benefit from a synthetic tool that would be meaningful for both ecologists and managers in the tradition encouraged by Leopold (1934).

Experimental efforts to determine the biological and physical variables that affect seagrass growth have been successful in providing a general idea of how nutrient enrichment, temperature, light, and sediment type may affect productivity. A number of numerical models have been designed to provide better insight into how physical variables combine to influence overall growth of seagrasses (e.g. Short 1980; Wetzel and Neckles 1986; Bach 1993; Buzzelli et al. 1999; Cerco and Moore 2001; Zharova et al. 2001; Eldridge et al. 2004; Adams et al. 2017). Fewer studies have addressed the larger scale processes that influence population dynamics and landscape level changes in seagrass meadows (Carr et al. 2016; Ewanchuk 1995; Olesen and Sand-Jensen 1994; Neckles et al. 2005), and only a rare study has been completed to create models that link small-scale physiological processes with community level interactions that occur at the 1–100 m^2 scale (Baird et al. 2016).

The modeling efforts described in the following chapters are a first attempt to link a mechanistic, time-varying, physiological model of individual eelgrass growth rates with a two-dimensional, individual based model (IBM) that uses "rules" based on our current understanding of how resource allocation to roots and shoots responds to local environmental conditions. Such "rules-based" models have been more commonly applied to animal and/or terrestrial plant populations, often describing behavior and interactions between species (Grimm and Railsback 2013). A few examples exist for seagrass but do not incorporate physiological rates (Kuusemäe et al. 2018; Lai et al. 2024). Applying this strategy to simulate growth and colonization potential for a seagrass meadow rests upon a renewed appreciation for seagrasses as clonal plants that exhibit morphological plasticity in response to changing environmental conditions. While many successful restorations have focused on seeds and seedlings, stewardship and conservation of eelgrass habitat ultimately rests on having a deep understanding of its clonal growth and expansion. Using rules to govern how new growth is allocated to roots, rhizomes, leaves, and lateral shoot production and the resulting, emergent phenotypic plasticity can be interpreted as a substitution for the more commonly seen "behavioral" rules of IBMs that simulate adaptive behavior in animal populations.

Zostera marina is an ideal model organism to explore this approach for several critical reasons including its widespread geographic distribution in temperate waters (Short et al. 2007), well-evaluated role in supporting fish communities (e.g. Orth et al. 2020), and multiple efforts to effectively annotate its genome (e.g. Olsen et al. 2016; Ma et al. 2021). *Zostera marina* has also been the subject of perhaps the most extensive experimental investigations of physiological response to environmental factors, lending robustness to model development. The output from this IBM is also used to drive a dynamic visualization program, based on a model developed by Sintes et al. (2005), which creates an animation of eelgrass clonal expansion according to rhizome elongation and lateral shoot production rates generated by the allocation rules, along with empirically derived branching angles for new lateral shoots. Together, the physiological specific growth rate model, the resource allocation rules, and the visualization program are used to create a "Virtual Eelgrass Meadow" (VEM) that provides a platform for performing virtual experiments to answer real questions regarding the dynamics of this important habitat in relation to time, space, and a heterogeneous environment. This approach also allows us to consider how the adaptive, morphological plasticity of individual ramets in a clonal population interact with physiological limits to growth imposed by the environmental variables of light, nutrients, temperature, and sediment type.

Construction of a predictive simulation model demands that we assemble and strive for the numerical representation of the functionality of a seagrass meadow and its environment in an effort that is analogous to the reality of actual restoration endeavors. Local knowledge regarding substrate conditions, wave energy, and light and temperature conditions are used to evaluate site suitability for transplant or seeding efforts. As such, the Virtual Eelgrass Meadow (VEM) provides a synthesis and test of our existing knowledge regarding this important habitat by evaluating the predictive capability of the physiological relationships that drive a mechanistic growth model, and the capacity of the rules-based model to include qualitative, expert intuition not incorporated into traditional seagrass models.

1.2 A Review

Duarte (1999) published a literature review of seagrass ecology that drew attention to trends in publication rates, research approaches, and study topics over the time period between 1989 and 1997. While the final years of the twentieth century were highlighted by an exponential increase in the number of papers published regarding seagrass ecology, there were noted biases toward particular approaches and research topics, and a conspicuous neglect of synthetic work (Duarte 1999). In the spirit of this review and using similar methods to those of Duarte (1999), we performed a search focusing specifically on *Z. marina* using the Web of Science database. The purpose of this survey was to take a historic look at the direction of eelgrass ecology, to identify publications useful for construction of the VEM, as well as to identify gaps and potential biases in this body of research.

The search used keywords "eelgrass" or "*Zostera marina*" for journal articles and reports published between 1989 and 2024. Citations for each publication were collected that included title, abstract, journal, year, authors, and the lead author's affiliated country. Using a personal library composed of over 300 eelgrass-specific references published within the search period, fifty random papers were used to cross-check the literature search, establishing a 100% accuracy rate for the search period between 1989 and 2022, with errors in 2023 and 2024 that reduced the time-series to an end year of 2022. This database of 4639 publications was then queried for topical areas that both overlapped with the Duarte (1999) analysis, and also updated to include genetics, disease, reproduction, and to identify studies that focused specifically on clonal characteristics of *Zostera marina* (Table 1.1). In

Table 1.1 Research topics used in literature review of eelgrass ecology (1989–2003)

Research Topic	*Description*
Associated Fauna	Eelgrass as habitat or in relation to animal species
Biogeochemistry	Cycling of nutrients, sediment chemistry, blue carbon
Contamination	Effects of anthropogenic pollution on eelgrass
Disease	Primarily dealing with the fungus *Labyrinthula zosterae*
Distribution	Spatial coverage, remote sensing, mapping techniques
Disturbance	Effects of anthropogenic or storm disturbance
Genetics	Taxonomic and evolutionary studies
Growth	Factors affecting growth and measurement techniques
Management	Policy, management, education, and evaluation techniques
Models	Specifically simulation models, excludes statistical modeling
Physics	Hydrodynamics, particle trapping
Physiology	Any aspect of physiology e.g., carbon metabolism, chemistry
Ramet	Clonal growth, life history, botanical considerations
Reproduction	Asexual and sexual reproduction, seed banks
Restoration	Techniques and success, evaluation

Categories are taken from Duarte (1999) except as noted in bold

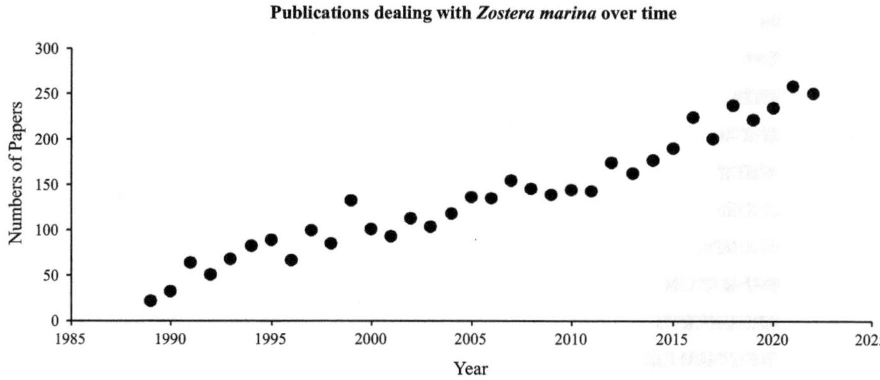

Fig. 1.1 Papers published in eelgrass ecology between 1989 and 2022. Cumulative papers = 4639

general, there has been a linear increase in per-year publications over the 30+ years reviewed, with approximately 6–7 papers added per year over this record (Fig. 1.1).

The overall distribution of publications by search topic is shown in Fig. 1.2 and mirrors the Duarte (1999) study with a dominance of those dealing with "associated fauna" of eelgrass, accounting for 27% of the publications. In this case, "associated fauna" include any invertebrates or fishes found within or having an impact on eelgrass meadows. Research on "management", "restoration", and "genetics" were all also quite high. Topics involving features related to plant dynamics such as growth, clonal characteristics, physiology, and reproduction each represented less than 5% of the totals, with a composite value of just 13% of all published studies (Fig. 1.2).

The body of literature that has attempted to describe the complex effects of water quality, temperature, and geochemistry is based on measurements of eelgrass standing stock biomass, density, metabolic rates, or shoot-growth rates. The literature search revealed that only a minority (<5%) of studies completed to test the effects of stressors and environment on eelgrass meadows examined life history or population characteristics such as lateral shoot production, mortality, or flowering frequency. These responses are crucial to understanding clonal plant responses and are necessary to determine whether a population is in equilibrium; balancing new shoot recruitment with mortality. As will be discussed in subsequent sections, this is especially important because the morphological plasticity of clonal plants such as *Z. marina* has been implicated as a life history trait that is particularly advantageous (De Kroon and Hutchings 1995), especially in an aquatic environment (Hutchinson 1975; Grace 1993). Without an integration of our detailed understanding of shoot--level physiology with a life-history, clonal perspective of eelgrass meadows, it will be difficult to complete a narrative of *Z. marina* decline and impossible to provide managers and conservationists with early warning and detection tools for determining meadow health.

The good news is that there has been an expansive attention to restoration and management in the literature over the past 30 years (Fig. 1.3). This has also been matched with large increases in studies on genetic populations, and modest increases

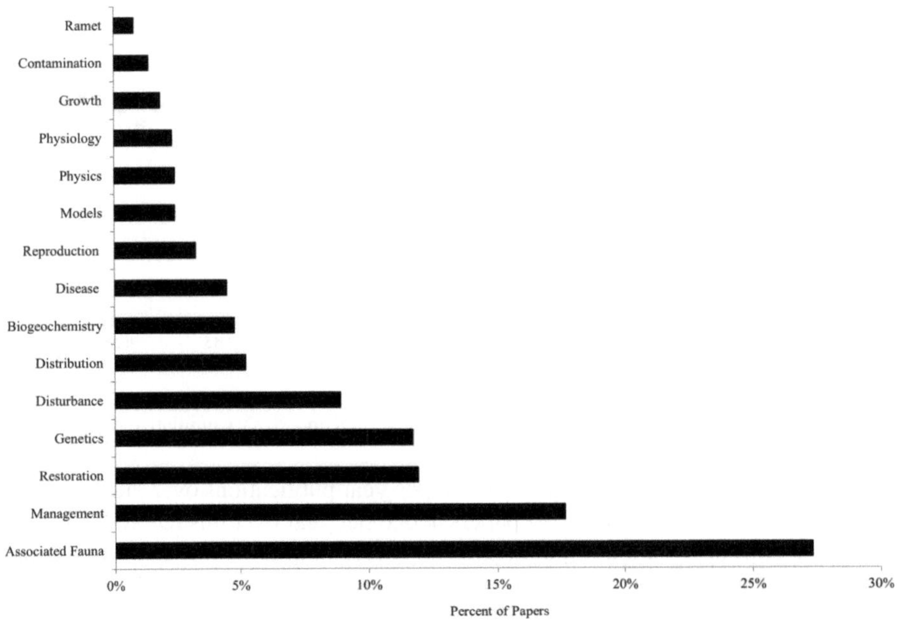

Fig. 1.2 Distribution of research topics covered in eelgrass literature (1989–2022)

in the past 15+ years around sexual reproduction and disease. Combined, these trends indicate a modern interest and motivation for understanding population dynamics and an evolution from studying the mechanisms of decline in eelgrass towards reckoning with how to manage, conserve, and restore this important habitat--forming species.

1.3 Mechanisms of Eelgrass Decline

As with other seagrass species, documented reductions in the historical distributions of *Z. marina* over the twentieth century occurred in coastal and estuarine areas such as the Chesapeake Bay (Orth and Moore 1983), Great Bay New Hampshire (Behm et al. 2003), the Wadden Sea (Den Hartog 1970), the Baltic Sea (Bostrom et al. 2003), Waquoit Bay (Short and Burdick 1996), Charlestown Pond (Short et al. 1996), and Narragansett Bay (Kopp et al. 1995). Over the past twenty-five years, we have witnessed a mix of recovery and continued decline or stasis in these systems. Modest recovery of *Zostera marina* in the polyhaline portion of the Chesapeake Bay system (Lefcheck et al. 2018) is complicated by its temperature sensitivity and the competitive advantage of *Ruppia maritima* (Hensel et al. 2023). Other systems show sustained losses (Wadden Sea; Rehlmeyer et al. 2024) or recent and sudden extensive losses (Great Bay; Routhier et al. 2024). The mechanisms and origin of such declines have received scrutiny by ecologists and funding agencies, often

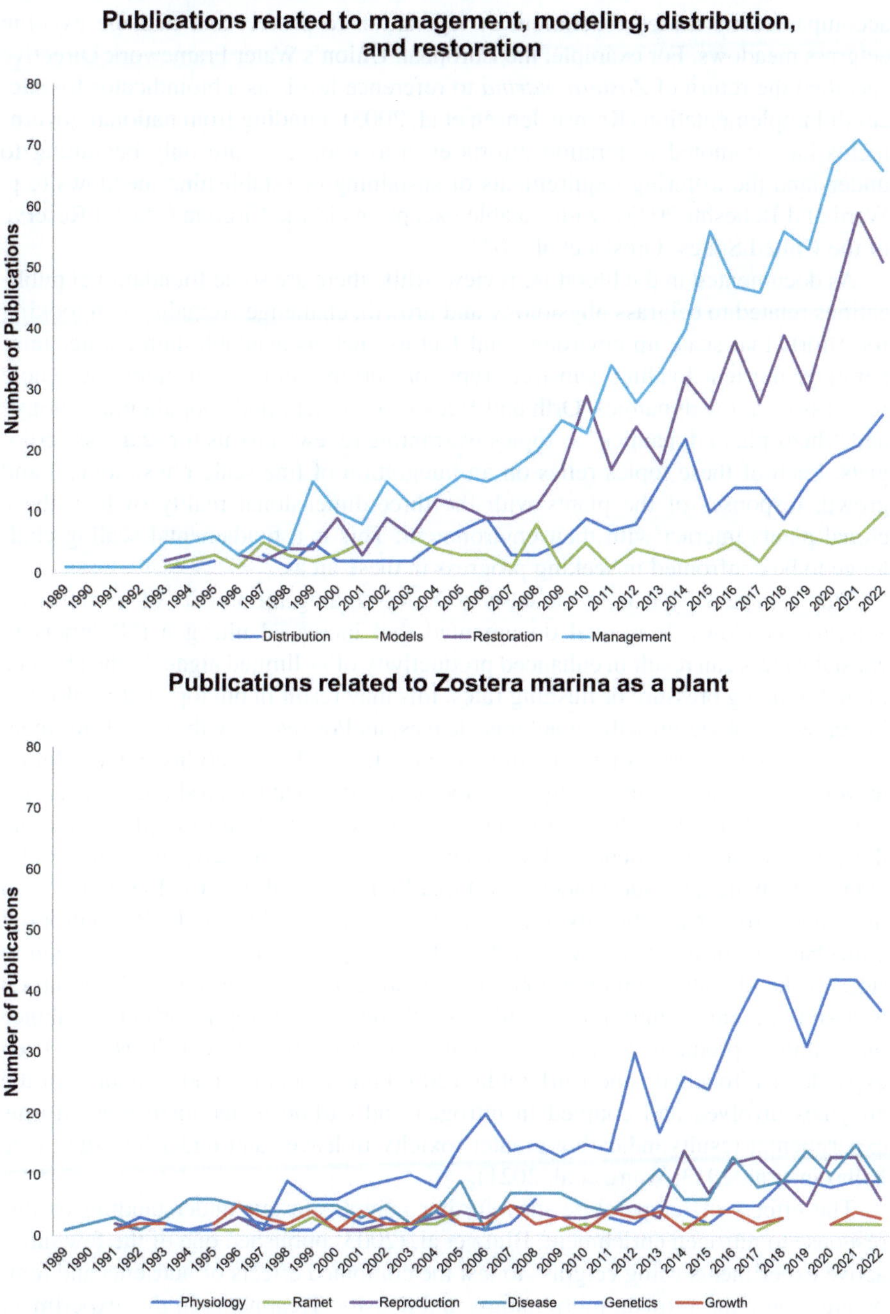

Fig. 1.3 Patterns in publication numbers over time (1989–2022) according to topic

accompanied by the establishment of legislation to protect and manage existing eelgrass meadows. For example, the European Union's Water Framework Directive specified the return of *Zostera marina* to reference levels as a bioindicator for successful implementation (Krause-Jensen et al. 2005). Funding from national governments has promoted restoration efforts even as ecologists are only beginning to understand the differing requirements of sustaining or establishing meadows (e.g. Ward and Beheshti 2023), with notable exceptions in the Virginia Coastal Reserve of the United States (Oreska et al. 2021).

As documented in the literature review, while there are some foundational publications related to eelgrass physiology and growth, challenges remain when looking for efforts that scale up environmental factors such as available light, water temperature, nutrient loading, substrate type, or current velocity on plant and whole seagrass meadow dynamics. Orth and Heck (2023) identified "population biology" and "rhizosphere dynamics" as topics warranting renewed focus for seagrass ecologists. Each of these topics relies on an integration of fine-scale physiological and growth responses of the plants with the three-dimensional reality of how these clonal plants interact with their environment. This is a fundamental scaling challenge to be confronted in seeking progress in these areas.

This is especially true in the case of understanding the impact of nutrients on eelgrass meadows. It is well documented that increased nitrogen (N) inputs to coastal waters can result in enhanced productivity of N-limited algae. In the absence of high grazing pressure or flushing rates, this may result in phytoplankton blooms, increased epiphyte growth on eelgrass leaves, and/or overgrowth by drifting macroalgae. All three forms of algal biomass can reduce light availability to the eelgrass leaves, thereby decreasing the light compensation depth at which shoots can survive (e.g. McGlathery et al. 2007). In addition to leading indirectly to light limitation, there is also some evidence (Burkholder et al. 1994; Touchette and Burkholder 2000; Touchette and Burkholder 2007) that high levels of water column dissolved inorganic nitrogen are directly toxic to *Z. marina*. Burkholder et al. (1994) propose a mechanism for this response that describes an apparent inability of *Z. marina* to stop uptake of water column nitrate, thus creating a continuous demand for carbon to assimilate nitrate into amino acids, and thereby producing a carbon imbalance that inhibits production of new structural material for growth. This has been expanded by Touchette and Burkholder (2007) into a detailed understanding of the enzymes involved and coupled in nitrogen and carbon metabolism that informs experimental results indicating greater toxicity in leaves and under low light (see Villazán et al. 2013; Wang et al. 2021).

The effects of temperature may further complicate our understanding of this response to nitrogen enrichment. Bintz et al. (2003) published one of the few interactive experiments using eelgrass to test the combined effects of nutrients and temperature on plant growth, morphology, and density. Treatments in this experiment included replicate tanks planted with eelgrass that were warm (3–4 °C above a mean daily temperature), cool (3–4 °C below a mean daily temperature), and tanks that approximated the mean temperature recorded in Rhode Island coastal lagoons. Bintz et al. (2003) also subjected duplicate warm and duplicate cool mesocosms to daily additions of nitrate (6 mmol m^{-2} d^{-1}) and phosphate in a molar ratio of 12:1. The adverse effects seen as a result of increased temperature and nutrient enrichment were multiplicative, where nutrient enrichment had a greater effect at warm temperatures than at cool temperatures. Complicating this narrative, Moreno-Marín et al. (2018) performed aquarium experiments manipulating temperature, light, and nitrogen and recorded results that were additive, not multiplicative and Kaldy (2014) reported no nitrogen toxicity or multiplicative impact of temperature. It is possible that these differing responses are the result of local adaptation, but even this possibility remains equivocal in the literature. For example, Dubois et al. (2022) performed transplant experiments across three populations and documented local thermal adaptation even as common garden experiments performed by Hattich et al. (2025) resulted in no clear population level effects of temperature on phenotypic adaptation. We highlight this as a clear next step and potential opportunity for expansion of this model, especially given growing understanding of the eelgrass genome.

Cultural eutrophication, as a result of nitrogen enrichment of coastal waters, also has the potential of increasing organic particulate loads to sediments within eelgrass meadows. The die-off of another seagrass species, *Thalassia testudinum,* has been linked to high concentrations of sediment sulfide in Florida Bay as a consequence of high organic loads to the sediments. Eldridge et al. (2004) framed this paradigm in a numerical model that examined the "cascade of effects" that follows from eutrophication. In this scenario, altered sediment geochemistry (due to increased organic inputs) combines with lowered light availability to stress the seagrass photosystem and lower productivity. This model was adapted to populations of *Zostera marina* on the west coast of the United States to test the applicability of such an alternate means of eelgrass decline (Kaldy et al. 2006). Pederson et al. (2004) documented extremely high concentrations of gaseous sulfide in a *Zostera marina* meadow. Holmer and Nielsen (1997) measured high rates of sulphate reduction in *Z. marina* vegetated versus unvegetated sediments. Over a shoot density gradient, they reported a positive linear correlation between increasing density and sulphate reduction (Holmer and Nielsen 1997). Such a correlation may be due not only to possible carbon inputs from belowground roots and rhizomes, but also to the hydrodynamic conditions that facilitate particle trapping by seagrass leaves along with direct trapping by leaf surface "stickiness" (Gacia and Duarte 2001). While *Z. marina* is capable of growing in highly organic sediments (Koch 2001), both the Kaldy et al. (2006) and Holmer and Nielsen (1997) studies advocate renewed attention to the effects of sediment geochemistry on eelgrass which is also encouraged by Orth and Heck (2023) in their emphasis on rhizosphere dynamics as a topic of future research.

In this context, it is important to highlight the lessons learned from ongoing restoration using seeds in the Virginia Coastal Reserve of the United States. Since 1999, a restoration in ocean-restricted lagoons using hand-broadcast seeds has resulted in the recovery of over 2500 hectares of *Zostera marina* (Orth et al. 2020). The success of this effort revealed that these lagoons may have suffered from recruitment challenges or unrecoverable seed banks (Orth et al. 2000, 2012). In this way, considering the reproductive strategy and population biology and dynamics becomes important to interpreting mechanisms of decline.

There is broad evidence that *Z. marina* is highly plastic to changes in its environment (Hemminga and Duarte 2000; Duarte et al. 2006), strategically allocating growth to either the roots or shoots or altering its own reproductive strategies (Jarvis et al. 2014). In order to understand the tolerances of *Zostera marina,* it is useful to be able to understand how rapidly this plasticity can occur to create greater resilience of a meadow that might prevent reduced distribution and die-offs. One well--documented example of an altered reproductive strategy used to cope with increased water temperatures is the emergence of *Z. marina* "annual meadows", such as those documented in North Carolina (Jarvis et al. 2012). While the individuals are not genetically annuals, they are able to persist amid stressful summer temperatures and yearly vegetation dieback by shifting their reproductive strategy to survive as seeds during unfavorable times of the year (Kim et al. 2014). Under this strategy, the individuals depend on the yearly production of reproductive shoots, a viable sediment seed bank, and successful seedling establishment (Jarvis et al. 2012). In this temperature stressed environment, seagrass individuals must be able to allocate resources to the formation of reproductive shoots, flower, and set seed for the next year's recruitment before taxing water temperatures lead to vegetative shoot mortality. This contrasts with more northerly populations, where meadows are maintained by a much higher rate of clonal reproduction and expansion, with some sexual reproduction.

Warmer water temperatures have been documented globally in estuarine settings (Prum et al. 2024) and are projected to increase. Having tools to predict how eelgrass might respond with the potential for increasing rates of sexual reproduction and a heavier reliance on annual growth, recruitment, and establishment of seedlings, or responses to light and nitrogen availability, will aid our restoration and management strategies. According to an investigation by Furman and Peterson (2015), the need to link recruitment mechanisms to coverage changes (meadow development and small-scale disturbance recovery) occurring at landscape scales continues to remain a challenge for seagrass ecologists and managers alike. We need a better understanding of the impacts of reproductive biology, phenology, and whole plant ontogeny on the maintenance of existing meadows in the face of a changing climate.

The complexity that emerges from this long period of eelgrass research reinforces the need for synthetic tools to aid our understanding of *Z. marina*. Perhaps no other species has received as much attention within the seagrass research community as *Z. marina* (Duarte 1999; Orth and Heck 2023), especially with respect to attempts to model eelgrass growth and biomass. While the brief review of eelgrass stressors here emphasizes the multiple mechanisms of decline or nonlinear response to restoration, a review of overall eelgrass understanding may be achieved by an evaluation of the extensive library of existing eelgrass models and the varied attempts to numerically synthesize our knowledge into a modeling framework.

1.4 Existing *Zostera marina* Models

The first numerical model constructed to describe eelgrass growth was developed by Short (1975) while a student at the University of Rhode Island Graduate School of Oceanography, and later published as a monograph chapter (Short 1980). The diagram pictured in Fig. 1.4 describes the variables and processes used to simulate carbon flow in an eelgrass shoot for this model and reflects the fact that the approaches taken were very similar to those used to model phytoplankton growth in Narragansett Bay (i.e. Kremer and Nixon 1978) and other systems. The production rate essentially relies on the analogous application of Steele's (1962) equation for phytoplankton to the production-irradiance curve for *Zostera marina*. Short (1980) applies this formulation as a limitation factor, scaled between 1 and 0, by which a maximum growth rate is reduced under declining light availability. This maximum growth rate is also temperature limited by a Q_{10} of 2.0 below 25 °C, and the empirical relationship between current velocity and production is described as a third limitation factor to compute daily specific growth rates. The specific growth rate was then multiplied by the available leaf biomass to predict a growth rate that decreased according to calculations of nighttime respiration, and as wind stress/disturbance caused leaf breakage and a decline in biomass. Aboveground biomass in the first example of this model included five compartments for each of the (potentially)

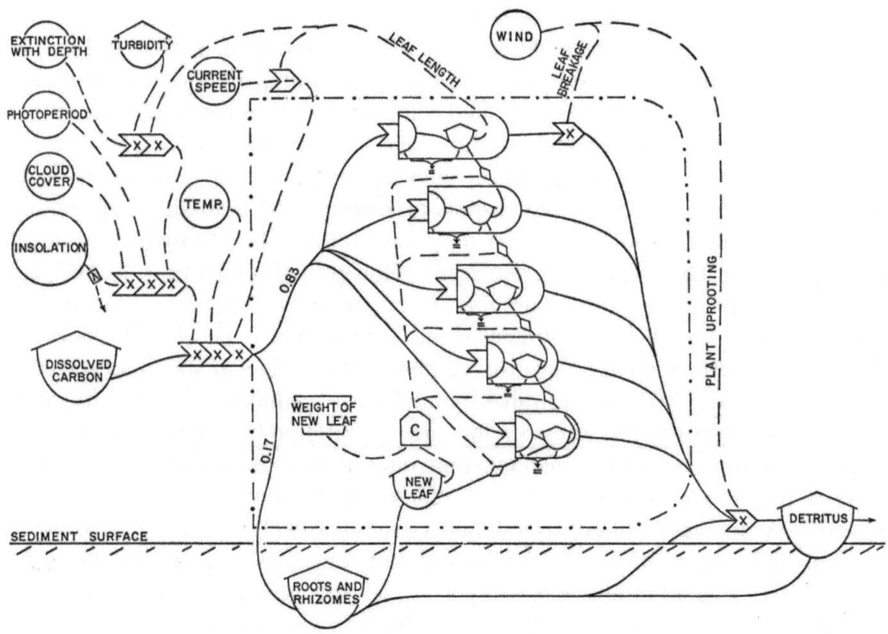

Fig. 1.4 Energy Diagram used to design Short (1980) eelgrass model

growing eelgrass leaves. A constant translocation of carbon from leaves to roots/rhizomes was set at 17%, as described by McRoy (1974).

This hybrid approach of combining empirically-derived limitation factors within the framework of mechanistically derived stressors and growth factors has been repeated several times over the past 30 years for *Zostera marina*. Typically, biomass is simulated on an area basis and may be divided between above and belowground portions. As a part of this study, we undertook a review of a subset of available eelgrass models that combine environmental forcing functions, growth, and some description of plant characteristics and have compiled fourteen of these in Table 1.2, along with their state variables and forcing functions. Other eelgrass models not included in Table 1.2 are formulations that focus on a specific component or response of eelgrass growth, habitat suitability GIS tools, statistical models, or those focused on ecosystem impacts like trophic transfer. For example, this list excludes models specifically focused on leaf movement and hydrodynamic impacts (Dijkstra and Uittenbogaard 2010), food webs (Plummer et al. 2013), species competition (Bocci et al. 1997), habitat suitability index models (Staehr et al. 2019) and a generalized dynamic Bayesian network model (Hatum et al. 2022). Finally, this list does not include the studies that have gone on to develop and apply these core formulations to other applications and simulation frameworks, instead focusing on the original studies, equations, and approaches that informed many of these (e.g. Carr et al. 2010; Kuusemäea et al. 2018). The exception to this is the Jarvis et al. (2014) model that provided a substantial step forward for representing sexual reproduction and ontogenetic processes.

A common approach applied by many of the reviewed models listed in Table 1.2 is the use of a maximal growth rate, limited by stressors, and the translocation of carbon production from the aboveground component to belowground roots and rhizomes. Values for these parameters (μ_{max} and β, respectively) are also listed in Table 1.2. Because we were particularly interested in population processes of reproduction (flowering or asexual lateral shoot production) and mortality, notes on how these factors were handled are also included in Table 1.2. Most of the models include state variables describing above and belowground compartments of eelgrass biomass. Temperature and light are the most commonly used forcing functions to limit production, with the exception of the Zimmerman et al. (1987) model that focused on nutrient uptake and use. A remarkable range of maximum specific growth rates (μ_{max}) were used in these models with a minimum of 0.03 d^{-1} and a maximum of 0.20 d^{-1}. The translocation rates (β) differed by almost a factor of two with minimum values of 17% and maximal rates of 30%. Nearly all biomass losses were a function of temperature, and reproductive processes were largely not included. As indicators of our overall understanding of eelgrass, Table 1.2 provides a surprisingly varied picture of the forcing functions, growth rates, and processes important to eelgrass production. Consensus appears only to include our belief that temperature and light affect plant growth, although the precise mechanism of this effect varies between models as outlined below. We emphasize that this lack of consensus is not because any given study is incorrect, but perhaps because there is a wide range of responses possible.

Table 1.2 Comparisons of existing *Zostera marina* models listed chronologically

Study	Model type	Location	State variables	Forcing functions	μ_{max}	β	Reproductive processes	Shoot mortality
Short (1980)	Physiological growth	Charlestown Pond, USA	$B_L \times 5$ B_{NL} B_B	T I W V	0.201 d^{-1} Carbon	0.17	None	B_L losses function of T driven respiration, wave energy, and translocation B_B loss due to wave energy
Short (1981) [Short (1980)]	Physiological growth	Izembek Lagoon, USA	B_A B_B	T I W $NH4_W$ $NH4_S$ $NO3_W$	0.005 h^{-1} Dry weight	0.17	None	B_L losses function of T driven respiration, wave energy, and translocation B_B loss due to wave energy
Verhagen and Nienhuis (1983)	Physiological growth, Reproductive processes, Some spatial	Lake Grevelingen, Netherlands	SB_V SB_{VF} B_B B_A N	T I W Age Space	0.08 d^{-1} Carbon	0.19	Shoots classified as "generative" and "vegetative" as well as 220 age classes. Dependent on T, PAR, Space, Age.	SB loss function of T, W, and age (SB_V 40 d, SB_{VF} 70 d) B_B loss function of new shoot production
Wetzel and Neckles (1986)	Physiological growth	Chesapeake Bay, USA	B_A EPI Grazers	T I CO_2 Space	*Derived from T* *Max ~0.1* d^{-1} Carbon	0.17	None	B_A loss function of T driven respiration and mortality, as well as translocation to roots and rhizomes

(continued)

Table 1.2 (continued)

Study	Model type	Location	State variables	Forcing functions	μ_{max}	β	Reproductive processes	Shoot mortality
Zimmerman et al. (1987)	Physiological	NA	NU_A NU_B NU Uptake NU_W NU_S	NU I	0.03 d^{-1} Dry weight	0.20	None	None—Runs for only 7–10 days. All validation, output reported for Nutrient Uptake Rates
Bach (1993)	Physiological growth, Asexual reproduction	Kattegat Estuary, Denmark	B_A B_B N	T I W	0.095 d^{-1} Carbon	0.3	MSP_{max} = 23 shoots m^{-2} d^{-1} Dependent on same forcing functions as growth rate.	*Estimated by calibration*
Bocci et al. (1997)	Physiological growth	Lagoon of Venice, Italy	B_A B_B NU_{AB}	T I $NH4_W$ $NH4_S$ $NO3_W$ $NO3_S$ Space	0.06 Dry weight	0.25	None	B_A loss function of T driven respiration and translocation B_B loss function of T driven respiration
Zharova et al. (2001)	Physiological growth, Asexual reproduction	Lagoon of Venice, Italy	B_A B_B B_S N	T I Space	0.043 d^{-1} Carbon	0.21	MSP_{max} = 0.028 d^{-1} Dependent on same T and PAR forcing functions as G_A as well as space limitation above and belowground	B_A loss function of T B_B loss function of uprooting and shoot production N loss = .0072 d^{-1}

Best et al. (2001) [Buzzelli et al. (1999)]	Physiological growth	Chesapeake Bay, USA	B_A B_B NU_A NU_B EPI	T I DIN	*Not reported* Carbon	0.25	None	B_A loss function of respiration and mortality, as well as translocation B_B loss function of respiration, mortality, and bed "storage"
Cerco and Moore (2001)	Physiological growth	Chesapeake Bay, USA	B_A B_B EPI	T I NU	0.06 d^{-1} Carbon	0.1–0.85	None	B_A loss function of sloughing, translocation B_B loss function of root respiration
Neckles et al. (2005)	Landscape model	Maquoit Bay, USA	*SPATIAL:* Presence/ absence in grid cells	Time	NA	NA	Constant rate of patch expansion/seedling recruitment for annual time step	No losses
Carr et al. (2012) [Zharova et al. (2001)]	Physiological growth	Hog Island Bay, USA	B_L, B_B, N, B_{NL} *leaf dynamics explicitly included*	T I	0.095 from Bach (1993)	0.3	Calibrated rate of recruitment set at 0.04 per day	6.5×10^{-3} per day, as well as threshold function when shoot density becomes low.
Jarvis et al. (2014)	Physiological growth, Reproductive processes	Chesapeake Bay, USA	SB_V, B_B, EPI, seed bank, seedlings	T I NU_w	Temp. dependent optimum	0.3	Explicitly modeled, including germination rates, transfer to seedling state variable, and transition to SBv biomass	Roots, Shoots, and seeds all parameterized with individual mortality rates

(continued)

Table 1.2 (continued)

Study	Model type	Location	State variables	Forcing functions	μ_{max}	β	Reproductive processes	Shoot mortality
Salinas and Solano--Arellano (2021)	Individual-based model	Punta Banda Estuary, Mexico	N, RL Individual--based model Rhizome elongation	T I Air Exposure	Data Assimilation Methods	NA	Clonal branching only	Age dependent mortality

Review of eelgrass simulation models: B_L leaf biomass, B_{NL} leaf Initiation biomass, B_B root and rhizome biomass, SB_V aboveground vegetative shoot biomass, SB_{VF} “Annual” shoot biomass, *N* number of shoots, *RL* rhizome length, *EPI* epiphytes, NU_A aboveground nutrient content, NU_B belowground nutrient content, NU_W water column nutrient concentration, NU_S sediment nutrient concentration, *T* temperature, *I* light, *W* wind, *V* current speed, μ_{max} specific growth rate, β belowground growth allocation percentage

Development of the pioneering model of Short (1980) continued and included the additional limitation factor of nutrients in a simulation scenario designed for Izembek Lagoon, Alaska (Short 1981). In addition, the five leaf compartments were combined into one aboveground state variable and the current speed limitation factor was eliminated. Due to the nature of the available field data, state variables were simulated using units of grams dry weight m^{-2} rather than the carbon units used for the original model. No reproductive processes were included in either of these endeavors, although Short (1981) concludes that including these traits are a clear necessity for future models. Losses included belowground respiration and uprooting caused by wind/wave energy. It is also important to note that in this model, as in all other similar studies completed to date, translocation of material produced in the leaves to roots and rhizomes is considered as a constant proportion. In the case of Short (1980, 1981), this value was set at 17% and ranged between 17% and 30% for all the studies considered in Table 1.2.

In the same time period, Verhagen and Nienhuis (1983) created a simulation environment for *Z. marina* that included the most integrated example of population dynamics and physiology completed to date for this species. Sets of differential equations were described for the state variables that included an "average" eelgrass shoot, the numbers of shoots, and belowground biomass. Eelgrass shoots were differentiated by those that were primarily vegetative and those that eventually flower (SB_V and SB_{VF}). These were then further identified by an age class based on the time step when they were produced in the simulation exercise. Production of the aboveground portions of these shoots was similar to the format of other models, with limitation factors based on temperature, light, and wave energy. However, in addition to these environmental factors, the issues of age and crowding were considered along with the expense to belowground biomass caused by new shoot production.

In many ways, this early example is the most similar to the approach taken with the Virtual Eelgrass Meadow presented in this book. Rather than simulating the variability of production in a number of shoots, the mean growth rate and losses to one shoot is modeled and output is multiplied by a shoot density to arrive at areal biomass. Reproduction is considered as well as density dependent growth limited by space. However, a fatal flaw affects the use of space limitation in the Verhagen and Nienhuis (1983) model. Because space is not explicitly modeled, state variables are confined to simulation conditions within a square meter area with units of g C m^{-2}. This also means that in a given square meter compartment of simulated shoot density, new shoot production is limited once a specified carrying capacity is reached. This carrying capacity also uses units of C m^{-2} or shoots m^{-2}. Regardless of how this is parameterized, it neglects the reality that within a virtual square meter area, if conditions are crowded, *a new shoot may colonize adjacent areas*. This may also explain the puzzlement of the authors when simulated coverage of eelgrass did not match the area expansion of actual meadows measured in Lake Grevelingen, Netherlands (Verhagen and Nienhuis 1983). The authors attempt to explain this via recruitment of seedlings, a process not included in the model but certainly a potential source of increased eelgrass coverage. However, it seems likely that another explanation is simply that the colonization potential of the eelgrass was not properly incorporated within the modeling environment. Despite these oversights, it is certainly a sophisticated example of a combined population-physiology model for eelgrass.

In the United States, Wetzel and Neckles (1986) elaborated upon the efforts of Short (1980, 1981) to enhance the physiological equations describing production to include epiphytes, grazers, CO_2 limitation, and a density dependence on leaf biomass for populations found in the Chesapeake Bay. A systems diagram using the energy circuit language developed by Odum (1971) for this simulation model is shown in Fig. 1.5. This model illustrates the varied approaches to simulating light, arguably the most important environmental factor considered in eelgrass models. Short (1980) used forcing functions to simulate reduced light in response to a constant water column light extinction coefficient and also introduced a sophisticated integration formulation to describe how light availability decreases from the top of the eelgrass canopy to the base of the leaves. Wetzel and Neckles (1986) considered the biological interference of epiphytic algae and the relation between grazing rates and epiphyte load. The emphasis on coupling relatively simple eelgrass growth models with increasingly complicated simulations of light based on biological processes (phytoplankton, epiphytes) and other ecosystem components affected by

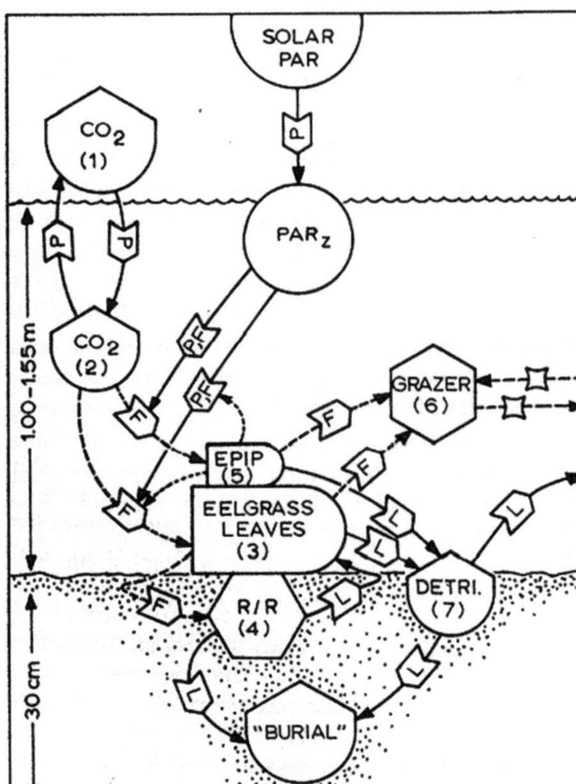

Fig. 1.5 Energy flow diagram for eelgrass model reprinted from Wetzel and Neckles (1986) with permission from Elsevier

eutrophication was common for Chesapeake Bay examples (Best et al. 2001; Cerco and Moore 2001).

As can be seen in Table 1.2, these Chesapeake Bay models include more state variables and slightly more complex ways of simulating forcing functions even though growth rates and loss processes remain true to traditional techniques. One difference to note is the alternative way that shoot biomass growth is modeled by Cerco and Moore (2001). In all other growth models reviewed for Table 1.2, a specific growth rate is predicted based on the law of multiplicative factors (Swartzman and Bentley 1977) that takes μ_{max} and multiplies by various limitation factors. A distressing consequence of this approach is that growth declines as additional factors are included. Instead, Cerco and Moore (2001) applied Liebig's Law of the Minimum to a temperature-dependent μ_{max}. This μ_{max} is then multiplied by the minimum of light, nitrogen, or phosphorus limitation factors. The contextual significance of these models is found within the hypotheses phrased by their unique combinations of state variables and links to hydrodynamic or water quality models that signify an increasing understanding of the complexity of eelgrass decline (see previous section).

In contrast to the expanded state variables and links to more complicated water quality simulations considered by Chesapeake Bay models, Zimmerman et al. (1987) undertook a modeling exercise examining the role of nutrients in eelgrass growth that consisted of a thoroughly theoretical approach. Rather than simulating a particular location or set of circumstances, Zimmerman et al. (1987) set out to understand uptake kinetics of nutrients and the balance of nutrient source uptake between leaves and roots. Previous models had only considered nutrients indirectly via water column light attenuation, and growth rates were solely dependent on light and temperature limitation factors. Zimmerman et al. (1987) considered light and water column nutrients as limitation factors and simulations were run for a brief 7–10 day time period. Output parameters reported in the publication included only those state variables associated with the Michaelis-Menton kinetics of nutrient uptake, rather than the more evolved state variables of biomass or shoot density that consider both growth rates and a plethora of (usually) calibrated losses due to mortality or respiration. Within the tradition of seagrass modeling, this novel approach of developing a model exclusively to test a hypothesis considers the simulation exercise as a creative environment that may provide information or insight not readily available from experimental results. This example is worth noting in a larger volume of modeling examples that tend to be more descriptive in nature and are designed to simulate a particular place and set of conditions.

Beginning in the early 1990s a series of models were published based on field settings in Europe (Bach 1993; Bocci et al. 1997; Zharova et al. 2001). Perhaps more directly influenced by the Verhagen and Nienhuis (1983) study due to geography, these studies are more likely to include asexual reproduction as a state variable (Table 1.2). Bach (1993) modeled shoot production rates in a similar fashion as specific growth rates, including a maximum lateral shoot production rate (23 shoots m^{-2} d^{-1}) that is modified by the same growth rate limitation factors of light, temperature, and wind energy. Zharova et al. (2001) also applied this approach, although maximum shoot production state variables were modeled with units of areal biomass rather than density. As with the Verhagen and Nienhuis (1983) model, space limitation was considered with a carrying capacity confined to a square meter area and would have the same effect of limiting colonization as previously mentioned. Despite the problems with applying this limitation approach directly to asexual reproduction, it is probably reasonable to consider that aboveground leaf production can be limited by this description of carrying capacity because shoots continue to produce new leaves and are generally stationary. It's also important to note that the loss of material in the root and rhizome compartment to production of new shoots is a significant mechanistic detail included by both Zharova et al. (2001) and Verhagen and Nienhuis (1983). Carbon produced by the leaves is translocated belowground, a portion of which goes to root and rhizome growth with some losses occurring when a new shoot is formed. This partitioning of materials between parent and branching lateral shoot units is one of the few truly clonal characteristics described by any of these models. Carr et al. (2012) created significant developments to the Zharova et al. (2001) model by creating explicit state variables for the leaves of each shoot and incorporating more sophisticated tracking between the number of shoots, aboveground growth, and leaf length.

Three additional models are critical to expand on here as providing either significant advances or differing approaches to modeling eelgrass. First, we include Neckles et al. (2005) because it represents modeling efforts with a focus on population and landscape processes (i.e. Kendrick et al. 1999; Fonseca et al. 2004; Sintes et al. 2005). Neckles et al. (2005) tracked recruitment and bed expansion for twenty years within a dredging scar created in an eelgrass meadow located in Maine. A simulation designed to predict dredge scar recovery rates considered various rates of patch expansion and seedling recruitment, but did not model growth or physiology in terms of environmental forcing functions. By considering both of these means of recovery, the authors could test the relative importance of asexual versus sexual reproduction to the reestablishment of the eelgrass meadow. Within the mean values of both parameters measured in the field, Neckles et al. (2005) found that asexual reproduction was more important to recovery. This hypothesis-driven modeling exercise is similar to the way in which numerical simulation techniques were used by Zimmerman et al. (1987) to evaluate the relative contribution of leaves versus roots to nutrient uptake. However, as is the case with many modeling efforts focused on population dynamics, the Neckles et al. (2005) formulation does not consider physiology or a mechanistic description of growth rates or asexual reproduction.

Jarvis et al. (2014) are also included because of the significant contribution of the addition of sexual reproduction to a seagrass model. Jarvis et al. (2014) provides a robust example of a reproduction model that includes formulations for reproductive shoot production, seed production, seed-bank density, seed viability, and seed germination. The model by Jarvis et al. (2014) offers estimates for key parameters, which are derived from several sources and model calibrations (Silberhorn et al. 1983; Fishman and Orth 1996; Harwell and Orth 2002; Bintz and Nixon 2001). The Jarvis model does not, however, track seedling above and belowground biomass through the first year of growth citing a lack of information on seedling parameters. This model highlighted the need to include sexual reproduction within traditional *Z. marina* production models as model output could more accurately predict loss and recovery processes (Jarvis et al. 2014).

Lastly, Salinas and Solana-Arellano (2021) developed an individual-based model to simulate rhizome length and branching in *Zostera marina*. This model is significant as it represents the first published individual-based model for eelgrass and focuses on simulating rhizome elongation in response to temperature, light, and air exposure as a means to understand how continuous growth rates connect to more discrete patterns of shoot and branching dynamics. This model used a data assimilation approach to leverage a dataset of internode and elongation rates for growth model selection to inform rhizome elongation. This was then connected to class objects in the individual-based model to describe the shoot module (phytomere), branch characteristics, and individual characteristics.

1.5 The Rules-Based Approach

Numerical models applied to marine aquatic systems are commonly divided between those taking a population approach (focusing on variations of Lotka-Volterra sets of equations) and systems ecology modeling. Even during the early days of creating numerical simulations within a computing environment, Levins (1966) argued that no model is capable of meeting all our goals in ecology. His essay brought considerable attention to the tradeoffs between attaining generality, precision, and reality in a numerical environment where it is often possible to target only one of these ambitious goals. The debate that evolved surrounding the Levins (1966) essay implicated systems ecologists, population and evolutionary biologists, and was symptomatic of the philosophical crisis underway in the field of ecology during the 1960s. Population and theoretical biologists argued for generality while systems ecologists advocated mechanistic, realistic descriptions (Odenbaugh 2005). Some of the debate over Levins' proposal has persisted as detailed by Orzack and Sober (1993), who argue against any apparent conflict of these three goals, and a response by Odenbaugh (2005) that focuses on the historical context of the original Levins essay. More recently Beni (2022) revisits Levins' framing with a call for harmony between generality and accuracy. This philosophical divide has extended from modelers to include subdivisions within the field of ecology, such as community ecology, population ecology, and evolutionary ecology that can be especially segregated, especially amongst terrestrial specialists.

The development and application of Individual Based Models (IBMs) signifies one clear attempt to provide a basis for some unification among these various subdisciplines (Huston et al. 1988). IBMs were developed as ecologists identified a need for simulation environments that considered local interactions and the behavior of individuals to bring about emergence of patterns at the ecosystem level. In some cases, this was a pragmatic approach, illuminated by field observations implicating the importance of local interactions. Foresters identified individual-based responses in trees, such as competition between different trees in a forest (i.e. JABOWA, Botkin et al. 1972), and the response of mangroves to the spatial distribution of salinity gradients (Berger and Hildenbrandt 2000). In the case of imagining a model for *Z. marina* that combines both population dynamics and mechanistically driven growth rates, using the IBM approach seems natural and practical for some of the same reasons that foresters applied the technique to trees; a desire to model local interactions between individuals and a spatially heterogeneous environment. In hindsight, this choice of modeling technique has also resulted in an added theoretical dimension to the endeavor that is possible because of well-established heuristics for applying IBMs to ecological settings (Huston et al. 1988; Uchmanski and Grimm 1996; Grimm and Railsback 2013; Railsback and Grimm 2019). While ecologists today use both "agent based model" and "individual based model", we use the individual based definitions in this monograph to signify the emphasis of the Virtual Eelgrass Meadow in simulating the eelgrass itself, with less emphasis on its impacts and behavioral impact on its ecosystem. For example, an IBM of seagrass that offers feedbacks on the sediment dynamics of its ecosystem might more properly be termed as an agent based model.

Just as ecological IBMs were struggling to define a coherent theory, the rise of complexity science resulted in a boom of publications and studies in the mid to late 1990s (Axelrod 1997; Holland 1998). The science of complex systems considers how simple, adaptive rules operating on small scales can lead to complex, emergent patterns at very large scales. This evolving field has helped ecologists using IBMs to develop what is now termed "Individual Based Ecology" (IBE: Grimm and Railsback 2013), providing clear guidelines that describe how IBMs should be used and their value to the field of ecology in general. Importantly, this IBE also differentiates between models that are true IBMs and those that are "individually-oriented". As the field has evolved, Uchmanski and Grimm (1996) first offered criteria for defining a model as individually based followed by a "conceptual design checklist" outlined by Grimm and Railsback (2013) that illuminates the various characteristics that should be considered in an IBM.

Within this checklist, further elaborated by Railsback and Grimm (2019), some processes must be modeled that are "emergent". Emergence is defined here as a pattern that can only be explained by the collective action of simple rules followed on the scale of the individual. In addition, the authors encourage the use of adaptive rules to create this emergent behavior. In this case "adaptive" rules are those that respond dynamically to internal or external environmental change with the ultimate goal of the fitness of an individual. The checklist reminds IBM designers that even a concept such as fitness can, and often should, be adaptive in an IBM due to ontogeny or migration patterns. Grimm and Railsback (2013) also emphasize that this application of natural selection theory in terms of fitness must be especially considerate of the individual's point of view. What processes might enable an individual to "predict" its personal fitness or success? Are these processes included in the model? How does an individual interact with other individuals and its environment?

Today, the computational limits to IBMs may be less critical as they were in the past. However, the computational power needed to simulate cascading and exponentially expansive processes and individuals over time and space can still be a challenge, requiring some thoughtfulness about tradeoffs in accessibility, simulation time, and whether high performance computing is warranted. In the crafting of this work, Scott Nixon often asked that this simple test be done: "Is the model faster than pulling up my lawn chair and watching the eelgrass grow? How much faster?" Indeed. There are approaches to reducing computational investments that include aggregating groups of individuals into collectives and the issue of simulating rules that would occur concurrently in the real world, but must be scheduled within the computer environment. A personal computer is unable to process actions simultaneously, so any software or programming effort should consider how tasks are ordered in a program "schedule" that determines at what point and in what order a particular calculation or updated state variable action should take place.

Initially, the potential of using IBM techniques was appealing for *Zostera marina* because of the opportunity to merge population dynamics with physiology. However, this type of model would straddle an uneasy "individual-oriented" modeling world that would not be particularly useful from either a classical population modeling or a systems based approach. Instead, additional questions must be answered to take advantage of the new outlook offered by the IBM techniques. Are we aware of any "adaptive" behavior in *Zostera marina*? What types of emergent patterns could be used to validate the rules we specified? Are there mechanisms that a plant might possess for sensing its own fitness or environment? What new perspective about eelgrass might be emergent based on exploring this approach?

Despite the early development of forest models, most plant IBMs are relatively simple and neglect one of the key aspects of IBE; adaptive behavior (see Grimm and Railsback 2013; Railsback and Grimm 2019 for review). In contrast to animal IBMs, it is certainly less intuitive to consider a plant following behavioral rules, with the exception of interactive rules that might govern how different species respond to each other. In fact, the plant IBMs typically focus on competition and have included examples for mangroves (Berger and Hildenbrandt 2000) and the well-used and widely-adapted forest model named SORTIE (Pacala and Silander 1993). In their review of plant community models, Grimm and Railsback (2013) suggest several aspects of plant ecology that are particularly suited to an IBM. These might include adaptive behavior of resource allocation and using the well-known pattern of self-thinning in monocultures as an emergent pattern that would be useful as a tool for validation. Both of these suggestions are particularly prescient for a model of eelgrass, as described below.

1.6 Clonal Plants and the Virtual Eelgrass Meadow

Despite a new interest in the life history and population characteristics of seagrasses (Marba and Duarte 2003; Olesen et al. 2004; Sintes et al. 2005; Vermaat 2009; Salinas and Solana-Arellano 2021; Orth and Heck 2023), the vast majority of the eelgrass literature does not emphasize their clonal nature (see literature review). Limnologists have long recognized that clonal plants are ideally adapted to an aquatic environment (Hutchinson 1975; Grace 1993). Among the advantages of clonal growth is the ability to reproduce asexually, a factor that enables colonization in lakes (or marine environments) where a heterogeneous aquatic environment creates a lower probability that seed dispersal will result in recruitment to an appropriate site for growth (Grace 1993).

Another benefit of the clonal plant strategy is the potential for shared resource acquisition amongst individual shoots (ramets) via partitioning of materials through connected rhizomes. Alpert and Stuefer (1997) have shown that such resource sharing can lead to a spatial division of labor similar to that predicted by economic trade theory. In such a scenario, certain ramets within a genet (genetically identical collection of connected ramets) have the capacity to take advantage of a locally plentiful resource. This may lead to morphological plasticity within an individual shoot as it responds to local conditions. Resource allocation and morphology also vary for a terrestrial non-clonal plant, but the morphological changes are often targeted at capturing scarce resources (Bloom et al. 1985), as would be the case for a shade plant that develops larger surface area leaves to intercept more sunlight. In the case of clonal plant spatial division of labor, a ramet will allocate more growth to the portion of its morphology that captures the most abundant resource (Alpert and Stuefer 1997).

These aspects of clonal growth would be considered adaptive within the context of IBE and present an avenue to include adaptive behavior. In addition, the use of the self-thinning law as an emergent behavior is well suited to *Zostera marina*. This phenomenon has been used for two other species of seagrass in a functional structural model that is one of the few seagrass models that explicitly models the clonal nature of these plants (Brun et al. 2006). The focus of this effort was to evaluate how different architectural constraints translate into morphological features of the seagrass module to describe how simple features of branching and rhizome structures interact to result in a given space-occupying feature for a species. Thus, the morphology itself becomes an emergent feature that becomes partially explanatory for the self-thinning law.

The phenomenon of density-dependent production and/or mortality in plant communities has traditionally been examined in the context of the "thinning law". Data describing the average weight of plants found at their highest densities is closely correlated both within and among species and has generally been attributed to an upper limit on individual biomass production resulting from competition for resources under crowded conditions (Yoda et al. 1963; White 1981; Duarte and Kalff 1987). Amazingly, the empirical description of the thinning law between terrestrial species is closely correlated across 10 orders of magnitude (Enquist et al. 1998) and suggests that mechanistic processes governing rates of resource acquisition follow a universal law.

The development of allometric scaling rules in plant communities was initially motivated by foresters' attempts to use easily measured components of trees (e.g. trunk diameter) to estimate tree parts that were difficult to measure (belowground biomass, branching, crown diameter). This application has also been used to estimate dry weight from leaf length and/or width in *Zostera marina* (McRoy 1970; Hamburg and Homann 1986; Solana-Arellano et al. 1998), as well as *Thalassia testudinum* (Patriquin 1973). In contrast, zoologists have used power laws between animal size and metabolic rate to advance general theories that have lead us progressively to a greater understanding of evolution and ecology (Peters 1983; Odum 1994). Theoretically derived power rules of the relationships between size and metabolism have been successfully tested against empirical data describing all scales of life, from bacteria to sequoias (West et al. 1997; Enquist et al. 1998).

Plant ecologists in the twenty-first century focused on re-examining allometric data from a new perspective, relating productivity to life-history variability, using scaling properties to explain ecosystem organization in forests (Enquist and Niklas 2001), and proposing a mechanistic explanation for correlation of metabolism and stem diameter in vascular plants based on the fractal geometry of branching networks within the context of the "metabolic theory of ecology" (MTE) (Brown et al. 2004). All of these approaches emphasize an understanding of physiological processes performed at very small scales to explain large-scale community dynamics and spatial patterns.

In contrast to terrestrial botanists, the application of scaling data available for marine plants is still in need of exploration and expansion. Exceptions to this are the papers of Marba and Duarte (1998, 2003) that examined the allometry of various seagrass species in terms of rhizome elongation, and shoot size and density to propose implications at the seagrass population level regarding clonal growth. The MTE was also directly applied to marine phytoplankton by adding measurements of marine phytoplankton to a terrestrial dataset comparing maximum population density to body size (Belgrano et al. 2002). However, the Belgrano et al. (2002) oceanic data do not span the range of sizes captured in the terrestrial dataset (Enquist et al. 1998), do not include seagrasses, and are in contrast to steeper estimates of the slope of this relationship for larger aquatic plants (Duarte and Kalff 1987). If resource acquisition in marine plants is governed by a mechanism similar to that found in terrestrial systems, numerical descriptions of these systems in simulation models might benefit from an allometric perspective. By constructing a simulation model that uses allometry as an emergent property, along with resource allocation and physiological parameters, further insight may be possible in structuring the explanation of universal scaling laws (see Harris et al. 2006).

Because the terrestrial self-thinning law can be derived using these first principles, it seems useful to document its applicability to aquatic plants as a way to provide a theoretical foundation for validation of our model. We have collected a preliminary database that covers a wider range of sizes and densities than those reported by Belgrano et al. (2002). These data are shown in Fig. 1.6, along with the terrestrial data points compiled by Enquist et al. (1998) to describe maximum reported densities of plant stands and average individual biomass of plants. The slope for the dataset including marine plants does not differ significantly from that calculated using the Enquist et al. (1998) data alone.

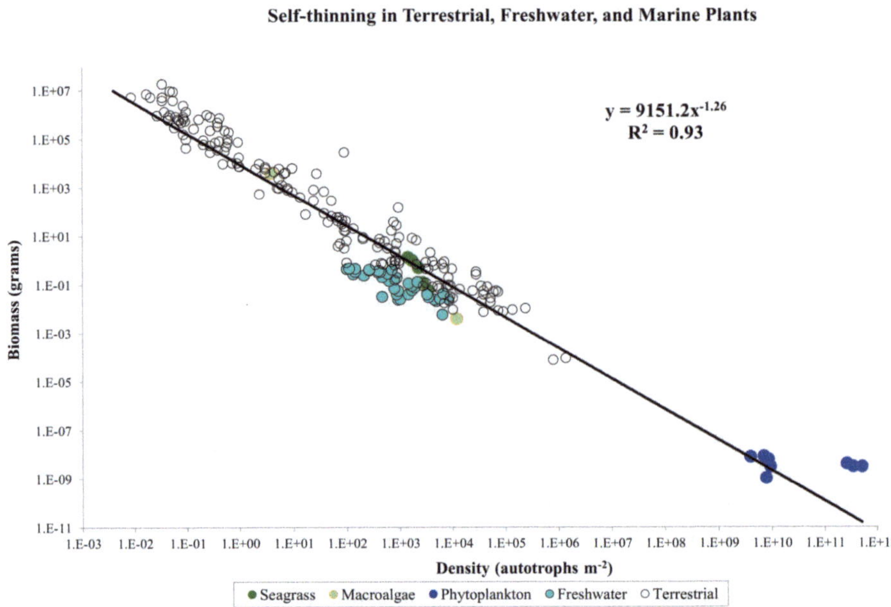

Fig. 1.6 Relationship between maximum plant density and average body mass. Data for aquatic plants compiled by author to compare with terrestrial database of Enquist et al. (1998). Units are grams dry weight

In addition to establishing that this self-thinning law applies to eelgrass in the same manner as other plants, self-thinning trajectories have been established for two life history stages that exhibited density dependent reproduction rates. Granger et al. (2000) planted seeds of *Z. marina* at various densities and reported reduced germination and growth at the highest densities. During the summer of 2000, we completed experiments in lagoon mesocosms that measured production in varying densities of eelgrass. Growth and lateral shoot production varied with shoot densities, with lower lateral shoot production and higher plastochrone intervals occurring at higher shoot densities (Fig. 1.6). The results of these experiments suggest that competition and crowding by neighbors affects overall productivity.

The Virtual Eelgrass Meadow relies on these observations to bring together a unique combination of modeling techniques. Historical formulations of eelgrass models that included mechanistic descriptions of specific growth rates based on environmental parameters are desirable processes to include in any modeling effort. However, it is equally clear that merging these growth rates with an IBM approach that uses adaptive rules of resource allocation to govern translocation of carbon will provide a valuable perspective on how eelgrass meadows respond to changes. By focusing on exploring mechanistic bases for formulating and parameterizing these processes, the Virtual Eelgrass Meadow also advances the rich history of systems-oriented modeling and advances using clonal and individual-oriented approaches reviewed in Table 1.2. The MTE basis for the self-thinning law also creates a firm emergent pattern upon which to base our modeling efforts and perform validation exercises. Because space and colonization patterns are so important to the use of an IBM approach, the output from the resource allocation rules will be used to drive parameterization of a visualization model for seagrasses that is adapted to the minimal, simple rules formulated for a clonal growth model of the seagrass *Cymodocea nodosa* (Sintes et al. 2005). The remaining chapters describe each of the sub-models and their validation.

Finally, the purpose of this extensive introduction is to also call attention to a critical first step in any modeling study. Each modeling initiative must be derived from a deep exploration for what motivates creation of a new model, a thorough review of both the challenges and questions being tackled, and an extensive literature review and evaluation of the work that has come before. To focus and accelerate our efforts to advance knowledge, it is only at that point when we can push to ideate and create new advances, combine existing approaches, and articulate clear objectives to move ahead to model development.

1.7 Suggestions for Use in Modeling or Course Design

This chapter's main lessons are in the value of a thorough literature review that is directed by a larger question or theme. Here are some candidate exercises that might be used to apply this perspective to your model or a course design using this book.

Identify the Ecological Challenge and Question
In this chapter, we apply an approach that presumes writing is its own tool for synthesizing available information regarding the decline and prospects for restoration for *Zostera marina*. Collecting critical literature and forming a narrative that points to the major themes and findings is an essential critical thinking skill. A first step is to identify a combination of literature that includes both the most well cited studies related to the model organism, as well as papers published very recently on relevant topics. In a review of these studies, appropriate guidance for students might include:

- Direction in best practices for reading scientific literature
- Exposure to good tools for developing a database of relevant literature and citation managers
- Use of a writing outline to organize thoughts and themes from the literature review
- Proper guidelines for referencing literature sources in writing

Using Published Databases to Quantify and Describe Trends in Research for Your Study Organism
In addition to a discerning and targeted literature search, the review we describe here follows the example of Duarte (1999) and can lend a more objective approach to assessing trends and gaps in knowledge. A similar exercise can be extended to

any candidate organism, or even topic (e.g. Testa et al. 2017). Replicating this approach might involve:

- An examination of a variety of search databases and their similarities and differences (Web of Science used here, but many others available)
- An exploration of the capacities of advanced searches. For this example, we could export results in.csv files, use Boolean operators to make searches include "and"/"or" operators to better narrow search conditions. This enabled the development of our own resulting database that informed the graphs and findings we describe.
- A discipline in model development around data curation; even when we are collecting literature information and not data from experiments or field measurements. An emphasis here is on basic quality control approaches, such as checking to be sure papers aren't missing from database results, insuring the captured papers do represent the study subject, and generally querying results to insure they are what the data collector believes them to be.
- Data visualization using graphs or tables from these results can also be an early exercise to be sure students can produce basic time series visualizations and continue to practice their work to derive themes and synthesize generalized findings from across a broad literature.

Make Bold Decisions for a Research Path Forward

Of course, a literature review can be helpful in any research for providing context and recognizing past work. A literature review can also be used to synthesize and draw greater insights that might accelerate advancement of the discipline. After a literature review is completed, appropriate questions to ask include:

- Where is the most agreement in the scientific literature around understanding this organism?
- Where might there be the biggest gaps in understanding or available data?
- How do these findings relate to the identified challenge or big picture question?
- And perhaps most challenging, where might the field boldly go next?

References

Adams MP, Collier CJ, Uthicke S, Ow YX, Langlois L, O'Brien KR (2017) Model fit versus biological relevance: evaluating photosynthesis-temperature models for three tropical seagrass species. Sci Rep 7(1):39930

Alpert P, Stuefer JF (1997) Division of labour in clonal plants. In: de Kroon H, van Groenendael J (eds) The ecology and physiology of clonal plants. Backhuys Publishers, Leiden

Axelrod R (1997) The complexity of cooperation: agent-based models of competition and collaboration. Princeton University Press, Princeton

Bach HL (1993) A dynamic model describing the seasonal variations in growth and the distribution of eelgrass (*Zostera marina* L.) I. Model theory. Ecol Model 65:31–50

Baird ME, Adams MP, Babcock RC, Oubelkheir K, Mongin M, Wild-Allen KA, Skerratt J, Robson BJ, Petrou K, Ralph PJ, O'Brien KR (2016) A biophysical representation of seagrass growth for application in a complex shallow-water biogeochemical model. Ecol Model 325:13–27

Behm PM, Boumans RMJ, Short FT (2003) Spatial modeling of eelgrass distribution in Great Bay, New Hampshire. In: Costanza R, Voinov A (eds) Spatially explicit landscape simulation modeling. Springer, New York

Belgrano A, Allen AP, Enquist BJ, Gillooly JF (2002) Allometric scaling of aximum population density: a common rule for marine phytoplankton and terrestrial plants. Ecol Lett 5:611–613

Beni MD (2022) Dosis sola facit venenum: reconceptualising biological realism. Biol Philos 37(6):54

Berger U, Hildenbrandt H (2000) A new approach to spatially explicit modeling of forest dynamics: spacing, ageing and neighbourhood competition of mangrove trees. Ecol Model 132:287–302

Best EPH, Buzzelli CP, Bartell SM, Wetzel RL, Boyd WA, Doyle RD, Campbell KR (2001) Modeling submersed macrophyte growth in relation to underwater light climate: modeling approaches and application potential. Hydrobiologia 444:43–70

Bintz JC, Nixon SW (2001) Responses of eelgrass Zostera marina seedlings to reduced light. Mar Ecol Prog Ser 223:133–141

Bintz JC, Nixon SW, Buckley BA, Granger SL (2003) Impacts of temperature and nutrients on coastal lagoon plant communities. Estuaries 26:765–776

Bloom AJ, Chapin FS, Mooney HA (1985) Resource limitation in plants—an economic analogy. Annu Rev Ecol Syst 16:363–392

Bocci M, Coffaro C, Bendoricchio G (1997) Modelling biomass and nutrient dynamics in eelgrass (*Zostera marina* L.):applications to the Lagoon of Venice (Italy) and Oresund (Denmark). Ecol Model 102:67–80

Boström C, Baden S, Krause-Jensen D (2003) Scandinavia and the Baltic Sea Region. In: Green EP, Short FT, Spalding MD (eds) World atlas of seagrasses: present status and future conservation. California Press, Berkeley

Botkin DB, Janak JF, Wallis JR (1972) Some ecological consequences of a computer model of forest growth. J Ecol 60:849–872

Brown JH, Gillooly JF, Allen AP, Savage VM, West GB (2004) Toward a metabolic theory of ecology. Ecology 85:1771–1789

Brun FG, Vergara JJ, Peralta G, García-Sánchez MP, Hernández I, Pérez-Lloréns JL (2006) Clonal building, simple growth rules and phylloclimate as key steps to develop functional–structural seagrass models. Mar Ecol Prog Ser 323:133–148

Burkholder JM, Glascow HB, Cooke JE (1994) Comparative effects of water column nitrate enrichment on eelgrass *Zostera marina*, shoalgrass *Haloduli wrightii*, and widgeon grass *Ruppia marina*. Mar Ecol Prog Ser 105:121–138

Buzzelli CP, Wetzel RL, Meyers MB (1999) A linked physical and biological framework to assess biogeochemical dynamics in a shallow estuarine system. Estuar Coast Shelf Sci 49:829–851

Carr J, D'Odorico P, McGlathery K, Wiberg PL (2010) Stability and bistability of seagrass ecosystems in shallow coastal lagoons: role of feedbacks with sediment resuspension and light attenuation. J Geophys Res Biogeosci 115(G3)

Carr JA, D'Odorico P, McGlathery KJ, Wiberg PL (2012) Modeling the effects of climate change on eelgrass stability and resilience: future scenarios and leading indicators of collapse. Mar Ecol Prog Ser 448:289–301

Carr JA, D'Odorico P, McGlathery KJ, Wiberg PL (2016) Spatially explicit feedbacks between seagrass meadow structure, sediment and light: habitat suitability for seagrass growth. Adv Water Resour 93:315–325

Cerco CF, Moore K (2001) System-wide submerged aquatic vegetation model for Chesapeake Bay. Estuaries 24:522–534

De Kroon H, Hutchings MJ (1995) Morphological plasticity in clonal plants: the foraging concept reconsidered. J Ecol 83:143–152

Den Hartog C (1970) The seagrasses of the world. North Holland Publishing Company, Amsterdam

Dijkstra JT, Uittenbogaard RE (2010) Modeling the interaction between flow and highly flexible aquatic vegetation. Water Resour Res 46(12)
do Amaral Camara Lima M, Bergamo TF, Ward RD, Joyce CB (2023) A review of seagrass ecosystem services: providing nature-based solutions for a changing world. Hydrobiologia 850(12):2655–2670
Duarte CM (1999) Seagrass ecology at the turn of the millennium: challenges for the new century. Aquat Bot 65:7–20
Duarte CM, Kalff J (1987) Weight-density relationships in submerged macrophytes: the importance of light and plant geometry. Oecologia 72:612–617
Duarte CM, Fourqurean JW, Krause-Jensen D, Olesen B (2006) Dynamics of seagrass stability and change. In: Seagrasses: biology, ecology and conservation. Springer, Dordrecht, pp 271–294
Duarte CM, Conley DJ, Carstensen J, Sánchez-Camacho M (2009) Return to Neverland: shifting baselines affect eutrophication restoration targets. Estuar Coasts 32(1):29–36
DuBois K, Pollard KN, Kauffman BJ, Williams SL, Stachowicz JJ (2022) Local adaptation in a marine foundation species: implications for resilience to future global change. Glob Chang Biol 28(8):2596–2610
Dunic JC, Brown CJ, Connolly RM, Turschwell MP, Côté IM (2021) Long-term declines and recovery of meadow area across the world's seagrass bioregions. Glob Chang Biol 27(17):4096–4109
Eldridge PM, Kaldy JE, Burd AB (2004) Stress response model for the tropical seagrass *Thalassia testudinum*: the interactions of light, temperature, sedimentation, and geochemistry. Estuaries 6:923–937
Enquist BJ, Niklas KJ (2001) Invariant scaling relations across tree-dominated communities. Nature 410:655–660
Enquist BJ, Brown JH, West GB (1998) Allometric scaling of plant energetics and population density. Nature 395:163–165
Ewanchuk P (1995) Population growth of eelgrass (*Zostera marina* L.): the relative importance of sexual versus asexual reproduction. Masters thesis. San Diego University, California
Fishman JR, Orth RJ (1996) Effects of predation on Zostera marina L. seed abundance. J Exp Mar Biol Ecol 198(1):11–26
Fonseca MS, Whitfield PE, Kenworthy WJ, Colby DR, Julius BE (2004) Use of two spatially explicit models to determine the effect of injury geometry on natural resource recovery. Aquat Conserv Mar Freshwat Ecosyst 14:281–298
Furman BT, Peterson BJ (2015) Sexual recruitment in Zostera marina: progress toward a predictive model. PLoS One 10(9):e0138206
Gacia E, Duarte CM (2001) Elucidating sediment retention by seagrasses: sediment deposition and resuspension in a Mediterranean (*Posidonia oceanica*) meadow. Estuar Coast Shelf Sci 52:505–514
Grace JB (1993) The adaptive significance of clonal reproduction in angiosperms: an aquatic perspective. Aquat Bot 44:159–180
Granger S, Traber MS, Nixon SW (2000) Propagation of *Zostera marina* L. from seed. In: Shepard C (ed) Seas at the millennium: an environmental evaluation. Elsevier, Oxford
Grimm V, Railsback SF (2013) Individual-based modeling and ecology. Princeton University Press, Princeton
Hamburg SP, Homann PS (1986) Utilization of growth parameters of *Zostera marina*, for productivity estimates under laboratory and *in situ* conditions. Mar Biol 93:299–303
Harris LA, Duarte CM, Nixon SW (2006) Allometric laws and prediction in estuarine and coastal ecology. Estuar Coasts 29:340–344
Harwell M, Orth R (2002) Seed bank patterns in Chesapeake Bay Eelgrass (Zostera marina L.): a bay-wide perspective. Estuaries 25(6):1196–1204
Hattich GS, Jahnke M, Enge S, Niemi N, Bernal-Gómez M, De Wit P et al (2025) Small-scale thermal habitat variability may not determine seagrass resilience to climate change. Limnol Oceanogr

Hatum PS, McMahon K, Mengersen K, Wu PPY (2022) Guidelines for model adaptation: a study of the transferability of a general seagrass ecosystem Dynamic Bayesian Networks model. Ecol Evol 12(8):e9172
Hauxwell J, Cebrian J, Valiela I (2003) Eelgrass *Zostera marina* loss in temperate estuaries: relationship to land-derived nitrogen loads and effect of light limitation imposed by algae. Mar Ecol Prog Ser 247:59–73
Hemminga MA, Duarte CM (2000) Seagrass ecology. Cambridge University Press
Hensel MJ, Patrick CJ, Orth RJ, Wilcox DJ, Dennison WC, Gurbisz C, Hannam MP, Landry JB, Moore KA, Murphy RR, Testa JM (2023) Rise of Ruppia in Chesapeake Bay: climate change–driven turnover of foundation species creates new threats and management opportunities. Proc Natl Acad Sci 120(23):e2220678120
Holland J (1998) Emergence: from chaos to order. Addison-Wesley Publishing Company, Reading
Holmer M, Nielsen SL (1997) Sediment sulfur dynamics related to biomass-density patterns in *Zostera marina* (eelgrass) beds. Mar Ecol Prog Ser 146:163–171
Huston M, DeAngelis D, Post W (1988) New computer models unify ecological theory. Bioscience 38:682–691
Hutchinson GE (1975) A treatise on limnology volume III: limnological botany. Wiley, New York
Jarvis JC, Moore KA, Kenworthy WJ (2012) Characterization and ecological implication of eelgrass life history strategies near the species' southern limit in the western North Atlantic. Mar Ecol Prog Ser 444:43–56
Jarvis JC, Moore KA, Kenworthy WJ (2014) Persistence of Zostera marina L.(eelgrass) seeds in the sediment seed bank. J Exp Mar Biol Ecol 459:126–136
Kaldy JE (2014) Effect of temperature and nutrient manipulations on eelgrass Zostera marina L. from the Pacific Northwest, USA. J Exp Mar Biol Ecol 453:108–115
Kaldy JE, Eldridge PM, Cifuentes LA, Jones WB (2006) Utilization of DOC from seagrass rhizomes by sediment bacteria:^{13}C-tracer experiments and modeling. Mar Ecol Prog Ser 317:41–55
Kendrick GA, Eckersley J, Walker DI (1999) Landscape-scale changes in seagrass distribution over time: a case study from Success Bank, Western Australia. Aquat Bot 65:293–309
Kim SH, Kim JH, Park SR, Lee KS (2014) Annual and perennial life history strategies of Zostera marina populations under different light regimes. Mar Ecol Prog Ser 509:1–13
Koch E (2001) Beyond light: physical, geological and geochemical parameters as possible submersed aquatic vegetation habitat requirements. Estuaries 24:1–17
Kopp BA, Doherty AM, Nixon SW (1995) A guide to site-selection for eelgrass restoration projects in Narragansett Bay, Rhode Island. Final report submitted to the Rhode Island Aquafund Program, Department of Environmental Management, Division of Water Resources, Providence
Krause-Jensen D, Greve TM, Nielsen K (2005) Eelgrass as a bioindicator under the European Water Framework Directive. Water Resour Manag 19(1):63–75
Kremer JN, Nixon SW (1978) A coastal marine ecosystem: simulation and analysis. Springer, New York
Kuusemäe K, von Thenen M, Lange T, Rasmussen EK, Pothoff M, Sousa AI, Flindt MR (2018) Agent Based Modelling (ABM) of eelgrass (Zostera marina) seedbank dynamics in a shallow Danish estuary. Ecol Model 371:60–75
Lai S, Teo TZE, Rullyanto A, Low J, Tun K, Todd PA, Yaakub SM (2024) An agent-based model approach to assessing the role of vegetative fragments in seagrass connectivity. Ecol Model 487:110528
Lefcheck JS, Orth RJ, Dennison WC, Wilcox DJ, Murphy RR, Keisman J et al (2018) Long-term nutrient reductions lead to the unprecedented recovery of a temperate coastal region. Proc Natl Acad Sci 115(14):3658–3662
Leopold A (1934) The arboretum and the university. Parks Recreat 18:59–60
Levins R (1966) The strategy of model building in population biology. Am Sci 54:421–431
Lotze HK, Lenihan HS, Bourque BJ, Bradbury RH, Cooke RG, Kay MC et al (2006) Depletion, degradation, and recovery potential of estuaries and coastal seas. Science 312(5781):1806–1809

Ma X, Olsen JL, Reusch TB, Procaccini G, Kudrna D, Williams M et al (2021) Improved chromosome-level genome assembly and annotation of the seagrass, Zostera marina (eelgrass). F1000Research 10:289
Marba N, Duarte CM (1998) Rhizome elongation and seagrass clonal growth. Mar Ecol Prog Ser 174:269–280
Marba N, Duarte CM (2003) Scaling of ramet size and spacing in seagrasses: implications for stand development. Aquat Bot 77:87–98
Maxwell PS, Eklöf JS, van Katwijk MM, O'Brien KR, de la Torre-Castro M, Boström C, Bouma TJ, Krause-Jensen D, Unsworth RK, van Tussenbroek BI, van der Heide T (2017) The fundamental role of ecological feedback mechanisms for the adaptive management of seagrass ecosystems—a review. Biol Rev 92(3):1521–1538
McGlathery KJ, Sundbäck K, Anderson IC (2007) Eutrophication in shallow coastal bays and lagoons: the role of plants in the coastal filter. Mar Ecol Prog Ser 348:1–18
McRoy CP (1970) Standing stocks and other features of eelgrass (*Zostera marina*) populations on the coast of Alaska. J Fish Res Board Can 27:1811–1821
McRoy CP (1974) Seagrass productivity: carbon uptake experiments in eelgrass, *Zostera marina*. Aquaculture 4:131–137
Moreno-Marín F, Brun FG, Pedersen MF (2018) Additive response to multiple environmental stressors in the seagrass Zostera marina L. Limnol Oceanogr 63(4):1528–1544
Neckles HA, Short FT, Barker S, Kopp BS (2005) Disturbance of eelgrass *Zostera marina* by commercial mussel *Mytilus edulis* harvesting in Maine: dragging impacts and habitat recovery. Mar Ecol Prog Ser 285:57–73
Nixon SW (2009) Eutrophication and the macroscope. Hydrobiologia 629(1):5–19
Nordlund L, Koch EW, Barbier EB, Creed JC (2016) Seagrass ecosystem services and their variability across genera and geographical regions. PLoS One 11(10):e0163091
Nordlund LM, Jackson EL, Nakaoka M, Samper-Villarreal J, Beca-Carretero P, Creed JC (2018) Seagrass ecosystem services—what's next? Mar Pollut Bull 134:145–151
Odenbaugh J (2005) Idealized, inaccurate but successful: a pragmatic approach to evaluating models in theoretical ecology. Biol Philos 20:231–255
Odum HT (1971) An energy circuit language for ecological and social systems, its physical basis. In: Patten B (ed) Systems analysis and simulation in ecology, vol 2. Academic, New York
Odum HT (1994) Ecological and general systems. an introduction to systems ecology,. 2nd edn. Revised edition. University Press of Colorado
Olesen B, Sand-Jensen K (1994) Patch dynamics of eelgrass *Zostera marina*. Mar Ecol Prog Ser 106:147–156
Olesen B, Marba N, Duarte CM, Savela RS, Fortes MD (2004) Recolonization dynamics in a mixed seagrass meadow: the role of clonal versus sexual processes. Estuaries 27:770
Olsen JL, Rouzé P, Verhelst B, Lin YC, Bayer T, Collen J et al (2016) The genome of the seagrass Zostera marina reveals angiosperm adaptation to the sea. Nature 530(7590):331–335
Oreska MP, McGlathery KJ, Wiberg PL, Orth RJ, Wilcox DJ (2021) Defining the Zostera marina (eelgrass) niche from long-term success of restored and naturally colonized meadows: Implications for seagrass restoration. Estuar Coasts 44(2):396–411
Orth RJ, Heck KL Jr (2023) The dynamics of seagrass ecosystems: history, past accomplishments, and future prospects. Estuar Coasts 46(7):1653–1676
Orth RJ, Moore KA (1983) Chesapeake Bay: an unprecedented decline in submerged aquatic vegetation. Science 222:51–53
Orth RJ, Harwell MC, Bailey EM, Bartholomew A, Jawad JT, Lombana AV et al (2000) A review of issues in seagrass seed dormancy and germination: implications for conservation and restoration. Mar Ecol Prog Ser 200:277–288
Orth RJ, Moore KA, Marion SR, Wilcox DJ, Parrish DB (2012) Seed addition facilitates eelgrass recovery in a coastal bay system. Mar Ecol Prog Ser 448:177–195
Orth R, Lefcheck J, McGlathery K, Aoki L, Luckenbach M, Moore K, Lusk B (2020) Restoration of seagrass habitat leads to rapid recovery of coastal ecosystem services. Sci Adv 6(41):eabc6434

Orzack SH, Sober E (1993) A critical look at Richard Levins' "The strategy of model building in population biology". Q Rev Biol 68:533–546

Pacala SW, Canham CD, Silander JAJ (1993) Forest models defined by field measurements: I. The design of a northeastern forest simulator. Canadian J For Res 23:1980–1988

Paling EI, Fonseca M, van Katwijk MM, Keulen MV (2009) Seagrass restoration. Elsevier, Coastal Wetlands, pp 687–713

Patriquin D (1973) Estimation of growth rate, production and age of the marine angiosperm *Thalassia testudinum* Konig. Caribb J Sci 13:111–121

Pedersen O, Binzer T, Borum J (2004) Sulfide intrusion in eelgrass (Zostera marina L.). Plant Cell Environ 27:595–602. https://doi.org/10.1111/j.1365-3040.2004.01173.x

Peters RH (1983) The ecological implications of body size. Cambridge University Press, Cambridge/New York

Plaisted HK, Shields EC, Novak AB, Peck CP, Schenck F, Carr J et al (2022) Influence of rising water temperature on the temperate seagrass species eelgrass (Zostera marina L.) in the Northeast USA. Front Mar Sci 9:920699

Plummer ML, Harvey CJ, Anderson LE, Guerry AD, Ruckelshaus MH (2013) The role of eelgrass in marine community interactions and ecosystem services: results from ecosystem-scale food web models. Ecosystems 16:237–251

Prum P, Harris L, Gardner J (2024) Widespread warming of Earth's estuaries. Limnol Oceanogr Lett 9(3):268–275

Railsback SF, Grimm V (2019) Agent-based and individual-based modeling: a practical introduction. Princeton University Press

Rehlmeyer K, Franken O, Van Der Heide T, Holthuijsen SJ, Meijer KJ, Olff H et al (2024) Reintroduction of self-facilitating feedbacks could advance subtidal eelgrass (Zostera marina) restoration in the Dutch Wadden Sea. Front Mar Sci 11:1253067

Rindi L, Mintrone C, Ravaglioli C, Benedetti-Cecchi L (2024) Spatial signatures of an approaching regime shift in Posidonia oceanica meadows. Mar Environ Res 198:106499

Routhier M, Grizzle R, Goddard T, Ward K (2024) Eelgrass distribution in the Great Bay Estuary and Piscataqua River for 2023 Final Project Report. PREP Reports and Publications, p 477.

Salinas H, Solana-Arellano E (2021) Importance of elongation and organogenesis on the rhizome length of Zostera marina in an individual-based simulation model. Estuar Coast Shelf Sci 261:107530

Short FT (1975) Eelgrass production in Charlestown pond: an ecological analysis and numerical simulation model. Masters thesis. University of Rhode Island, Kingston

Short FT (1980) A simulation model of the seagrass production system. In: Phillips RC, McRoy CP (eds) Handbook of seagrass biology: an ecosystem perspective. Garland STPM Press, New York

Short FT (1981) Nitrogen resource analysis and modelling of an Eelgrass (*Zostera marina* L.) Meadow in Izembek Lagoon, Alaska. Ph.D. dissertation. University of Alaska.

Short FT, Burdick DM (1996) Quantifying eelgrass habitat loss in relation to housing development and nitrogen loading in Waquoit Bay, Massachusetts. Estuaries 19:730–739

Short FT, Mathieson AC (1985) Wasting disease: eelgrass decline in the Great Bay Estuary. Estuaries 8:49

Short FT, Burdick D, Granger S, Nixon SW (1996) Long-term decline in eelgrass, *Zostera marina* L., linked to increased housing development. In: Kuo J, Walker D, Kirkman H (eds) Seagrass biology: proceedings of an international workshop. Faculty of Sciences, University of Western Australia, Perth

Short F, Carruthers T, Dennison W, Waycott M (2007) Global seagrass distribution and diversity: a bioregional model. J Exp Mar Biol Ecol 350(1–2):3–20

Silberhorn GM, Orth RJ, Moore KA (1983) Anthesis and seed production in Zostera marina L.(eelgrass) from the Chesapeake Bay. Aquat Bot 15(2):133–144

Sintes T, Marba N, Duarte CM, Kendrick GA (2005) Nonlinear processes in seagrass colonization explained by simple clonal growth rules. Oikos 108:165–175

Solana-Arellano E, Borbon-Gonzalez DJ, Echavarria-Heras H (1998) A general allometric model for blade production in *Zostera marina* L. Bull South Calif Acad Sci 97:39–49
Staehr PA, Göke C, Holbach AM, Krause-Jensen D, Timmermann K, Upadhyay S, Ørberg SB (2019) Habitat model of eelgrass in Danish coastal waters: development, validation and management perspectives. Front Mar Sci 6:175
Steele JH (1962) Environmental control of photosynthesis in the sea. Limnol Oceanogr 7:137–150
Swartzman GL, Bentley R (1977) A comparison of plankton models with emphasis on application to assessing non-radiological nuclear plant impacts on plankton in natural ecosystems. US Nuclear Regulatory Commission Technical Report UW-NRC-1.126
Testa JM, Kemp WM, Harris LA, Woodland RJ, Boynton WR (2017) Challenges and directions for the advancement of estuarine ecosystem science. Ecosystems 20(1):14–22
Touchette BW, Burkholder JM (2000) Review of nitrogen and phosphorus metabolism in seagrasses. J Exp Mar Biol Ecol 250:133–167
Touchette BW, Burkholder JM (2007) Carbon and nitrogen metabolism in the seagrass, Zostera marina L.: environmental control of enzymes involved in carbon allocation and nitrogen assimilation. J Exp Mar Biol Ecol 350(1–2):216–233
Uchmański J, Grimm V (1996) Individual-based modelling in ecology: what makes the difference? Trends Ecol Evol 11(10):437–441
Unsworth RK, Rees SC (2025) The road to seagrass restoration at scale using engineering. Ecol Eng 215:107607
Unsworth RK, Collier CJ, Waycott M, Mckenzie LJ, Cullen-Unsworth LC (2015) A framework for the resilience of seagrass ecosystems. Mar Pollut Bull 100(1):34–46
van Katwijk MM, Thorhaug A, Marbà N, Orth RJ, Duarte CM, Kendrick GA, Althuizen IH, Balestri E, Bernard G, Cambridge ML, Cunha A (2016) Global analysis of seagrass restoration: the importance of large-scale planting. J Appl Ecol 53(2):567–578
Verhagen JHG, Nienhuis NPH (1983) A simulation model of production, seasonal changes in biomass and distribution of eelgrass (*Zostera marina*) in Lake Grevelingen. Mar Ecol Prog Ser 10:187–195
Vermaat JE (2009) Linking clonal growth patterns and ecophysiology allows the prediction of meadow-scale dynamics of seagrass beds. Perspect Plant Ecol Evol Syst 11(2):137–155
Villazán B, Pedersen MF, Brun FG, Vergara JJ (2013) Elevated ammonium concentrations and low light form a dangerous synergy for eelgrass Zostera marina. Mar Ecol Prog Ser 493:141–154
Wang H, Tang X, Chen J, Shang S, Zhu M, Liang S, Zang Y (2021) Comparative studies on the response of Zostera marina leaves and roots to ammonium stress and effects on nitrogen metabolism. Aquat Toxicol 240:105965
Ward M, Beheshti K (2023) Lessons learned from over thirty years of eelgrass restoration on the US West Coast. Ecosphere 14(8):e4642
West GB, Brown JH, Enquist BJ (1997) A general model for the origin of allometric scaling laws in biology. Science 276:122–126
Wetzel RL, Neckles HA (1986) A model of *Zostera marina* L. photosynthesis and growth: simulated effects of selected physical-chemical variables and biological interactions. Aquat Bot 26:307–323
White J (1981) The allometric interpretation of the self-thinning rule. J Theor Biol 89:475–500
Yoda K, Kira T, Ogawa H, Hozumi KJ (1963) Self-thinning in overcrowded pure stands under cultivated and natural conditions. J Biol Univ Osaka Ser D 14:107–129
Zharova N, Sfriso A, Voinov A, Pavoni B (2001) A simulation model for the annual fluctuation of *Zostera marina* biomass in the Venice lagoon. Aquat Bot 70:135–150
Zimmerman RC, Smith RD, Alberte RS (1987) Is growth of eelgrass nitrogen limited? A numerical simulation of the effects of light and nitrogen on the growth dynamics of *Zostera marina*. Mar Ecol Prog Ser 41:167–176

Chapter 2
The Specific Growth Rate Submodel

2.1 Introduction

The early development of models to simulate seagrass growth and biomass borrowed heavily from the conceptual approach used for numerical models of marine phytoplankton production in the previous decade (DiToro et al. 1971; Kremer and Nixon 1978). In general, these models take dynamically simulated or forced environmental conditions such as light and temperature and use them as parameters in equations that describe mass-specific growth rates. Specific growth rate (μ) is defined here as the amount of new material (grams carbon or grams dry weight (gDW)) produced per unit time (t), per unit of existing plant material (B).

$$\mu = \frac{\Delta B}{B\Delta t} \tag{2.1}$$

This mass-specific growth rate can serve as a parameter in the classic growth equation attributed to Lotka (1922) and Volterra (1926) and depicted below in Eqs. 2.2 and 2.3 to characterize specific growth rates as a function of birth (b) minus death (d).

$$\frac{\Delta \boldsymbol{B}}{\Delta t} = B\left(b - d\right) \tag{2.2}$$

$$\mu = b - d \tag{2.3}$$

$$B_t = B_0 e^{\mu t} \tag{2.4}$$

Equation 2.4 describes the integrated form of Eq. 2.2 for growth and is represented by the amount of plant material present at time zero (B_0), combined with the base e of natural logarithms, the specific growth rate (μ), and time, to predict the amount

© Springer Nature B.V. 2026

L. A. Harris et al., *Ramet Rules*, Aquatic Ecology Series 9,
https://doi.org/10.1007/978-94-024-2365-5_2

of material present at time t (B_t). With the perspective of a systems approach rather than the population dynamics characteristic of classical Lotka-Volterra equations, Riley (1946, 1947) presented further elaborations of these equations to predict standing stock biomass for phytoplankton that included a mechanistically derived specific growth rate (as a function of environmental parameters), and additional loss terms to represent zooplankton grazing and respiration. In the tradition of these efforts to simulate plankton growth, models of seagrass systems generally use similar specific growth rate equations and substitute various other death processes, such as mechanical loss due to wave energy (Short 1980), in place of the zooplankton grazing term.

$$B_t = B_0 e^{\mu t} - \text{loss terms} \tag{2.5}$$

If the output from one of these models is tested, it is far more common to focus validation efforts on the comparison of final predicted standing stock biomass (B_t in Eq. 2.5) with field data of phytoplankton (mg Chl L^{-1}) or seagrass biomass (g C m^{-2}) than it is to test the specific growth rate output (μ). For example, Pastres et al. (2004) tested a model of eelgrass (*Zostera marina*) dynamics previously calibrated against two locally available datasets of temperature and light (Zharova et al. 2001) by running the simulation with alternative datasets of these forcing functions not used in the original model calibration. Standing stock biomass and shoot density of the modeled eelgrass were then compared with field data measured under conditions similar to the simulated forcing functions. Such an exercise examines the generality of the calibrated parameters by evaluating performance in the context of environmental conditions not used in the original model development. Other validation efforts are typically simpler and focus on plotting field data of biomass against that predicted by the original model (e.g. Short 1980; Cerco and Moore 2001) in an effort to test precision of the simulated results.

However, there are limitations and cautions to consider in these common validation strategies of testing only the model output of biomass/standing stock against field measurements. Brush et al. (2002) completed a rigorous examination of phytoplankton production rates predicted by the Eppley Curve relationship with temperature (Eppley 1972), that is often used to derive specific growth rates. This alternative test of production ***rates***, rather than modeled ***standing stock*** output, highlighted several flaws in the specific growth rate parameters and formulation. It appears that problems with specific growth rate calculations can be masked by the loss terms, which are often themselves calibrated to fit a local dataset, as is the case for several eelgrass models (e.g. Bach 1993; Cerco and Moore 2001). Indeed, an analysis performed with at least one of these eelgrass models has revealed particularly sensitive respiration loss terms (Bocci et al. 1997). Both Short (1981) and Wetzel and Neckles (1986) have acknowledged that mortality, respiration, and wind loss terms retain great uncertainties. If we have any ambition to ensure that the numerical descriptions in these models approximate a true mechanism driving plant growth, it is important that we test our models at various levels of prediction and output.

Growth of an individual eelgrass shoot within the virtual eelgrass meadow (VEM) begins with a specific growth rate sub-model that uses simulated environmental conditions to derive a mechanistic, physiological description of ramet growth rates. The VEM then integrates this traditional, specific growth rate model with a new, individual-based approach that specifies rules that direct new growth to various morphological features of the ramet, as well as asexual reproduction. This chapter describes efforts to ensure that the specific growth rate formulation techniques developed in the past are amenable (with some modification) to providing the growth rate values that drive the individual based model. Borrowing again from the strategies forged by phytoplankton models and the example set by Brush et al. (2002), this chapter re-examines specific growth rate models previously designed for eelgrass, tests predicted rates against field measurements of eelgrass growth rates, and proposes some changes and reflections on past strategies. We note here that our use of μ_{max} overlaps with use elsewhere in the literature of G_{max}, with both representing a weight-specific growth rate in simplified units of d^{-1} that can be dimensionally expanded to gDW gDW^{-1} d^{-1}.

2.2 Specific Growth Models and the Legacy of μ_{max}

The first step in many formulations of specific growth includes specifying a maximum specific growth rate. For phytoplankton the "Eppley curve" formulation predicts maximum production as μ_{max} (or photosynthesis, P_{max}) as a function of temperature under optimal, 24-h illumination and abundant nutrients (Eppley 1972). In contrast, seagrass models have most often used the maximum published production/growth rate available from a literature search or unpublished collections of data. These values have been measured using a variety of methods such as oxygen evolution, ^{14}C uptake experiments, or field and laboratory growth incubations carried out under a wide range of environmental conditions. The Wetzel and Neckles (1986) model is the only eelgrass model reviewed here that follows a temperature-linked "Eppley curve" equation to set μ_{max} in a manner similar to many of the traditional phytoplankton models. A study completed by Wetzel and Penhale (1983), and used for parameter estimation by Wetzel and Neckles (1986), showed a poor correlation between temperature and P_{MAX} values calculated for photosynthesis-irradiance curves; the use of a temperature-set maximum is thus surprising in this 1986 model.

Regardless of whether this growth rate is linked to temperature, or simply taken as a fixed value from the literature, it may then be reduced by multiplication with various factors scaled between 1 and 0 that represent fractions of the maximum potential by which primary production is limited in respect to the light, nutrient, or other environmental parameter that the factor represents.

$$\mu = \mu_{max} \times f(I) \times f(NU) \times f(S) \quad (2.6)$$

In the example equation above, μ_{max} is then multiplied by light (*f*(*I*)), nutrient (*f*(*NU*)), and sulfide toxicity (*f*(*S*)) limitation factors. For phytoplankton, the equation associated with *f*(*NU*)) might approximate a Michaelis and Menten (1913) hyperbolic relationship while *f*(*I*) would classically follow the photosynthesis-light curve response described by Steele (1962). This phytoplankton example is the approach that Kremer and Nixon (1978) applied to Narragansett Bay and represents an early effort to synthesize the multiplicative effects of the three major environmental parameters considered especially crucial to phytoplankton growth rates.

Specific growth models for *Zostera marina* have followed this example, beginning with the work of Short (1980) and reported for all but two of the papers described in Table 1.2. The bed expansion model of Neckles et al. (2005) does not simulate shoot growth, so no μ_{max} is reported. Cerco and Moore (2001) applied Liebig's law of the minimum to select the one limitation factor (at any given time step) representative of the most limiting environmental condition, rather than multiplying μ_{max} by all possible limitation factors.

In addition to a historical legacy, adapting the phytoplankton formulation to seagrass models remains a valuable means of adding mechanistic, dynamic features to a time-varying model. As new knowledge is gained regarding the effects of various environmental conditions such as light, temperature, nutrients, or sediment conditions, new limitation factors may be added or existing functions altered.

However, there are some intrinsic disadvantages to using such a specific growth rate model. The addition of new limitation factors can only serve to cause growth rates to decrease. The predictions are also very sensitive to the selection of the value for μ_{max}, a vulnerability also exposed by Behrenfeld and Falkowski (1997) for phytoplankton models. No analogous "Eppley curve" is available for eelgrass, so μ_{max} is typically selected from experiments that measure production rates at what is considered an optimum temperature and light environment, and temperature is then added as an additional limitation term.

Perhaps most revealing in a review of this μ_{max} approach as applied to eelgrass has been selection of the maximum specific growth value itself. Phytoplankton μ_{max} or P_{max} rates are based on photoperiods of 24 h, so some adjustment for photoperiod must be made within the specific growth rate calculation. This has most frequently been accomplished by including a limitation factor that represents the light fraction of a day, assuming a linear relationship between photoperiod and growth. Unfortunately, only four of the ten models reviewed in Table 1.2 specified the photoperiod represented by their chosen μ_{max} values (Short 1980, 1981; Verhagen and Nienhuis 1983; Wetzel and Neckles 1986). Of these four models, only Short (1980, 1981) included an explicit term to reduce μ_{max} to the photoperiod appropriate to the simulation time-step. Wetzel and Neckles (1986) used hourly, rather than daily timesteps, but no description is given for simulation of photoperiod so it is unclear whether photoperiod varied in their simulated annual cycle.

Both Bocci et al. (1997) and Zharova et al. (2001) relied on previously used μ_{max} values from older models but do not appear to have taken into account the relevant photoperiod. For example, the Verhagen and Nienhuis (1983) μ_{MAX} estimate is based on ^{14}C measurements made in the laboratory under a constant 9:15 Light:Dark cycle and was used along with other published rates to estimate a value for the Bocci et al. (1997) and Zharova et al. (2001) models. However, neither Bocci et al. (1997) nor Zharova et al. (2001) acknowledge or appear to adjust for this lower photoperiod. Bach (1993) and Zimmerman et al. (1987) calculated their own μ_{max} values based on direct measurement or calibration, yet neither study included details on the assumed photoperiod for the specified μ_{max}. Short (1980) defined a μ_{MAX} photoperiod of 12 h while also reporting the highest maximum specific growth rate (0.201 d^{-1}). Given the range of values for μ_{max} reported in Table 1.2, and the history of using values with photoperiods within a natural range, it is unlikely that the unspecified μ_{MAX} day lengths follow the example of the phytoplankton 24-h illuminated μ_{MAX} values. Peer-reviewed journal articles are limited due to space constraints, but the generosity of modern digital platforms around supplemental materials means we have an opportunity to rectify this with thorough documentation or shared code so that onward progress can more easily grapple with these important details.

After carefully reviewing the publications upon which many of the eelgrass models based their μ_{max} value, it is also clear that certain methods used to determine eelgrass production may not be appropriate for a vascular plant that is clonal in nature. For example, oxygen evolution measurements performed by Evans et al. (1986), and used by Wetzel and Neckles (1986), involved only pieces of eelgrass leaves separated from rhizomes and roots. The photosynthesis versus irradiance curves that depend on measuring oxygen evolution may be more appropriate for unicellular phytoplankton or non-vascular macroalgae that do not possess lacunar gas spaces. The early μ_{MAX} estimates that used growth rates often measured new leaf growth in terms of surface area rather than weight, neglecting below ground production (e.g. Short 1981).

Luckily, none of these issues represent insurmountable problems for using a similar μ_{MAX} formulation for the Virtual Eelgrass Meadow (VEM), provided appropriate photoperiod factors and growth units are used. However, the clonal emphasis of the VEM exposes one significant flaw in the transfer of this phytoplankton modeling technique to eelgrass. How do we define and measure growth of a single ramet for a model that will translocate some of this growth to neighbors, new shoots, and variable belowground production? Does the current combination of rhizome and leaf tagging growth measurement techniques provide an appropriate estimate of growth for a ramet that is connected to, and shares resources with, its neighbors?

Unfortunately, the answer to this last question is most certainly "no" as can be revealed by a simple examination of commonly used growth tagging methods. Beginning in 2000, all experiments completed at the University of Rhode Island's Graduate School of Oceanography Lagoon Mesocosm Facility measured the production rates of *Zostera* rhizomes, leaves, and lateral shoots using a combination of rhizome tagging techniques modified from Bulthuis and Woelkerling (1983) and

Dennison (1987), and leaf piercing techniques described in Kentula and McIntire (1986) and Dennison (1990). Initial tagging involves placing a 3-inch colored cable tie around the shoot rhizome just below the first root node. The plant is then pierced with a hollow syringe needle below the youngest sheath scar. This creates pierced holes in all leaves growing within the sheath and serves as a marker for new growth. In addition, the second and third youngest leaves are stapled. Upon retrieval, the presence of staples on tagged plants ensures that no new leaf material was lost due to sloughing. Morphological features are measured, and new growth material is then dried to calculate production of dry weight for a given shoot. Figure 2.1 provides an illustration of this technique.

Provided that no material produced in the leaves is translocated past the cable-tie tag on the rhizome, or shuttled into the production of a new daughter lateral shoot, this technique will measure net production of a given ramet. However, if a new shoot is produced, or translocation of materials moves beyond the rhizome tag, a μ_{MAX} estimated from these types of measurements will underestimate growth for the purposes of the VEM. It is also possible that materials translocated to a tagged shoot from other ramets within a given genet will increase the potential growth of the tagged shoot. The fundamental integration of *Zostera marina* ramets as clonal plants thus presents a conundrum for assigning an appropriate maximum growth rate using current tagging methods.

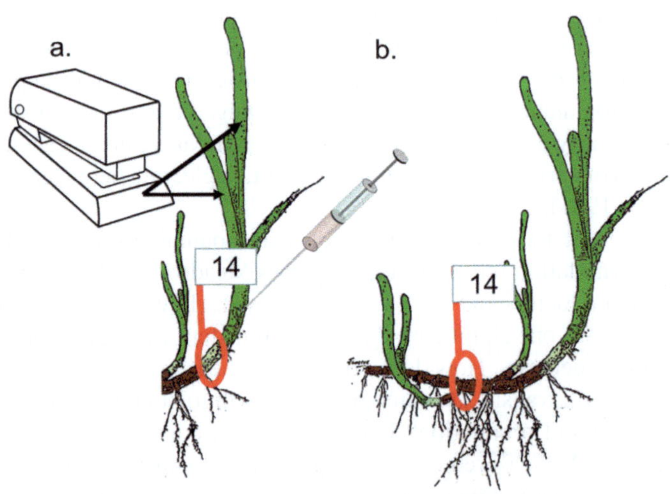

Fig. 2.1 Illustration of combined leaf marking and rhizome tagging technique. (**a**) Eelgrass ramets are tagged with a plastic cable tie, identifying number below first internode. The second and third leaves are stapled and a syringe is used to pierce all leaves just below sheath mark. (**b**) After periods of 3–5 weeks, the plants are collected and new growth is measured through cutting material using the scars and drying to constant weight. (Picture adapted from Thayer et al. (1984) with permission)

2.3 Assigning μ_{max} for the Virtual Eelgrass Meadow

As we look ahead to the goal of creating a VEM that considers eelgrass ontogeny and morphology, ecophysiology—the manner in which an individual functions in its environment—is a valuable framework for approaching growth rate formulation. Generally, plant ecophysiology describes the relationships of the essential resources of light, water, temperature, and nutrients in the context of varied climate conditions. This field of study dates far back to the work of Theophrastus, an ancient Greek native c. 300 BC, who took extensive notes of how seed nutrition, germination, and plant growth are affected by the growing environment. Having spent considerable time critiquing the specific growth rate formulations of past eelgrass models, we humbly find ourselves arriving at the same body of literature and resources upon which to estimate a μ_{max} for the VEM, and the same essential approach of plant ecophysiology championed by Theophrastus! By deciding to apply the multiplicative addition of limitation factors as in previous models, this selection must also appreciate the prospect of adding new terms for nutrient and sediment sulfide limitation, which will ultimately act to further decrease growth rates as described previously. Let us proceed with this work with our eyes open, considering that this model-awareness might serve to create added rigor and provide opportunities for clearly outlining both detail and the necessary assumptions and simplifications that are a part of any numerical model.

As a set of goals grounded in this mindset; the μ_{max} estimate must be explicit in terms of photoperiod, as rigorous as possible in terms of measurement techniques, while also including an estimate of unmeasured translocation and its effect on ramet growth. There must also be a holistic appreciation for the overall purpose of the VEM and the mechanisms and processes that this model is designed to highlight; primarily the inherently clonal and spatial nature of eelgrass meadows. This includes considering the role of ontogeny in plant growth, which ultimately translates to providing two growth rate parameterizations that separate adult ramets from seedlings.

2.3.1 Adult Eelgrass Specific Growth Rate Formulation

Unfortunately, no perfect study exists that executes the type of experiment necessary for absolute confidence in the selection of this parameter. Even in an ideal experiment where connected ramets might be incubated under optimum temperature, light, and nutrient conditions, with measurements of both individual and between ramet growth and translocation, it is likely that estimates would be susceptible to the same uncertainty reported for cultured phytoplankton experiments carried out in optimized settings (Behrenfeld and Falkowski 1997; Brush et al. 2002). Even as controlled experiments are carried out under optimal conditions, laboratories and mesocosms are necessarily artificial and include inherent biases that may affect growth rates (Oviatt 1994).

Fortunately, there is one experiment published which approaches the conditions most amenable to parameter estimation for μ_{max} in the VEM. Olesen and Sand-Jensen (1993) performed a series of laboratory experiments to examine minimum light requirements for eelgrass growth. Whole ramets (up to five internodes) were collected and planted in pots in the laboratory with the addition of slow-release fertilizers and sediments. These plants were grown under 16:8 h Light:Dark cycles at a range of light intensities (0–300 μmol m^{-2} s^{-1}) and temperatures (7, 15, and 21 °C). Specific growth rates were calculated at the end of the experiments as both dry weight and ash-free organic dry weight, reported as milligram dry weight gram dry weight^{-1} d^{-1} (mgDW gDW^{-1} d^{-1}). Growth measurements included leaf, root and rhizome production, and Olesen and Sand-Jensen (1993) report a strong correlation between specific growth rates and temperature. This is in contrast to the difficulties encountered by Wetzel and Penhale (1983) in correlating ^{14}C determined P_{max} values with temperature. The apparent discrepancy between the two studies may be explained by the fact that specific growth rates effectively integrate photosynthesis and respiration. Marsh et al. (1986) found that respiration in eelgrass was more sensitive to temperature than photosynthetic rates, a response that would presumably impact the net growth of a plant. In addition, Olesen and Sand-Jensen (1993) note that many processes implicated in plant growth involve temperature sensitive enzymes that could decrease growth rates at low temperatures regardless of the pace of photosynthesis or respiration. It should be noted that the temperature range for the Olesen and Sand-Jensen (1993) experiment did not include the temperature previously determined to elevate respiration rates higher than photosynthesis (~25 °C; Zimmerman et al. 1989), or the temperature threshold of 28.6 °C computed by Berger and Berg (2024).

Olesen and Sand-Jensen (1993) applied the following model after Baly (1935) to estimate specific growth rates using the growth response data measured at various light levels for each of the temperature treatments. This approach adapts the rectangular hyperbola model typically used to model photosynthetic rates from Photosynthesis-Irradiance curves with similar parameters from their Growth-Irradiance curves.

$$\mu = \frac{\mu_{MAX}\alpha I}{\mu_{MAX} + \alpha I} + loss_0 \tag{2.7}$$

Where μ_{MAX} is the maximum specific growth rate at light saturation, α is the slope of the growth versus irradiance curve at low light levels and represents the efficiency of light use, and I is photon flux density. The parameter $loss_0$ is negative and represents the rate of biomass loss in the dark. As demonstrated in Fig. 2.2, all parameters measured from this model relationship in the Olesen and Sand-Jensen (1993) experiments can be correlated with temperature to create predictive, temperature

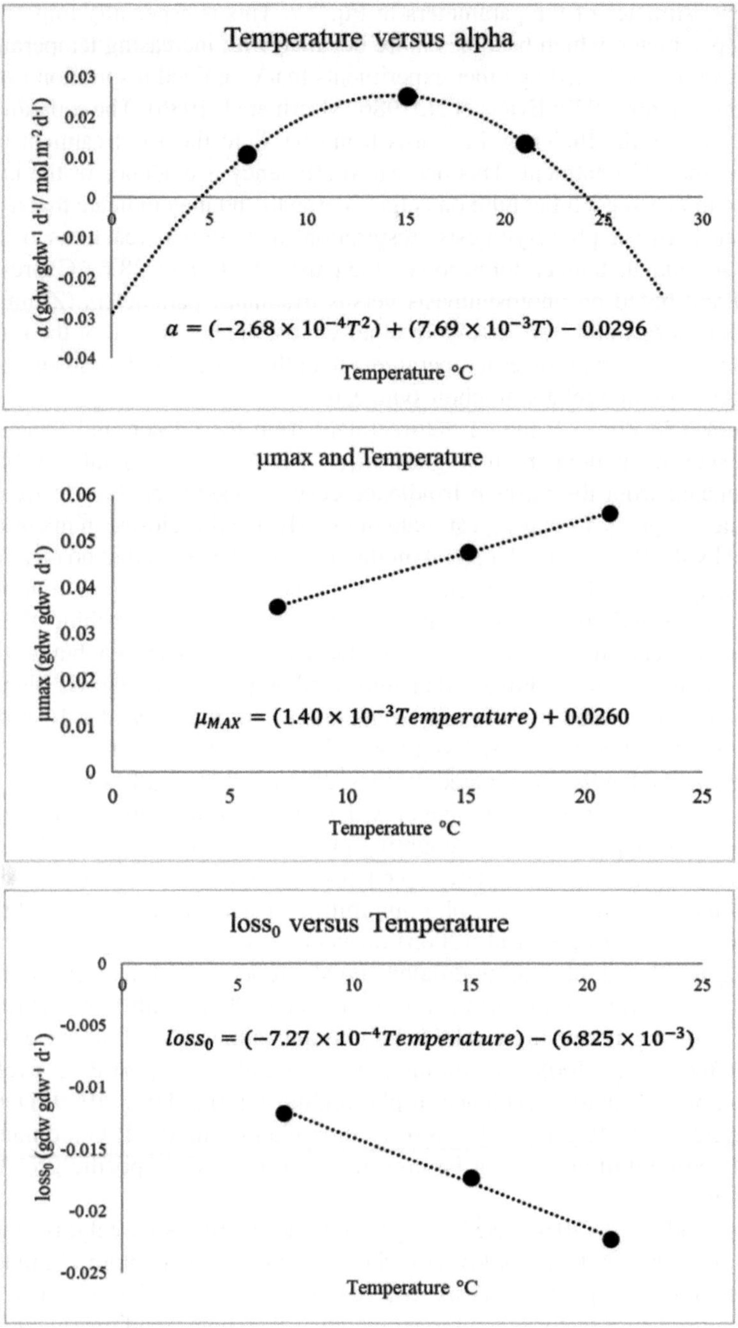

Fig. 2.2 Relationships between parameters of growth versus irradiance curves with temperature using data collected by Olesen and Sand-Jensen (1993)

dependent estimates of the parameters in Eq. 2.7. This is especially important for the $loss_0$ parameter, which becomes more negative with increasing temperature, as has been well established by other experiments that examined respiration rates and temperature (Drew 1979; Evans et al. 1986; Marsh et al. 1986). The α parameter, a measure of growth efficiency, increases from the 7° to the 15° treatment only to decline in the 21° treatment. This decreased efficiency is evidence of the negative impact of increasing temperature on eelgrass growth and may indicate that a carbon imbalance between photosynthesis, respiration, and growth reactions occurs in *Zostera marina* at temperatures lower than the 25 °C and 28.6 °C previously reported and based on photosynthesis versus irradiance parameters (Zimmerman et al. 1989; Berger and Berg 2024). In other words, the net growth of the ramets is likely to be impacted at lower temperatures than those identified as absolute limits for oxygen evolution related to photosynthesis.

As shown in Fig. 2.2, the 21 °C treatment from the Olesen and Sand-Jensen (1993) experiments predicts the highest μ_{MAX}. The highest μ_{MAX} value, 0.056 d^{-1}, was estimated from the Growth-Irradiance curves created for the 21° treatment. This value is a proxy for a μ_{MAX} estimate in the VEM and is closest in magnitude to that used by the Zharova et al. (2001) model. It should be noted that no clear photoinhibition appears to have occurred, as is often the case for phytoplankton production. Rhode Island summer maximum irradiance intensities reaching the water surface may exceed the light levels used by Olesen and Sand-Jensen, but with water column attenuation it is unlikely that light reaching subtidal eelgrass plants will surpass the range tested in this study (maximum light intensity of a 16-h day for Olesen and Sand-Jensen (1993) 300 $\mu mol\ m^{-2}\ s^{-1} = 17.28\ E\ m^{-2}\ d^{-1}$).

Experiments that have evaluated more traditional photosynthesis versus irradiance curves of *Z. marina* (rather than growth rates versus irradiance) have reported evidence both supporting and discounting photoinhibition at high irradiance levels. McRoy (1974) used ^{14}C determined photosynthetic rates under a range of light intensities to demonstrate photoinhibition at irradiance values higher than 580 $\mu mol\ m^{-2}\ s^{-1}$. Boese et al. (2005) measured relative photosynthetic rates *in situ* using a pulse amplitude modulated (PAM) fluorometer for eelgrass growing in the Pacific Northwest in various intertidal zones. Photoinhibition was reported in plants growing at low intertidal tide heights at irradiance levels above 200 $\mu mol\ m^{-2}\ s^{-1}$ (Boese et al. 2005). In contrast, many studies that report P vs. I relationships do not demonstrate evidence of photoinhibition (i.e. Drew 1979; Dennison and Alberte 1985; Marsh et al. 1986; Zimmerman et al. 1994; Goodman et al. 1995). Photoinhibition will not be considered in the VEM specific growth rate sub-model.

Berger and Berg (2024) used ecosystem-scale measures of eelgrass meadow oxygen combined with the eddy covariance technique to explore a model that included computing photosynthesis as a function of light, which was then multiplied by a limitation factor related to temperature thresholds, and finally added to a calculated respiration rate to simulate ambient oxygen concentrations. Their approach was especially interesting because the intent of the model was to use the dataset to compute the temperature limitation and identify whole eelgrass meadow thermal tolerances. This is essentially a diagnostic model focused on identification of the model parameter value. An important assumption was that thermal impacts only occurred at high temperatures. Model fitting resulted in the identification of an average thermal threshold of 28.6 °C. This is useful for our understanding of thermal constraints around net primary production using oxygen indicators, but without a connection to growth of the ramets in the studied meadow we return to studies using growth as a predicted variable.

For the purposes of the VEM, the growth versus irradiance model described by Olesen and Sand-Jensen (1993) and shown in Eq. 2.7 will be used to set a specific growth rate based on simulated daily irradiance values. The units reported by Olesen and Sand-Jensen (1993) were converted to standard units for the Virtual Eelgrass Meadow; specific growth parameters as gDW gDW^{-1} d^{-1}, and light in units of E m^{-2} d^{-1}. Because ash-free dry weights are not as commonly available as dry weights, parameters for Eq. 2.7 were converted to dry weights based on the proportion of ash-free dry weight to the dry weight reported in Olesen and Sand-Jensen (1993) of 75%, a value similar to the 73–77% range measured at the University of Rhode Island Lagoon Mesocosm Facility by Bintz (2002). Olesen and Sand-Jensen (1993) reported slightly lower percentages of organic dry weight at low light intensities. This may be explained by increased respiration of organic compounds at low light intensities (Olesen and Sand-Jensen 1993). The parameters used to calculate this specific growth rate are set as a function of temperature using the following equations and displayed graphically in Fig. 2.2.

$$\mu_{MAX} = \left(1.40 \times 10^{-3}\,Temperature\right) + 0.0260 \tag{2.8}$$

$$\begin{gathered} \alpha = \left(-2.68 \times 10^{-4}\,Temperature^2\right) + \left(7.69 \times 10^{-3}\,Temperature\right) - 0.0296 \\ \text{If}\,Temperature < 7\,\text{then}\,\alpha = 1.11 \times 10^{-3} \\ \text{Elseif}\,Temperature > 21\,\text{then}\,\alpha = 0.0136 \end{gathered} \tag{2.9}$$

$$loss_0 = \left(-7.27 \times 10^{-4}\,Temperature\right) - \left(6.825 \times 10^{-3}\right) \tag{2.10}$$

By using this series of equations to parameterize Eq. 2.7, many of the ideal conditions reviewed previously are achieved. These include appropriate consideration of photoperiod (16 h) by converting both α and simulated irradiance to have light units of mol m^{-2} day^{-1}, measurements of growth that included both above and below ground production, and incubation in experimental treatments with ramets grown in sediments under adequate nutrient availability. The quadratic function defined for α is given limits that fall within the temperatures tested by Olesen and Sand-Jensen (1993) and α is initially set as a constant below 7° and above 21° using the values measured for these temperatures to constrain output to the data used to develop these equations. We also recognize this is not ideal because photosynthetic light efficiency will not decline with lower or higher temperatures than these limits and have created the option to release this restriction at higher temperatures given the findings of Zimmerman et al. (1989) and Berger and Berg (2024).

Features unique to the clonal nature of the experimental plants, such as translocation or integration between ramets, were not directly measured. Olesen and Sand-Jensen (1993) described the growth response of leaves, roots, and rhizomes in addition to total plant growth, with the various predicted parameters of Eq. 2.7 reported at the three experimental temperatures. Using these parameters, we produced a series of growth versus irradiance curves to demonstrate the difference between above and below ground specific growth rates (Fig. 2.3). Plants grown at low temperatures under shaded light conditions show some evidence of higher specific growth rates in rhizomes than in the leaves. In contrast, a comparison of the three graphs reveals increasing disparities between above and belowground specific growth rates among the three temperature treatments at moderate to high light levels,

Olesen and Sand-Jensen (1993) hypothesize that different specific growth rates between leaves and belowground rhizomes and roots represent biomass allocation that adjusts to the respiratory demands of higher temperatures and the storage needs of overwintering plants. Physiologically, this agrees well with our conceptual model of how the carbon balance between photosynthesis and respiration shifts under increasing temperatures (Marsh et al. 1986; Zimmerman et al. 1989). At high temperatures, it appears that there is simply less excess carbon available, after accounting for temperature dependent respiratory demands, to translocate carbohydrates belowground for root and rhizome growth. Because of the individual-based modeling capabilities of the VEM, this pattern will be explored and modeled explicitly using rules specified in Chap. 3, which allows the use of parameters estimated from total plant growth (Eqs. 2.8, 2.9, and 2.10) to calculate temperature and irradiance adjusted maximum specific growth rates from Eq. 2.6.

2.3.2 *Seedling Specific Growth Rate Formulation*

A seedling specific growth rate model was developed separately from the adults using a Jassby-Platt formulation (Jassby and Platt 1976) and as described in Foley (2017). This formulation was developed originally as a photosynthesis-light (PI) curve for phytoplankton, and parameterized with eelgrass seedling data by Abe et al. (2008). Given that associated seedling growth data was already parameterized to this Jassby-Platt formulation, it was more suitable to use for the seedlings than the adult formulation. The equation includes a maximum specific growth rate ($\mu Seedling_{max}$) designated from the literature, which describes the rate at which seedlings will grow under optimal conditions. The $\mu Seedling_{max}$ is then limited by a derived and normalized interactive function of light and temperature, and a sediment sulfide toxin limitation factor (Eq. 2.11).

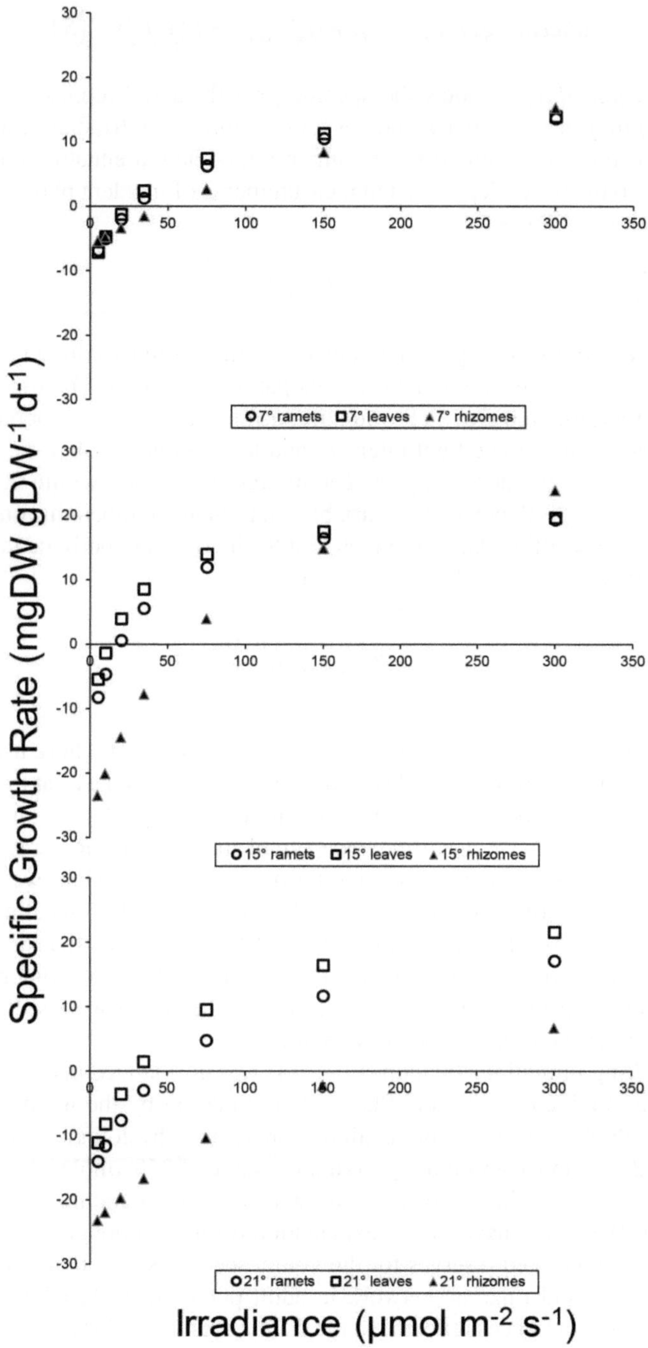

Fig. 2.3 Predicted growth versus irradiance for plants at three different temperatures (7°, 15°, and 21°) using model from Olesen and Sand-Jensen (1993)

$$\mu Seedling(I,T,S) = \mu Seedling_{max} * f(I,T) * f(S) \tag{2.11}$$

In Eq. 2.11, *μSeedling* denotes the specific growth rate, *I* represents underwater irradiance (μmol m^{-2} s^{-1}) and *T* denotes temperature (°C). Irradiance at depth was calculated using Beer-Lambert's Law where a modeled attenuation coefficient, k, was applied to the water depth (z) and measurements of incident photosynthetically active radiation (PAR) as I_o:

$$I_z = I_o * e^{-kz} \tag{2.12}$$

While sulfide toxicity is suggested as a mechanism limiting seedling growth, we do not have studies to craft this function or its parameterization. The time step in the model (and therefore the growth formulation) is one day, allowing for daily changes in photoperiod and average light intensity and temperature to alter the growth rate of seedlings each day out of the year. The limitation function within the governing equation (Eq. 2.11) is dependent on variables of light and temperature and is derived using published seedling data (Abe et al. 2008) fitted to a hyperbolic tangent function originally described by Jassby and Platt (1976).

$$P(I) = P_{\max g} * \tanh\left(\frac{I}{I_k}\right) + R \tag{2.13}$$

This is an averaged photosynthesis-irradiance curve, similar to those used to model phytoplankton production, where P(I) indicates net photosynthesis at irradiance (μL O_2 cm^{-2} h^{-1}), $P_{max\,g}$ is the maximum gross photosynthesis (μL O_2 cm^{-2} h^{-1}), I_k is light saturation (μmol m^{-2} s^{-1}), I is irradiance (μmol m^{-2} s^{-1}) and R is respiration (μL O_2 cm^{-2} h^{-1}). Temperature proxies in the form of linear regressions were derived to represent the values of I_k, R, and P_{max} to fit the Abe et al. (2008) seedling photosynthetic rate data across changing temperatures of 5–35 °C. Only the seedling photosynthetic rate data from the final day 6 of the Abe et al. (2008) experiment were used as measurements prior to this day suggested that the plants were still undergoing thermal acclimation to the temperature treatments.

The resulting limitation equation (Eq. 2.14) was normalized between 0 and 1 by dividing the modified Jassby and Platt (1976) equation by the net photosynthesis maximum, which occurred at the seedling's presumed physiological optimum temperature of 25 °C and at a saturating irradiance value of 250 μmol m^{-2} s^{-1} (Abe et al. 2008). This sets the optimum for seedlings at a higher temperature than adult plants in the VEM. We do not have a clear explanation for this, although it may be related to the carbohydrate seed reserves for the young seedlings, respiratory demand of a greater belowground rhizome network in adult plants, or population scale differences in thermal tolerances reflected in the differences in site locations for Abe et al. (2008) versus Olesen and Sand-Jensen (1993).

Following normalization, this unitless limitation function was then multiplied by the selected $\mu Seedling_{max}$ of 0.03 gDW gDW^{-1} day^{-1} to determine the specific growth rate of an individual seedling for a particular day. This normalization permits the use of photosynthesis data to formulate the light limitation function. The limitation equation uses an "if, else" statement in the model due to an optimum temperature threshold at 25 °C, which substitutes into the f(I,T) portion of the seedling specific growth rate formulation (Eq. 2.11) above. These formulations are also described in Foley (2017).

$$
\begin{gathered}
\textit{If}\, T \le 25 \textit{then} \\
\frac{(0.97T - 0.75) * \tanh\left(\dfrac{I_z}{4.59T + 3.34}\right) + (-0.949T - 1.0503)}{20.02} \\
\textit{else} \\
\frac{\left((-2.8T + 94.3) * \tanh\left(\dfrac{I_z}{4.5978T + 3.347}\right) + (-0.949T - 1.0503)\right)}{20.02}
\end{gathered}
\tag{2.14}
$$

2.3.3 *Nutrient Limitation*

As reviewed in Chap. 1, three basic hypotheses exist that may describe a documented decline of *Zostera marina* in response to anthropogenic increases in nutrient loading to coastal waters. On the one hand, blooms of nitrogen limited algae (phytoplankton, epiphytes, and/or macroalgae) may result in decreased light availability to eelgrass leaves and subsequent declining production. Elevated water column nitrogen may also result in direct toxicity to plants (Burkholder et al. 1992; Touchette and Burkholder 2000) and impact the mechanical strength of leaves (Kopp 1999). Finally, insights regarding loss of *Thalassia testudinum* in Florida Bay in response to sediment sulfide toxicity (potentially created by increased biomass and organic inputs due to cultural eutrophication) have led to the proposition that similar mechanisms may act in temperate waters to impact eelgrass meadows (Kaldy et al. 2006).

There has also been an intensive effort on the part of estuarine managers to develop empirical, practical, predictive relationships between estimates of land--based nitrogen loading to coastal embayments and eelgrass coverage. These efforts have been largely motivated by the Total Maximum Daily Load (TMDL) program requirements of the U.S. Environmental Protection Agency (USEPA). Regardless of which hypothesis, or combination of hypotheses, may account for eelgrass decline under increased nitrogen (N) inputs, it is unlikely that a universal threshold of area-based N loading exists. In the case of the secondary effects of light limitation, ongoing efforts to develop water quality models that reflect the light requirements of seagrass (Biber et al. 2005) reveal a wide spectrum of water column optical properties, often differing with geographic location and land use in area watersheds. For example, the water of Chesapeake Bay may be dominated by phytoplankton blooms and watershed sediment inputs, whereas lagoons in the northeast may have optical properties characterized by tannin organic inputs from forested watersheds and light attenuation caused by epiphytes and/or drifting macroalgae blooms.

Direct nitrogen toxicity in *Zostera marina* has been suggested as the result of intolerably high levels of intracellular ammonia created when sediment and water column ammonium concentrations were enhanced in mesocosm experiments (Touchette and Burkholder 2000). Experimental evidence has also documented internal carbon limitation under water column nitrate enrichment, perhaps as a result of a limited carbon supply from photosynthesis that cannot keep pace with unlimited N-uptake (Burkholder et al. 1992). Nitrate acquired by the leaves is quickly reduced to nitrite and ammonium, and then assimilated as amino acids, with no apparent "shut-off" capacity (Touchette and Burkholder 2000). Burkholder et al. (1992) and Touchette and Burkholder (2000) suggest that this rapid assimilation prevents toxic levels of intracellular ammonia and may also be an adaptive feature to oligotrophic waters, even as it can result in a negative carbon balance under elevated nitrate levels. The nitrate and ammonium concentrations that result in either carbon limitation or ammonia toxicity are ultimately set by N uptake rates as well as light and temperature-limited rates of photosynthesis and respiration. Therefore, the N-loading limit for *Zostera marina* would differ with local temperature ranges and light availability. Likewise, linking N-inputs to sediment sulfide levels also involves a number of complex interactions with such factors as water column depth, residence time, particle trapping rates, and location specific sediment characteristics which all affect the rate of organic inputs and bacterial activity within meadow sediments.

Nevertheless, it is worthwhile to revisit the literature that has examined growth rates of *Zostera marina* in response to nutrient enrichment in order to fully evaluate the possibility of including a nutrient limitation factor in the VEM specific growth submodel. Once again, the growth measurements used to parameterize such a limitation factor must comply with the basic approach of the VEM, at a minimum including measurements of both above and below ground production.

Unfortunately, as noted by Bintz (2002), growth studies of *Z. marina* generally measure either leaf or rhizome production, and rarely both. In fact, there is very little standardization or agreement on how production of eelgrass should be measured. Some have focused on timing the interval between leaf initiation (the plastochrone interval) via leaf marking or internode tracking (Cebrian et al. 1994; Duarte et al. 1994). Indeed, the studies published on the topic of nitrogen and eelgrass growth employ a number of measurement techniques. The majority of these studies exclusively document leaf production (Orth 1977; Burkholder et al. 1992; Williams and Rucklehaus 1993). Pedersen (1995), Short et al. (1995), and Wang et al. (2021) used leaf marking techniques to report either total new leaf growth or leaf elongation rates in response to various experiments designed to test the response of eelgrass to nutrient enrichment. Other studies with a similar experimental focus document plastochrone interval response (Murray et al. 1992; Bintz et al. 2003), while some enrichment studies have converted leaf growth into weight specific leaf growth rates (Neckles et al. 1993; Van Lent et al. 1995; Moore and Wetzel 2000).

There are a few valuable studies looking at the impacts on flowering (Van Lent et al. 1995; Jackson et al. 2017). Qin et al. (2021) provides a notable exception with an experiment focused on porewater enrichment where above and below ground specific growth rates are measured alongside reproductive metrics. While many of these experiments measure the effects of nitrogen additions on shoot density, none directly measure rates of asexual lateral shoot production or shoot mortality.

Of the sixteen studies reviewed that performed experiments to evaluate the effects of nitrogen loading on eelgrass growth, only one included measurement techniques appropriate for the VEM (Hauxwell et al. 2003). Rather than incubating eelgrass shoots in laboratory tanks or mesocosms under a gradient of nutrient additions, Hauxwell et al. (2003) estimated watershed loadings of N to seven embayments located in Waquoit Bay, Massachusetts with ranges from 5 to 400 kg N ha^{-1} $year^{-1}$. This design allows us to translate responses to a metric that is more easily available than, for example, porewater nitrogen concentrations that are unlikely to be available for many simulated locations. Eelgrass was found growing in four of these embayments and annual estimates of both above and below ground production of plants were measured using a combination of rhizome tagging and leaf marking techniques. The four embayments are unable to satisfy the statistical rigor provided by classical hypothesis testing in an experimental laboratory or mesocosm setting. However, as the published studies to date have largely neglected belowground production, the Hauxwell et al. (2003) data characterize the clonal growth of the plants in the most complete format available while including a range of N loadings. Interestingly, no statistically significant differences between the four embayments were reported for specific growth rates of leaves, rhizomes, or roots (Hauxwell et al. 2003).

Further analyses of the Waquoit Bay dataset revealed that shoot density was the only measured parameter to consistently vary (decline) with increasing watershed N loading (Hauxwell et al. 2006). The Waquoit Bay specific growth rates and N loadings (Hauxwell pers. Comm.) are plotted in Fig. 2.4 along with tagging data from Ninigret Pond (Bintz 2002). Estimates of N loading to the R. I. ponds are based on USGS groundwater inputs and a dissolved inorganic nitrogen concentration of 200 μM. Again, there appears to be no significant effect of nitrogen loading on specific growth rates for *Zostera marina*, even when including the rates measured in the highly loaded waters of Ninigret Pond. Short et al. (1995) also reported no difference between specific growth rates of eelgrass grown under ambient and nutrient enrichment conditions using experimental mesocosms. Indeed, the older eelgrass literature is more likely to report enhanced growth following nutrient additions, although these studies do not include belowground growth (Orth 1977; Roberts et al. 1987; Williams and Ruckleshaus 1993; Pederson 1995).

The growth measurements reported in the literature are at odds with the evidence we have that nutrient addition acts as an eelgrass stressor. Short et al. (1996) documented widespread decline of areal eelgrass coverage in response to increased housing density and associated septic system development. Valiela and Bowen (2002) reviewed a number of cases where increased nitrogen loading from the watershed resulted in the loss of eelgrass. In this case, it is possible that the specific

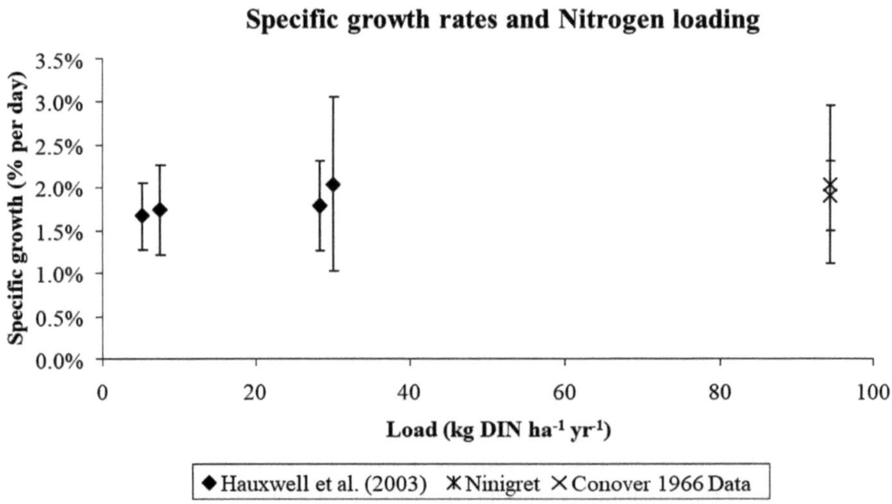

Fig. 2.4 Watershed nitrogen loading versus measured specific growth rates. Data for *Zostera marina* and collected by Hauxwell et al. (2003) and unpublished data (Traber and Granger, *personal communication*)

growth rate calculation is obscuring the overall effect of nutrient enrichment. It is possible to have comparable specific growth rates in plants experiencing vastly different absolute production of new plant material. Indeed, there is ample evidence that eelgrass ramet morphology does change in response to N loading, as was the case in the experiments of Bintz et al. (2003), where leaves increased in length and total belowground biomass declined between the start and end of a nutrient enrichment mesocosm experiment.

Qin et al. (2021) do report both absolute biomass production and specific growth rates for plants experiencing porewater nutrient enrichment. Their results indicate no statistically significant impact on specific growth rates with N enrichment, even as areal productivity was statistically increased under N enrichment. Morphological data also indicated the ramets produced longer leaves. In this study, the lack of significance is just as important to parse as the significant differences. Individual ramet sizes did not statistically change, meaning that the significance in areal productivity increases under N enrichment is largely due to an increase in shoot density and a change in individual leaf morphology to longer leaves, although unfortunately no lateral branching rates were measured. A significant increase in reproductive shoots may also explain the change in areal productivity, with flowering shoots weighing more than vegetative aboveground biomass. And finally, while Qin et al. (2021) offers tantalizing insights, translating these to understanding the overall impact of nitrogen enrichment and resulting eutrophic conditions for *Zostera marina* is limited by the focus on sediment enrichment.

For now, no direct nutrient limitation term will be included in the VEM specific growth model, instead we will focus on the impact of changing leaf morphology.

This is likely to impact shoot density given the prediction of the self-thinning rule, creating a path forward to explore nutrient impacts even if the needed consensus to drive a direct limitation term is lacking in the literature. Instead, the individual based modeling capabilities of the VEM described in the following chapter will allow us to explore the details of this morphological plasticity and will ultimately help us to understand how such a simple rule of leaf growth might affect overall ramet survival.

2.3.4 Sediment Sulfide Limitation

The VEM will not attempt to simulate the complex biogeochemistry involved in the transformation of low organic sediments to high organic, anoxic, sulfide-rich environments that may occur in response to eutrophic conditions. An entire monograph has been written on the subject (DiToro et al. 1971), although even this treatment does not consider the complications that arise in an eelgrass meadow that is capable of modifying its hydrodynamic environment (Koch 1993) or creating sticky substances on leaves for more effective particle trapping (Gacia and Duarte 2001). However, concerns that enhanced sediment sulfide levels in eutrophic estuaries could affect eelgrass negatively have been raised in several studies (Kaldy et al. 2006; Berger et al. 2024). In fact, sulfide is the most prevalent and important phytotoxin found in the eelgrass environment, produced due to the unique nature of marine bacterial communities in reducing sediments (Koch 2001).

The body of work investigating the effects of sulfide on eelgrass growth and survival is noticeably smaller than that available for the forcing functions reviewed so far. Kenworthy and Fonseca (1977) performed reciprocal transplants of *Z. marina* between sand and silt substrates, with the assumption that oxygen availability was lower (and sulfide concentrations presumably higher) in the silty sediments. While growth measurements were restricted to the leaves, the total weight of the plants was slightly higher in shoots transplanted from silty to sandy sediments (Kenworthy and Fonseca 1977). In a review by Terrados et al. (1999), the cessation of translocation from leaves to roots under anoxic conditions (Zimmerman and Alberte 1996) is invoked as a protective response of *Z. marina* to elevated sulfide levels.

Goodman (1992) and Goodman et al. (1995) completed experiments designed specifically to measure the photosynthetic response of eelgrass to sediment sulfide. Intact cores of *Z. marina* were held in outdoor mesocosms where sediment sulfide levels were manipulated to represent three different levels (low, ambient, enriched) and screens were deployed to create low and high irradiance treatments. In particular, they found that levels of P_{MAX} predicted from empirically derived photosynthesis versus irradiance curves declined with increasing sulfide levels. Using data published in Goodman's thesis (1992), the measurements of P_{MAX} versus sulfide levels are plotted in Fig. 2.5 and reveal a power relationship with sulfide concentration. The oxygen evolution measurement technique used to create the P-I curves by Goodman (1992) and Goodman et al. (1995) was previously reviewed critically

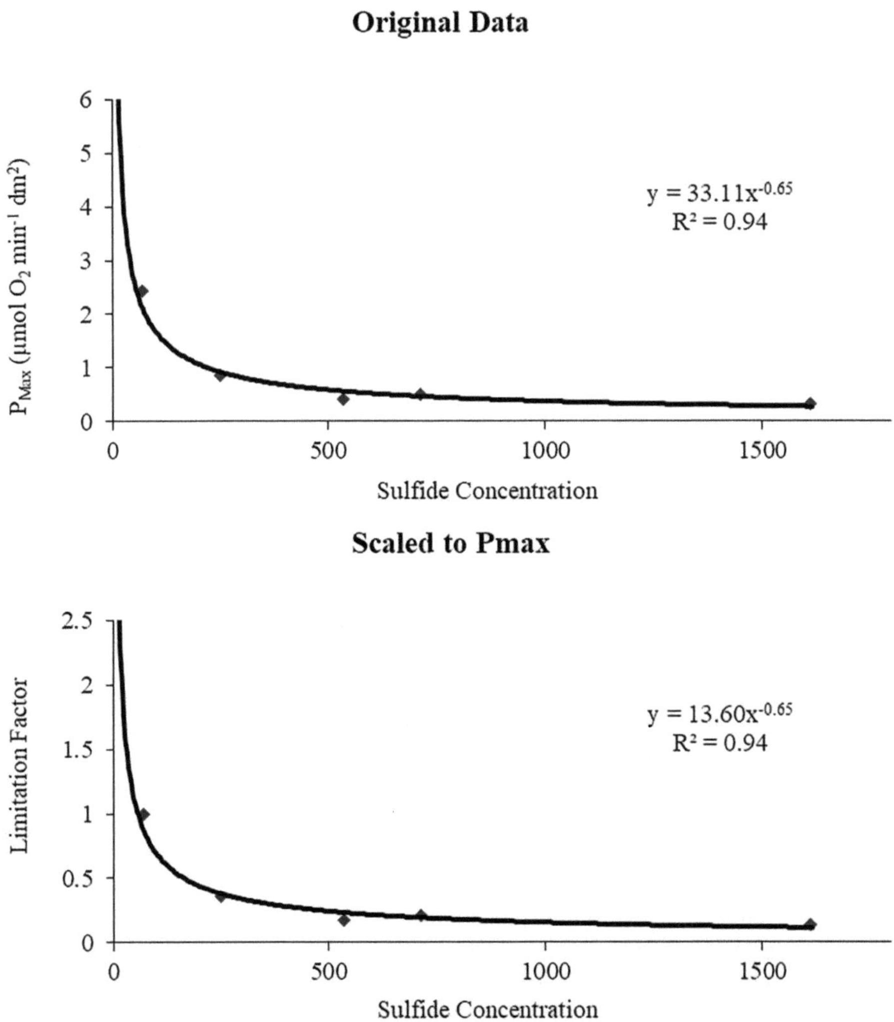

Fig. 2.5 Relationship between PMAX and sulfide concentration (Goodman 1992). Bottom graph scales relationship between 1 and 0 for limitation factor in model

when considering formulations for the μ_{MAX} value. The same problems of sampling only a small piece of leaf tissue and the issue of lacunar air spaces are implicated with these measurements. However, with no other similar experiments to draw upon, the results from Goodman (1992) are our best attempt at parameterizing a sediment sulfide limitation term. It is also true that this additional limitation term will be scaled from 1 to 0 as a dimensionless parameter by which the specific growth rate predicted from the light and temperature conditions will be multiplied. Therefore, it is the shape of the relationship between the P_{MAX} value and sulfide concentrations, as pictured in Fig. 2.5, which will ultimately influence the predicted specific growth rate in VEM simulations and as such the precision of its measurement values is not as important as its ability to capture a general response of the plants to this stressor. The value of this limitation after scaling between 1 and 0 is listed in Eq. 2.15:

$$\begin{gathered} SULFIDELIMIT = 13.6 \times sulfideconcentration^{-0.65} \\ \text{If } sulfideconcentration \text{ is less than } 55.45\,\mu M \text{ then } SULFIDELIMIT = 1 \\ \text{If } sulfideconcentration \text{ is more than } 2000\,\mu M \text{ then } SULFIDELIMIT = 0 \end{gathered} \tag{2.15}$$

The upper limit for the sulfide concentration of 2000 μM is also supported by work of Pregnall et al. (1984) and Smith et al. (1988) as the concentration when carbon stores from the roots and rhizomes are used under conditions of no net photosynthesis.

The seedling sediment sulfide (*S*) limitation displayed in Eq. 2.16 was calculated using data from field and laboratory experiments performed by Dooley et al. (2013) on eelgrass seedlings and normalized between 0 and 1.

$$If\ S \leq 1\ then\ 1\ elseif\ S \geq 2000\ then\ 0\ else\ 1.0239 * e^{(-0.002*S)} \tag{2.16}$$

In this equation, S represents porewater sediment sulfide concentrations in units of μM of hydrogen sulfide (H_2S).

2.4 Adult Specific Growth Rate Validation

In order to proceed with confidence to the description of resource allocation rules in Chap. 3, it is necessary at this stage to ensure that the specification of the adult specific growth rate submodel is tested against field data. It would also be of interest to compare this new attempt at modeling specific growth with other models of eelgrass production where parameters are available to run simulations using similar forcing functions and conditions, as other modeling exercises have done (e.g. Ehrich and Harris 2015). Here again, we are following the example of Brush et al. (2002) and their testing of modeled phytoplankton production rates against the traditionally used Eppley Curve (Eppley 1972).

The Specific Growth Model was programmed using SIMILE (Simulistics Incorporated), a declarative, visual modeling software that can integrate systems dynamics modeling within an individual-based approach. Three existing models were chosen for comparison; the first eelgrass modeling attempt of Short (1980), the Verhagen and Nienhuis (1983) quasi-population based model, and efforts of Zharova et al. (2001) to simulate the Lagoon of Venice eelgrass populations. These three models are reviewed extensively in Chap. 1. The complete list of equations used for the VEM specific growth rate model is available in Table 2.1. Details regarding

Table 2.1 Essential equations for specific growth rate model

Adult specific growth rate submodel:	
$\mu = \mu_{max} \times f(I) \times f(Nuts) \times f(S)$	Eq. 2.6
$\mu = \frac{\mu_{MAX}\alpha I}{\mu_{MAX} + \alpha I} + loss_0$	Eq. 2.7
$\mu_{MAX} = (1.40 \times 10^{-3} Temperature) + 0.0260$	Eq. 2.8
$\alpha = (-2.68 \times 10^{-4} Temperature^2) + (7.69 \times 10^{-3} Temperature) - 0.0296$ If *Temperature* < 7 then $\alpha = 1.11 \times 10^{-3}$ Elseif *Temperature* > 21 then $\alpha = 0.0136$	Eq. 2.18
$loss_0 = (-7.27 \times 10^{-4} Temperature) - (6.825 \times 10^{-3})$	Eq. 2.10
$SULFIDELIMIT = 13.6 \times sulfideconcentration^{-0.65}$ If *sulfideconcentration* is less than 55.45 μM then *SULFIDELIMIT*=1 If *sulfideconcentration* is more than 2000 μM then *SULFIDELIMIT*=0	Eq. 2.15
Seedling Specific Growth Rate Submodel:	
$\mu Seedling(I, T, S) = \mu Seedling_{max} * f(I, T) * f(S)$	Eq. 2.13
If $T \leq 25$ *then* $f(I,T)$= $\frac{\left(0.97T - 0.75\right) * \tanh\left(\frac{I_z}{4.59T + 3.34}\right) + \left(-0.949T - 1.0503\right)}{20.02}$ *else* $f(I,T)$= $\frac{\left(\left(-2.8T + 94.3\right) * \tanh\left(\frac{I_z}{4.5978T + 3.347}\right) + \left(-0.949T - 1.0503\right)\right)}{20.02}$	Eq. 2.14

μ Sets value of μ_{MAX} in relation to light and temperature environment. Units are mgdw gDW^{-1} d^{-1}
μ_{MAX} Maximum adult or seedling growth rate from Growth-Irradiance Curves. Units are mgDW gDW^{-1} d^{-1}
α Slope of Growth-Irradiance Curve. Units are mgDW mol PAR^{-1} m^{-2} d^{-1}
I Irradiance value in units of mol PAR m^{-2} day^{-1}
$loss_0$ Weight loss of growing plants in the dark. Units are mgDW gDW^{-1} d^{-1}
T All temperature terms are in degrees Celsius
S Sulfide limitation in the seedling is not formulated or parameterized

equations and parameterization for the three pre-existing models are listed in the Appendix.

To standardize comparisons, the same descriptions of the light and temperature forcing functions were used for all simulations. Because data for validation of this comparative exercise are most readily available to the authors from Rhode Island (RI), USA, forcing functions were selected to simulate RI light and temperature conditions most closely. Hourly light data are collected at the Eppley Laboratory in Newport and were integrated to produce daily values and then transformed from units of langleys using a 0.47 multiplication factor to Einsteins Photosynthetically Active Radiation (PAR) m^{-2} d^{-1} after Vollenweider (1974). Some missing values due to instrumentation problems were estimated by randomly assigning a value from a range based on the mean and standard deviation of measurements taken five days before and after the missing value date. Figure 2.6 displays the annual cycle of irradiance values used for this forcing function.

The water temperature was simulated using the equation of Short (1980) to describe Ninigret Pond as shown in Eq. 2.17 below.

$$Temperature = 14.2 - 12.8 * \cos \frac{2\pi(Dayofyear - 32)}{365} \tag{2.17}$$

To ensure that this formulation remains accurate for current temperatures recorded in Rhode Island Coastal Ponds, predicted values for a year were compared with available temperature records taken from the Salt Pond Coalition's "Pondwatchers" monitoring program between 1985 and 1993. Additional measurements taken during the summer of 2001 in both Green Hill and Ninigret Ponds were also added for comparison and are included in Fig. 2.7 While the function described by Eq. 2.17 may overestimate temperatures at some stations during the summer months, it captures the general temperature pattern and misses only 7 recorded temperatures with higher values.

For the Verhagen and Nienhuis (1983) and Zharova et al. (2001) models, these are the only two environmental parameters used as forcing functions. The Short (1980) model also includes current speed, which has been optimized in the

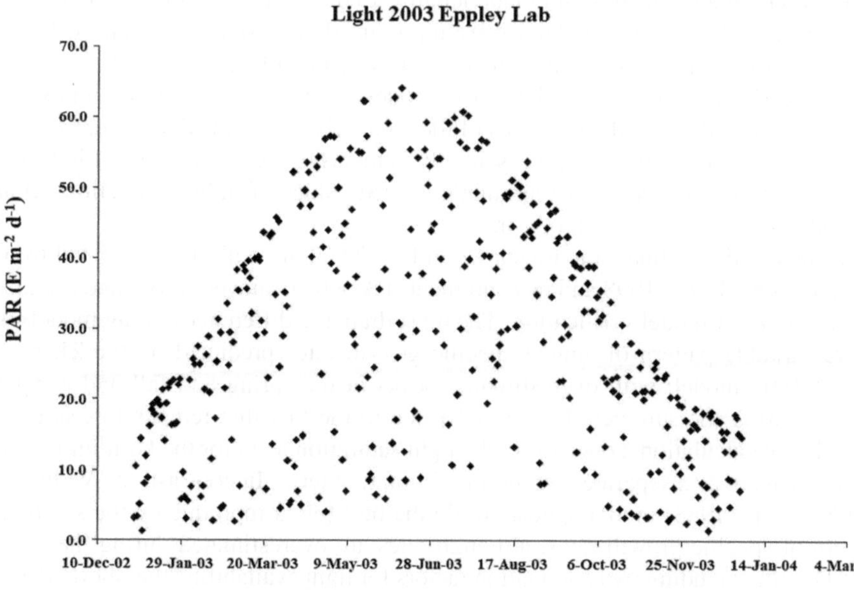

Fig. 2.6 Solar irradiance data from Newport Eppley Lab for 2003. Original data integrated to provide daily values and converted from langleys to PAR

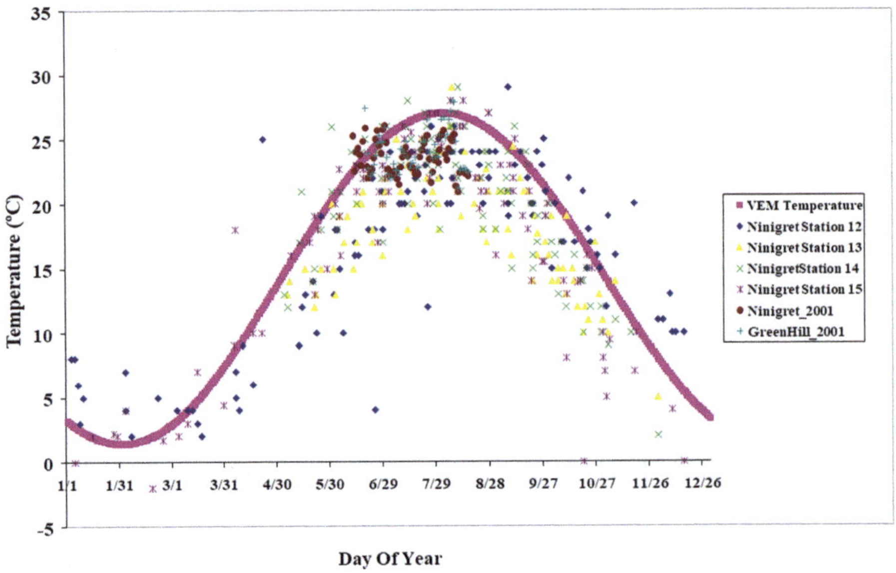

Fig. 2.7 Temperature simulated in VEM and compared with field measurements from Ninigret and Green Hill ponds. Station data courtesy of PondWatchers

simulation for the purposes of this comparison (Current Speed Limitation Factor = 1). Shoot densities and blade lengths used by Short (1980) in simulations of his Station C in Ninigret Pond were reproduced (200 shoots m^{-2} and 0.14 m, respectively) to satisfy the additional attenuation term with canopy height included in his earliest eelgrass model. All models were converted to units of mgDW $gDWt^{-1}$ d^{-1}. For the purposes of the comparison, the VEM sediment sulfide term is optimized so that we are essentially comparing the Temperature-Light formulations between models. All simulations used values of light attenuation (k) at 0.5 and a water column depth of 1 m.

Results of the comparison are shown in Fig. 2.8 along with data collected from Ninigret Pond during 1998 and measurements taken by Conover (1961) and used by Short (1980) for model verification. The most dramatic difference among models is the remarkable pattern of annual specific growth rates predicted by the Zharova et al. (2001) model, with overestimated peaks in the spring and fall and a rapid decline during the summer. This may be due to the fact that temperature is used twice in the calculations; once to set the light saturation level for the light limitation term and again as a separate temperature limitation term. In contrast, the Verhagen and Nienhuis (1983) model appears to do the best job at reproducing the seasonal pattern of specific growth rates, although rates are overestimated during the summer. Despite including two attenuation factors for light availability, the Short (1980) model still overestimates specific growth rates for the majority of the spring, summer, and fall months (Figs. 2.8 and 2.9).

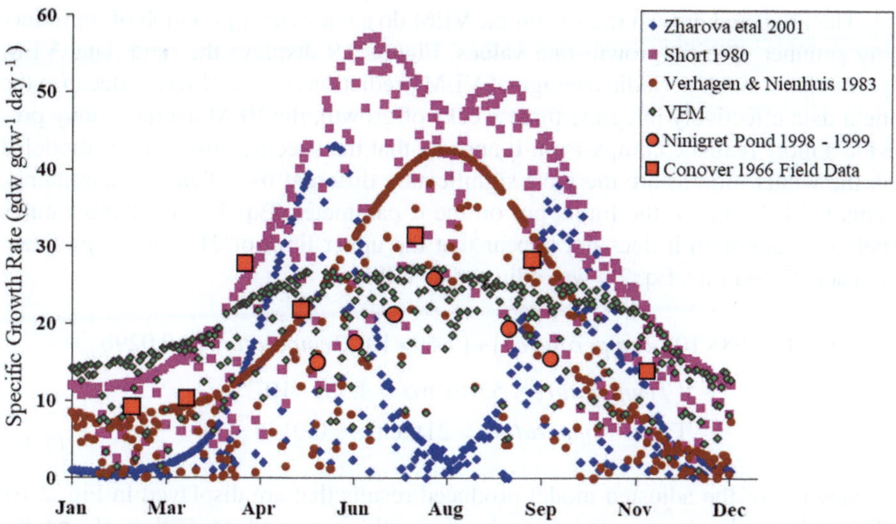

Fig. 2.8 Model comparisons of simulated specific growth rates from the VEM and previously published eelgrass models with field data collected in Ninigret Pond. Eelgrass models include those of Short (1980), Zharova et al. (2001), and Verhagen and Nienhuis (1983). Field data collected in Ninigret Pond by Conover (1961) and Bintz (2002)

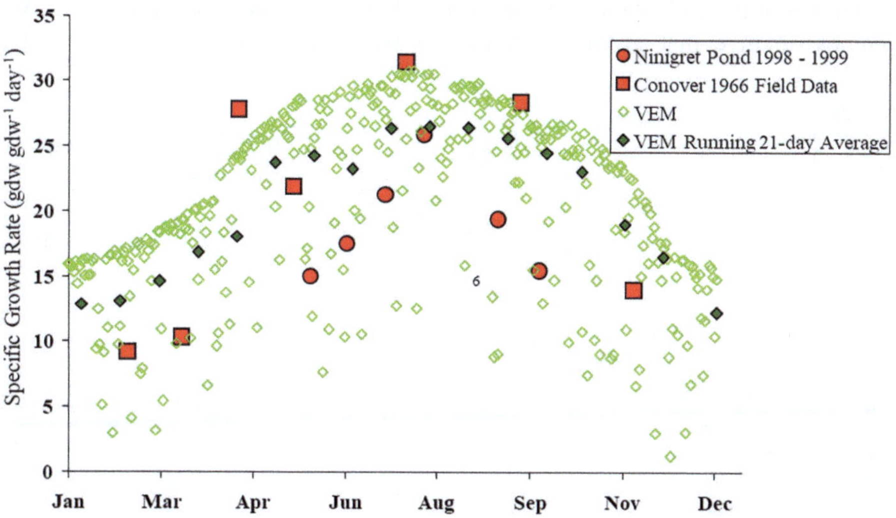

Fig. 2.9 VEM specific growth rate output compared with data collected from Ninigret Pond by Conover (1961) and Bintz (2002)

The predicted growth rates from the VEM do a reasonably good job of reproducing summer specific growth rate values. Figure 2.9 displays the field data, VEM predictions, and a periodic average of VEM predictions every 21 days. Because the field data effectively integrate three weeks of growth, the VEM averages may provide a more realistic comparison. It appears that the specific growth rates modeled in the winter months are the most significantly different from field measurements. This is likely due to the limits put on the α parameter (Eq. 2.9) for temperatures below 7° although it does not appear that the upper limit of 21° has a significant impact. To test this, Eq. 2.9 was adjusted as follows.

$$\begin{gathered}\alpha = \left(-2.68\times10^{-4}\,Temperature^{2}\right)+\left(7.69\times10^{-3}\,Temperature\right)-0.0296\\ \text{If}\,Temperature < 5.5\,\text{then}\,\alpha = 4.582\times10^{-3}\\ \text{Elseif}\,Temperature > 21\,\text{then}\,\alpha = 0.0136\end{gathered}\tag{2.18}$$

A new run of the adjusted model produced results that are displayed in Fig. 2.10. This minor adjustment appears to have greatly improved prediction of specific growth rates during the winter months and will be used for the remaining simulations performed with the VEM, replacing Eq. 2.9 with that defined by Eq. 2.18. Reliability of the model would be greatly improved by experiments that measure specific growth rates at these low temperatures in a similar fashion to the Olesen and Sand-Jensen (1993) study. However, it seems reasonable to conclude that photosynthetic efficiency under very low temperatures is reduced, therefore supporting an extension of the variable to encompass a slightly wider range of temperatures. We emphasize here that given the results of Berger and Berg (2024), it is also

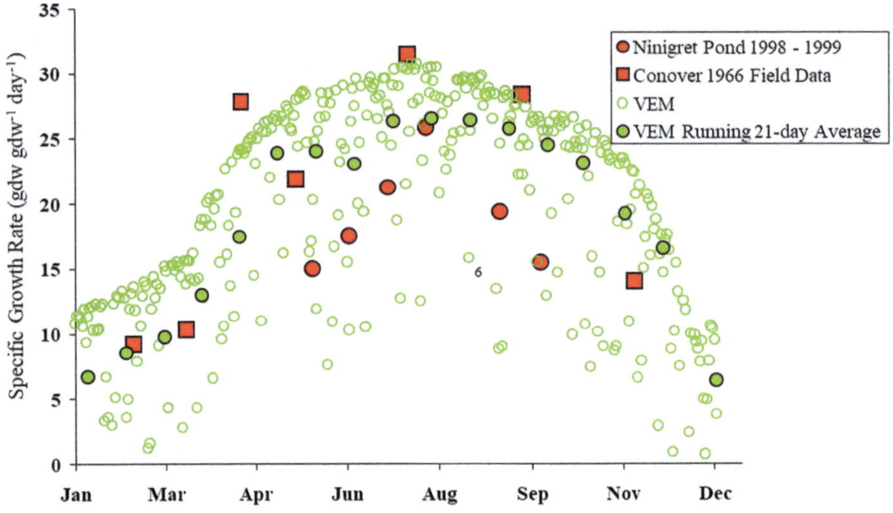

Fig. 2.10 VEM specific growth rate output after adjusting parameter to include effects of lower temperatures. Comparison with field data from Ninigret Pond collected by Conover (1961) and Bintz (2002)

reasonable to consider elimination of an upper temperature bound, and this simply involves a change setting the **Elseif** value above 21 to line one of Eq. 2.18.

The model comparison demonstrated that the VEM specific growth model approaches field values more closely than other formulations which consistently overestimated production rates for the greater part of the simulated year. The over-prediction of production rates has also been a factor in phytoplankton models as outlined by Brush et al. (2002). As reviewed in previous sections, the uncertainty and calibration techniques used to "tune" losses in numerical models using the specific growth formulation approach may mask serious errors in how productivity is modeled. The example presented here provides further evidence that numerical models benefit from being tested at multiple stages, not only the final output of biomass or standing stock values currently used in most validation exercises. In particular, we point to rigorous validation of rate processes, in particular pulling apart formulations that might combine multiple production or consumption terms to result in predicted net rates. For example, evaluating both predicted gross photosynthesis and respiration formulations, even if they are later combined in a model to produce a net primary production term. These combined formulations, if tuned, run the risk of losing the capacity of the models to be used in a diagnostic manner, as it then becomes difficult to assess which term is responsible for a resulting rate process.

2.5 Seedling Specific Growth Rate Validation

Seedling specific growth rate predictions were directly compared against growth rate and biomass data collected by Bintz (2002) from a 12 week seedling mesocosm experiment in Narragansett, Rhode Island. Model forcing functions, parameter values, and initial conditions were defined in these simulation scenarios to replicate Rhode Island conditions as provided in Bintz (2002). During the 12-week Rhode Island mesocosm validation run, the modeled average VEM seedling biomass output fit well against the observed average biomass values recorded in the Rhode Island experiment (Fig. 2.11). A small divergence in the average biomass results was seen in June, although the VEM seedling formulation caught up with the Rhode Island observed biomass results by the end of the 12 week mesocosm experiment with an average of 0.268 gDW shoot^{-1}; nearly identical to the Rhode Island biomass of 0.267 gDW shoot^{-1}. Despite a small decline in average biomass in early August due to stressful water temperatures, the average specific growth rates over the 12 week validation run in the VEM and in Rhode Island were also very similar, 0.0283 gDW gDW^{-1} d^{-1} and 0.027 gDW gDW^{-1} d^{-1}, respectively.

We also chose to test the sensitivity of two state variables, total biomass and the first day of adulthood, to a +/−5%, +/−10%, and +/−20% change in the seedling maximum specific growth rate or $\mu Seedling_{max}$ parameter. The goal for performing the analysis was to assess the degree to which the model output changed per changes in $\mu Seedling_{max}$. All of the sensitivity simulation runs began on January 1, 2007,

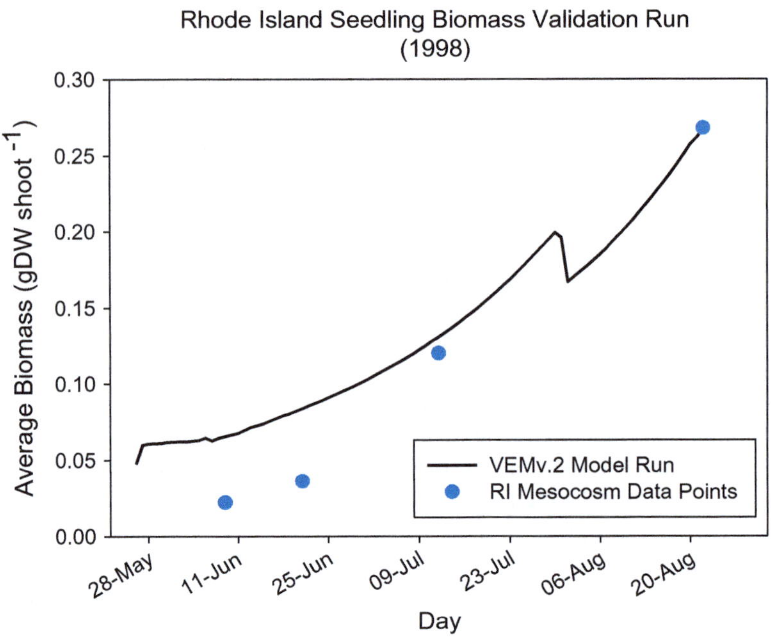

Fig. 2.11 Seedling specific growth rate formulation modeled results versus observed biomass from a Rhode Island mesocosm study (Bintz 2002)

continued for 120 days, and were forced with conditions representing Virginia's South Bay. Complete results are displayed in Table 2.2, including those that detail changes in the day a seedling transitions to adulthood, which is slightly more sensitive to changes in $\mu Seedling_{max}$ than total biomass. Results show that with a +/−20% change in $\mu Seedling_{max}$ there is a 4% change in total biomass. This was a surprising realization. In addition, there is a difference in the sensitivity of aboveground biomass versus belowground biomass to $\mu Seedling_{max}$. Belowground biomass is slightly more influenced by changes in μmax than the aboveground values. Finally, the most significant result this sensitivity analysis revealed was related to a 20% decrease in $\mu Seedling_{\mathrm{max}}$, which resulted in a 10% shift later in the year for the timing of the transition of a seedling to an adult.

2.6 Suggestions for Use in Modeling or Course Design

There are numerous, small, but impactful decisions that we make as modelers in both the work of developing formulations, but also the implementation of the simulations in our code that can impact our models. Beginning a modeling exercise with a focus on thoroughly describing and understanding a central rate process like specific growth rate guards against a tendency to take prior formulations and tune to a new organism or setting without deep consideration of mechanism.

Table 2.2 Results from seedling specific growth rate sub-model sensitivity analysis

μmax seedling (gDW gDW^{-1} d^{-1})	% change in μmax	Biomass (gDW shoot-1)	% change in total biomass (gDW shoot^{-1})	AG Biomass (gDW shoot^{-1})	% change in AG biomass (gDW shoot^{-1})	BG Biomass (gDW shoot^{-1})	% change in BG biomass (gDW shoot^{-1})	Day of year transition to adulthood	% change transition to adulthood
0.03	**0%**	0.00690	0%	0.00539	0%	0.00151	0%	147	0%
0.0315	**5%**	0.00697	1%	0.00543	1%	0.00154	2%	146	−1%
0.033	**10%**	0.00704	2%	0.00548	2%	0.00157	4%	142	−3%
0.036	**20%**	0.00718	4%	0.00555	3%	0.00163	8%	137	−7%
0.0285	**−5%**	0.00684	−1%	0.00536	−1%	0.00148	−2%	149	1%
0.027	**−10%**	0.00678	−2%	0.00531	−1%	0.00146	−3%	158	7%
0.024	**−20%**	0.00665	−4%	0.00525	−3%	0.00141	−7%	161	10%

Choose Your Rate Process

What is the rate process you have identified as a central driver for your organism? Are you choosing to focus on a direct metabolic rate such as photosynthesis or respiration? Or will your organism be better suited to simulation of growth rates as done in the VEM? Making this choice is a critical one and might depend on knowing:

- What studies are available for photosynthesis, respiration, or growth rates and do they describe plant responses to the environmental variables of interest?
- Are the units of measurement from these studies easily converted or compared to the units of interest for your model?
- Do the authors provide enough information in their empirical studies to enable parameterization or needed formulation?

Carefully Parameterize Your Driving μ_{max}, P_{max}, or R_{max}

You will have a robust literature to draw on for the parameterization of the maximum value of this process. Use this to carefully select this parameter, as it has an outsized impact on your simulation. Consider the following:

- How were the data collected that you are using for this parameter and are those empirical methods aligned with the assumptions and understanding you are hoping to replicate mathematically in your formulated model?
- Can the units of the study be used or converted easily in the model framework? Yes, this is a repetitive suggestion! Units are everything. Growth can often be measured in absolute units (gDW d^{-1}), limiting its use in parameterization of a weight specific rate.

Create Your Specific Growth Rate Formulation

This is an opportunity to combine creativity with the boundaries of a mathematical formulation to describe how environmental factors affect growth and metabolism of your organism. Many of the tasks in this work are by now second nature; what studies are available and do their units and methods work well with the modeling framework? However, there is also the capacity to be more expansive, for example asking:

- Are there formulations for limitation factors from other organisms or settings that might be useful to evaluate here? A limitation factor is scaled from 0 to 1, and in this way the shape and nature of the quantitative relationship (linear, exponential, logarithmic) may be most critical.
- How much of the rate process is driven by a given environmental factor and at what scale does a process have an impact important to model? As an example, the VEM has not chosen to simulate trace metals even though many are essential for metabolic functions in plants. The choices of what to omit are just as important as what to include.
- Do you need to separate your organism into different life stages as we have done here? This question is also dependent on the organism and challenge or research questions you have framed for your model.

Validate Your Formulation and Parameterization
Here we have used a combination of model comparisons and validation against separate empirical data to explore our confidence in the formulations alongside some sensitivity analyses. Decide on your approach as a function of available data and the intention of your validation. It is unlikely validation will yield perfection! Use the results to adjust parameterization informed by the literature or mechanistic understanding, and be prepared to modify and communicate the assumptions or boundaries within which your model works well.

References

Abe M, Yokota K, Goto M, Kurashima A, Maegawa M (2008) Relationship between distribution patterns of shoots and light conditions on population floor in Zostera marina population. Fish Sci 74:299–307

Bach HL (1993) A dynamic model describing the seasonal variations in growth and the distribution of eelgrass (*Zostera marina* L.) I. Model theory. Ecol Model 65:31–50

Baly ECC (1935) The kinetics of photosynthesis. Proc R Soc Lond Ser B 117:218–239

Behrenfeld MJ, Falkowski PG (1997) A consumer's guide to phytoplankton primary productivity models. Limnol Oceanogr 42:1479–1491

Berger AC, Berg P (2024) Eelgrass meadow response to heat stress. I. Temperature threshold for ecosystem production derived from in situ aquatic eddy covariance measurements. Mar Ecol Prog Ser 736:35–46

Berger AC, Berg P, McGlathery KJ, Aoki LR, Kerns K (2024) Eelgrass meadow response to heat stress. II. Impacts of ocean warming and marine heatwaves measured by novel metrics. Mar Ecol Prog Ser 736:47–62

Biber PD, Paerl HW, Gallegos CL (2005) Evaluating indicators of seagrass stress to light. In: Bortone SA (ed) Estuarine indicators. CRC Press, Boca Raton

Bintz JC (2002) The ecology and morphology of eelgrass (*Zostera marina* L.) and its associated macrophyte community in relation to environmental variables. Ph.D dissertation. University of Rhode Island

Bintz JC, Nixon SW, Buckley BA, Granger SL (2003) Impacts of temperature and nutrients on coastal lagoon plant communities. Estuaries 26:765–776

Bocci M, Coffaro C, Bendoricchio G (1997) Modelling biomass and nutrient dynamics in eelgrass (*Zostera marina* L.): applications to the Lagoon of Venice (Italy) and Oresund (Denmark). Ecol Model 102:67–80

Boese BL, Robbins BD, Thursby G (2005) Desiccation is a limiting factor for eelgrass (*Zostera marina* L.) distribution in the intertidal zone of a northeastern Pacific (USA) estuary. Bot Mar 48:274–283

Brush MJ, Brawley JW, Nixon SW, Kremer JN (2002) Modeling phytoplankton production: problems with the Eppley curve and an empirical alternative. Mar Ecol Prog Ser 238:31–45

Bulthuis D, Woelkerling W (1983) Seasonal variation in standing crop, density and leaf growth rate of the seagrass *Heterozostera tasminica*, in western Port and Port Phillip Bay, Victoria Australia. Aquat Bot 16:111–136

Burkholder JM, Mason KM, Glasgow HB (1992) Water-column nitrate enrichment promotes decline of eelgrass *Zostera marina*: evidence from seasonal mesocosm experiments. Mar Ecol Prog Ser 81:163–178

Cebrian J, Marba N, Duarte CM (1994) Estimating leaf age of the seagrass *Posidonia oceanica* (L.) Delile using the plastochrone interval index. Aquat Bot 49:59–65

Cerco CF, Moore K (2001) System-wide submerged aquatic vegetation model for Chesapeake Bay. Estuaries 24:522–534

Conover RJ (1961) A study of Charlestown and Green Hill Ponds, Rhode Island. Ecology 42:119–140

Dennison WC (1987) Effects of light on seagrass photosynthesis growth and depth distribution. Aquat Bot 27:15–26

Dennison WC (1990) Seagrasses: chlorophyll content. In: Phillips RC, McRoy CP (eds) Seagrass research methods. UNESCO, Paris

Dennison WC, Alberte RS (1985) Role of daily light period in the depth distribution of *Zostera marina* (eelgrass). Mar Ecol Prog Ser 25:51–61

DiToro DM, O'Conner DJ, Thomann RV (1971) A dynamic model of the phytoplankton population in the Sacramento-San Joaquin Delta. In: Hem JD (ed) Nonequilibrium systems in natural waters. Advances in chemistry series. American Chemical Society, Washington, DC

Dooley FD, Wyllie-Echeverria S, Roth MB, Ward PD (2013) Tolerance and response of Zostera marina seedlings to hydrogen sulfide. Aquat Bot 105:7–10

Drew EA (1979) Physiological aspects of primary production in seagrasses. Aquat Bot 7:139–150

Duarte C, Marba N, Agawin N, Cebrian J, Enriquez S, Fortes MD, Gallegos ME, Merino M, Olesen B, Sand-Jensen K, Uri J, Vermaat J (1994) Reconstruction of seagrass dynamics: age determinations and associated tools for the seagrass ecologist. Mar Ecol Prog Ser 107:195–209

Ehrich MK, Harris LA (2015) A review of existing eastern oyster filtration rate models. Ecol Model 297:201–212

Eppley RW (1972) Temperature and phytoplankton growth in the sea. Fish Bull 70:1063–1085

Evans A, Webb KL, Penhale PA (1986) Photosynthetic temperature acclimation in two coexisting seagrasses, *Zostera marina* L. and *Ruppia maritima* L. Aquat Bot 24:185–197

Foley JL (2017) Using an individual based model to evaluate the effects of climate change on the reproductive phenology of eelgrass (Zostera marina L.) along a latitudinal gradient. Master's thesis, University of Maryland, College Park

Gacia E, Duarte CM (2001) Elucidating sediment retention by seagrasses: sediment deposition and resuspension in a Mediterranean (*Posidonia oceanica*) meadow. Estuar Coast Shelf Sci 52:505–514

Goodman JL (1992) Photosynthetic responses of eelgrass (*Zostera marina* L.) to light and sediment sulfide in a shallow Barrier Island Lagoon. Masters thesis. College of William and Mary, Virginia

Goodman JL, Moore KA, Dennison WC (1995) Photosynthetic responses of eelgrass (*Zostera marina* L.) to light and sediment sulfide in a shallow barrier island lagoon. Aquat Bot 50:37–48

Hauxwell J, Cebrian J, Valiela I (2003) Eelgrass *Zostera marina* loss in temperate estuaries: relationship to land-derived nitrogen loads and effect of light limitation imposed by algae. Mar Ecol Prog Ser 247:59–73

Hauxwell J, Cebrian J, Valiela I (2006) Light dependence of *Zostera marina* annual growth dynamics in estuaries subject to different degrees of eutrophication. Aquat Bot 84:17–25

Jackson LJ, Furman BT, Peterson BJ (2017) Morphological response of Zostera marina reproductive shoots to fertilized porewater. J Exp Mar Biol Ecol 489:1–6

Jassby AD, Platt T (1976) Mathematical formulation of the relationship between photosynthesis and light for phytoplankton. Limnol Oceanogr 21(4):540–547

Kaldy JE, Eldridge PM, Cifuentes LA, Jones WB (2006) Utilization of DOC from seagrass rhizomes by sediment bacteria:^{13}C-tracer experiments and modeling. Mar Ecol Prog Ser 317:41–55

Kentula ME, McIntire CD (1986) The autoecology and production dynamics of eelgrass (*Zostera marina* L.) in Netarts Bay, Oregon. Estuaries 9:188–199

Kenworthy WJ, Fonseca M (1977) Reciprocal transplant of the seagrass *Zostera marina* L.: effect of substrate on growth. Aquaculture 12:197–213

Koch EW (1993) Hydrodynamics of flow through seagrass canopies: biological, physical and geochemical interactions. Ph.D. dissertation. University of South Florida, Tampa

Koch EW (2001) Beyond light: physical, geological and geochemical parameters as possible submersed aquatic vegetation habitat requirements. Estuaries 24:1–17

Kopp B (1999) Effects of nitrate fertilization and shading on physiological and biomechanical properties of eelgrass (*Zostera marina* L.). Ph.D. dissertation. University of Rhode Island

Kremer JN, Nixon SW (1978) A coastal marine ecosystem: simulation and analysis. Springer, New York

Lotka AJ (1922) Contribution to the energetics of evolution. Proc Natl Acad Sci 8:147–150

Marsh JA, Dennison WC, Alberte RS (1986) Effects of temperature on photosynthesis and respiration in eelgrass (*Zostera marina* L.). J Exp Mar Biol Ecol 101:257–267

McRoy CP (1974) Seagrass productivity: carbon uptake experiments in eelgrass, *Zostera marina*. Aquaculture 4:131–137

Michaelis L, Menten ML (1913) Der kinetik der invertinwirkung. Biochem Z 49:333–369

Moore K, Wetzel RW (2000) Seasonal variations in eelgrass (*Zostera marina* L.) responses to nutrient enrichment and reduced light availability in experimental ecosystems. J Exp Mar Biol Ecol 244:1–28

Murray L, Dennison WC, Kemp WM (1992) Nitrogen versus phosphorus limitation for growth of an estuarine population of eelgrass (*Zostera marina* L.). Aquat Bot 44:83–100

Neckles HA, Wetzel RL, Orth RJ (1993) Relative effects of nutrient enrichment and grazing on epiphyte–macrophyte (*Zostera marina* L.) dynamics. Oecologia 93:285–295

Neckles HA, Short FT, Barker S, Kopp BS (2005) Disturbance of eelgrass *Zostera marina* by commercial mussel *Mytilus edulis* harvesting in Maine: dragging impacts and habitat recovery. Mar Ecol Prog Ser 285:57–73

Olesen B, Sand-Jensen K (1993) Seasonal acclimatization of eelgrass *Zostera marina* growth to light. Mar Ecol Prog Ser 94:91–99

Orth JR (1977) Effect of nutrient enrichment of growth of eelgrass *Zostera marina* in the Chesapeake Bay, Virginia, USA. Mar Biol 44:187–194

Oviatt C (1994) Biological considerations in marine enclosures experiments: challenges and revelations. Oceanography 7:45–51

Pastres R, Brigolin D, Petrizzo A, Zucchetta M (2004) Testing the robustness of primary production models in shallow coastal areas: a case study. Ecol Model 179:221–233

Pederson MF (1995) Nitrogen limitation of photosynthesis and growth: comparison across aquatic plant communities in a Danish Estuary (Roskilde Fjord). Ophelia 41:261–272

Pregnall AM, Smith RD, Kursar TA, Alberte RS (1984) Metabolic adaptation of *Zostera marina* (eelgrass) to diurnal periods of root anoxia. Mar Biol 83:141–147

Qin LZ, Suonan Z, Kim SH, Lee KS (2021) Growth and reproductive responses of the seagrass Zostera marina to sediment nutrient enrichment. ICES J Mar Sci 78(3):1160–1173

Riley GA (1946) Factors controlling phytoplankton populations on Georges Bank. J Mar Res 6:54–73

Riley GA (1947) Seasonal fluctuations of the phytoplankton population in New England coastal waters. J Mar Res 6:114–125

Roberts M, Orth RJ, Moore KA (1987) Growth of *Zostera marina* L. seedlings under laboratory conditions of nutrient enrichment. Aquat Bot 20:321–328

Short FT (1980) A simulation model of the seagrass production system. In: Phillips RC, McRoy CP (eds) Handbook of seagrass biology: an ecosystem perspective. Garland STPM Press, New York

Short FT (1981) Nitrogen resource analysis and modelling of an eelgrass (*Zostera marina* L.) meadow in Izembek Lagoon, Alaska. Ph.D. dissertation. University of Alaska

Short F, Burdick DM, Kaldy JE III (1995) Mesocosm experiments quantify the effects of eutrophication on eelgrass, *Zostera marina*. Limnol Oceanogr 40:740–749

Short FT, Burdick D, Granger S, Nixon SW (1996) Long-term decline in eelgrass, *Zostera marina* L., linked to increased housing development. In: Kuo, Phillips R, Walker D, Kirkman H (eds) Seagrass biology: proceedings of an international workshop. Faculty of Sciences, University of Western Australia, Perth

Smith RD, Pregnall AM, Alberte RS (1988) Effects of anaerobiosis on root metabolism of the seagrass *Zostera marina* (eelgrass). Mar Biol 98:131–141

Steele JH (1962) Environmental control of photosynthesis in the sea. Limnol Oceanogr 7:137–150

Terrados D, Duarte CM, Kamp-Nielsen L, Agawin NSR, Gacia E, Lacap D, Fortes MD, Borum J, Lubanski M, Greve T (1999) Are seagrass growth and survival constrained by the reducing conditions of the sediment? Aquat Bot 65:175–197

Touchette BW, Burkholder JM (2000) Review of nitrogen and phosphorus metabolism in seagrasses. J Exp Mar Biol Ecol 250:133–167

Valiela I, Bowen JL (2002) Nitrogen sources to watersheds and estuaries: role of land cover mosaics and losses within watersheds. Environ Pollut 118:239–248

Van Lent F, Verschuure JM, van Veghel MLJ (1995) Comparative study on populations of *Zostera marina* L. (eelgrass): *in situ* nitrogen enrichment and light manipulation. J Exp Mar Biol Ecol 185:55–76

Verhagen JHG, Nienhuis NPH (1983) A simulation model of production, seasonal changes in biomass and distribution of eelgrass (*Zostera marina*) in Lake Grevelingen. Mar Ecol Prog Ser 10:187–195

Vollenweider RA (1974) A manual on methods for measuring primary production in aquatic environments, 2nd edn. IBP handbook No. 12. Blackwell Scientific Publications, Oxford

Volterra V (1926) Fluctuations in the abundance of species, considered mathematically. Nature 118:558–560

Wang H, Tang X, Chen J, Shang S, Zhu M, Liang S, Zang Y (2021) Comparative studies on the response of Zostera marina leaves and roots to ammonium stress and effects on nitrogen metabolism. Aquat Toxicol 240:105965

Wetzel RL, Neckles HA (1986) A model of *Zostera marina* L. photosynthesis and growth: simulated effects of selected physical-chemical variables and biological interactions. Aquat Bot 26:307–323

Wetzel R, Penhale PA (1983) Production ecology of seagrass communities in the Lower Chesapeake Bay. Mar Technol Soc J 17:22–31

Williams SL, Ruckelshaus MH (1993) Effects of nitrogen availability and herbivory on eelgrass (*Zostera marina*) and epiphytes. Ecology 74:904–918

Zharova N, Sfriso A, Voinov A, Pavoni B (2001) A simulation model for the annual fluctuation of *Zostera marina* biomass in the Venice lagoon. Aquat Bot 70:135–150

Zimmerman RC, Alberte RS (1996) Effect of light/dark transition on carbon translocation in eelgrass *Zostera marina* seedlings. Mar Ecol Prog Ser 136:305–309

Zimmerman RC, Smith RD, Alberte RS (1987) Is growth of eelgrass nitrogen limited? A numerical simulation of the effects of light and nitrogen on the growth dynamics of *Zostera marina*. Mar Ecol Prog Ser 41:167–176

Zimmerman RC, Smith RD, Alberte RS (1989) Thermal acclimation and whole-plant carbon balance in *Zostera marina* L. (eelgrass). J Exp Biol Ecol 130:93–109

Zimmerman RC, Cabello-Pasini A, Alberte RS (1994) Modeling daily production of aquatic macrophytes from irradiance measurements: a comparative analysis. Mar Ecol Prog Ser 114:185–196

Chapter 3
The Ramet

3.1 Introduction

The specification of programming "rules" that apportion growth to various plant organs within an eelgrass ramet constitutes the most original contribution of the Virtual Eelgrass Meadow (VEM). Whereas parameterizing the VEM specific growth rate described in Chap. 2 entailed a disciplined and rigorous modeling exercise, the following descriptions of the VEM individual-based model (IBM) rules are representative of the more creative aspect of numerical simulation, where the computing environment allowed for the creation of a virtual, visual world of growing and colonizing eelgrass shoots. While this description may conjure a task comparable to cartoon animation, the process of developing the VEM was grounded with empirical data and general biological knowledge of how these plants grow and reproduce. At a moment in time when our technological tools enable ever more sophisticated images and visualizations, it should be emphasized that the value of the VEM is as a computationally enumerated hypothesis that may test our understanding and serve as a starting point for further investigations of eelgrass autoecology.

To some degree, selecting units of grams dry weight (rather than carbon or other units of photosynthesis) in the specific growth model has already raised the mechanistic description of production from the sub-cellular scale, that requires explicit consideration of respiration, to the level of "individual" shoot (ramet) growth for the purposes of creating an IBM. However, the rules regarding the expenditure of this growth currency to sustain and/or propagate ramets depend upon botanical details of clonal growth that have heretofore been frequently simplified in existing seagrass models. Such a ramet-level depiction of resource allocation should be capable of producing emergent behavior that describes genet colonization and eelgrass bed expansion without explicitly modeling the colonization processes, thus meeting the classification criteria of an individual-based model (Grimm and Railsback 2005), while also providing insight into processes operating at the ecosystem scale.

© Springer Nature B.V. 2026

L. A. Harris et al., *Ramet Rules*, Aquatic Ecology Series 9,
https://doi.org/10.1007/978-94-024-2365-5_3

There are eight fundamental processes accounted for in the VEM, which will be described in detail and are depicted in Tables 3.1 and 3.2. Conceptual diagrams are also provided in Fig. 3.1. In the context of an individual-based modeling framework, these processes are simulated by equations ***or*** simple rules, and our programming uses a schedule for the order of operations these actions are taken in to result in a simulated eelgrass ramet and clone at each time step. For the VEM, these are scheduled in the following order: (1) distinct seedling and adult ramet specific growth rates are computed, (2) these growth rates are translated into biomass, and (3) subsequently partitioned separately to either aboveground (leaves) or belowground (roots and rhizomes) biomass. Concurrently, the model dictates (4) the occupation of space and location of new shoots along growing rhizomes and in an expanding meadow landscape. As individual densities increase, (5) the model limits population size via a set of self-thinning rules. Finally, (6) the production of offspring via asexual reproduction (i.e. the creation of daughter ramets) is tracked in

Table 3.1 Flow process rules and schedule for VEM

<table>
<tr><th colspan="4">Process schedule for VEM growth and space</th></tr>
<tr><td colspan="4">↓</td></tr>
<tr><td colspan="2">Compute specific growth rate for all adults</td><td colspan="2">Compute specific growth rate for seedlings</td></tr>
<tr><td colspan="2">↓</td><td colspan="2">↓</td></tr>
<tr><td colspan="2">Multiply by individual ramet's biomass to compute new growth</td><td colspan="2">Multiply by individual seedling's biomass to compute new growth</td></tr>
<tr><td>↓</td><td>↓</td><td>↓</td><td>↓</td></tr>
<tr><td>Apportion into leaves</td><td>Apportion into rhizomes</td><td>Apportion into leaves</td><td>Apportion into rhizomes</td></tr>
<tr><td>↓</td><td>↓</td><td>↓</td><td>↓</td></tr>
<tr><td colspan="4">Leaf production and nodes are translated into rules that move the location of the rhizomes for each individual across the sediment surface, changing the x,y coordinates of the ramet in 2-D space. This is done by converting rhizome biomass into allometrically determined rhizome length</td></tr>
<tr><td colspan="4">↓</td></tr>
<tr><td colspan="4">Individual ramets check how many neighbors they have in a 10 cm radius and this local density either increases or decreases their individual available light, providing a feedback from the meadow scale to individual ramet as this light availability impacts growth rates</td></tr>
<tr><td colspan="2">↓</td><td colspan="2">↓</td></tr>
<tr><td colspan="2">Adult Ramets also keep track of number of nodes to trigger a branching rule, alternating which direction the daughter branch takes, but maintaining branching angle</td><td colspan="2">Seedlings become adults at first branching of a daughter ramet. In programming rules the mother ramet then transitions from the seedling to adult submodel</td></tr>
<tr><td colspan="4">↓</td></tr>
<tr><td colspan="4">Adults become flowers as a function of temperature and cumulative growing degree days. Sexual reproduction rules are detailed in Flow (Table 3.2)</td></tr>
<tr><td colspan="4">↓</td></tr>
<tr><td colspan="4">The primary mortality process in the model is described by senescence of flowers</td></tr>
</table>

Table 3.2 VEM sexual reproduction rules modified from Jarvis et al. (2014)

Schedule for sexual reproduction
↓
Count how many days there are in the year above the 20°C average thermal stress threshold
↓
Use those days to set the individuals' probability of flowering that year (30%, 50%, 90% chance)
↓
When daily average temperature increases to 15°C after winter, flowering commences
↓
During flowering, multiply the # of flowering shoots by 10 seeds per shoot
↓
The seeds produced enter the sediment seed bank
↓
Any reproductive shoots die after 60 days post flowering
↓
Seeds remain dormant in the seed bank during high summer temperatures
↓
Only 40% of the seeds in the seed bank remain viable at time of germination
↓
When temperature decreases below 20 °C, viable seeds germinate
↓
X # of germinated seeds are recruited as new seedlings per m^2 in the model

addition to (7) the incidence of sexual reproduction (flowering, seed production, seed dormancy and germination) and subsequent (8) seedling recruitment and establishment in the model. Here, we go into detail regarding the thought processes, literature review, and fundamental questions we are asking with the VEM around how resource allocation impacts growth and how plastochrone intervals ultimately control the occupation of space and biomass predicted for a given set of environmental conditions.

3.2 The Ramet Module

The morphology of clonal plants is best described by a modular architecture (De Kroon and van Groenendael 1997) where the genet may grow larger by producing more ramet modules via asexual reproduction of lateral branches. While non-clonal plants may also exhibit modular morphology (leaf, stem, root), the ramet module of a clonal plant is based on a higher order of organization that consists of root-shoot couplings (i.e. a module of combined leaf, stem, & root modules) capable of independent existence (Alpert and Stuefer 1997). For plants such as *Zostera marina*, ramets are reiterated along a rhizome (analogous to a horizontal stem) composed of

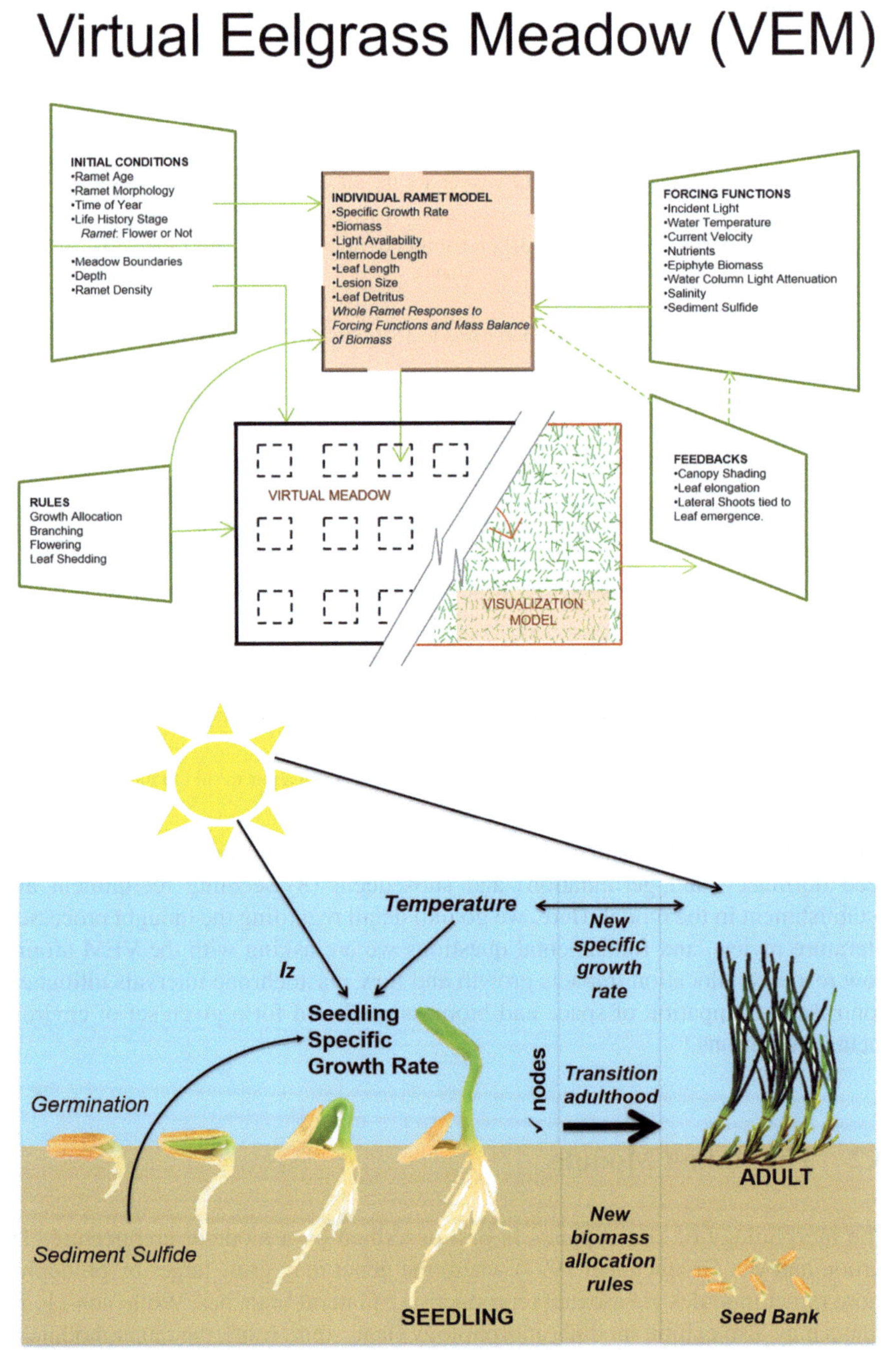

Fig. 3.1 Conceptual diagram of VEM. Growth is allocated to leaves and rhizome. Leaf length is affected by the local light environment and acts as the ramet "clock" to time emergence of new internodes and lateral shoots. X-Y spatial coordinates keep track of internode growth and new ramets. Local Shoot Density creates feedback to affect downwelling light availability. A sexual reproduction module adds to the population via seed germination and seedling growth

repeating internodes that create spaces between individuals and encourage colonization of a horizontal surface (Tomlinson 1974). The length and frequency of internodes, associated roots, nodes, and leaf sheaths, the rate of branching at lateral buds, and the angle that daughter shoots diverge from mother rhizomes all coalesce to produce features such as shoot density and expansion rates of seagrass patches (Bell and Tomlinson 1980; Marba and Duarte 1998).

The ramet-module perspective agrees with the "meristem dependence" of seagrasses emphasized by Tomlinson (1974). Salinas and Solano-Arellano (2021) apply the "phytomer" module definition to their model of rhizome elongation after definitions taken from the literature for terrestrial grasses. As for the VEM, the Salinas and Solano-Arellano (2021) model emphasizes a modular perspective and highlights a critical reality that the ramet or phytomer unit is described by features that are both continuous (internode length) and discrete (lateral branches, leaf bundles "shoots", nodes). It is this reality that invites a hybrid individual-based modeling approach that includes growth rate formulations as well as rules-based programming.

Eelgrass and many other seagrass species depend primarily on vegetative growth to maintain shoot densities and areal coverage. As monocots, all new growth is supported by the apical meristem, which produces basal growth of leaves and associated internodes enclosed within a sheathed bundle. This growth habit enables the combined rhizome tagging/leaf marking measurement technique described in Chap. 2 where the meristem is pierced and subsequent growth-mediated movement of the piercing scar allows for measurement of leaf growth. For *Zostera marina*, which possesses only horizontal rhizomes, the combined leaf bundle/apical meristem constitutes what is commonly referred to as a "shoot" and here will be considered the "ramet individual" along with an associated portion of rhizome and internode within the VEM.

Setchell (1929) completed a thorough description of this growth, including descriptive sketches of eelgrass development that are adapted to illustrate the chronology of rhizome elongation in Fig. 3.2. By observing the growth of an individual from germination, it is simple to understand the sequence of leaf elongation, internode growth, and the potential of a meristem to branch and form a new rhizome/meristem unit. Indeed, Setchell (1929) recognized the importance of meristem branching in creating overall patterns of eelgrass meadow colonization, contrasting the effect of indeterminate rhizome elongation meristem leaf/internode production in perennial ramets with the determinate, terminal growth of annual shoots that flower and die in their second year. Figure 3.3 depicts a reproduction of figures from Setchell (1929) that were used to diagrammatically illustrate this modular growth in a manner that clearly demonstrates a nascent desire to simulate eelgrass meadow expansion. While not conceived within a computing environment, this visualization can certainly be considered an early "model", as it was a representation of reality useful in Setchell's investigation of pattern formation and the effect of flowering on overall generational, seasonal sequences of eelgrass growth. From Fig. 3.3 it is also clear that *Zostera marina* exhibits monopodial branching, with one clear "parent" ramet creating the main axis/rhizome and dichotomic branching of new ramets to

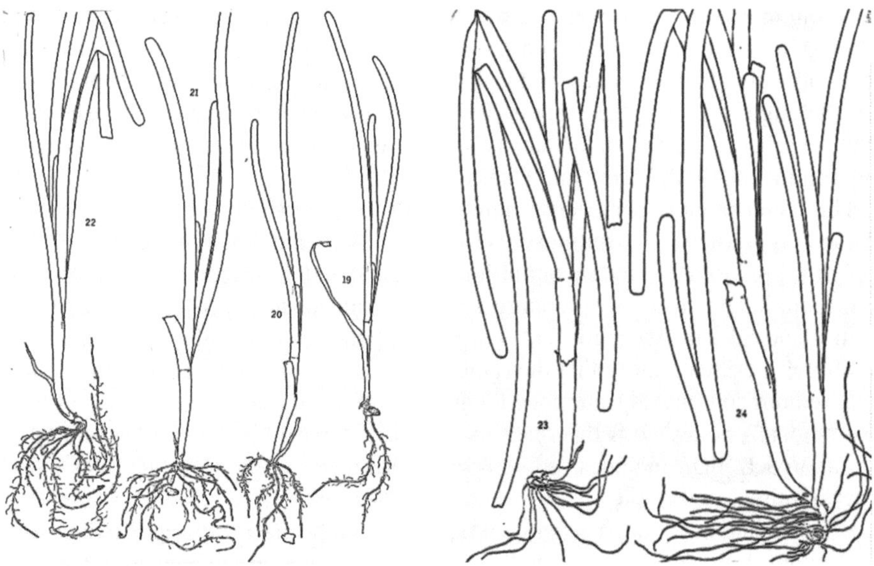

Fig. 3.2 Reproduction of Setchell's (1929) hand drawings of eelgrass development. Shoots numbered 19-22 chronicle the shedding of the seed coat, emergence of leaves, and growth of rhizome and root material. Shoots 23 and 24 document the continued elongation of the rhizome and subsequent production of a new lateral shoot

either side. It is this ordered, sequential pattern of colonization that has enabled demographic growth analysis (Duarte et al. 1994) and the estimation of plastochrone intervals for leaf, shoot, and rhizome modules.

Seventy plus years after the Setchell (1929) study, a focus on clonal plant growth as a repetitive succession of rhizome spacers separating shoot ramets has been described by computer models and simulations for several terrestrial examples (e.g. Bell et al. 1979; Oborny and Cain 1997; Oborny et al. 2001; Winkler and Fischer 2002). In particular, the rules approach of the VEM is most similar to that described by Bell et al. (1979), who recommended that the construction of computer programs simulating branching plants should parallel the architectural rules governing the plant.

Clonal seagrass models in this tradition include the work of Marba and Duarte (1998), who emphasized rhizome growth and meristem dependence by creating spatially explicit simulations of three seagrass species (*Halophila ovalis, Thalassodendron ciliatum, Posidonia oceanica*). Marba and Duarte (1998) used deterministic parameters (internodal length, branching angle, and internode productivity) and one stochastic parameter (for the probability of branching) to model vegetative growth. This comparative study produced important insights regarding the effect of size on various architectural components of a given seagrass species and the implications of this size-dependency on variation in colonization rates among species.

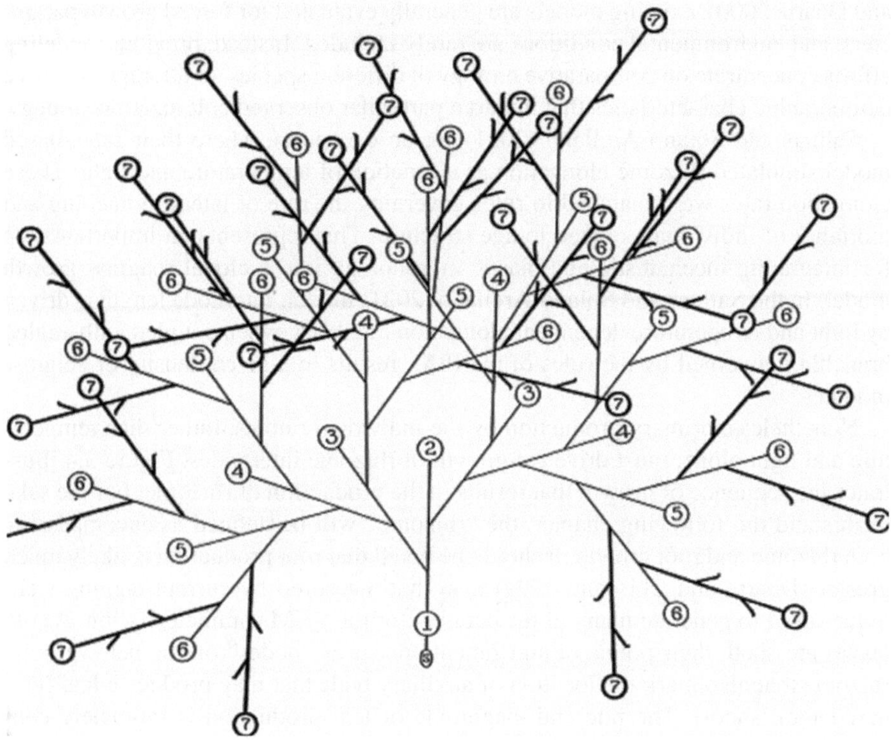

Fig. 3.3 Early efforts by Setchell (1929) to visualize the demographics of clonal growth in eelgrass. Eelgrass genet is classified into various generations of branching ramets over the course of a Californian summer. Generations progress from oldest (1) to youngest (7). Note alternate branching pattern of lateral shoots

Sintes et al. (2005) added to the Marba and Duarte (1998) model using the species *Cymodocea nodosa* by including programming rules that create a radius of exclusion around shoots to penalize overlapping, colonizing rhizome apices. The stochastic branching rate parameter in the Marba and Duarte (1998) example was replaced with values randomly selected from a Gaussian distribution associated with an empirical mean and standard deviation measured in the field. This empirical distribution approach was repeated for the parameters of spacer length between shoots, branching angle, and rhizome production. Although this model used minimal parameters, the Sintes et al. (2005) simulations produced complex, nonlinear results, where patch expansion rates varied with patch size, and branching angle emerged as a sensitive parameter.

Despite these significant contributions to modeling clonal plants, neither the terrestrial nor the seagrass examples have integrated the rules governing vegetative growth of ramets with a mechanistic description of how physical factors such as light, temperature, or nutrients drive growth. Although intraspecific plasticity of these ramet rules is widely accepted (De Kroon and Hutchings 1995; Hemminga and Duarte 2000), existing models are generally evaluated for forced growth parameters, and environmental conditions are rarely included. Instead, previous modeling efforts concentrate on comparative biology of different species, or attempts to derive demographic characteristics that impart a particular observed colonization strategy.

Salinas and Solano-Arellano (2021) are an exception, where their rules-based model simulated rhizome elongation as a function of temperature and light. These elongation rates were matched to rules governing the rate of lateral branching and mortality of individuals related to age structure. This represents an important step for integrating mechanistic and plastic morphology into a clonal seagrass growth model. In the Salinas and Solano-Arellano (2021) model, internode length is driven by light and temperature dependent elongation rates that, when coupled with angled branching governed by the rules of the IBM, results in a given density of eelgrass modules.

Nonetheless, primary production by the individual ramets, rather than temperature and light alone, must drive the growth of rhizome internodes. Figure 3.4 illustrates the sequence of growth that results in the production of rhizome. For the sake of this and the following chapter, the "rhizome" will be defined as encompassing both rhizome and root growth. It should be noted that root production is likely much greater (Duarte and Chiscano 1999) than that measured by current tagging techniques used to generate many of the datasets for the VEM parameterization. As old leaves are shed, their points of attachment appear as "nodes" on the belowground rhizome that also mark the location of auxiliary buds that may produce a leaf (or a new lateral shoot). The rate and magnitude of leaf production is intimately connected to the amount of material in-between nodes (the internode), which ultimately dictates the horizontal spaces between shoots and genet morphogenesis. This is the mechanism that ultimately underpins the ability of the Salinas and Solano-Arellano (2021) model to use rhizome elongation as a proxy for clonal growth. For the VEM, we choose to focus on leaf growth as it also allows us to explore several other environmental factors that can influence ramet morphology and affect eelgrass success in a given habitat.

Table 3.1 and Fig. 3.1 describes the schedule followed by the VEM from specific growth rates modeled according to environmental conditions, to apportioning the new growth between above and belowground modules and ultimately linking leaf production with node/internode development and colonization of a horizontal surface by the rhizome via an apical meristem. The following description of the VEM programming rules attempts to reproduce this sequence of growth for the eelgrass ramet within the computer environment. Conventions used in this description include the capitalization of state variables and the use of italics for other parameters and flows. A complete list of equations used in the vegetative portion of the VEM is included in Table 3.3, with associated parameters and state variables provided in Table 3.4. While we use many of the conventions of traditional system dynamics modeling to describe the VEM, the peculiarities of the individual based modeling approach may stand out in the following description. In particular, the transition or "flows" from one state variable to another often occur in sudden increments according to the scheduled rules of the VEM. As such, the use of difference

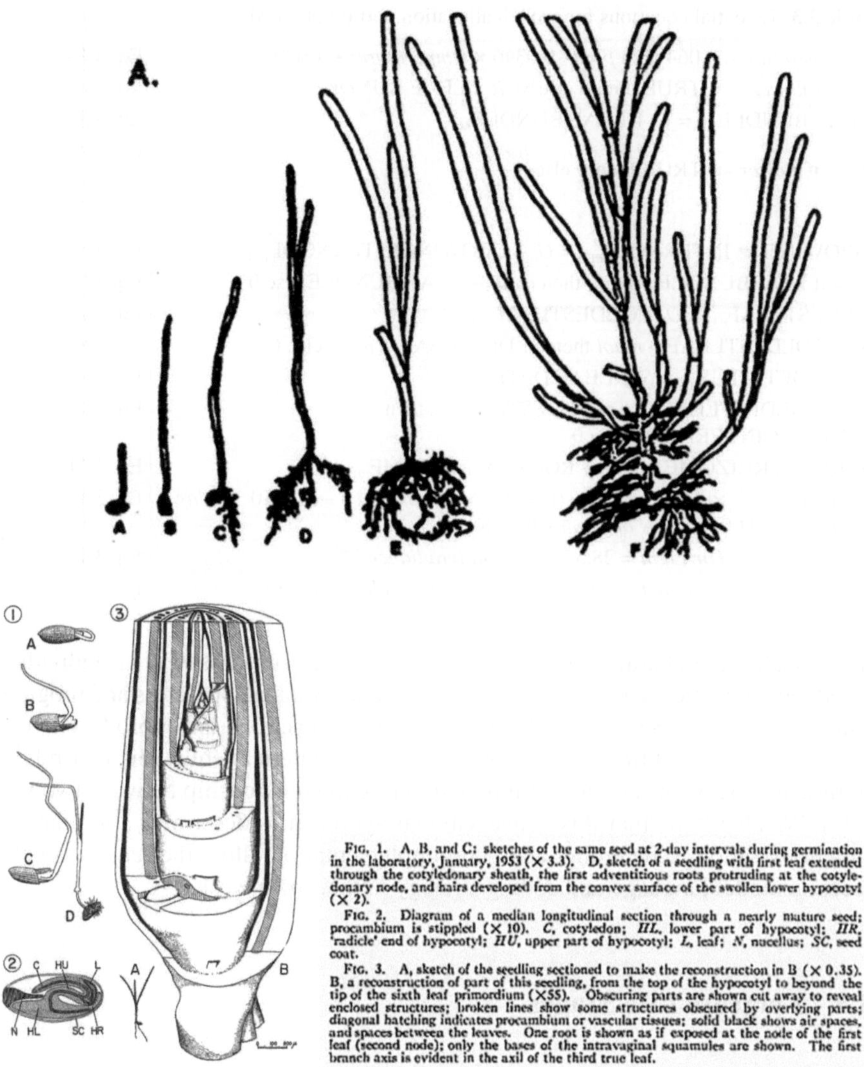

Fig. 3.4 This drawing by Taylor (1957) depicts early life history stages for *Zostera marina* in detail. Section 1 of the image reproduces Taylor's sketches of seeds at 2-day intervals following germination through the emergence of the first leaf through the cotyledonary sheath alongside the first roots. Section 2 of the drawing includes a section drawing of a nearly mature seed to reveal the cotyledon, hypocotyl, leaf, nucellus, and seed coat. Section 3 is a section of a seedling focused on revealing the hypocotyl through the primordium of the sixth leaf. This final drawing illustrates the basal meristematic growth of this species

equations to describe changes in biomass or other ramet features was the most appropriate formulation. Subtext associated with state variables generally references the 1-day timestep (e.g. t(0) or t(1)) to describe these difference equations.

Table 3.3 Essential equations for growth allocation portion of VEM

If temperature < 8.064 *then* $\beta = (-0.0346 \times temperature) + 1.029$	Eq. 3.1
G_l = if *flower* = = TRUE then 0 else *SGR* × LEAF BUNDLE	Eq. 3.2
$\text{LEAF BUNDLE}_{t(1)} = G_l + \text{LEAF BUNDLE}_{t(0)}$	Eq. 3.3
$G_r = \text{if } flower == \text{TRUE then 0 else} \dfrac{b \times G_l}{1-b}$	Eq. 3.4
$\text{GROWING} \rightleftarrows \text{INTERNODE}_{t(1)} = G_r + \text{GROWINGINTERNODE}_{t(0)}$	Eq. 3.5
O_l = if LEAFBUNDLE > *malb* then *malb* – LEAF BUNDLE else 0	Eq. 3.6
$\text{OLDESTLEAF}_{t(1)} = O_l + \text{OLDESTLEAF}_{t(0)}$	Eq. 3.7
S_l = if OLDESTLEAF > *maol* then OLDESTLEAF – *maol* else 0	Eq. 3.8
$\text{LEAF DETRITUS}_{t(1)} = S_l + \text{LEAF DETRITUS}_{t(0)}$	Eq. 3.9
G_i = if $\text{OLDESTLEAF}_{t(n-1)} > \text{OLDESTLEAF}_{t(n)}$ then GROWINGINTERNODE else 0	Eq. 3.10
$\text{ROOTS \& RHIZOME}_{t(1)} = G_i + \text{ROOTS \& RHIZOME}_{t(0)}$	Eq. 3.11
$k = (-4 \times 10^{-11} \times day\ of\ year^4) + (6 \times 10^{-8} \times day\ of\ year^3) - (3 \times 10^{-5} \times day\ of\ year^2) + (0.0045 \times day\ of\ year) + 0.3324$	Eq. 3.12
$Canopy\ Height\ For\ Light = 28.55 \times Percent\ Irradiance^{-0.60}$	Eq. 3.13
$Nutrient\ Elongation\ Factor = [0.206 Ln(Nitrogen\ Loading)] + 0.84$	Eq. 3.14

Additionally, the characterization of certain botanical processes in an individual-based model is often achieved by using conditional Boolean operators and programming conventions. Several of the VEM Boolean functions are reproduced (with explanations) in addition to the more traditional numerical equations that rely on empirical regressions or curve-fitting to describe the relationship between two variables. We also hope that this conversational approach to describing formulations, parameterization, scheduling, and code implementation allow the reader to better access a model language and coding strategy in their own work.

3.3 Eelgrass Life Stages

Prior to model formulation, we also need to define the three main ontogenetic life stages of *Z. marina* represented in the model (seed, seedling, adult), both botanically and functionally, so that operational model definitions are explicitly characterized. This largely draws from work also described by co-author Foley (2017). One immediate challenge with this exercise is that in botany the terms "seed", "seedling", and "adult" carry no hard botanical description. Perhaps the reader now sees that even seemingly simple assumptions that go into decisions regarding model structure require deep research! According to Webster's Seventh New Collegiate Dictionary (1967), for example, a seedling (botany) is "a young plant grown from seed". For the purposes of model application, this definition is neither specific nor informative enough to be effective. Furthermore, a literature review (Table 3.5) of

Table 3.4 VEM growth allocation parameter and state variable definitions

Parameter	Description	Units
β	Percent of total growth allocated belowground to growing internode	No units
G_l	New Leaf Growth	grams dry weight day^{-1}
LEAF BUNDLE	State variable for leaves contained in ramet leaf bundle, excluding the oldest leaf	grams dry weight
flower	Boolean variable for status of individual ramet; "true" for flower, "false" for vegetative shoot	Boolean
G_r	New belowground growth for Growing Internode	grams dry weight day^{-1}
GROWING INTERNODE	State variable for developing internode	grams dry weight
O_l	Transition of leaf material from Leaf Bundle to Oldest Leaf status. Represents maturation of leaves	grams dry weight day^{-1}
malb	Maximum Allowable Leaf Biomass. Dynamic variable that sets the threshold for the Leaf Bundle to indicate when an old leaf ages into the Oldest Leaf compartment	grams dry weight
maol	Dynamic variable that sets the maximum allowable oldest leaf biomass. Once this threshold is reached, the ramet will shed its oldest leaf	grams dry weight
OLDEST LEAF	State variable to keep track of oldest leaf biomass	grams dry weight
S_l	Sloughing of Oldest Leaf into detrital pool	grams dry weight day^{-1}
LEAF DETRITUS	State variable to keep track of leaf detritus. Detritus does not decompose in the VEM	grams dry weight
G_i	Transition of Growing Internode material into Roots & Rhizome. Occurs simultaneously with leaf sloughing	grams dry weight day^{-1}
ROOTS & RHIZOME	State variable to track size of a ramet's living belowground biomass	grams dry weight
k	Dynamic light extinction coefficient	meters^{-1}
Canopy Height for Light	Height of longest leaf set to amount of incoming light	cm
Nutrient Elongation Factor	Factor to incorporate elongating effect of Nitrogen loading	No units—scaled from 100% up
Percent Irradiance	Amount of sunlight reaching leaves	No units
Nitrogen Loading	Dissolved Inorganic Nitrogen loading to water body from watershed	g Nm^{-2} d^{-1}
In	Creation of new node	# Nodes day^{-1} (0 or 1)

Table 3.5 A literature review on the description of the term "eelgrass seedling" confirmed multiple inconsistencies in how the seedling life stage was denoted

Study	Seedling definition
Ochieng et al. (2010)	Three month old plants, age identified by the presence of seed coat still attached to cotyledon and by # of leaves. Allowed for 103 days of growth after 22 day transplant recovery in mesocosm
Jarvis et al. (2012)	[<1 year of growth] Seedlings reached maximum biomass within 4 months
Niu et al. (2012)	Collected and germinated seeds. The germinated seeds were cultured for two days in 20 °C until the cotyledon grew up right out of the seed coat up to 0.5 cm. Study used 800 seedlings with cotyledon length 0.78 ± 0.20 cm. Experiment lasted only 30 days
Rasmussen at al. (2012)	Seedlings identified as small shoots with 2–5 narrow 1–2 mm leaves and no rhizome present. Many of the collected seedlings still had the seed coat attached to the hypocotyl. Collected seedlings 7.9 ± 2.3 cm in height
Abe et al. (2008)	Mature seeds buried in sand laid at bottom of culture bottles. After 2 months culture, many seedlings appeared and grew to a length of 10 cm under 15 °C and 50 μmol photons m^{-2} s^{-1}. Seedlings then held at different light treatments for 6 days. Sample seedlings in study ranged from 10.1 to 16.4 cm in total length
Jarvis et al. (2014)	In model, once germinated, seedlings were then converted back to above and below ground carbon values using fixed conversion factors. When above ground vegetative *Z. marina* biomass was <0.44 g C m^{-2} all above and below ground seedling biomass was transferred to the vegetative shoot and root stocks. If more than this, then seedling mortality 100%. Relationship based on inhibitory effect of shading
Tanner and Parham (2010)	Seeds were considered germinated when the seed coat split and the hypocotyl and cotyledon exposed. Seedlings were recognized by the appearance of photosynthetic leaves and adventitious roots. Seeds vernalized for 1–4 weeks before planting. Time to germination: 3–29 days (fastest germination in low salinity treatments). Development into seedlings with green leaves took 16–56 days. Most seedlings emerged in 50 days. 1000 seeds planted, 90 days after planting there were 26,000 shoots, of which approximately 15,000 met specifications to harvest and transplant (shoots > 12.25 cm tall, rhizome > 2.5 cm long). Fertilization enhanced growth rates of seedlings, proliferation of lateral shoots, and shortened period of time necessary to reach planting size
J. Bintz dissertation (2002)	Seeds planted late December, allowed seeds to germinate and seedlings began to emerge within the month. Within 4 months seedlings reached a mean height of 4 cm and were transplanted to outdoor tanks

the term "eelgrass seedling" confirmed multiple inconsistencies in defining the seedling life stage using both chronological age and biomass measurements as indicators.

In-depth botanical descriptions of *Z. marina* development and structure by Taylor (1957) are shown in Fig. 3.4. The precise morphological and cellular descriptions of the species' life stages occurs at a level of resolution that is too fine for the scale at which the VEM is formulated, and associated calibration and validation data are not available to distinguish these ontogenetic phases. A seagrass seedling is the earliest part of the juvenile phase; typically, no more than a few weeks old, usually where evidence of attachment to the seed is still present.

Lacking a formal, published definition, we chose to designate the ramet plastochron interval (PI), or the first instance of clonal reproduction (i.e. fecundity), as the point of transition or biological threshold separating an eelgrass seedling from adulthood (Foley 2017). Fecundity is under both genetic and environmental control and is a measure of fitness, providing a clear biological threshold separating the two life stages in the model. Furthermore, the PI threshold is intimately connected to the rate and magnitude of leaf production, as opposed to chronological age. Terrestrial botanists have also long understood the principle that a plant's ontogenetic life stage or "biological age" (Robbins 1957) is a better measure than calendar age (Gatsuk et al. 1980). For these reasons, the subsequent creation of new internodes in the model appropriately allows it to act as a biological age clock. The biological feedback loop is visualized in Fig. 3.5. For model purposes, once a growing seedling reaches this PI threshold, then the "seedling" is considered an "adult" in the model and subject to the adult specific growth rate formulation and other adult-related IBM rules (Table 3.1).

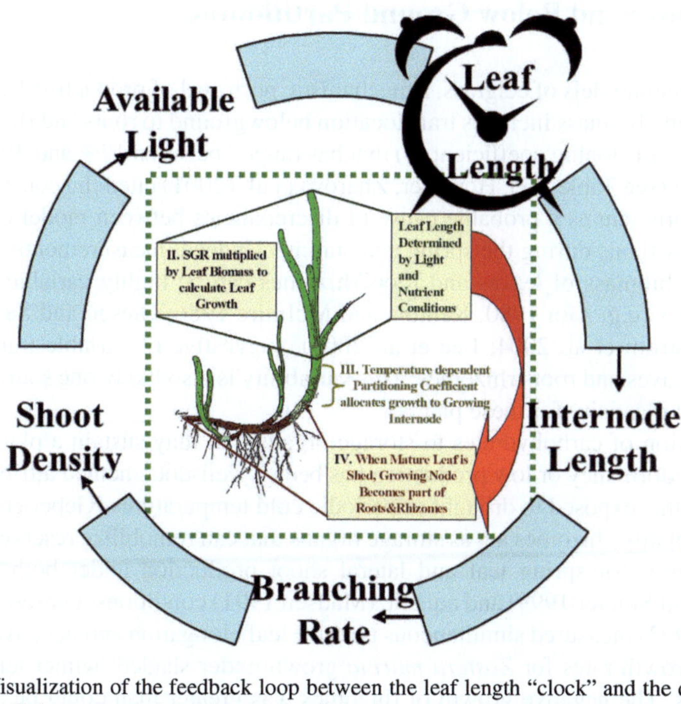

Fig. 3.5 Visualization of the feedback loop between the leaf length "clock" and the dependency of available light on local shoot density. As light decreases with increasing shoot density, leaf length increases and may limit further crowding by (a) decreasing the rate at which new branches are formed and (b) increasing the length of spacer-internodes. (Drawing of *Z. marina* from Thayer et al. (1984) used with permission)

Lastly, the operational model definition of "seed" used in the VEM is a state variable produced from the product of the flowering shoots variable and a parameter setting the number of seeds produced per flowering shoot (Foley 2017). The flowering shoots variable is calculated by summing how many total shoots flowered on the first flowering day. To obtain the total number of seeds produced each year, the seeds are summed and stored in a sediment seed bank until the seeds lose their viability (i.e. rot) or germinate. While stored in the seed bank, only a portion of the original seeds survive through the summer dormancy period until temperatures fall below 20 °C and trigger the remaining stored seeds to germinate and recruit into the population as new seedling individuals. Asexual and sexual reproduction occurred in the model via clonal growth of new ramets and anthesis, seed development, and germination. A list of the VEM sexual reproduction model rules, which were formed using a modified version of the sexual reproduction model developed by Jarvis et al. (2014), are shown in Table 3.2. We elaborate on the specific details related to these life history stages and reproduction in the VEM, and the work by Jarvis et al. (2014), in Chap. 4's *Modeling Reproduction.*

3.4 Above and Below Ground Partitioning

In non-clonal models of eelgrass, a mechanistic portrayal of production by leaves or aboveground biomass includes translocation belowground to roots and rhizomes via a constant partitioning coefficient (β) that has ranged between 17% and 30% of total production (see Table 1.2). However, Zharova et al. (2001) cited the constant nature of this coefficient as a probable cause of discrepancies between model output and field observations during the spring and summer. Indeed, measurements of relative growth or biomass of leaves and roots/rhizomes can be highly variable over seasonal cycles (e.g. Aioi 1980; Kentula and McIntire 1986; Olesen and Sand-Jensen 1993; Bostrom et al. 2004; Lee et al. 2005), suggestive of variable translocation between leaves and roots/rhizomes. This variability is also likely one source of morphological plasticity for these plants.

Allocation of carbohydrates to storage organs that may sustain a plant through periods of dormancy or low production has been a well-documented attribute in terrestrial plants exposed to drought or periodic cold temperatures (Geber et al. 1997). In clonal plants, rhizomes act as storage organs that can remobilize reserves (reverse translocation) for spring leaf and lateral shoot production under both terrestrial (Suzuki and Stuefer 1999) and aquatic (Madsen 1991) conditions. Olesen and Sand-Jensen (1993) measured simultaneous positive leaf elongation and negative rhizome specific growth rates for *Zostera marina* grown under shaded, winter temperature conditions. The negative growth of rhizomes was greater than could be accounted for by respiration alone and is most likely accounted for by translocation. While basipetal translocation of resources tends to be most prevalent in clonal plants, movement of materials from rhizomes to aboveground structure has been documented in *Zostera marina* (Touchette and Burkholder 2000). Using economic theory, Bloom et al. (1985) predicted that allocation to plant organs continues until the marginal revenue generated from this storage is equal to the marginal cost. Respiring belowground organs might be considered too costly for continued storage or allocation under high temperature or other stressful conditions (when respiration increases). Indeed, Olesen and Sand-Jensen (1993) found that high temperatures and low light resulted in greater decreases in rhizome than leaf biomass.

Bintz (2002) measured production of eelgrass under varying temperature and nutrient enrichment treatments in experimental mesocosms. Figure 3.6 uses data from these measurements to examine the relationship between temperature and percent allocation to leaf and rhizome growth. It is clear from these graphs that ramets allocate more growth to rhizomes under cold temperatures and less under high temperatures, confirming the hypothesis of Bloom et al. (1985) and in agreement with

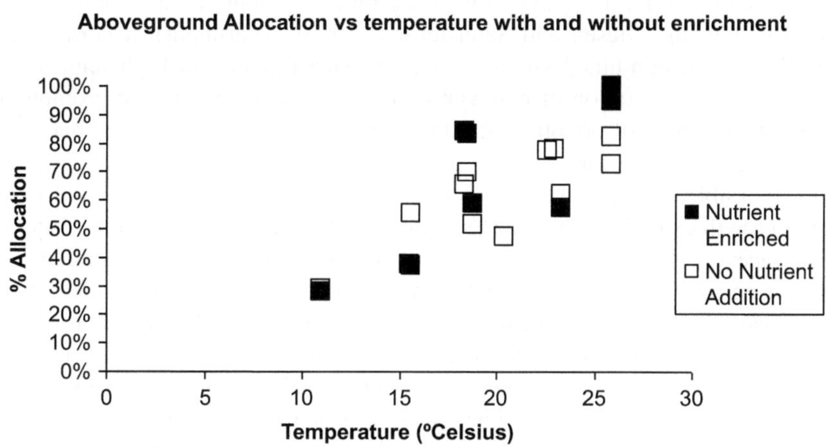

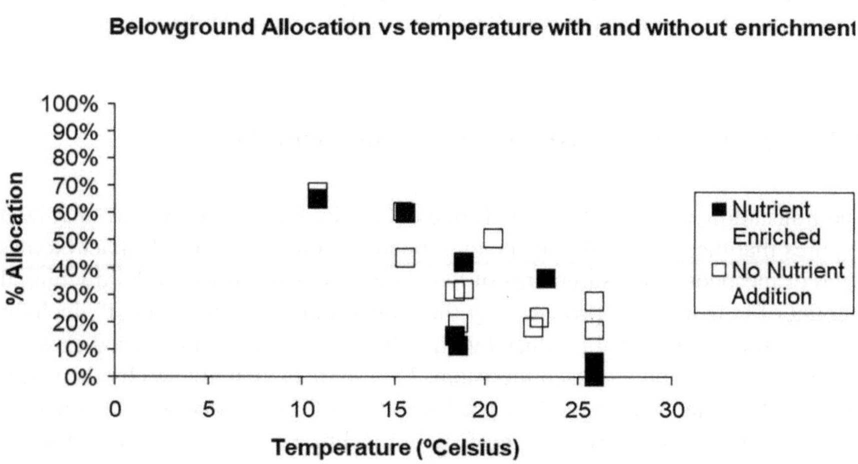

Fig. 3.6 Relationship between allocation of above and below-ground growth and temperature under ambient and enriched nutrient conditions. (Data from Bintz 2002)

field observations for both terrestrial and aquatic perennials. Regression analysis did not reveal significant differences between the nutrient treatments ($p > 0.05$), suggesting that the presence or absence of N and P nutrient additions does not affect total biomass partitioning. The VEM will proceed with using the regression equation derived from the complete dataset of ambient and nutrient enriched treatments described by Eq. 3.1 for the percentage of growth allocated to rhizomes (β), although a maximum value of 0.75 is specified to limit allocation in the cold months.

$$\begin{aligned} &\textit{If temperature} < 8.064 \text{ then } 0.75 \text{ else} \\ &\beta = \left(-0.0346 \times \textit{temperature}\right) + 1.029 \end{aligned} \tag{3.1}$$

It should be noted that despite the lack of statistical support for an effect of nutrients on this partitioning, only the treatments undergoing nutrient enrichment exhibited 100% allocation to leaves with no rhizome growth. Without measurements of respiration (as with the Olesen and Sand-Jensen (1993) experiment), it is difficult to determine if the combined stress of nutrient enrichment and high temperatures resulted in re-mobilization of belowground reserves aboveground to promote leaf growth. This aspect of adaptive translocation is a feature of eelgrass that should merit future research efforts.

It is possible that the plasticity observed in partitioning of above and belowground growth extends to the translocation of materials between ramets. Using isotopic tracers, Marba et al. (2002) measured significant translocation from neighboring ramets, contributing between 5% and 40% to rhizome and leaf carbon and nitrogen. Unfortunately, the datasets upon which the VEM must rely for parameterization do not differentiate between the growth that occurred as the result of a neighboring ramet and that produced by an individual. The discovery of these relationships has not yet extended to documenting seasonal cycles of this translocation. These gaps in our understanding create challenges to incorporating a translocation term in the VEM which will not be resolved in this version of the model.

3.5 Leaves and Root-Rhizome State Variables

The translation of a specific growth rate (SGR) into growth of leaves or rhizome requires that the simulated SGR be multiplied by some measure of ramet biomass. Field or mesocosm measurements of SGR are generally calculated by dividing the amount of new material produced by the biomass of the "whole shoot", including the new rhizome material produced within the measurement time period as well as the leaves and sheath enclosed meristem. This value is then divided by the number of days the plant was tagged to produce units of grams dry weight grams dry weight^{-1} day^{-1}. The reproduction of such a technique within the daily time step of the simulation requires a somewhat arbitrary specification of "shoot biomass". Of course, the "leaves" growing on the plant must be included, but the amount of rhizome material to be included in the "shoot biomass" by which SGR is multiplied is much less clear. According to the field measurement technique, only the rhizome growth that has occurred since the last time step (i.e. one day of belowground growth) should be included in the "shoot mass" by which SGR is measured.

However, in cases where no leaves exist this would still result in growth, clearly an unrealistic scenario. Fortunately, the belowground partitioning coefficient allows the VEM to avoid explicit rules to calculate shoot size for purposes of the growth calculations. Instead, leaf growth (G_l) is first determined according to Eq. 3.2 with the implicit assumption that the amount of leaf material present (LEAF BUNDLE) determines how much new material is produced.

$$G_l = SGR \times \text{LEAF BUNDLE} \tag{3.2}$$

$$\text{LEAF BUNDLE}_{t(1)} = G_l + \text{LEAF BUNDLE}_{t(0)} \tag{3.3}$$

The G_l term acts as the flow into the LEAF BUNDLE state variable, characterizing the rate-of-change parameter in the difference-equation for the growth of LEAF BUNDLE. Within the same time step, this leaf growth term is used along with the belowground partitioning coefficient to calculate rhizome growth (G_r) as demonstrated with the derivation below.

$$\begin{aligned} G_r &= b \times [G_l + G_r] \\ G_r &= (b \times G_l) + (b \times G_r) \\ G_r - (b \times G_r) &= b \times G_l \\ G_r \times [1 - b] &= b \times G_l \\ G_t &= \frac{b \times G_l}{1 - b} \end{aligned} \tag{3.4}$$

$$\text{GROWINGINTERNODE}_{t(1)} = G_r + \text{GROWINGINTERNODE}_{t(0)} \tag{3.5}$$

This process is the same for an individual defined as a seedling, but uses the specific growth rate described in Chap. 2 for seedlings instead of adults.

3.6 Light, Nitrogen, and Adaptive Partitioning

A node produced on an eelgrass rhizome marks the former attachment point of a leaf that has been shed from a ramet. The rhizome segment in-between consecutive nodes is defined as the internode and represents the amount of belowground material produced between the shedding of two leaves. Within the VEM it seems appropriate to use rules that link the maturation and shedding of a leaf with the production of nodes and internodes. The amount of belowground growth that is produced in the time period from the shedding of one mature leaf to the shedding of the next will be moved from the GROWING INTERNODE state variable compartment to a new compartment that contains the living rhizome material; "ROOTS & RHIZOME". This flow of material is tied to the size of the mature leaf and its associated leaf bundle. The programmed link between mature leaf shedding and the growth of the internode should be interpreted only as a simulation timing device. Even though flow from individual leaves belowground is not explicitly modeled, the translocation of materials to the rhizome from all of the older leaves is implied by the biomass dependent specific growth rate.

An eelgrass leaf bundle is enclosed by the leaf sheath; a tube of leaf material that encircles the meristem and nodes of growing leaves that have not developed significant internode material (Hemminga and Duarte 2000). Figure 3.7 illustrates the maturation of the oldest leaf, separation from the leaf bundle, and the elongation of its associated internode. The node insertion points for new leaves result in a pattern where the youngest leaf grows in the center of the laterally compressed leaf bundle and older leaves alternate in age between the left and right of this center leaf. The distribution of leaf lengths among the various leaves follows a positive age-length relationship only for the leaves enclosed in the leaf bundle. The oldest leaf appears shorter because the associated internode, previously enclosed in the leaf bundle

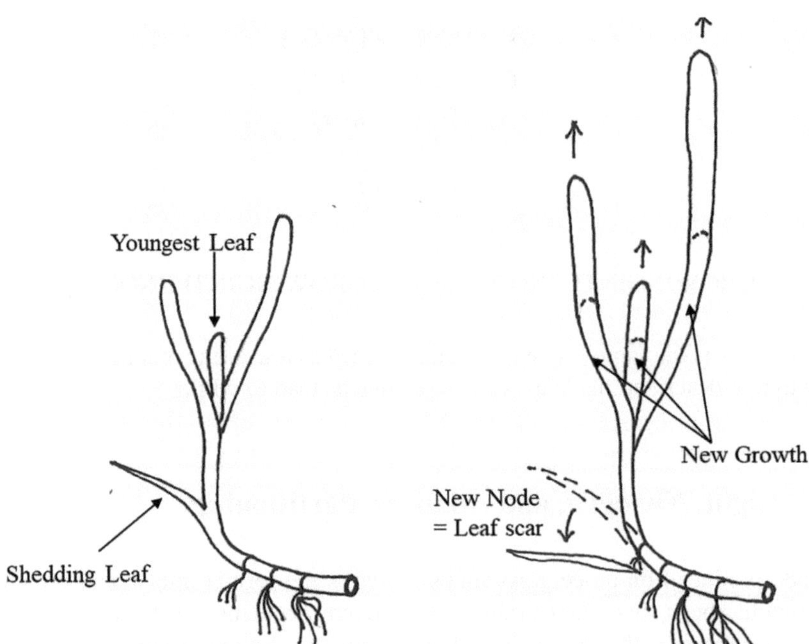

Fig. 3.7 Drawing to illustrate leaf bundle, leaf maturation and shedding, and the emergence of the leaf scar (node) and internode. (Drawing by S. Galczynski and used with permission)

sheath, has now matured into a rhizome segment. As such, the GROWING INTERNODE state variable in the VEM actually represents the material on Fig. 3.7 between the node of the mature leaf and the leaf bundle sheath.

In order to determine when a mature leaf is shed (and the subsequent appearance of an internode), it is necessary to determine the distribution of biomass among leaves. This is important because of the non-linear distribution of lengths/weights among leaves as they age; a leaf does not reach some maximum biomass and then fall off, instead the shedding of this mature leaf is linked to the transition of GROWING INTERNODE material from within the leaf bundle into a rhizome internode, resulting in an apparent decrease in leaf size. Rather than explicitly model each leaf, the VEM can use the average distribution of leaf sizes, standardized to the size of the oldest leaf, to set a maximum allowable total biomass for the leaf bundle and the oldest leaf. Flow (O_l) from the LEAF BUNDLE compartment into the OLDEST LEAF will be permitted once the LEAF BUNDLE biomass exceeds the maximum allowable leaf bundle biomass (*malb*) and the OLDEST LEAF compartment will slough (S_l) into a LEAF DETRITUS pool once the OLDEST LEAF biomass exceeds the maximum allowable oldest leaf biomass (*maol*). The sloughing of a mature leaf will also trigger the flow of internode material (G_i) from GROWING INTERNODE to the ROOTS&RHIZOMES compartment.

$$O_l = \text{if LEAFBUNDLE} > malb \text{ then } malb - \text{LEAF BUNDLE else } 0 \tag{3.6}$$

$$\text{OLDESTLEAF}_{t(1)} = O_l + \text{OLDESTLEAF}_{t(0)} \tag{3.7}$$

$$S_l = \text{if OLDESTLEAF} > maol \text{ then OLDESTLEAF} - maol \text{ else } 0 \tag{3.8}$$

$$\text{LEAF DETRITUS}_{t(1)} = S_l + \text{LEAF DETRITUS}_{t(0)} \tag{3.9}$$

$$G_i = \text{if OLDESTLEAF}_{t(\mathrm{n}-1)} > \text{OLDESTLEAF}_{t(n)} \text{ then GROWINGINTERNODE else } 0 \tag{3.10}$$

$$\text{ROOTS \& RHIZOME}_{t(1)} = G_i + \text{ROOTS \& RHIZOME}_{t(0)} \tag{3.11}$$

The rule for the G_i parameter (Eq. 3.10) uses the "emptying" of the OLDEST LEAF compartment to signal the transition of the biomass held within the GROWING INTERNODE compartment into the mature ROOTS&RHIZOME state variable. The reader is reminded that these rules must specify discrete events to work within the individual-based modeling environment, even though it is important to acknowledge that growth and translocation are continuous processes.

Using data from Bintz (2002) and measurements collected in the Rhode Island Coastal Ponds during the summer of 2001, we calculated the distribution of leaf lengths standardized to the size of the oldest leaf (% oldest leaf). This standardization allows comparison of eelgrass ramets that were growing in a variety of

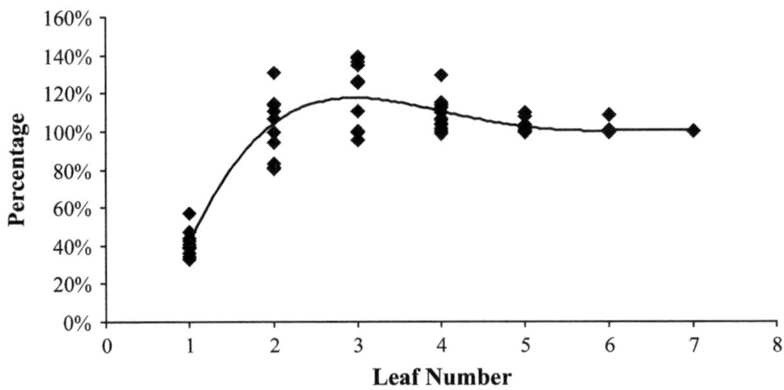

Fig. 3.8 Distribution of mass among leaves, standardized to oldest leaf mass. Older leaves "shorten" as their internodes (previously enclosed in the leaf sheath) become part of the ramet's rhizome. Data from Bintz (2002) and other experiments in the lagoon mesocosm facility

conditions and with varying morphological characteristics (i.e. canopy heights) during the summer months. Leaves were pooled in drying pans for these experiments so only leaf lengths were available for individual leaves. Figure 3.8 displays these data according to leaf number, ordered from the youngest to the oldest leaf. The third leaf was consistently the longest of all leaves, with slightly shorter, older leaves as would be predicted by the growth sequence described above. The mean percentage (as standardized to the oldest leaf) for each leaf was calculated using the combined datasets. The sum of these means predicts that total leaf length of a ramet with five leaves is best represented by 470% of the oldest leaf length.

Bintz (2002) reported that most shoots in southern Rhode Island possessed five leaves during the summer months (May–August). Although number of leaves per shoot is generally considered one of the most conservative features of seagrass morphology (Marba and Duarte 1998), the number of leaves on an eelgrass ramet may vary over seasonal cycles (Kentula and McIntire 1986; Sfriso and Marcomini 1997; Bintz 2002; Lee et al. 2005; Hauxwell et al. 2006). Data from an annual survey of eelgrass production (Bintz 2002) in Ninigret Pond documented a reduction in the number of leaves during the coldest months by approximately one leaf. From November through March, four leaves will be used to set the *malb* and *maol* parameters.

The lack of data detailing individual leaf biomass has inadvertently created an opportunity in the VEM to use leaf length as a morphologically plastic feature of the eelgrass ramet. Elongation of eelgrass leaves has been reported in response to shading (Bintz and Nixon 2001) as well as nitrogen enrichment (Bintz et al. 2003). This response indicates that a rule could be described to associate canopy height (as defined by the longest leaf length) with the light and nutrient regime experienced by a ramet. The third leaf is most commonly the longest leaf (Fig. 3.8) and therefore represents the canopy height of the ramet according to this definition. A quantitative relationship between light, nutrient regime, and canopy height could be combined with the leaf distributions described previously to calculate dynamic *malb* and *maol* biomass values that respond to a ramet's local environment.

Leaf length measurements taken in a number of site-specific descriptive studies suggest a tentative hypothesis to explain changing leaf length in response to water depth or time of year. For example, Dennison and Alberte (1986) and Bostrom et al. (2004) report increasing leaf length with water depth. Lee et al. (2005) recorded various features of *Zostera marina* production over annual cycles at two sites in Korea, one of the few studies to measure growth over entire annual cycles. During the winter months, light reaching the seagrass increased while shoot length decreased (Fig. 3.9, data from Lee et al. 2005). Kentula and McIntire (1986) also measured dramatic declines in leaf surface area between the late summer and winter months.

While it is certainly true that the daily solar irradiance is lower during the winter months in temperate regions, several studies have demonstrated that water column attenuation above seagrass meadows is higher during the summer when increased temperatures and sunlight enhance phytoplankton production and contribute to decreased water clarity (e.g. Olesen and Sand-Jensen 1994; Björk et al. 2021). Between 1997 and 1998, Oviatt et al. (2002) collected water quality data at 16 stations in Narragansett Bay, Rhode Island. These included unpublished light attenuation coefficients that are reproduced in Fig. 3.10 (Oviatt *unpublished data*) and which seem to indicate decreased light attenuation in the fall and early winter months when nutrient depletion, grazing, and/or low temperatures suppress phytoplankton production.

Certainly, it is likely that the lower specific growth rates observed under cold temperatures and shorter photoperiod conditions are partially responsible for the shorter leaf lengths observed during the winter. With shorter and fewer leaves, it is likely that self-shading is also reduced. However, the apparent plasticity of this

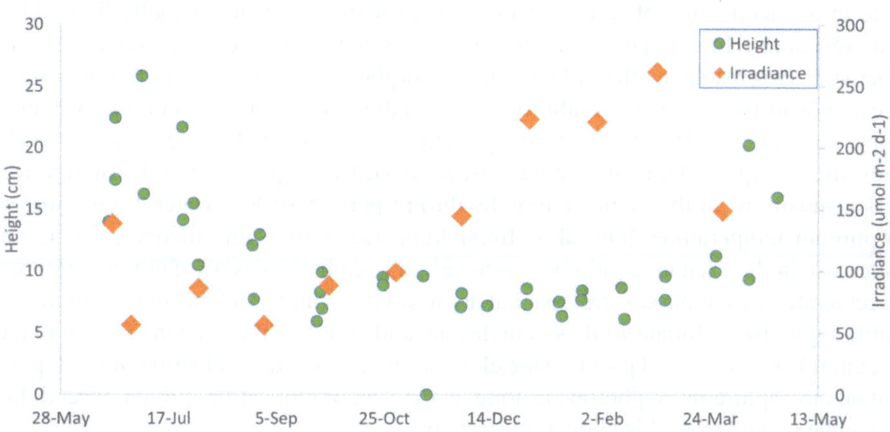

Fig. 3.9 Seasonal pattern of irradiance reaching eelgrass canopy and ramet leaf lengths. Data from Lee (2005). Note pattern of apparent decline in leaf length under high irradiance conditions in fall and winter

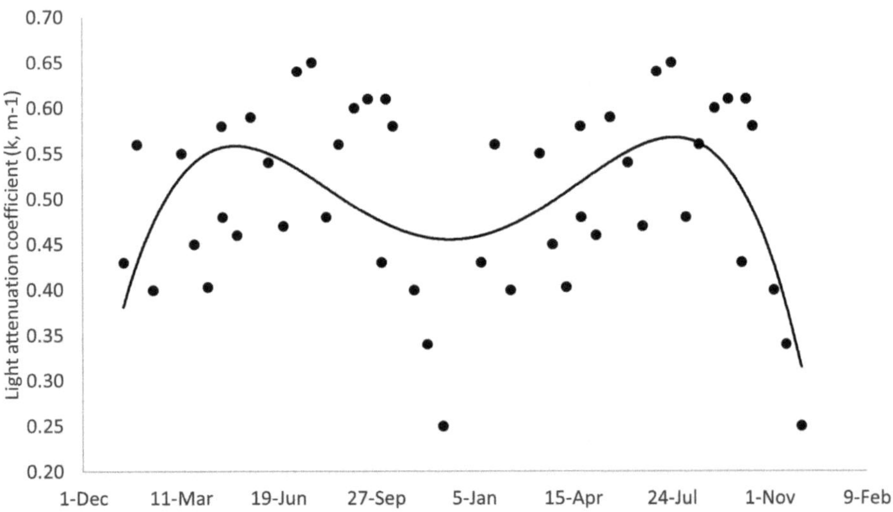

Fig. 3.10 Measurements of light attenuation coefficients at Station 1 in Narragansett Bay are used to describe an annual trend. Original values were measured from April 1997 to April of 1998 but are manipulated here to describe values from January 1st to December 31st. The curve is used to model a dynamic attenuation of light in the VEM

morphological response is also related to the capacity of a ramet to capture light. Leaf elongation represents an investment by the plant that enhances acquisition of photons under light-limiting conditions that may not be necessary under the higher water clarity winter conditions. Wong and Dowd (2025) revealed these general patterns in a meta-analysis of eelgrass traits in relation to temperature and light, reinforcing the patterns described here.

Bloom et al. (1985) predicted that plants optimize investment in structures that aid in the acquisition of resources until the growth of a plant is equally limited by all resources. In this economic framing, it is the exchange ratio (relative cost) between two resources that affects ramet morphology as allocation of new growth responds to the seasonal variability and availability of light, temperature, or nutrients (Bloom et al. 1985). The exchange ratio will ultimately be determined by each resource's supply, demand, and the cost incurred by the plant to build structure for its acquisition. In the summer months during periods of low water clarity, under optimum temperatures but sub-optimal light availability, this theory predicts an increase in the exchange ratio between carbon and photons as warmer temperatures accelerate rates of photosynthesis that are ultimately limited by the amount of available light. To acclimate to these conditions and stabilize the exchange ratio, plant economic theory would promote the elongation of leaves or production of photopigments to capture more photons as long as the cost of elongation did not exceed the revenue gained from this allocation strategy.

With the combined empirical and theoretical support for a response of leaf elongation to decreased light availability, it is possible to consider formulating a variable canopy height as well as light attenuation coefficients that simulate seasonal fluctuations in the VEM. Light extinction coefficients (k) measured by Oviatt (*unpublished data*) at Station 1 in Narragansett Bay will be used to describe this parameter in the VEM. Station 1 is located in the mid-West Passage of Narragansett Bay off the northwest coast of Conanicut Island. Figure 3.10 plots the k value against day of the year which was used for polynomial curve-fitting of the following time-varying function.

$$k = \left(-4\times10^{-11}\times day\,of\;year^{4}\right)+\left(6\times10^{-8}\times day\,of\;year^{3}\right) \\ -\left(3\times10^{-5}\times day\,of\;year^{2}\right)+\left(0.0045\times day\,of\;year\right)+0.3324 \qquad (3.12)$$

The selection of a variable light extinction coefficient using field data forces seasonality to the underwater light environment that allows the VEM to consider a dynamic response of eelgrass ramet leaf length. Solar irradiance in simulations will vary in magnitude according to both changing photoperiod and light extinction through the water column without explicitly modeling the phytoplankton community. Certainly, a user of the VEM can couple forced light extinction values with a mechanistic model for phytoplankton, but we recommend generation of forcing values separately rather than integration of a dynamic phytoplankton model to reduce model complexity.

Dennison and Alberte (1986) completed a transplant experiment to examine the adaptation of eelgrass shoots to depth, which reported an elongation of leaves along the depth gradient (Fig. 3.11). Short et al. (1995) performed a shade experiment that recorded declining leaf length with an increase in the percent of surface light received by eelgrass plants. Ideally, this work could be used to numerically parameterize the relationship between percent irradiance and longest leaf length. However, the Dennison and Alberte (1986) study did not measure light and the linear regression equation reported by Short et al. (1995) indicated an unrealistic intercept of 49.2 as illustrated by Fig. 3.11. This contrasts with frequent reports of leaf lengths in excess of two meters for *Zostera marina* (e.g. Lee et al. 2005) and also contradicts an intuition that the relationship between light and leaf length is nonlinear. Without additional data to assign a relationship between leaf length and irradiance, we can make an educated guess that there is an exponential or power relationship between percent irradiance and leaf length that parallels the exponential attenuation of light with increasing water depth. Using data from the Short et al. (1995) study, this relationship might look something like Eq. 3.13, which is further described by the curve shown in Fig. 3.12.

$$CanopyHeightForLight = 28.55\times PercentIrradiance^{-0.60} \qquad (3.13)$$

This is clearly a less than satisfactory parameterization of canopy height, but it does allow for a hypothesis regarding the general behavior of the ramet to declining irradiance in the form of the *Canopy Height* variable. One of the advantages of the individual-based approach is the ability to incorporate “expert” intuition/experience

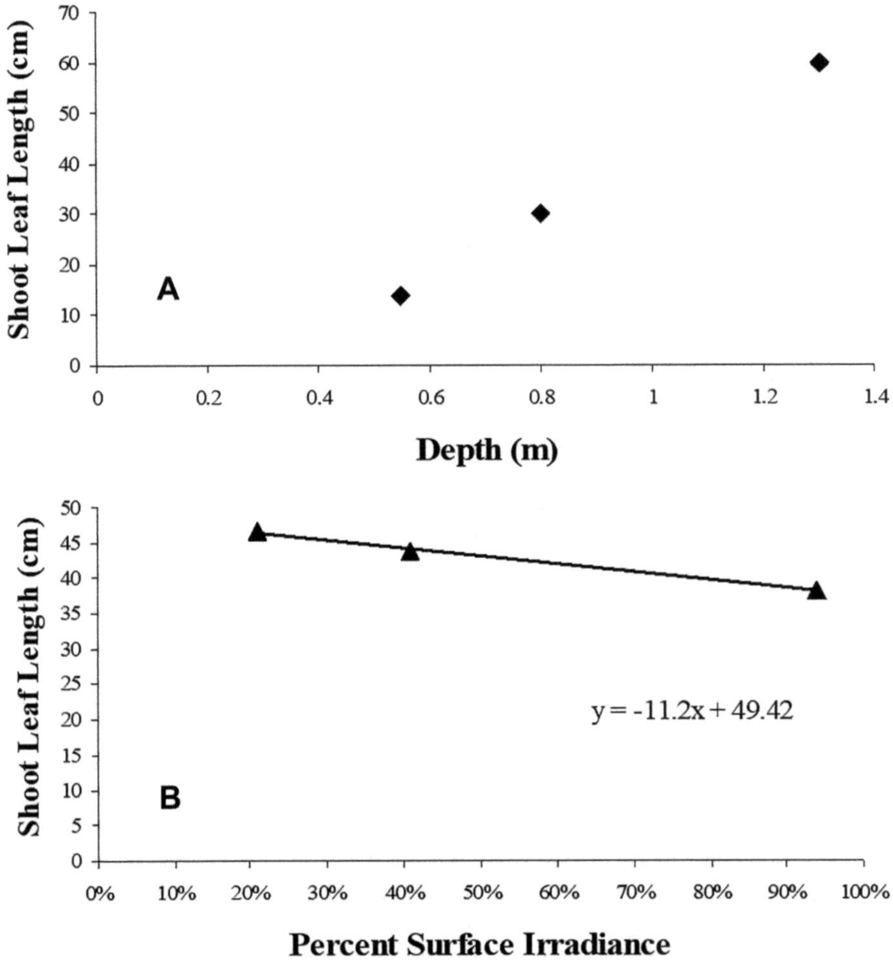

Fig. 3.11 (**a**) Relationship between leaf length and depth (Dennison and Alberte 1986) and (**b**) response of leaf length to percent surface irradiance (Short et al. 1995)

of the ecology of an organism into the modeling process (Grimm and Railsback 2005). In addition to the evidence outlined above for eelgrass, many authors have documented a similar relationship between light and leaf length in other aquatic plants (e.g. Barko et al. 1982; Chambers and Kalff 1987; Goldsborough and Kemp 1988; Strand and Weisner 2001). Santamaria (2002) illustrated the plasticity of leaf length under turbid water column conditions with the example of *Potamogeton pectinatus*, which also exhibits elongated internodes under shaded conditions. Because of the manner in which internode production is modeled in the VEM, the analogous elongation of *Zostera* internodes is implicit in the coupling of canopy height to Eqs. 3.6, 3.7, 3.8, 3.9, 3.10, and 3.11. If the morphology of a ramet responds to reduced light by elongating leaves, the associated internode will also elongate due

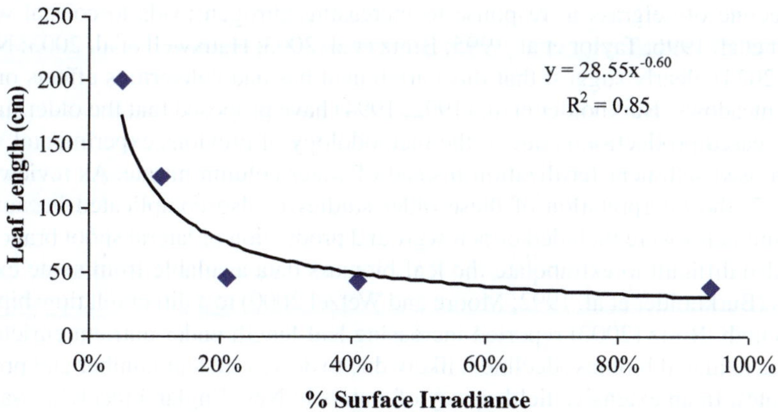

Fig. 3.12 Relationship between percent surface irradiance and canopy height used in the VEM to set mature leaf mass. Data points less than 20% irradiance based on "best guess", other data from Short et al. (1995).

to the longer time interval required for the OLDEST LEAF to slough into the LEAF DETRITUS pool, which triggers the GROWING INTERNODE biomass to empty into the mature ROOTS&RHIZOME compartment to create a new internode segment.

Of course, it is also possible that other environmental conditions affect leaf length. Schanz and Asmus (2003) observed longer eelgrass leaf lengths in sheltered, low velocity conditions than were measured from plants growing in high energy intertidal environments. As mentioned previously, Bintz et al. (2003) documented leaf elongation in response to nutrient enrichment. One approach to including additional environmental conditions when modeling this morphologically plastic feature would be the incorporation of limitation factors scaled between 1 and 0, or in the case of increasing leaf length as "elongation" factors which would multiply a minimum canopy height by values greater than 1. This adaptation of the "limitation factor" strategy followed in Chap. 2 (and many other models) to calculate specific growth rates appears appropriate for this morphological feature of the VEM. At this point in time, there is only limited support for the use of an elongation factor related to current speed. However, there is a much larger literature to draw upon for a nutrient factor. Because no mechanistic detail of nutrient effects was included in the VEM specific growth model, a leaf length elongation factor will also enumerate a hypothesis that links ramet morphology to nutrient enrichment.

It is enlightening to review the extensive literature regarding eelgrass biology and nutrients over a period of time that encompasses the growing awareness of cultural eutrophication as an effect of nutrient enrichment in coastal and estuarine waters. Early work that experimentally increased nutrient enrichment to eelgrass ramets generally report nutrient limitation and enhanced production with fertilization, including leaf elongation in enriched versus control treatments (Orth 1977; Short 1983; Roberts et al. 1987; Murray et al. 1992). Reports have long documented the decline of eelgrass in response to increasing nitrogen loads to coastal waters (Short et al. 1996; Taylor et al. 1995; Bintz et al. 2003; Hauxwell et al. 2003; Novak et al. 2023) clearly suggest that this enrichment has had deleterious effects on eelgrass meadows. Burkholder et al. (1992, 1994) have proposed that the older finding of increased production is due to the methodology of previous experimental work, which used sediment fertilization instead of water column nitrate. As reviewed in Chap. 2, the interpretation of these older studies is also complicated because no measurements were included of belowground production or lateral shoot branching. It is also difficult to extrapolate the leaf biomass data available from some experiments (Burkholder et al. 1992; Moore and Wetzel 2000) to a direct relationship with leaf length. Bintz (2002) reported increasing leaf length under nutrient enrichment even as total leaf biomass declined, likely due to decreased leaf number and production rates. In an extensive field survey of waters in New England receiving varying levels of nutrient loading, Lee et al. (2004) also found it difficult to relate many morphological parameters to enrichment.

One of the practical reasons that there is widespread confusion and debate regarding the direct versus indirect effects of nutrient enrichment on eelgrass is certainly the apparent contradiction between older studies documenting enhancement of leaf growth at the ramet-level and with work which has demonstrated a severe, and often drastic, effect of fertilization on larger-scale features such as shoot density or area-calculated production rates. To truly decipher the demographic history of seagrasses that leads to a given shoot density, it is necessary to examine several measures of population dynamics including lateral branching, seedling recruitment, and mortality (Hemminga and Duarte 2000). We propose that these contrary findings can be reconciled by considering the dependencies between individual, ramet-level production of leaves and internodes, the morphology of these features dictated by the ambient environment, and the rates of asexual lateral branching imprinted within the internal blueprints of a clonal plant.

It is possible, as Hauxwell et al. (2006) suggest, that the decline in shoot density and the observed reduction in eelgrass meadow coverage under increasing nitrogen loading is entirely related to the declining water clarity caused by blooms of phytoplankton and/or macroalgae in response to fertilization. However, the early studies, with their focus on nutrient limitation of eelgrass growth as observed in leaf elongation, suggest a tantalizing alternative hypothesis. Touchette and Burkholder (2000) review the implications of increased water column nitrate concentrations and their impact on the carbon balance of eelgrass ramets, described in detail in Chap. 2. Within the economic analogy discussed previously, an increase in nitrogen to carbon exchange ratios would also promote the allocation of more resources to leaf elongation to capture more light energy. In this instance, the shift in allocation would represent an adaptation to harness enough light energy so that excess nitrogen could be fully used to reach a more stable exchange ratio where all resources are limited more equitably. The balance of this exchange ratio would be all the more imperative to reach if excess nitrate became toxic for the plants (Touchette and Burkholder 2000). As with decreased light availability, these longer leaves will also result in longer rhizome internodes.

In this case we can use the measurements of leaf elongation from older studies to parameterize an elongation factor, which will then extend within the VEM rules structure to influence belowground biomass and production. The work of Roberts et al. (1987) provided the most extensive description of leaf length response to nutrient additions under controlled experimental conditions. Nitrogen additions were converted to areal loading rates by assuming a constant rate of release by the osmocote fertilizer. Figure 3.13 displays the relationship between leaf length and loading rate along with a separate graph scaling these to the lowest, ambient nutrient treatment so that the *nutrient elongation factor* is equal to 1 for this lowest loading. The

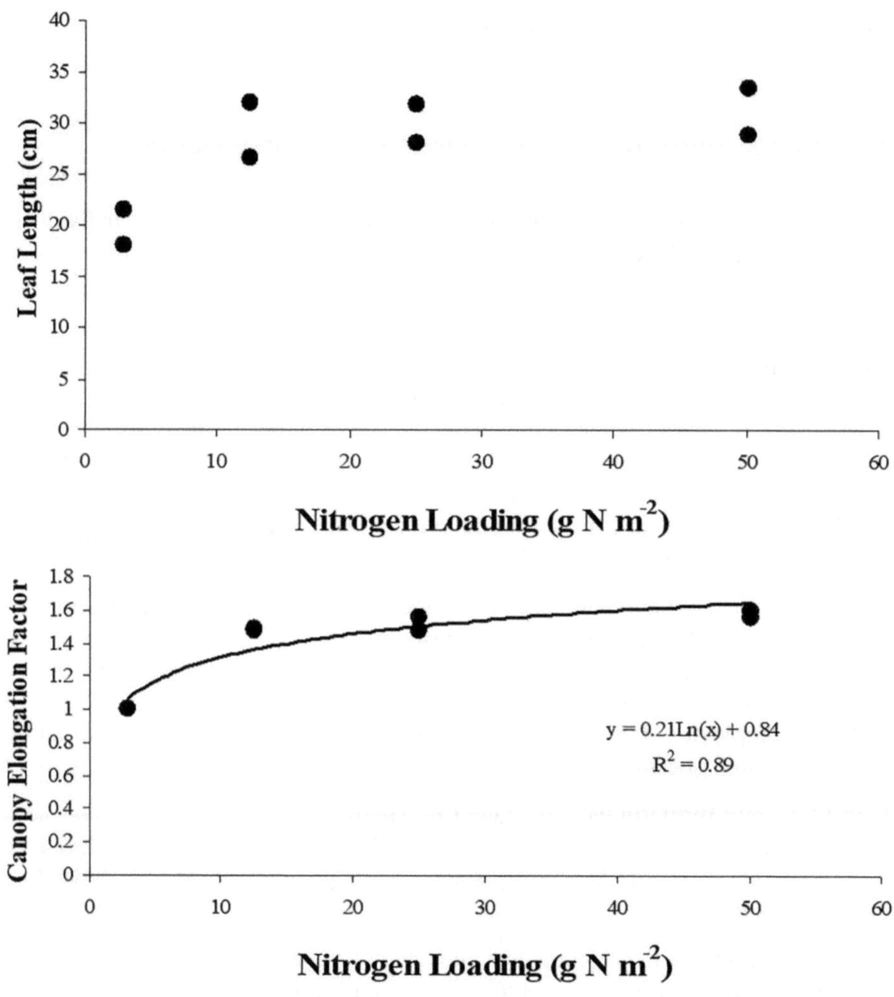

Fig. 3.13 Relationship between leaf length and nitrogen loading used to parameterize the *Canopy Elongation Factor*. Top graph displays data from Roberts et al. (1987) that was scaled to the elongation factor in the lower graph so that the lowest loading would experience a factor of 1

VEM uses this *nutrient elongation factor* multiplied by the *CanopyHeight* variable described previously to estimate a longest leaf length.

$$NutrientElongationFactor = \left[0.206\log\left(NitrogenLoading\right)\right] + 0.8408 \tag{3.14}$$

The implications for the VEM of this link between leaf and internode length are clearly significant. Because the specific growth rate model specifies the magnitude of production in response to the dynamic light and temperature variables, it is difficult to know how total biomass or root to shoot ratios might change. However, within a modular, clonal architecture, the potential for an elongated leaf to produce a longer internode length may also result in increased spacing between shoots, thereby creating the potential for lower shoot density.

3.7 Suggestions for Use in Modeling or Course Design

This chapter provides a roadmap for how to begin considering classes of individuals to describe from an IBM perspective. One of the first tasks in extending this approach to your work or within a classroom might be to delve into a definition of your individuals.

Define Your Module

Where will your individual begin and end? If you are simulating a clonal organism, it will help to clearly define components and think about what information you might have to describe how these might grow or change, or be related to one another. In an ecosystem model, we always define boundaries, here you are just doing this at multiple scales that also consider the individual. This will help you to define submodels that are best to identify before extensive programming.

- We focus on a ramet/phytomer here but there are opportunities to expand to consider plants with greater below ground storage (tubers)
- For floating vegetation, having a separate module for canopy that lays on the surface versus that submerged may be more appropriate
- Is the complexity of growth and morphological plasticity of leaves important to your research question?

Consider Your Individuals and Their Life History

Here we present both sexual and asexual reproductive processes, but the decisions made to divide these into life history stages, while justified, could vary depending on model intention.

- What is known of the reproductive phenology for your organism?
- Are there clear thresholds for ontogenetic change that lend themselves to a rules-based approach?

- Might there be advantages to having different classes of individuals to track changes in growth or sexual reproduction in an IBM that counts each instance of a population?
- What computational tradeoffs might occur from expanding the number of individual classes in your model?

What Questions Are You Asking and Do Your Rules Help You to Answer Them?

Here we were interested in temperature impacts and eutrophication as they might affect both existing meadows and restoration efforts. The processes included in the model sought to test hypotheses associated with these. We also wanted to leverage the benefits of an IBM to have population level feedbacks to individuals and vice versa.

- What processes are you investigating that would most benefit from an IBM model that simulates growth? Is this modeling approach necessary for your goals?
- How are you building in the potential for emergence in your IBM? The purpose here is to avoid deterministic formulations and insure that the spatial and individual-based framework lends itself to new insights.

References

Abe M, Yokota K, Goto M, Kurashima A, Maegawa M (2008) Relationship between distribution patterns of shoots and light conditions on population floor in Zostera marina population. Fish Sci 74:299–307

Aioi K (1980) Seasonal change in the standing crop of eelgrass (*Zostera marina* L.) in Odawa Bay, central Japan. Aquat Bot 8:343–354

Alpert P, Stuefer JF (1997) Division of labour in clonal plants. In: de Kroon H, van Groenendael J (eds) The ecology and physiology of clonal plants. Backhuys Publishers, Leiden

Barko J, Hardin DG, Matthews MS (1982) Growth and morphology of submersed freshwater macrophytes in relation to light and temperature. Can J Bot 60:877–887

Bell AD, Tomlinson PB (1980) Adaptive architecture in rhizomatous plants morphology. Bot J Linn Soc 80:125–160

Bell AD, Roberts D, Smith A (1979) Branching patterns: the simulation of plant architecture. J Theor Biol 81:351–375

Bintz JC (2002) The ecology and morphology of eelgrass (*Zostera marina* L.) and its associated macrophyte community in relation to environmental variables. Ph.D dissertation. University of Rhode Island

Bintz JC, Nixon SW (2001) Responses of eelgrass *Zostera marina* seedlings to reduced light. Mar Ecol Prog Ser 223:133–141

Bintz JC, Nixon SW, Buckley BA, Granger SL (2003) Impacts of temperature and nutrients on coastal lagoon plant communities. Estuaries 26:765–776

Björk M, Asplund ME, Deyanova D, Gullström M (2021) The amount of light reaching the leaves in seagrass (Zostera marina) meadows. PLoS One 16(9):e0257586

Bloom AJ, Chapin FS, Mooney HA (1985) Resource limitation in plants—an economic analogy. Annu Rev Ecol Syst 16:363–392

Bostrom C, Roos C, Ronnberg O (2004) Shoot morphometry and production dynamics of eelgrass in the northern Baltic Sea. Aquat Bot 79:145–161

Burkholder JM, Mason KM, Glasgow HB (1992) Water-column nitrate enrichment promotes decline of eelgrass *Zostera marina*: evidence from seasonal mesocosm experiments. Mar Ecol Prog Ser 81:163–178

Burkholder JM, Glascow HB, Cooke JE (1994) Comparative effects of water column nitrate enrichment on eelgrass *Zostera marina*, shoal grass *Haloduli wrightii*, and widgeon grass *Ruppia marina*. Mar Ecol Prog Ser 105:121–138

Chambers PA, Kalff J (1987) Light and nutrients in the control of aquatic plant community structure. I. *in situ* experiments. J Ecol 75:611–619

De Kroon H, Hutchings MJ (1995) Morphological plasticity in clonal plants: the foraging concept reconsidered. J Ecol 83:143–152

De Kroon H, van Groenendael J (eds) (1997) The ecology and physiology of clonal plants. Backhuys Publishers, Leiden

Dennison WC, Alberte RS (1986) Photoadaptation and growth of *Zostera marina* L. (eelgrass) transplants along a depth gradient. J Exp Mar Biol Ecol 98:265–282

Duarte CM, Chiscano CL (1999) Seagrass biomass and production: a reassessment. Aquat Bot 65:159–174

Duarte C, Marba N, Agawin N, Cebrian J, Enriquez S, Fortes MD, Gallegos ME, Merino M, Olesen B, Sand-Jensen K, Uri J, Vermaat J (1994) Reconstruction of seagrass dynamics: age determinations and associated tools for the seagrass ecologist. Mar Ecol Prog Ser 107:195–209

Foley JL (2017) Using an individual based model to evaluate the effects of climate change on the reproductive phenology of eelgrass (Zostera marina L.) along a latitudinal gradient. Master's thesis, University of Maryland, College Park

Gatsuk LE, Smirnova OV, Vorontzova LI, Zaugolnova LB, Zhukova LA (1980) Age states of plants of various growth forms: a review. J Ecol 68:675–696

Geber MA, Watson MA, de Kroon H (1997) Organ preformation, development, and resource allocation in plants. In: Grace J, Bazzaz FA (eds) Plant resource allocation. Academic, San Diego

Goldsborough WJ, Kemp WM (1988) Light responses of a submersed macrophyte: implications for survival in turbid waters. Ecology 69:1775–1786

Grimm V, Railsback SF (2005) Individual-based modeling and ecology. Princeton University Press, Princeton

Hauxwell J, Cebrian J, Valiela I (2003) Eelgrass *Zostera marina* loss in temperate estuaries: relationship to land-derived nitrogen loads and effect of light limitation imposed by algae. Mar Ecol Prog Ser 247:59–73

Hauxwell J, Cebrian J, Valiela I (2006) Light dependence of *Zostera marina* annual growth dynamics in estuaries subject to different degrees of eutrophication. Aquat Bot 84:17–25

Hemminga MA, Duarte C (2000) Seagrass ecology. Cambridge University Press, Cambridge

Jarvis JC, Moore KA, Kenworthy WJ (2012) Characterization and ecological implication of eelgrass life history strategies near the species' southern limit in the western North Atlantic. Mar Ecol Prog Ser 444:43–56

Jarvis JC, Brush MJ, Moore KA (2014) Modeling loss and recovery of Zostera marina beds in the Chesapeake Bay: the role of seedlings and seed-bank viability. Aquat Bot 113:32–45. https://doi.org/10.1016/j.aquabot.2013.10.010

Kentula ME, McIntire CD (1986) The autoecology and production dynamics of eelgrass (*Zostera marina* L.) in Netarts Bay. Oregon Estuaries 9:188–199

Lee K, Short FT, Burdick DM (2004) Development of a nutrient pollution indicator using the seagrass *Zostera marina*, along nutrient gradients in three New England estuaries. Aquat Bot 78:197–216

Lee K, Park SR, Kim J (2005) Production dynamics of the eelgrass, *Zostera marina* in two bay systems on the south coast of the Korean peninsula. Mar Biol 147:1091–1108

Madsen JD (1991) Resource allocation at the individual plant level. Aquat Bot 41:67–86

Marba N, Duarte CM (1998) Rhizome elongation and seagrass clonal growth. Mar Ecol Prog Ser 174:269–280

Marba N, Hemminga MA, Mateo MA, Duarte CM, Mass YEM, Terrados J, Gacia E (2002) Carbon and nitrogen translocation between seagrass ramets. Mar Ecol Prog Ser 226:287–300

Moore K, Wetzel RW (2000) Seasonal variations in eelgrass (*Zostera marina* L.) responses to nutrient enrichment and reduced light availability in experimental ecosystems. J Exp Mar Biol Ecol 244:1–28

Murray L, Dennison WC, Kemp WM (1992) Nitrogen versus phosphorus limitation for growth of an estuarine population of eelgrass (*Zostera marina* L.). Aquat Bot 44:83–100

Niu S, Zhang P, Liu J, Guo D, Zhang X (2012) The effect of temperature on the survival, growth, photosynthesis, and respiration of young seedlings of eelgrass Zostera marina L. Aquaculture 350:98–108.

Novak AB, Plaisted HK, Hughes ZJ, Mittermayr A, Molden E (2023) Eelgrass (Zostera marina L.) populations are threatened by high sea-surface temperatures and impaired waters on Nantucket Island, USA. Mar Pollut Bull *197*:115689

Oborny B, Cain ML (1997) Models of spatial spread and foraging in clonal plants. In: de Kroon H, van Groenendael J (eds) The ecology and evolution of clonal plants. Backhuys, Leiden

Oborny B, Czaran T, Kun A (2001) Exploration and exploitation of resource patches by clonal growth: a spatial model on the effect of transport between modules. Ecol Model 141:151–169

Ochieng CA, Short FT, Walker DI (2010) Photosynthetic and morphological responses of eelgrass (Zostera marina L.) to a gradient of light conditions. J Exp Mar Biol Ecol 382(2):117–124

Olesen B, Sand-Jensen K (1993) Seasonal acclimatization of eelgrass *Zostera marina* growth to light. Mar Ecol Prog Ser 94:91–99

Olesen B, Sand-Jensen K (1994) Patch dynamics of eelgrass *Zostera marina*. Mar Ecol Prog Ser 106:147–156

Orth JR (1977) Effect of nutrient enrichment of growth of eelgrass *Zostera marina* in the Chesapeake Bay, Virginia, USA. Mar Biol 44:187–194

Oviatt C, Keller A, Reed L (2002) Annual primary production in Narragansett Bay with no bay-wide winter-spring phytoplankton bloom. Estuar Coast Shelf Sci 54:1013–1026

Robbins WJ (1957) Physiological aspects of aging in plants. Am J Bot 44:289–294

Roberts M, Orth RJ, Moore KA (1987) Growth of *Zostera marina* L. seedlings under laboratory conditions of nutrient enrichment. Aquat Bot 20:321–328

Salinas H, Solana-Arellano E (2021) Importance of elongation and organogenesis on the rhizome length of Zostera marina in an individual-based simulation model. Estuar Coast Shelf Sci 261:107530

Santamaría L (2002) Why are most aquatic plants broadly distributed? Dispersal, clonal growth and small-scale heterogeneity in a stressful environment. Acta Oecol 23:137–154

Schanz A, Asmus H (2003) Impact of hydrodynamics on development and morphology of intertidal seagrasses in the Wadden Sea. Mar Ecol Prog Ser 261:123–134

Setchell WA (1929) Morphological and phenological notes on *Zostera marina* L. Univ Calif Publ Bot 14:389–452

Sfriso A, Marcomini AM (1997) Macrophyte production in a shallow coastal lagoon. Part I: coupling with chemico-physical parameters and nutrient concentrations in waters. Mar Environ Res 44:351–375

Short FT (1983) The seagrass, *Zostera marina* L.: plant morphology and bed structure in relation to sediment ammonium in Izembek Lagoon, Alaska. Aquat Bot 16:149–161

Short F, Burdick DM, Kaldy JE III (1995) Mesocosm experiments quantify the effects of eutrophication on eelgrass, *Zostera marina*. Limnol Oceanogr 40:740–749

Short FT, Burdick D, Granger S, Nixon SW (1996) Long-term decline in eelgrass, *Zostera marina* L., linked to increased housing development. In: Kuo J, Phillips R, Walker D, Kirkman H (eds) Seagrass biology: proceedings of an international workshop. Faculty of Sciences, University of Western Australia, Perth

Sintes TN, Marba C, Duarte M, Kendrick GA (2005) Nonlinear processes in seagrass colonization explained by simple clonal growth rules. Oikos 108:165–175

Strand JA, Weisner SEB (2001) Morphological plastic responses to water depth and wave exposure in an aquatic plant (*Myriophyllum spcatum*). J Ecol 89:166–175

Suzuki JI, Stuefer JF (1999) On the ecological and evolutionary significance of storage in clonal plants. Plant Species Biol 14:11–17

Tanner CE, Parham T (2010) Growing Zostera marina (eelgrass) from seeds in land-based culture systems for use in restoration projects. Restor Ecol 18(4):527–537.

Taylor ARA (1957) Studies of the development of Zostera marina l.: I. the embryo and seed. Can J Bot *35*(4):477–499

Taylor DI, Nixon SW, Granger SL, Buckley BA, McMahon JP, Lin H-J (1995) Responses of coastal lagoon plant communities to different forms of nutrient enrichment—a mesocosm experiment. Aquat Bot 52:19–34

Thayer GW, Kenworthy WJ, Fonseca MS (1984) *The ecology of eelgrass meadows of the Atlantic coast: a community profile*. Fish and Wildlife Service, US Department of the Interior.

Tomlinson BF (1974) Vegetative morphology and meristem dependence - the foundation of productivity in seagrasses. Aquaculture 4:107–130

Touchette BW, Burkholder JM (2000) Review of nitrogen and phosphorus metabolism in seagrasses. J Exp Mar Biol Ecol 250(1-2):133–167

Webster's Seventh New Collegiate Dictionary (1967) Gove, Philip (ed). G & C Merriam Co

Winkler E, Fischer M (2002) The role of vegetative and seed dispersal within habitats for optimal life histories of clonal plants: a simulation study. Evol Ecol 15:281–301

Wong MC, Dowd M (2025) Eelgrass (Zostera marina) trait variation across varying temperature-light regimes. Estuar Coasts 48(1):13

Zharova N, Sfriso A, Voinov A, Pavoni B (2001) A simulation model for the annual fluctuation of *Zostera marina* biomass in the Venice lagoon. Aquat Bot 70:135–150

Chapter 4
The Virtual Meadow

4.1 Introduction

The Virtual Eelgrass Meadow modeling framework first needs to simulate the amazing feat of manufacturing plant structure from solar energy using existing plant infrastructure (Chap. 2's Specific Growth Rate), followed by steps to direct that new growth to various features of the ramet itself (Chap. 3's focus on leaves, internodes, rhizomes). This chapter is then left with the task of crafting a simulated environment where the clonal nature of these plants is extended into space, with the life and death processes related to lateral branching, flowering, seed germination, and mortality programmed into at least a two-dimensional space. As a reminder, the full schedule of these processes are outlined in Tables 3.1 and 3.2.

We have spent time discussing many aspects of clonal growth, the ramet and phytomer unit, and the interconnection between the rhizome and leaf production. Another critical aspect is the capacity to optimize resource capture using plant architecture and clonal expansion. For some in the plant ecology community, adaptive responses signal characteristics of complex behavior more frequently attributed to mobile animals (Trewavas 2003; Latzel and Münzbergová 2018). The VEM takes some of this perspective, understanding that adaptive rules propel the plant across the sediment surface through a complex combination of growth, morphology, and environmental response. Here we critically examine how the combination of plant architecture and availability of light might lead to larger scale patterns of eelgrass meadow structure, especially rates of asexual lateral shoot branching and density dependence. To realistically simulate the eelgrass meadow, we must also include mechanisms for sexual reproduction, and here we modify and expand the work of Jarvis et al. (2014), while also proposing flowering as driving natural mortality.

© Springer Nature B.V. 2026

L. A. Harris et al., *Ramet Rules*, Aquatic Ecology Series 9,
https://doi.org/10.1007/978-94-024-2365-5_4

4.2 Lateral Branching

We ended Chap. 3 highlighting the potential for morphological plasticity associated with leaf elongation to produce a longer internode length, thus resulting in a direct potential impact to plant architecture in response to light, temperature, sulfide, and nutrient conditions. Before exploring the consequences of a variable internode length on larger scale features such as density or patch expansion rates in the VEM, it is necessary to designate rules regarding when the meristem should divide to result in lateral branching and the initiation of a new ramet. The frequency of branching in eelgrass is generally measured by recording the number of days separating the production of new lateral shoots. This measure constitutes an example of a plastochrone interval, which is defined as the number of days between initiation of a plant module such as a leaf, or in this case the ramet itself.

The branching frequency of eelgrass typically follows a seasonal pattern, with shorter shoot plastochrone intervals in the summer than during the winter months (Olesen and Sand-Jensen 1994). In a review of the entire seagrass flora, Marba and Duarte (1998) reported 34% within-species variability of this feature and a strong correlation with size among the various species surveyed. Across the terrestrial clonal plants, most species respond to higher resource availability with increased branching rates (De Kroon and Hutchings 1995). This has been idealized as a "behavior" of the clonal ramet that can result in perceived foraging for resources such as light, water, or nutrients (Oborny 1994; De Kroon and Hutchings 1995).

During the summer of 2000, we completed experiments in the lagoon mesocosms at the University of Rhode Island's Graduate School of Oceanography that were designed to measure predation rates of prey fish in varying densities of eelgrass and macroalgal cover (Harris et al. 2004). During this experiment, measurements of eelgrass production based on the rhizome tagging techniques described in Chap. 2 were taken at shoot densities of 75, 200, 500 and 1000 shoots m^{-2}. Plants were tagged for 6 weeks, collected, and returned to the laboratory where the number of lateral shoots and new nodes were counted. Lateral shoot production declined with increasing shoot densities, with longer shoot plastochrone intervals occurring at higher shoot densities (Fig. 4.1). This suggests that competition and crowding by neighbors affects overall productivity, with plants responding with density--dependent production that lead to self-thinning. Data describing the average weight of plants found at their highest densities is closely correlated both within and among species as pictured in Fig. 4.2 (data from Enquist et al. 1998), and has generally been attributed to an upper limit of individual biomass production resulting from competition for resources under crowded conditions (Yoda et al. 1963; White 1981; Duarte and Kalff 1987). Whether the measured phenomenon of self-thinning may be attributable to crowding induced mortality or lower rates of reproduction is still under debate (Li et al. 2000; Berger et al. 2002; Weiner 2004). However, it appears that branching rates are intimately related to this feature in *Zostera marina*, a mechanism which has been previously proposed but not measured in field populations of

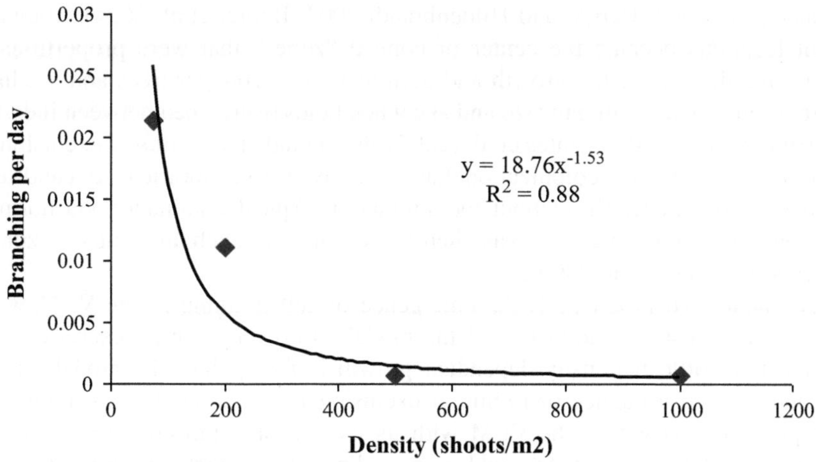

Fig. 4.1 The effect of shoot density on lateral shoot production. Data from plant tagging during the summer of 2000 lagoon mesocosm experiment

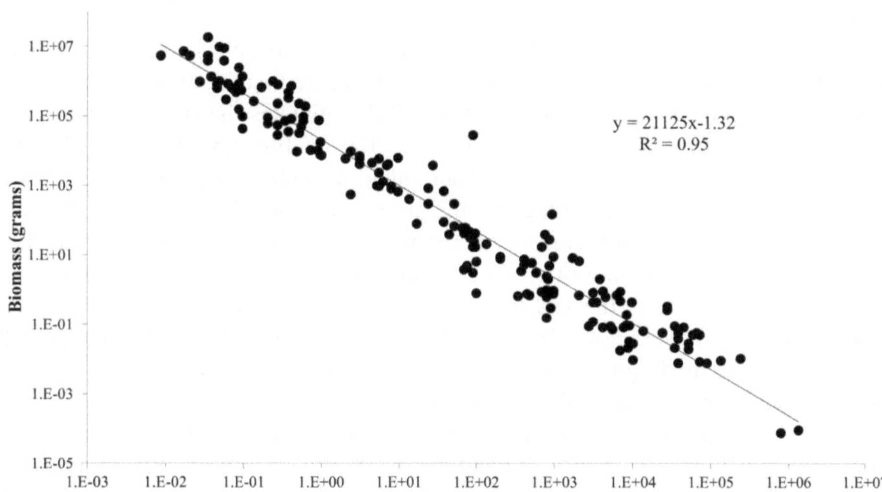

Fig. 4.2 Data from terrestrial plants describing "self-thinning law". (Data from Enquist et al. 1998). Density is defined as number of individual plants per square meter and biomass represents the biomass of an individual

this species (Olesen and Sand-Jensen 1994; Poumian-Tapia and Ibarra--Obando 1999).

Berger and Hildenbrandt (2000) overcame significant computational challenges in an individual-based model to simulate self-thinning in mangroves using a "field--of-neighborhood" approach which has now been extended to several other models

(Bauer et al. 2002; Berger and Hildenbrandt 2003; Berger et al. 2024). Mangrove point locations became the center of conical "zones" that were proportional to mangrove size, while the growth and germination of younger trees and seedlings were penalized according to size and age when fields overlapped between individuals (Berger et al. 2002). Sintes et al. (2005) also included a "radius of exclusion" in their model of seagrass colonization that was derived from empirical data and set as a constant parameter throughout the simulation. Apical dominance via hormone mediated growth suppression was cited as evidence for such an exclusion zone in seagrasses (Sintes et al. 2005).

As mentioned in Chap. 1, the emergence of self-thinning in the VEM would serve as a robust validation test of the model. However, such an exercise would demonstrate little if density-dependent growth is forced into the model with an explicit zone-of-influence or radius of exclusion formulation. The exploration of this phenomenon within the VEM with its mechanistic, physiological underpinnings should help us to understand how crowding might affect measured shoot densities and branching rates without including a density-specific mortality term. This approach emphasizes an understanding of physiological processes *and* architectural rules enacted at very small scales to explain large-scale community dynamics and spatial patterns.

We hypothesize that the ramet plastochrone interval is correlated with the leaf plastochrone interval. Within the VEM, this would mean that the dynamic morphology of leaf length serves as a type of "clock" that dictates the rate at which new internodes and new branches are formed as visualized in Fig. 3.5. The canopy height specified by local light conditions is further linked with physical parameters of temperature and sediment type via the specific growth rate model to determine the rate at which new leaves, and therefore internodes and lateral shoots, are formed. By linking the lateral branching rule to leaf formation, a more elaborate hypothesis is also suggested that tests the self-thinning law at the mechanistic, first-principled level elucidated by West et al. (1999). In this scenario, the modular rules that clonal plants follow are finely tuned, likely over evolutionary time scales, to allow adaptation to available resources so that an optimum density and biomass can be reached according to local conditions. Rather than the forester's version of the self-thinning law, where seedlings are shaded out and die due to the size-dominance of an older neighbor, our hypothesis predicts that the plasticity of clonal plant morphology and modular rules is designed to avoid mortality due to crowding by predetermining the appropriate spatial configuration, size, and density of the plants for a given set of environmental conditions.

Empirical evidence supporting the dependence of lateral shoot branching on leaf production is shown in Fig. 4.3 and includes measurements taken in Rhode Island coastal ponds. When one or two lateral shoots were produced, Fig. 4.3 shows that these branches were most often associated with the fifth internode. Ramets producing three lateral shoots in this time frame were rare and were most frequently associated with the fourth, fifth and sixth nodes. It was also common to see two sequential lateral shoots on nodes immediately adjacent to one another, branching dichotomously to the left and right of the parent rhizome.

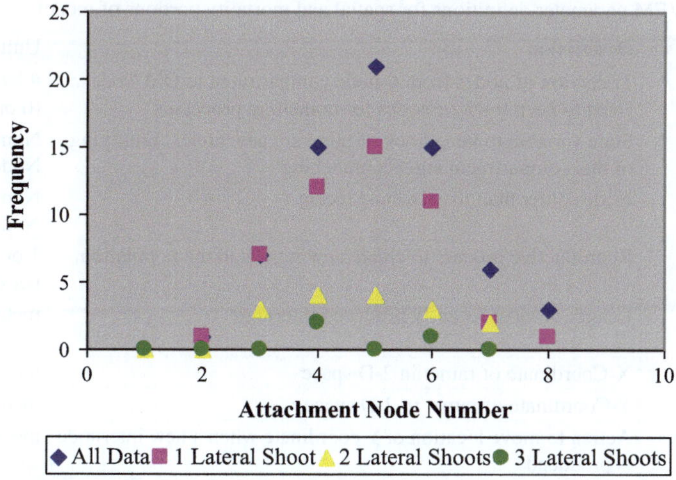

Fig. 4.3 Frequency distribution of lateral shoot's attachment node on the mother ramet. Data from lagoon tagging in Rhode Island coastal ponds. Differences between number of "offspring" from mother ramet are color coded

To incorporate this information into the VEM, a rule is specified to ensure that the ramet will branch every fourth and fifth internode that is transferred from the GROWINGINTERNODE compartment to the ROOTS&RHIZOME state variable. To accomplish this computationally, two new state variables are specified; NODES and OLDNODES. The NODES compartment will hold up to six nodes so that the branching rule can keep track of the fourth and fifth internodes. After the second branch is produced, the six nodes will be transferred to the OLDNODES compartment. The definitions for variables and parameters are provided in Table 4.1 and equations for these actions are reproduced below and compiled in Table 4.2.

$$I_n = \text{if OLDESTLEAF}_0 > \text{OLDEST LEAF}_1 \text{ then } 1 \text{ else } 0 \tag{4.1}$$

$$\text{NODES}_1 = \text{NODES}_0 + I_n \tag{4.2}$$

$$I_o = \text{if NODES}_1 == 6 \text{ then } 6 \text{ else } 0 \tag{4.3}$$

$$\text{OLD NODES}_1 = \text{OLD NODES}_0 + I_o \tag{4.4}$$

$$\begin{aligned} \mathit{BRANCH} = \text{if NODES}_1 == 6 \text{ and NODES}_0 == 5 \text{ then } 1 \\ \text{else if NODES}_1 == 5 \text{ and NODES}_0 == 4 \text{ then } 1 \text{ else } 0 \end{aligned} \tag{4.5}$$

The first flow (I_n) into the NODES compartment triggers the growth of a node once the oldest leaf is shed from the Ramet as described in Eqs. 4.1 and 4.2. The NODES state variable empties once it has reached a threshold of six nodes (Eq. 4.3), at which point these six nodes are placed in the OLD NODES compartment

Table 4.1 VEM parameter definitions for spatial and mortality portions of model

	Description	Units
I_O	Transition of nodes from 6-node compartment to Old Nodes. Used to keep track of nodes for branching processes	# Nodes/day (0 or 1)
NODES	State variable to keep track of up to six new nodes. Emptying of this compartment signals branching	Number of Nodes
OLD NODES	Nodes older than the six most recent	Number of Nodes
BRANCH	Reproductive process to create new ramets in the population	1 or 0 branches per day
Internode Length	Length of most recently produced internode	meters
X	X-Coordinate of ramet in 2-D space	meters
Y	Y-Coordinate of ramet in 2-D space	meters
MoveYApex	Action to move location of Y-coordinate when a new internode is produced	meters day^{-1}
MoveXApex	Action to move location of X-coordinate when a new internode is produced	meters day^{-1}
k_{canopy}	Light extinction coefficient for eelgrass canopy, dependent on density and leaf length	$meters^{-1}$
FLOWER	Class of Individuals in Model that are flowering	
FLOWER CLOCK	State variable to keep track of the 41 days that a ramet will live and occupy one location in space once it has been classified as a flower	days
flowertime	Flow into Flower Clock that marks one day	day
DEATH	Population process that removes one ramet from population after it has been a flower for 41 days	1 or 0
Density	Local shoot density within a quarter meter square area of an individual shoot	shoots $meter^{-2}$
Canopy Height	Length of longest leaf	centimeters
temperature	Water temperature	°C

(Eq. 4.4). A separate asexual reproductive function *BRANCH* uses the NODES compartment to add a new ramet to the simulation at the transition between nodes 4–5 and 5–6 (Eq. 4.5).

4.3 Sexual Reproduction

Sexual reproduction was programmed (Table 4.3) with procedures and parameters modified into a rules-based approach from the eelgrass reproduction model developed by Jarvis et al. (2014) and previously described in Foley (2017). The Jarvis et al. model (2014) highlighted the need to include sexual reproduction within traditional *Z. marina* production models as model output could more accurately

Table 4.2 Essential equations governing spatial implementation

I_n = if OLDESTLEAF$_0$ > OLDEST LEAF$_1$ then 1 else 0	Eq. 4.1
NODES$_1$ = NODES$_0$ + I_n	Eq. 4.2
I_o = if NODES$_1$ = = 6 then 6 else 0	Eq. 4.3
OLD NODES$_1$ = OLD NODES$_0$ + I_o	Eq. 4.4
BRANCH = if NODES$_1$ = = 6 and NODES$_0$ = = 5 then 1	Eq. 4.5
elseif NODES$_1$ = = 5 and NODES$_0$ = = 4 then 1 else 0	
InternodeLength = if OLDESTLEAF$_0$ > OLDEST LEAF$_1$ then 0.31728*m*/*g* × GROWING INTERNODE	Eq. 4.7
MoveYApex = if random constant(0, 1) < 0.5 then *InternodeLength* × sin ((*MyMother'sDirection* + 1.326)) else *InternodeLength* × sin ((*MyMother'sDirection* − 1.326)	Eq. 4.8
MoveXApex = if random constant(0, 1) < 0.5 then *InternodeLength*×	Eq. 4.9
cos((*MyMother'sDirection* + 1.326)) else *InternodeLength*×	
cos((*MyMother'sDirection* − 1.326)	
Y = if *myage* < 2 then *MyMother'sY* else Y$_0$ + *MoveYApex*	Eq. 4.10
X = if *myage* < 2 then *MyMother'sX* else X$_0$ + *MoveXApex*	Eq. 4.11
k_{canopy} = 2.09 + (0.0018 × *Density* × 0.01 × *CanopyHeight*)	Eq. 4.12

Table 4.3 Essential equations governing sexual reproduction and mortality

FLOWER = if T >=15 and *NODES*>=3 and propabilityflower<=	Eq. 4.6
(if Daysabove20<=100 then 0.3 elseif Daysabove20>=150 then 0.9 else 0.5)	
then "true" else "false" (boolean)	
FLOWERCLOCK = if *flower* = = TRUE then 1 else 0	Eq. 4.13
flowertime = if *flower* = = TRUE then 1 else 0	Eq. 4.14
G_l = if *flower* = = TRUE then 0 else *SGR* × LEAVES	Eq. 3.2
$G_r \text{if } flower == \text{TRUE then 0 else} \dfrac{b \times G_l}{1-b}$	Eq. 3.3
DEATH = if FLOWERCLOCK = = *random*(41, 50)	Eq. 4.15
then TRUE else FALSE	

predict loss and recovery processes. The reproduction model influences the timing and magnitude of sexual reproductive events, including the production of flowering shoots, seeds, germination, and seedling establishment. Silberhorn (1983) published a valuable synthesis documenting reproductive phenology at a number of locations along a latitudinal gradient (Fig. 4.4). Despite differences in the time of year and latitude, the observance of key reproductive events (inflorescence primordia, anthesis, and mature fruit) across four different investigations were all intimately tied to temperature (Silberhorn et al. 1983). These sexual reproduction-temperature relationships were also confirmed and documented by Orth and Moore (1983; Table 4.4).

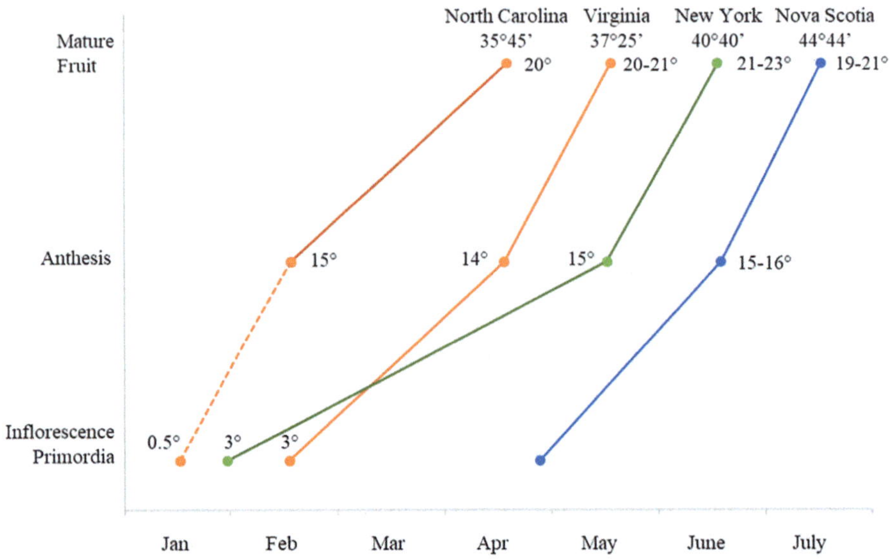

Fig. 4.4 Reproductive phenology of *Z. marina* at different locations (with latitude) along the East coast of the United States. (Data from Silberhorn et al. 1983)

Table 4.4 Relationships between *Z. marina* reproductive phenology and temperature (Orth and Moore 1983, Setchell 1929, Moore et al. 1993)

Development stage	Temperature (°C)
Spadix primordia (immature flowers)	0.5–3
Anthesis (flowering & pollination)	15
Mature fruit	20–21
Peak seed production	20–23
Seeds in sediment seed bank	0–30
Seed dormancy—no germination	>20
Seed germination	~15
Peak germination and presence of seedlings	5–15

One aspect not detailed in the Jarvis et al. (2014) model but incorporated in the VEM is the "growing degree days" (GDD) concept of thermal stress day accumulation (Foley 2017). One of the oldest and most studied ecological concepts, "growing degree days" (GDD) describe an accumulated degree-day phenological interaction (largely temperature and/or light) that drives a particular developmental event (Idso et al. 1978). This relationship has also been applied outside the field of plant ecology, such as with blue crab growth in the Chesapeake Bay (Brylawski and Miller 2006). Rates of flowering in clonal seagrasses typically increase with increased disturbance or stressful conditions, such as high water temperature (Kim et al. 2014).

We incorporated this relationship during parameterization of sexual reproduction in the model using a temperature threshold for accumulated “thermal stress days”. The threshold was set at 20 °C, the average temperature with which respiration begins to increase beyond productivity in *Z. marina* individuals (Marsh et al. 1986; Lee et al. 2017). As in other temperature dependent processes for *Zostera marina*, we recognize that there has been documented variability in the values for these thresholds and encourage end users of the VEM to adjust this parameter to their own population (e.g. Berger and Berg 2024).

This was accomplished practically by including a variable in the model that computes how many days in the growing season are above the 20 °C stress parameter (Foley 2017). The model then uses the number of days in the year above 20 °C to set the biological threshold and temperature proxy to determine the probability that an individual will flower. This conditional flowering probability is a hybrid mechanistic-stochastic parameter that determines if an individual should flower and is linked to temperature, time of year, number of nodes, and overall probability. Each year, individuals are assigned either a 30%, 50%, or 90% chance of flowering based on the number of thermal stress days accumulated over that year. If there were <=100 days with temperatures over 20 °C then an individual’s probability of flowering is 30%. If there were >= 150 days then the probability is 90% and if there was any amount in between then the probability of flowering is 50%. The probability of flowering is a value that affects the individual ramet and should not be confused with the percent of total individuals who flowered within the meadow during a given year. The programming rules for these processes are partially represented by Eq. 4.6:

$$\begin{aligned} &FLOWER = \text{if T >= 15 and } NODES \text{ >= 3 and propability flower <=} \\ &\left(\begin{array}{c}\text{if Daysabove20} \langle = 100 \text{ then } 0.3 \text{ else if Daysabove20} \rangle \\ = 150 \text{ then } 0.9 \text{ else } 0.5\end{array}\right) \text{then "true" else "false" (boolean)} \end{aligned} \tag{4.6}$$

In this programming, we are tracking whether there have been more than 100 or 150 days above 20° and then using a probability value to indicate whether a ramet will transition to being a flower. This only occurs if the current temperature is above 15° and the individual ramet has greater than 3 nodes.

The 100 day and 150 day temperature stress thresholds were selected based on a literature review of average temperatures against observed rates of reproductive shoots (Foley 2017). Information supporting these thresholds, however, are still lacking and there are inconsistencies in literature data with respect to eelgrass flowering and temperature. Still, several studies have shown that locations with higher water temperatures typically experience higher rates of flowering (i.e. North Carolina “annual” meadows) (Jarvis et al. 2012; Kim et al. 2014; Blok et al. 2018). An exception to this is a study by Qin et al. (2020) evaluating marine heat waves that may have resulted in lower flowering frequency. At present, the VEM does not account for marine heat wave (MHW) conditions, although a secondary MHW term could easily be added should additional data become available to best parameterize this effect. For example, flowering percentages could be multiplied by a limitation factor for every X days of temperatures above a well identified temperature threshold.

Percentages of reproductive shoots found within eelgrass meadows have been reported between 0% and 28% of total shoots (Jacobs and Pierson 1981; Silberhorn et al. 1983; Thayer et al. 1984; Olesen 1999), all the way up to 100% of total shoots flowering (Keddy and Patriquin 1978; Meling-López and Ibarra-Obando 1999; Jarvis et al. 2012; Qin et al. 2020). The flowering probability is applied once the optimal anthesis temperature is reached, a condition that is met when spring water temperatures increase from a daily average of 14 to 15 °C. This temperature threshold identifies the first flowering day (FFD), a time point that is declared in the model and at which time eligible shoots flower. It is important to note that a seedling with three or more nodes also has the ability to flower in the model, even if it is less than 1-year-old, as there is evidence that older seedlings can flower in their first year of growth (Jarvis et al. 2012; Johnson et al. 2017). The number of shoots that flower on the first flowering day are then multiplied by the average number of seeds per shoot (10) and placed in the model's sediment seed bank. While in the seed bank, the seeds remain dormant through the hot summer months until water temperatures decrease below 20 °C and near 15 °C (Moore et al. 1993). Only 40% of the original seeds that enter the seed bank remain viable to germinate after the period of dormancy (Jarvis et al. 2014). Once germinated, the individuals are considered newly "born" seedlings or individual recruits into the model and are assigned spatial coordinates. These young seedlings grow according to the seedling specific growth rate formulation and seedling biomass allocation rules until transition to adulthood (Foley 2017).

4.4 Simulating Space

Equations 4.1, 4.2, 4.3, 4.4, and 4.5 effectively describe branching that is linked to the growth of leaves in an eelgrass ramet. However, without including the spatial placement of branches, the VEM will be unable to simulate shoot density, radial expansion rates, or the effects of crowding on available resources. Past models of eelgrass growth have reported shoot density by using an empirical regression with simulated biomass values (e.g. Short 1980; Bach 1993; Zharova et al. 2001). However, this conversion from units of grams carbon per square meter to number of shoots per square meter assumes that ramets are stationary, permanently located within one square meter throughout the year. As reviewed in Chap. 2, the Verhagen and Nienhuis (1983) eelgrass model attempted to include population-level characteristics of eelgrass, including an effect of crowding. Although this model did attempt to consider space, the eelgrass shoots were once again "trapped" within the modeler's arbitrary square meter without any capacity to move or expand via rhizome elongation.

Using the IBM approach it is easy to fall into a similar trap of assuming stationary growth of the ramet. Most historical IBM plant models have simulated forests, and while three-dimensional models have considered dynamic crown height and trunk diameter, the trees are anchored to one location, as in reality. However, the modular perspective inherent to the VEM ramet once more recalls Setchell's (1929) early records of elongating rhizomes and mobile apical meristems colonizing the benthos. This also suggests a way forward for describing the spatial spread of each ramet in the model.

Using basic trigonometric functions, we can describe rhizome elongation and the movement of ramets based on X-Y coordinates that are linked to the length associated with each new internode and a branching angle that each new ramet takes from the mother's rhizome growth direction. Newly created ramets inherit their "mother" coordinates at the time of branching and combine this location with the new branching angle to initialize their own location in the Virtual Eelgrass Meadow. While necessitating the most complicated programming in the VEM, the conceptual basis of this spatial movement is exceedingly simple. Some empirical data were needed to stipulate a regression equation to convert biomass to rhizome length (Fig. 4.5), as well as a branching angle. The mean branching angle calculated from Rhode Island transplanted eelgrass plants and displayed in Fig. 4.6 is 76°, or 1.326 radians. While only limited measurements were made, this value is reinforced by the work of Marba and Duarte (1998) to develop allometric equations relating branching angle as the −1/3 power of rhizome diameter across the seagrass flora, a value also used by Salinas and Solana-Arellano (2021). The reported angle measured for *Zostera marina* and used along with other species to derive this allometry was 67°, a value encompassed by the range of values within one standard deviation of the empirically measured mean of 76° that will be used in this simulation. Figure 4.7 visualizes this combination of trigonometry and empirical parameterization.

To simplify the computational difficulties associated with inheriting a "birthplace" set of coordinates from the mother ramet, the X and Y coordinates are modeled as state variables with associated flows. In this way, the birthplace can serve as the initialization of an individual's X and Y coordinates. This significantly shortened simulation time by requiring the identification of a mother only once during

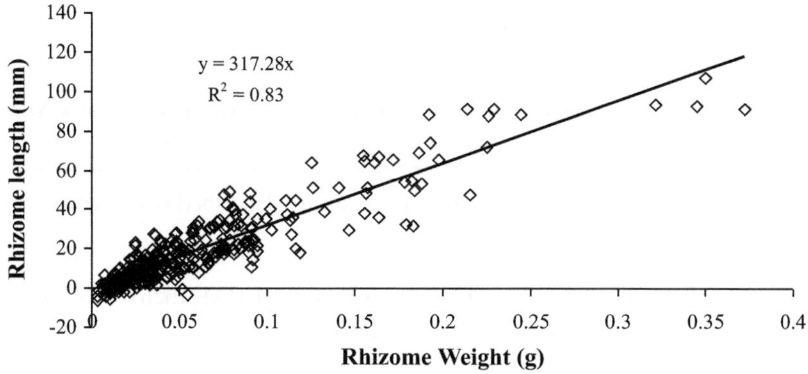

Fig. 4.5 Internode weight to rhizome length conversion used for spatial X-Y coordinates during elongation of VEM rhizomes. Data from lagoon mesocosms and Rhode Island coastal ponds

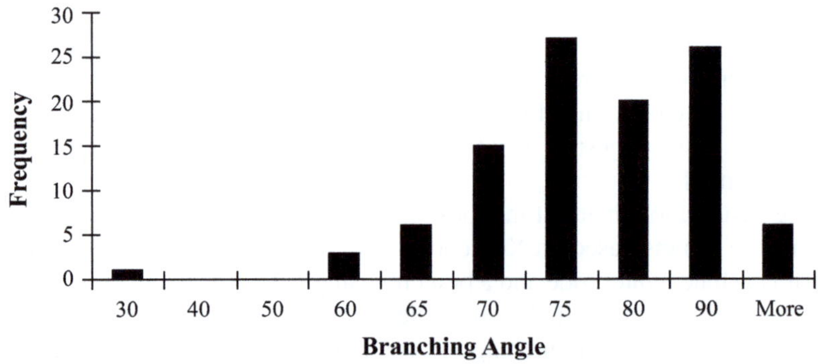

Fig. 4.6 Frequency distribution of lateral shoot branching angles in transplanted eelgrass shoots, Narragansett Bay, RI. n = 104

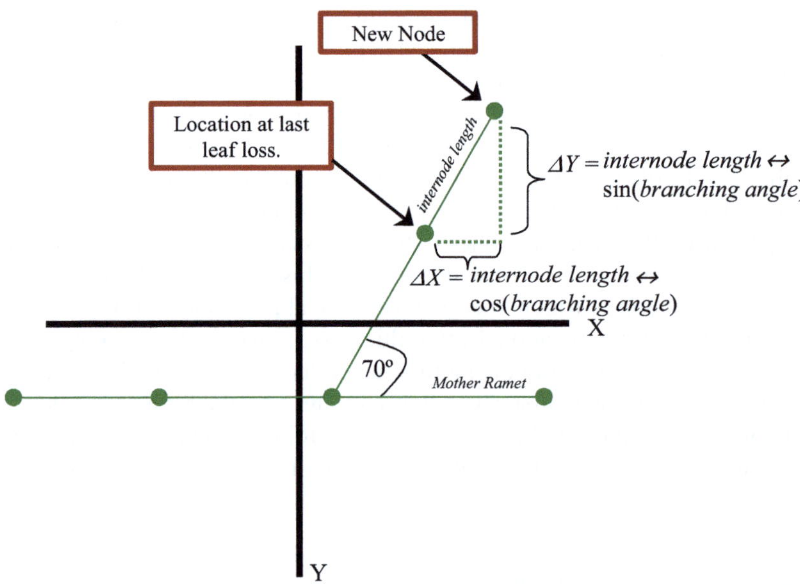

Fig. 4.7 Trigonometric functions used to move location of growing ramet in an X-Y coordinate system

the lifetime of the ramet. The programming rules are described below and compiled in Table 4.2.

$$InternodeLength = \text{if OLDESTLEAF}_0 > \text{OLDEST LEAF}_1 \text{ then } 0.31728 m/g \times \text{GROWING INTERNODE} \tag{4.7}$$

$$MoveYApex = \text{if random constant}(0,1) < 0.5 \text{ then } InternodeLength \times \sin\left(\left(MyMother'sDirection + 1.326\right)\right) \text{else } InternodeLength \times \sin(\left(MyMother'sDirection - 1.326\right) \tag{4.8}$$

$$MoveXApex = \text{if random constant}(0,1) < 0.5 \text{ then } InternodeLength \times \cos\left(\left(MyMother'sDirection + 1.326\right)\right) \text{else } InternodeLength \times \cos(\left(MyMother'sDirection - 1.326\right) \tag{4.9}$$

$$Y = \text{if } myage < 2 \text{ then } MyMother'sY \text{ else } \mathrm{Y}_0 + MoveYApex \tag{4.10}$$

$$X = \text{if } myage < 2 \text{ then } MyMother'sX \text{ else } \mathrm{X}_0 + MoveXApex \tag{4.11}$$

Equation 4.7 converts the biomass from GROWING INTERNODE to meters (length) when the OLDEST LEAF is shed, and in so doing keeps track of *internode length*. This parameter is analogous to the length converted value of G_i from Eq. 3.10 and is similarly zero when no flow occurs between the GROWING INTERNODE and ROOTS&RHIZOME compartments. Equations 4.8 and 4.9 use the sine and cosine functions to derive the change in X and Y associated with the new Internode Length by using the simple geometry illustrated in Fig. 4.7. To determine the angle to use for this calculation, 1.326 radians are added or subtracted to the mother ramet's angle of growth. Whether this value is added or subtracted will determine "left" or "right" branching from the mother rhizome. Because dichotomous branching occurs in eelgrass (Hemminga and Duarte 2000), the if-then statements in these equations are tied to a random constant between 0 and 1 that is set for each new instance of a ramet. The Gaussian distribution of the random number generator creates the probability that 50% of the time this constant will be below 0.5. This feature allows "left" branching via subtracting the 1.326 from the mother angle while values between 0.5 and 1 let the ramet know branching should occur to the "right" with the addition of the 1.326 angle. Equations 4.10 and 4.11 describe how the flow from *MoveYApex* and *MoveXApex* are used as difference equations to change the X and Y state variable values. During the first two timesteps of the new ramet's existence it shares the same X and Y coordinates as its mother's rhizome at the time of branching, these values change when a new internode is created.

4.5 Density Dependence

We have already detailed the argument that the occupation of space by the lateral branching of an eelgrass genet is controlled by the growth rate of leaves, the linked internode spacing length, branching angle, and rate of branching—rather than post-hoc mortality due to crowding. However, to adequately describe the documented self-thinning of eelgrass shoots, there must be a mechanism for decreasing the availability of resources with increased density. Both Duarte and Kalff (1987) and Olesen and Sand-Jensen (1994) suggest that increased density of shoots most likely limits the available light. The relationship between leaf area index and distribution of light through the canopy has been extensively studied and modeled in terrestrial plant communities (e.g. Gutschick and Weigel 1988). For seagrasses, Zimmerman (2003) developed a biooptical model of irradiance in relation to varying canopy heights and species-specific leaf optical properties. This model predicted detailed spectral properties of the downwelling and reflected light that are useful for remote sensing applications, as well as biomass-specific rates of photosynthesis. Both predictions and field values reported by Zimmerman (2003) provide ample evidence of dramatic light attenuation through the eelgrass canopy. A species-specific field study of *Thalassia testudinum* (Enriquez and Pantoja-Reyes 2005) measured a positive correlation between shoot density, leaf area index, and leaf biomass with the canopy attenuation coefficient (k_c). This study also documented an extensive set of measurements to characterize changing morphology with light availability. While it would be preferable to have reproduced the techniques used to relate density and leaf morphology with light attenuation in the *Thalassia* study, Short (1980) measured some of these parameters to use in his first eelgrass model. In particular, regression Eq. 4.12 relating k_c to shoot density and leaf length is available for use in the VEM.

$$k_c = 2.09 + \left(0.0018 \times Density \times 0.01 \times CanopyHeight\right) \tag{4.12}$$

To calculate light available to a particular ramet, k_c can be used to further attenuate the available light at depth previously computed using the dynamic water column k described in Eq. 3.12. This leaf irradiance is then used to compute the specific growth rate as well as the percent irradiance values that determine canopy height. This formulation predicts that increased shoot density will lead to increased canopy height as well as increased internode lengths.

To compute the local shoot density around a ramet, a relational submodel was created to keep track of an individual's neighbors within a 0.25 m radius of its location in space. This radius was chosen because it mimics the quadrat size used by Short (1980) to compute field densities. Each time step, a ramet searches for any neighbors plus or minus 0.125 m from its own X and Y coordinates. The number of individuals within this radius is then multiplied by 4 to calculate the *Density* parameter necessary for Eq. 4.11. This is a critical step in simulating a connection between shoot density and the light environment that an individual ramet receives. In this programming, the local shoot density determines how much light reaches an individual ramet via use of the k_c computed parameter. If there are more neighboring ramets in VEM simulated space, then there will be less light available. This is the fundamental mechanism for creating a feedback from meadow conditions back to individual growth rates for ramets.

4.6 Death of a Ramet

Storm disturbance, herbivory, flowering, and light limitation are all considered common mechanisms for mortality in eelgrass meadows, but rates and the significance of each of these processes are poorly documented. Both storm disturbance and burrowing invertebrates (Davis et al. 1998) may result in the uprooting of eelgrass shoots. Flowering is a terminal event for an apical meristem and in some populations may result in 100% mortality of shoots while creating large seed banks for germination of a new population in the next year, or later (Keddy 1987; Santamaria-Gallegos et al. 2000).

Estimates of flowering densities within meadows have been completed for eelgrass populations from geographic locations ranging between 33 and 65° latitude (see Olesen 1999; Blok et al. 2018; Qin et al. 2020; Guerrero-Meseguer et al. 2022). These studies are in general agreement that the latitudinal patterns observed in flowering phenology and first synthesized by Silberhorn et al. (1983) are most strongly related with temperature effects (Blok et al. 2018; Qin et al. 2020; Guerrero-Meseguer et al. 2022), with some indication that photoperiod or nutrients may also be implicated (Johnson et al. 2017; Lekammudiyanse et al. 2024). However, the continuous loss of reproductive shoots throughout the flowering season (April–August) decreases the confidence with which densities measured at one point in time can be used to predict this event in the VEM. Olesen (1999) tracked individual shoots in permanent plots located in a Danish eelgrass meadow. The local shoot density, lateral branching rate, and shoot size were compared with the incidence of flowering. In general, older and therefore larger shoots were more likely to flower and represented 10% of total shoot density, reinforcing the appropriateness of using flowering as the final life stage in the model. These studies provide a logical and mechanistic way of representing death for a ramet, and are already represented in the sexual reproduction module previously described in this chapter.

But what then of the time between flowering and senescence or death of the ramet? Olesen (1999) found that once a shoot became a flower it would persist for an average of 41 days. Guerrero-Meseguer et al. (2022) documented four reproductive stages of eelgrass based on morphology, and the data describing the frequencies of these stages follow a time course of approximately 50 days. Based on these observations, after a shoot is selected to flower, an internal "clock" will begin to trigger mortality at a randomly selected value between 41 and 50 days. During this time period, no growth will occur for that individual ramet, resulting in stationary X-Y coordinates. These programming rules are listed below and compiled in Table 4.1

$$\text{FLOWERCLOCK} = \text{if } flower == \text{TRUE then 1 else 0} \tag{4.13}$$

$$flowertime = \text{if } flower == \text{TRUE then 1 else 0} \tag{4.14}$$

$$G_l = \text{if } flower == \text{TRUE then 0 else } SGR \times \text{LEAVES} \tag{3.2}$$

$$G_r \text{if } flower == \text{TRUE then 0 else } \frac{b \times G_l}{1-b} \tag{3.3}$$

$$DEATH = \text{if FLOWERCLOCK} == random(41{,}50) \text{ then TRUE else FALSE} \tag{4.15}$$

Previously, we designated a new ramet life history stage of *flower* as indicated in Eq. 4.6. If this value is "TRUE" for a given ramet, the state variable FLOWER CLOCK is given a value of 1 (Eq. 4.13) and the equation *flowertime* begins to add 1 to this compartment after each time step (Eq. 4.14). Because growth of a flowering shoot must stop, Eqs. 3.2 and 3.4 are amended to halt flow into the LEAVES and GROWING INTERNODE compartments. Finally, when the FLOWER CLOCK reaches a value randomly selected between 41 and 50, the individual ramet dies and is eliminated from the population as indicated in Eq. 4.15. Daughter ramets that have branched from the flowering mother ramet remain alive. Although growth of the mother ramet stops during flowering, it is assumed that the daughter ramets continue to elongate their rhizomes without deleterious effects. Clearly, there are subtleties to this process that have not been included in the death processes of the VEM, including the impact of lost translocated material from a mother ramet and the effects of the towering, flowering shoots on the local light regime.

4.7 Implementation

The SIMILE software is developed by Simulistics, Ltd (www.simulistics.com). and was first created by Dr. Robert Muetzelfeldt and Dr. Jasper Taylor to support the MoDMED project, a multi-nation, multi-investigator endeavor to model Mediterranean Ecosystem Dynamics. While depending on a system dynamics approach similar to that used by STELLA, the SIMILE environment has added capabilities to construct object-oriented programs as implemented in its base language C++. This class of programming is essential to creating IBM's because the programming architecture mimics the same mind-set of the individual-based approach (Grimm and Railsback 2005). In this framework, the RAMET, FLOWER, SEED, or SEEDLING becomes a *Class* that is described by a set of state variables including its age, size, and location. *Submodels* assist in describing the methods and rules an individual should follow as well as relationships among individuals, while *schedules* decide the order of actions in the programming code. The scheduling of actions is particularly crucial when neighborhood or inheritance creates the potential for circular loops. To ensure that the flows into and out of compartments were considered as difference equations, a time-step of one day was specified. Figure 4.8 displays the visual modeling environment of this software and the VEM SIMILE diagram.

The inheritance of X and Y coordinates from a mother ramet was accomplished by creating a conditional submodel that existed only during the first time-step of a new ramet's existence and was used to "pass" the coordinates and direction of growth to the daughter ramet. This creates a unique list of mother-daughter pairs where the mother role is exclusive (a daughter can have only one mother). Shoots which are used to initiate a simulation are given an "EVE" status because they have no mother within the timeframe of the simulation, their X-Y coordinates and direction must be set with the initial conditions for each simulation.

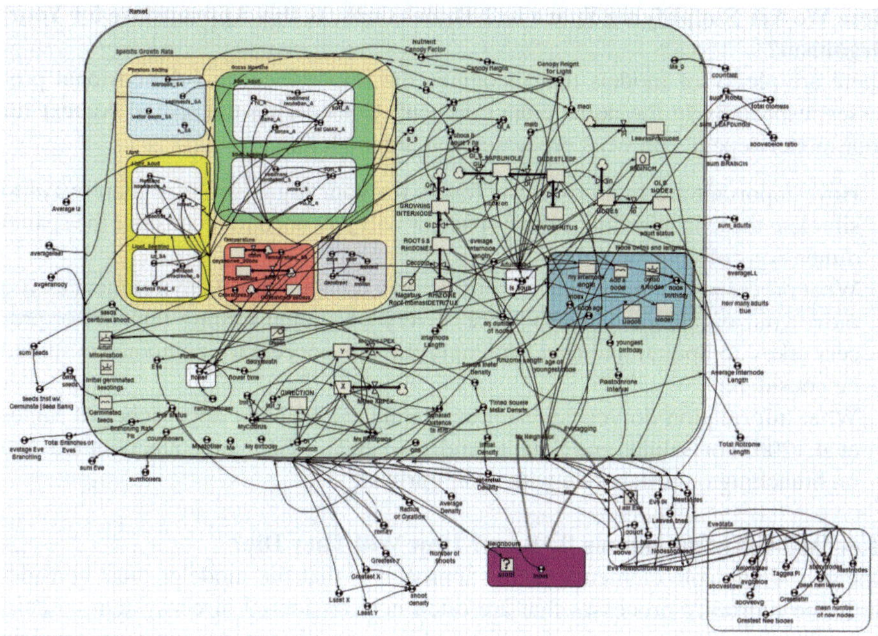

Fig. 4.8 Simile software visual environment for modeling the Virtual Eelgrass Meadow

To calculate the local density for an individual to use for the calculation of light attenuation through the canopy, another conditional submodel was created to associate each individual with any neighbors within a 25 cm radius. This aspect of the VEM will ultimately result in slowing simulation time significantly, as each timestep a ramet must consider its local neighbourhood to calculate shoot density.

Two additional submodels were included within the RAMET and SEEDLING class identities. The first included the formulations for the specific growth model described in Chap. 2 and the second was used to keep track of node locations and the timing of node placement so that an individual's leaf/node plastochrone interval could be calculated. Initial conditions and forcing functions will be described in Chap. 5 for each of the simulations.

4.8 Suggestions for Use in Modeling or Course Design

Much of this chapter is devoted to necessary elements of making the VEM function as a simulation. But in working out the ways these processes will be replicated in the computing environment, we are also able to pull together foundational aspects of how eelgrass colonize the sediment surface and sustain large populations.

Here We Are Simplifying Space to 2-Dimensions, Is this Appropriate for Your Organism?

There are plenty of models that recognize the importance of 3-dimensional processes, especially in the aquatic environment. Considering the spatial context for your model depends on what processes you are modeling.

- How important are hydrodynamic forces for your organism? Are there ways to simulate these in a 2-dimensional space or will you need to reconsider the spatial dimensions of your model?
- What processes are important to consider in a computational environment as you move your organisms through space? Every additional forcing function or process takes computational time, and only the most necessary components should be considered
- What information do you have for emulating the VEM or approaches of Sintes et al. (2005) or Salinas and Solana-Arellano (2021)? Can you collect limited data on branching or collaborate with an empiricist?

How Will Your Individuals Be Born? How Will They Die?

One of the valuable elements of this approach is that the modeler must consider birth and mortality processes that are often not considered in ecosystem models. Because you will have previously identified important life stages for your organism (Chap. 3), you should have an understanding of what information can be useful for characterizing population processes.

- Will your organism's birth and death processes be linked to environmental conditions, or randomly generated?
- Where will individuals appear in space when they are born? How will their location be tracked?

What Computational Environment Will You Use?

This will often come down to whether you use continuously varying functions like growth in your model or stick to discrete conditions and values. There are a range of modeling environments for IBMs.

- Does your model include continuous and discrete variables?
- How comfortable are you with coding? Do you prefer a windows interface?
- How many individuals do you anticipate modeling? With how many different classes and processes? Registering and tracking a large number of individuals and associated characteristics becomes computationally taxing, quickly.

Create Schedules and Track Equations

Finally, we highly recommend that you track programming through scheduling like those provided in Tables 3.1 and 3.2, preferably with greater detail. Taking some time to consider programming organization and how to order and execute processes is as critical to your model as formulating the correct rate process equations.

References

Bach HL (1993) A dynamic model describing the seasonal variations in growth and the distribution of eelgrass (*Zostera marina* L.) I. Model theory. Ecol Model 65:31–50

Bauer S, Berger U, Hildenbrandt H, Grimm V (2002) Cyclic dynamics in simulated plant populations. Proc R Soc Lond B 269:2443–2450

Berger AC, Berg P (2024) Eelgrass meadow response to heat stress. I. Temperature threshold for ecosystem production derived from in situ aquatic eddy covariance measurements. Mar Ecol Prog Ser 736:35–46

Berger U, Hildenbrandt H (2000) A new approach to spatially explicit modeling of forest dynamics: spacing, ageing and neighbourhood competition of mangrove trees. Ecol Model 132:287–302

Berger U, Hildenbrandt H (2003) The strength of competition among individual trees and the biomass-density trajectories of the cohort. Plant Ecol 167:89–96

Berger U, Hildenbrandt H, Grimm V (2002) Towards a standard for the individual-based modeling of plant populations: self-thinning and the field-of-neighborhood approach. Nat Resour Model 15:39–54

Berger U, Bell A, Barton CM, Chappin E, Dreßler G, Filatova T, Fronville T, Lee A, van Loon E, Lorscheid I, Meyer M (2024) Towards reusable building blocks for agent-based modelling and theory development. Environ Model Softw 175:106003

Blok SE, Olesen B, Krause-Jensen D (2018) Life history events of eelgrass Zostera marina L. populations across gradients of latitude and temperature. Mar Ecol Prog Ser 590:79–93

Brylawski BJ, Miller TJ (2006) Temperature-dependent growth of the blue crab (callinectes sapidus): a molt process approach. Can J Fish Aquat Sci 63(6):1298–1308

Davis RC, Short FT, Burdick DM (1998) Quantifying the effects of green crab damage to eelgrass transplants. Restor Ecol 6:297–302

De Kroon H, Hutchings MJ (1995) Morphological plasticity in clonal plants: the foraging concept reconsidered. J Ecol 83:143–152

Duarte CM, Kalff J (1987) Weight-density relationships in submerged macrophytes: the importance of light and plant geometry. Oecologia 72:612–617

Enquist BJ, Brown JH, West GB (1998) Allometric scaling of plant energetics and population density. Nature 395(6698):163–165

Enriquez S, Pantoja-Reyes NI (2005) Form-function analysis of the effect of canopy morphology on leaf self-shading in the seagrass *Thalassia testudinum*. Oecologia 145:234–242

Foley JL (2017) Using an individual based model to evaluate the effects of climate change on the reproductive phenology of eelgrass (Zostera marina L.) along a latitudinal gradient. Master's thesis, University of Maryland, College Park

Grimm V, Railsback SF (2005) Individual-based modeling and ecology. Princeton University Press, Princeton

Guerrero-Meseguer L, Veiga P, Rubal M (2022) Flowering effort and reproductive phenology of intertidal colonizing Zostera marina. Estuar Coast Shelf Sci *278*:108110

Gutschick VPG, Weigel FW (1988) Optimizing the canopy photosynthetic rate by patterns of investments in specific leaf mass. Am Nat 132:68–85

Harris LAB, Buckley SW, Nixon W, Allen BT (2004) Experimental studies of predation by bluefish *Pomatomus saltatrix* in varying densities of seagrass and macroalgae. Mar Ecol Prog Ser 281:233–239

Hemminga MA, Duarte C (2000) Seagrass ecology. Cambridge University Press, Cambridge

Idso SB, Jackson RD, Reginato RJ (1978) Extending the "Degree Day" concept of plant phenological development to include water stress effects. Ecology 59:431–433

Jacobs RPWM, Pierson ES (1981) Phenology of reproductive shoots of eelgrass, Zostera marina L., at Roscoff (France). Aquat Bot 10:45–60

Jarvis JC, Moore KA, Kenworthy WJ (2012) Characterization and ecological implication of eelgrass life history strategies near the species' southern limit in the western North Atlantic. Mar Ecol Prog Ser 444:43–56. https://doi.org/10.3354/meps09428

Jarvis JC, Brush MJ, Moore KA (2014) Modeling loss and recovery of Zostera marina beds in the Chesapeake Bay: the role of seedlings and seed-bank viability. Aquat Bot 113:32–45. https://doi.org/10.1016/j.aquabot.2013.10.010

Johnson AJ, Moore KA, Orth RJ (2017) The influence of resource availability on flowering intensity in Zostera marina (L.). J Exp Mar Biol Ecol 490:13–22

Keddy CJ (1987) Reproduction of annual eelgrass: variation among habitats and comparison with perennial eelgrass (*Zostera marina* L.). Aquat Bot 27:243–256

Keddy CJ, Patriquin DG (1978) An annual form of eelgrass in Nova Scotia. Aquat Bot 5:163–170

Kim SH, Kim JH, Park SR, Lee KS (2014) Annual and perennial life history strategies of Zostera marina populations under different light regimes. Mar Ecol Prog Ser 509:1–13

Latzel V, Münzbergová Z (2018) Anticipatory behavior of the clonal plant Fragaria vesca. Front Plant Sci 9:1847

Lee JS, Kang DJ, Hineva E, Slabakova V, Todorova V, Park J, Cho JH (2017) Estimation of net ecosystem metabolism of seagrass meadows in the coastal waters of the East Sea and Black Sea using the noninvasive eddy covariance technique. Ocean Sci J 52(2):243–256

Lekammudiyanse MU, Saunders MI, Flint N, Irving A, Aiken C, Clark DE, Berthelsen A, Hindmarsh B, Hooks R, Connolly RM, Sievers M (2024) Environmental drivers of flowering in the genus Zostera and spatio-temporal variability of Zostera muelleri flowering in Australasia. Aquat Conserv Mar Freshwat Ecosyst 34(2):e4068

Li BL, Wu H, Zou G (2000) Self-thinning rule: a causal interpretation from ecological field theory. Ecol Model 132:167–173

Marba N, Duarte CM (1998) Rhizome elongation and seagrass clonal growth. Mar Ecol Prog Ser 174:269–280

Marsh Jr JA, Dennison WC, Alberte RS (1986) Effects of temperature on photosynthesis and respiration in eelgrass (Zostera marina L.). Journal of Experimental Marine Biology and Ecology 101:257–267

Meling-López AE, Ibarra-Obando SE (1999) Annual life cycles of two Zostera marina L. populations in the Gulf of California: contrasts in seasonality and reproductive effort. Aquat Bot 65(1–4):59–69

Moore KA, Orth RJ, Nowak JF (1993) Environmental regulation of seed germination in Zostera marina L. (eelgrass) in Chesapeake Bay: effects of light, oxygen and sediment burial. Aquat Bot 45:79–79

Oborny B (1994) Spacer length in clonal plants and the efficiency of resource capture in heterogeneous environments: a Monte Carlo simulation. In: Soukupová L, Marshall C, Hara T, Herben T (eds) Plant clonality: biology and diversity. Opulus Press, Uppsala

Olesen B (1999) Reproduction in Danish eelgrass (*Zostera marina* L.) stands: size-dependence and biomass partitioning. Aquat Bot 65:209–219

Olesen B, Sand-Jensen K (1994) Patch dynamics of eelgrass *Zostera marina*. Mar Ecol Prog Ser 106:147–156

Orth RJ, Moore KA (1983) Seed germination and seedling growth of Zostera marina L.(eelgrass) in the Chesapeake Bay. Aquat Bot 15(2):117–131

Poumian-Tapia M, Ibarra-Obando SE (1999) Demography and biomass of the seagrass *Zostera marina* in a Mexican coastal lagoon. Estuaries 22:837–847

Qin LZ, Kim SH, Song HJ, Kim HG, Suonan Z, Kwon O, Kim YK, Park SR, Park JI, Lee KS (2020) Long-term variability in the flowering phenology and intensity of the temperate seagrass Zostera marina in response to regional sea warming. Ecol Indic 119:106821

Salinas H, Solana-Arellano E (2021) Importance of elongation and organogenesis on the rhizome length of Zostera marina in an individual-based simulation model. Estuar Coast Shelf Sci 261:107530

Santamaria-Gallegos NA, Sanchez-Lizaso JL, Felix-Pico EF (2000) Phenology and growth cycle of annual subtidal eelgrass in a subtropical locality. Aquat Bot 66:329–339

Setchell WA (1929) Morphological and phenological notes on *Zostera marina* L. Univ Calif Publ Bot 14:389–452

Short FT (1980) A simulation model of the seagrass production system. In: Phillips RC, McRoy CP (eds) Handbook of seagrass biology: an ecosystem perspective. Garland STPM Press, New York

Silberhorn GM, Orth RJ, Moore KA (1983) Anthesis and seed production in Zostera marina L. (eelgrass) from the chesepeak by. Aquat Bot 15(2):133–144

Sintes TN, Marba CM, Duarte M, Kendrick GA (2005) Nonlinear processes in seagrass colonization explained by simple clonal growth rules. Oikos 108:165–175

Thayer GW, Kenworthy WJ, Fonseca MS (1984) The ecology of eelgrass meadows of the Atlantic coast: a community profile. Fish and Wildlife Service, US Department of the Interior

Trewavas A (2003) Aspects of plant intelligence. Ann Bot 92(1):1–20

Verhagen JHG, Nienhuis NP (1983) A simulation model of production, seasonal changes in biomass and distribution of eelgrass (*Zostera marina*) in Lake Grevelingen. Mar Ecol Prog Ser 10:187–195

Weiner J (2004) Allocation, plasticity and allometry in plants. Perspect Plant Ecol Evol Syst 6:207–215

West GB, Brown JH, Enquist BJ (1999) A general model for the structure an allometry of plant vascular systems. Nature 400:664–667

White J (1981) The allometric interpretation of the self-thinning rule. J Theor Biol 89:475–500

Yoda K, Kira T, Ogawa H, Hozumi KJ (1963) Self-thinning in overcrowded pure stands under cultivated and natural conditions. J Biol Univ Osaka Ser D 14:107–129

Zharova N, Sfriso A, Voinov A, Pavoni B (2001) A simulation model for the annual fluctuation of *Zostera marina* biomass in the Venice lagoon. Aquat Bot 70:135–150

Zimmerman RC (2003) A bio-optical model of irradiance distribution and photosynthesis in seagrass canopies. Limnol Oceanogr 48:568–585

Chapter 5
The Restored Meadow

A model, once it is running reliably on a computer, is like a laboratory waiting to be used.

Anthony Starfield, Karl Smith, & Andrew Bleloch

It is a common fallacy to confuse scientists' models of reality with reality itself. A model is a map. A map is not the territory it describes.

Richard Casement - 1984

5.1 Introduction

The computing environment is far removed from actual eelgrass shoots and the shallow coastal regions they inhabit. And yet, in an attempt to demonstrate that the Virtual Eelgrass Meadow has some basis in reality, every assumption and decision made during formulation has been meticulously recorded and described in the preceding chapters. This process emphasizes the reduction of complexity that must occur when creating a numerical model, even in a complex model like the VEM.

Analogous simplifying decisions are made by scientists as we attempt to understand the workings of the system itself through experimental manipulations. It is equally possible that confounding effects or overlooked assumptions will hamper either a laboratory experiment or a computer simulation. From this point of view, it becomes possible to agree with Starfield et al. (1994) not only that a model "is like a laboratory" but also envision the laboratory as a model. Defining the simulation environment as a virtual laboratory also helps to identify the methodological and analytical steps necessary to produce an appropriate scenario to test and run an individual based model, the remaining tasks documented in this final chapter.

Existing, traditional seagrass models are typically developed by their authors for the purpose of describing or exploring the physiological mechanisms of production for a species under dynamic environmental conditions, often in the context of a particular geographical location that has undergone some environmental perturbation. Examples include the work of Bocci et al. (1997) to determine the competitive dynamics between macroalgae and eelgrass in the Lagoon of Venice, as well as the model of Cerco and Moore (2001) that links a Chesapeake Bay eutrophication

© Springer Nature B.V. 2026
L. A. Harris et al., *Ramet Rules*, Aquatic Ecology Series 9,
https://doi.org/10.1007/978-94-024-2365-5_5

model to simulations of *Zostera marina* and *Ruppia maritima* in an attempt to predict what level of nutrient and sediment loading would permit their growth and expansion. While both of these examples, and many others, are frequently designed to address a particular management problem, questions remain regarding the application of such models for the purpose of prediction (Duplisea 2000; Fulton et al. 2003; Ganju et al. 2016).

It may be instructive to consider detailed, mechanistic models more formally as numerical efforts to formulate hypotheses, or at a minimum consider them within a diagnostic framework (Testa et al. 2017). In the tradition of the empiricist's scientific method, model formulations enumerate the hypothesis and careful consideration of simulation scenarios (designed to mimic real-world conditions) serve as experiments to produce model output/predictions that are compared with actual measurements. This result may then be used to determine whether the hypothesis, in the form of the model equations, is accepted or rejected. In this framework, the disagreement of simulation output with reality requires that the model formulation be re-evaluated, rather than calibrating or tuning parameters to achieve better "predictive" capacity. Prediction becomes a long-term goal, while the act of modeling focuses on theory development.

For the manager that must develop quantifiable goals, such as for the Total Maximum Daily Load (TMDL) program, this approach may seem unwieldy when compared with calibrated models that appear to provide adequate predictive capacity. However, management decisions to achieve a mandated goal often include changes to a system that have not been attempted in the estuary of interest; i.e. large scale nutrient removal via tertiary treatment of sewage. Nixon (2009) advocated classification of these estuary-scale management manipulations as grand experiments of oligotrophication, the results of which are as yet unknown and therefore not included in the range of data and empirical relationships used to parameterize and formulate numerical models. Duarte et al. (2009) cautioned scholars of restoration to recall that responses may instead resemble instances of hysteresis or regime change given the non-linear nature of ecosystems. It is surely reasonable to believe that we have a good chance at making general predictions of system response to perturbations or changes that we have experienced and measured previously, but our capacity to foresee the results of such grand experiments under conditions that lie outside the range of our experience requires a thorough re-thinking of how we achieve prediction in ecology and the use of numerical models for the purposes of management (Harte 2002; Canham et al. 2003; Harris et al. 2006; Enquist et al. 2024).

In contrast to some traditional models, individual-based models do not allow the user or modeler the luxury of expecting that model output will mimic reality. Numerous evaluations of complex systems models have demonstrated that initial conditions specifying the spatial configurations of individuals can have as much, or more, of an effect on the final output of individual locations than some model parameters (Grimm and Railsback 2013; Wolfram 2002). Depending on the complexity of the IBM, this sensitivity to initial spatial locations may result in difficulty evaluating whether results that replicate (or contradict) real conditions are attributable to the model structure or a coincidence incurred from starting coordinates (Levin 1992; Moloney 1993; Petty 2018).

In addition, the unique features of individual-based models prevent speculation regarding the results of virtual experiments using this tool. By design, the VEM includes adaptive elements that will respond in unexpected ways to whatever combination of initial conditions and environmental forcings are provided for a given simulation. This element of surprise and the potential emergence of collective behavior may even provide the potential for new, unanticipated information and insight from the VEM. This unpredictable behavior and the possibility of emergent properties are considered hallmarks and advantages of IBMs even as they also necessitate careful consideration of initial conditions and simulation scenarios (Grimm and Railsback 2005).

In the case of the VEM these adaptive rules include the feedback between neighboring shoot density and leaf elongation on light availability to individual ramets, as well as the morphologically plastic allocation of resources created by the dynamic above-below ground partitioning coefficient. The latter rule is particularly difficult to evaluate prior to simulations because it is intricately connected to the rate of resource production indicated by the specific growth rate sub-model. Any resulting "behavior" of an individual ramet is therefore dependent on a multitude of factors that encompass spatial arrangement, environmental forcing functions, the initial size of the plants, and time of year; making it impossible to know what emergent properties will be produced by a model run. As discussed in the introductory chapter, the validation of an individual-based model (IBM) requires novel approaches. For example, spatial dynamics that can be evaluated by visualizing the position and spread of each individual ramet over 2-dimensional space do not have an appropriate analogue of empirical datasets with which comparisons can be made. Especially in the case of smaller plants, we do not regularly collect the level of detailed individual data on individual ramets that would be required to compare appropriately with model output. Instead, we are left to provide some picture of the collective behavior of individuals that may be described in the VEM output, using traditional parametric statistics such as means or measures of variance.

Despite its mechanistic specific growth rate formulation, the VEM is most appropriately classified as an IBM due to the rich structure of rules governing resource allocation, colonization, and neighbor interactions. Several existing IBMs have indicated that model output is far more sensitive to this structure than to parameter selection, at the same time demonstrating that this very complexity is frustratingly difficult to test (Grimm 1999; Grimm and Railsback 2005). In an effort to be mindful of the unique capabilities and limitations of the virtual "laboratory" created by the VEM, this final chapter will attempt to carefully construct appropriate hypotheses, virtual experimental design, sensitivity analyses, and testing procedures. While the following results of rigorous testing and examination of the VEM may affect our confidence in the model, they should not fool the reader (or the modeler) into imagining that such an exercise produces immovable truths or objectivity. A final expectation for the VEM can only be that new, potentially surprising, properties of the eelgrass meadow will emerge.

5.2 A Note on Software Testing

Evaluation of the VEM began early in the modeling process as coding and features of the modeling software were used to implement equations, programmed rules, and routines to enable visualization of the colonizing ramets in space. With so many parameters and an elaborate programming structure, it was far easier to perform checks on the software implementation during model development, before the complexity of the model itself overwhelmed our ability to test some of the simplest formulations. The known sensitivity of IBMs to programming structure indicates that these debugging tasks are far from insignificant, as even a minor error can result in behavior that may be difficult to attribute quickly to mistaken coding rather than a designed rule. In addition to the comparisons with field data of the specific growth rate model output outlined in Chap. 2, testing included repeated code review to ensure that equations were reproduced as intended in the Simile environment. Spot checks were also employed by hand-checking calculations of the partitioning coefficient and growth rates to the LEAF BUNDLE and GROWING INTERNODE state variables (G_l and G_r). Fortunately, the Simile software includes several graphic user interface (GUI) tools to monitor variables during simulations, and these were employed in early simulations using only one initial ramet to check the forcing functions, specific growth rate, partitioning coefficient, and growth rates to leaves and rhizomes.

A GUI designed to plot X-Y coordinates was used to ensure that key spatial processes associated with the location of an individual were working and connected to the state variable driving growth of internodes. For example, one feature of the visualization that was somewhat challenging to coordinate involved the dichotomous branching of shoots from the mother rhizome's axis. Figure 5.1a displays the results of visual tests of this feature when branching direction (left or right) from the axis was tied to a random variable, an approach that clearly did not create the desired dichotomous branching during the simulation. Once a variable was passed from mother to daughter ramet linking branching direction to node number, this problem was avoided and the daughter ramets proceeded to alternate branching direction as pictured in Fig. 5.1b. Without this available visual test, it is unlikely that such errors would have been caught before simulations were performed.

5.3 Hypothesis Testing with the VEM as a Diagnostic Model

Validation of traditional models is generally achieved by simulating a real-life scenario that is represented by adequate empirical data for parameterization and testing. Subsequent sensitivity analysis will often compare the results of this "standard run" with model output from the same basic scenario that is simulated multiple times after sequentially varying parameters by a specified percentage of their original value (Hamby 1994). The degree to which model output changes from the

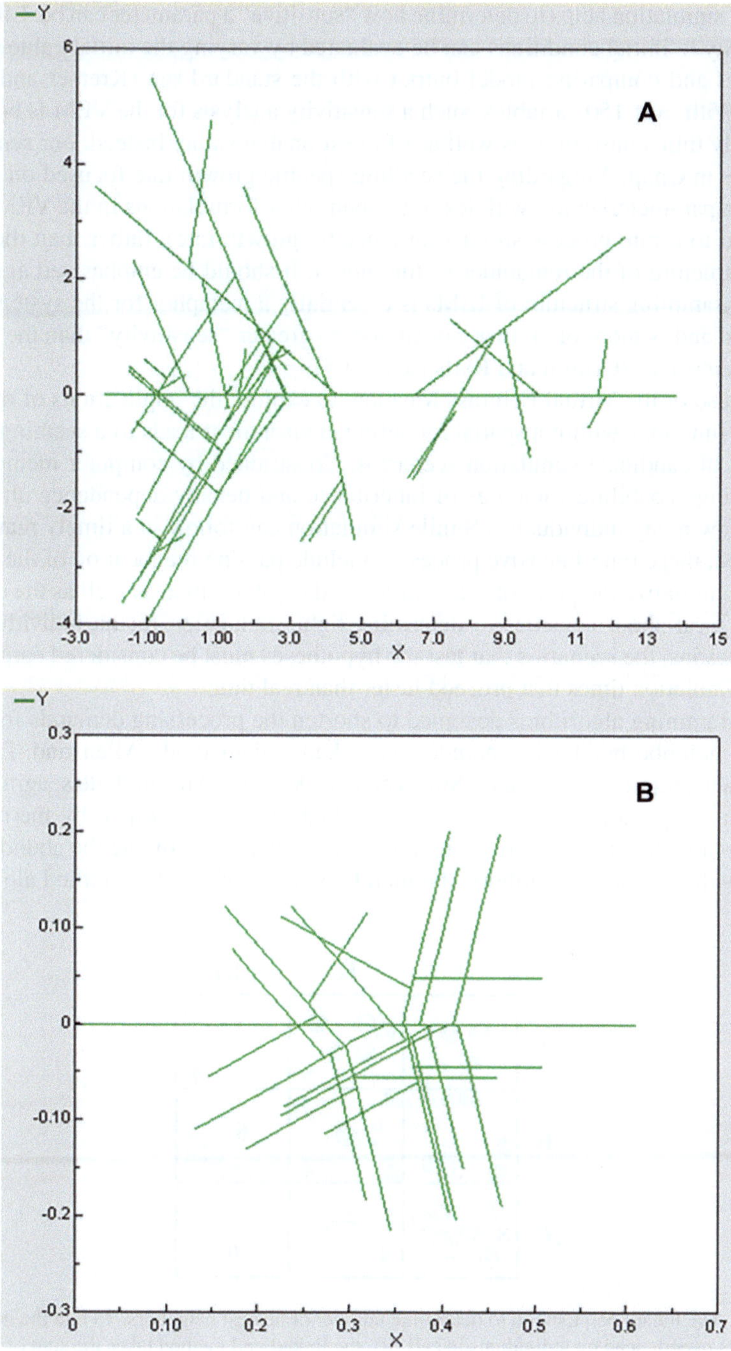

Fig. 5.1 Map of visual test to evaluate programming of alternate branching. Rhizomes colonize a two-dimensional surface delineated here by the X and Y axis, with distance measured in meters along each axis. Notice that image A does not have consistent alternate branching from Mother Rhizome. Programming was corrected and re-evaluated using the X-Y plotter in Image B

original simulation helps to determine how "sensitive" a parameter can be. Likewise, sensitivity to initial conditions can be evaluated by varying the initial value of state variables and comparing model output with the standard run (Kremer and Nixon 1978). With over 150 variables, such a sensitivity analysis for the VEM is both prohibitively time consuming as well as of questionable value. Instead, our sensitivity analyses in Chap. 2 regarding the seedling specific growth rate focused on evaluation of a parameterization with less data than other formulations in the VEM and is confined to a rate process simulation (specific growth rate), rather than the rules-based structure of the remainder of the model. It should be emphasized again that the programming structure of IBMs is essentially a metaphor for the system being modeled and is more often than not subject to greater "sensitivity" than the parameters themselves (Grimm and Railsback 2005).

The use of the Virtual Eelgrass Meadow to explore the implications of dynamic forcing functions within a spatial modeling environment leads to a seemingly endless list of candidate simulation scenarios. Constrained by computer memory and processing capabilities, features of inheritance and density dependence ultimately affect how many individuals a Simile simulation can follow in a timely manner. In the VEM, these time-intensive processes include passing the location of the mother ramet to initialize the point of branching of a daughter ramet, as well as the calculation of local shoot densities to determine light attenuation for an individual. For these reasons, the scenarios that test the hypotheses must be considered carefully to allow simulation times that proceed faster than real time.

Programming algorithms designed to shorten the processing demands for determining neighborhood lists include the linked-cell method (Allen and Tildesley 1987), a technique employed by Sintes et al. (2005, 2006) to simulate seagrass colonization. As pictured in Fig. 5.2, an individual ramet is identified by the row and column in which it is located within a gridded lattice. To estimate the abundance of an individual ramet's neighbors, the members of its grid cell are tallied along with

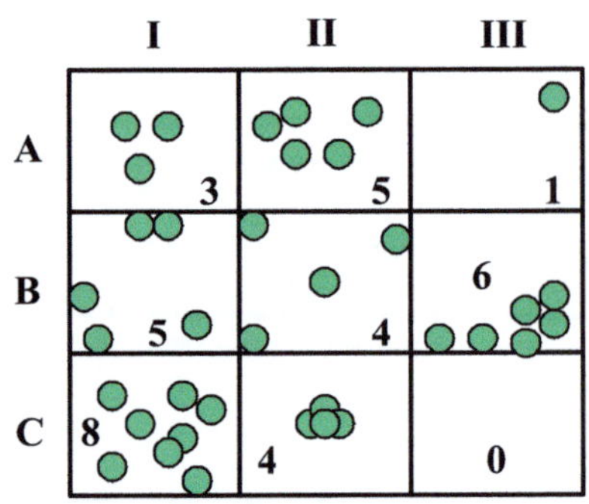

Fig. 5.2 The linked-cell method to determine number of nearest neighbors. To find the number of neighbors experienced by individuals in cell BII, the linked-cell method takes the sum of values in all eight neighboring cells along with the cell of interest. Large cell sizes can bias the density estimates made in this manner because the location of individuals within a cell are not taken into account

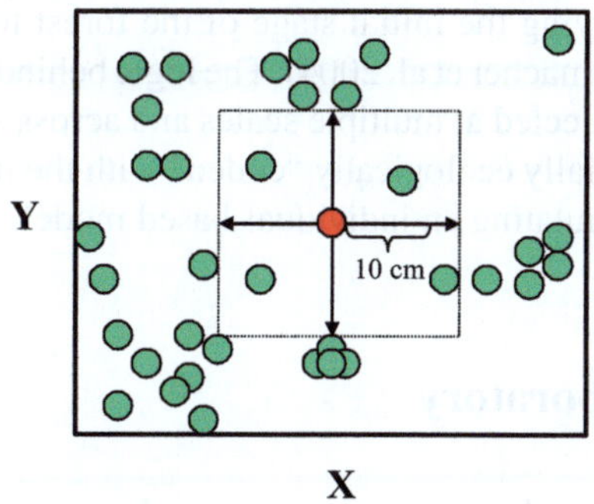

Fig. 5.3 Searching distance method used to find nearest neighbors in VEM. To find the number of neighbors experienced by individuals in the VEM, a "searching distance" is used to determine how many other individuals are within 10 cm of a ramet's X-Y coordinates. For example, the red circle above has 4 neighbors within a 0.40 m^2 area, resulting in a local density of 100 shoots m^{-2}

those in the surrounding cells. While this method does allow the simulation of a larger population of individuals, several unknown variables are introduced, including what size of grid cell to use. Like the Verhagen and Nienhuis (1983) model reviewed in Chap. 2, such a structure also introduces artificial boundaries and may result in biased estimates of local densities. Consequently, the programming structure of the VEM, instead specifies a searching distance to count neighbors for each individual within a grid as pictured in Fig. 5.3.

With these characteristics in mind, it is still necessary to outline a way forward for analysis of the VEM. Such an endeavor should consider careful experiments that can examine the structure of the model in detail, as well as scenarios with limited numbers of individuals so that simulation time and memory limits are not exceeded. The numerical and programmed formulation of the VEM described in Chaps. 3 and 4 provide the most thorough description of how we propose an eelgrass ramet operates in response to its physical, chemical, geological, and spatial environment. However, the evaluation of the model would benefit from a series of experiments communicated using the formalism of the scientific method. The hypotheses these simulations test will also serve to single out key processes or innovations considered particular to the VEM as a form of both model validation and sensitivity analysis.

The ecological (Grimm et al. 1996; Railsback and Harvey 2002; Wiegand et al. 2003; Gallagher et al. 2021) and complex systems literature (Grimm et al. 2005; An et al. 2021) has focused on developing strategies both to design and validate IBMs using pattern-oriented modeling (POM). This technique involves identifying ecological patterns that emerge in the real system that may serve both to orient model development and test the hypotheses posed by model structure. For example, successional patterns were used along with canopy gap structure to develop individual based "rules" of tree growth, death, and reproduction in a beech forest while also providing empirical patterns regarding size and distribution that were compared to model output (Rademacher et al. 2004). In addition to serving as validation tools, they may also act as tests of sensitivity (Grimm et al. 2005); in the case of the

BEFORE model by varying the initial stage of the forest to compare with successional trajectories (Rademacher et al. 2004). The logic behind using these approaches is that such patterns, collected at multiple scales and across varying examples of the same system, are essentially ecologically "coded" with the mechanistic information that should go into formulating an individual-based model.

5.4 A Virtual Laboratory

Using this approach to evaluate patterns as a mechanism of both using the model diagnostically and testing its validity, we outline four hypotheses below. It may benefit our ecological readers to understand that oceanography is one of the more common disciplines for the study of *Zostera marina*, and as a geoscience this field more commonly follows a history of descriptive research methods. We are intentionally framing these as hypotheses to reinforce the diagnostic approach, but are the first to acknowledge that these statements do not follow strict experimental design approaches, nor are they intended to embrace statistical frameworks for testing. Instead, we are leaning into hypotheses that clearly state a prediction we can evaluate with the VEM that is linked to a pattern and research question

As discussed extensively in previous chapters, the apparent density-dependence (see Table 3.1) of lateral shoot branching is a relevant pattern for the VEM and which helps to phrase the following hypothesis.

Hypothesis 1 *An increase in eelgrass ramet density will result in a decrease of light resources available to an individual ramet. In response to this changed light availability, leaves will elongate. With this altered resource allocation, production of new nodes will decrease, internodes will be produced less frequently but increase in length, and lateral branching will decrease.*

The canopy height elongation factor in the VEM is dependent on the percent of surface irradiance reaching the leaf of an individual ramet. Light is attenuated twice in the VEM, first by a water column light extinction coefficient and then by the effect of local shoot density and length of leaves, so it is reasonable to predict that elongation of leaves should occur under increased density. Because the length of the leaves serves as the "clock" for production of new nodes and branches, any process that increases the time taken to shed a mature leaf should result in slower node and branch production.

The lagoon mesocosm experiment performed during the summer of 2000 (measuring branching rates and node production of ramets under multiple shoot densities as described in Chap. 3) offers two measurements which might be used to compare with model output. The emphasis of this type of pattern-oriented modeling has so far been to search for qualitative similarities, and in the context of the branching rates displayed in Fig. 4.1 such an exercise would include first looking for an exponential decline of branching rates with increased initial ramet density. Because the programming structure of the VEM links this branching process to the production

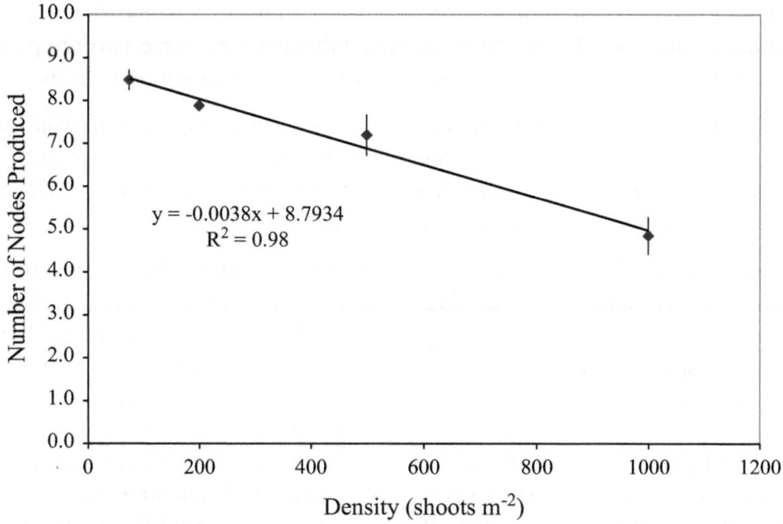

Fig. 5.4 Node production under varying shoot densities. Number of nodes produced over the tagging period used to measure ramet production during the summer of 2000 over 75 days (May–July) under varying shoot densities

of new nodes, a second pattern check may be performed by comparing simulated node production with that measured during the same density experiments. Figure 5.4 displays the number of nodes produced over the course of the mesocosm experiments, indicating that node production declined with increasing shoot density.

While it is fairly intuitive to imagine how Hypothesis 1 is included in the VEM, the relationship between temperature and eelgrass growth is more difficult to understand. The specific growth rate sub-model includes an interactive effect of light availability and temperature on overall production rates as reproduced below.

$$\mu = \frac{\mu_{MAX}\alpha I}{\mu_{MAX} + \alpha I} + loss_0 \tag{2.7}$$

The μ_{MAX}, α, and $loss_0$ terms are all temperature dependent, variable parameters. The loss term becomes more negative with increasing temperature, μ_{MAX} increases linearly and α is related to temperature parabolically (see Fig. 2.2). And of course, the overall rate is still dependent upon the amount of light received by an individual ramet via the Irradiance term (*I*). As related in Chap. 2, the implementation of these relationships in the VEM included limiting the value of the loss term to temperatures used in the Olesen and Sand-Jensen (1993) experiment from which they are taken. This limits the effects that very low and very high temperatures may have on decreasing the specific growth rate.

Adding to the complexity of the temperature effects within the VEM is the plastic partitioning coefficient (β) that allocates more of the growth produced at each timestep to leaves when temperatures are warm, and to roots and rhizomes when temperatures are cool. If growth were only influenced by these two temperature-dependent processes it might be possible to form the following hypothesis.

Hypothesis 2 *Warmer water temperatures will serve to increase specific growth rates and the production of new leaf material, thereby speeding up node and lateral shoot production. Extremely high temperatures may decrease a ramet's SGR, which may be compensated with an increased allocation to leaves.*

However, beyond these effects, node and lateral shoot production are subject to leaf loss rates. Because leaf sloughing is tied to the canopy height dictated by local light and nutrient conditions, a hypothesis describing how production will change under increased nitrogen loading, increased light attenuation, or temperatures in excess of optimal conditions is difficult to articulate. The lagoon mesocosm experiments performed by Bintz et al. (2003) to examine the interactive effects of nutrients and temperature demonstrated that increased water temperatures resulted in a decline in shoot density, shoot biomass, leaf production, branching rates, and above to belowground biomass ratios, the effects of which were amplified by the addition of nutrients. While it is difficult to know whether the VEM will reproduce this pattern, we can include this response as a third hypothesis that can be evaluated to see if relevant characteristics of a nutrient and temperature stressed eelgrass meadow are reproduced in VEM simulations.

Hypothesis 3 *Submitting eelgrass ramets to stressful temperatures will result in overall lower rates of ramet production, lateral branching, and an increased allocation to individual leaf biomass. The enrichment of ramets with nitrogen under high temperatures will enhance these effects by elongating leaves, resulting in decreases to shoot density greater than that predicted by nutrient enrichment alone.*

As for Hypothesis 2, results from the lagoon mesocosm experiments (Bintz 2002; Bintz et al. 2003) can be used to test this hypothesis. It is equally clear from the VEM formulation that the effects programmed to occur under enhanced temperatures and nutrient enrichment may cancel one another in a simulated scenario, as increased allocation to leaves coincides with the elongation of leaf length dictated by the Nutrient elongation factor. It is reasonable to consider that the light conditions induced by manipulation of the temperature and nutrient regimen will become more important to understanding how ramets might respond to such stresses. If water column attenuation in the virtual experiment is increased (as a result of macroalgae or phytoplankton blooms not explicitly modeled), it is even more likely that deleterious effects will occur making specification of the design of testing scenarios especially important.

Finally, one of the takeaways we hope readers who study *Zostera marina* will take from this book is the clonal nature of this plant and the complex life history that arises from considering a ramet perspective. This extends to the role of vegetative versus sexual reproduction. The use of growing degree day as a driver for flowering and seed related processes naturally leads to an opportunity to test the latitudinal patterns laid out by Silberhorn et al. (1983). Both photoperiod and temperature vary with latitude, and with the capacity to change both in the VEM we can evaluate how climate impacts may impact reproduction in *Zostera marina* via initiation of flowering and seed germination. Local climate determines whether these processes proceed in synchronicity to enable persistence of eelgrass meadows at low latitudes, and likewise determine the relative importance of seeds to high latitude meadows.

It is also true that many of the restoration efforts for eelgrass are focused on the use of seeds. Here we can combine questions regarding restoration trajectories in differing climate regimes using seeds with a pattern-oriented approach to testing whether temperature dependence can explain differences in rates of flowering across the latitudinal range where *Zostera marina* is found. The relative success of restoration using seeds may be connected to local temperature conditions.

Hypothesis 4 *Climate simulated across a latitudinal gradient will result in patterns of increasing probability and earlier flowering day in warmer conditions. Seedling biomass will respond to local climate in ways that predict persistence of the ramet over the growing season as a function of photoperiod and temperature conditions, where high latitude seedlings have lower predicted biomass for overwintering.*

In this instance, we can use data from New Hampshire, Virginia, and North Carolina to evaluate these latitudinal gradients accompanied by predictions of warming conditions under climate change. This final hypothesis originally articulated in Foley (2017) creates an opportunity to ask large scale questions about the geographic range of eelgrass and the relative risk at its low latitude range to temperature stress.

The remainder of this chapter will follow these hypotheses using the virtual laboratory of the VEM to design experiments that test each of these research questions. We use the structure of experimental design, results, and interpretation for each of these as a means to present these simulations, and also as a reminder that as in any experiment there are assumptions and limitations related to our findings.

5.5 Hypothesis 1: Self-Thinning

5.5.1 Experimental Design

To test the predictions of decreased branching rates under high eelgrass shoot density outlined by Hypothesis 1, we designed a series of simulation scenarios to reproduce mesocosm experiments performed during the summer of 2000 and previously described in Chap. 4 related to patterns of self-thinning in plants. The primary focus of that experiment was to test predator-prey relationships under varied eelgrass shoot densities as detailed in Harris et al. (2004). Because of this, not all environmental or initial conditions related to the shoots were recorded in detail for this particular experiment. Therefore, the following description of the simulation scenarios designed to test Hypothesis 1 use both details from the 2000 predator-prey experiment and data describing the previous summer's work in the lagoon mesocosms that are available from the doctoral dissertation of Bintz (2002) and a subsequent publication (Bintz et al. 2003). We note here that the predator-prey mesocosm experiment is being used for pattern-oriented validation, and so deploying forcing functions/environmental conditions similar to those experienced by the plants best aligns this virtual experiment. Likewise, we use some details of environmental forcing functions from the Bintz (2002) experiments to realistically portray initial conditions, but are avoiding use of measurements from these studies used to parameterize formulations or design rules in the model which might confound our efforts to validate the model.

In reality, only one half of each of the mesocosms was planted with eelgrass shoots, so the VEM restricted the virtual spatial extent of the plants to a 1.6 by 1.05 m area. The total area of this portion of the mesocosm is 1.68 m^2, a value used to select the initial number of ramets to plant in the virtual mesocosm. While the summer of 2000 experiments used densities of 75, 200, 500, and 1000 shoots m^{-2}, an additional density of 750 ramets m^{-2} was added to the design of the virtual experiments. It was assumed that shoots were planted at regular, even intervals to achieve the desired density, an initial condition reproduced to provide initial locations to the ramets in each virtual replicate run as pictured in Fig. 5.5.

So much of the VEM simulation depends on the canopy height of the plants that calculations of the initial biomass were based on this variable for the simulated ramets. Data collected in the spring of 1999 for an earlier mesocosm study describing the size of transplanted shoots indicate that canopy height ranged over the values reproduced in Fig. 5.6. It is likely that ramets planted in 2000 resembled those used in 1999 as eelgrass shoots were consistently collected at the same location and time to transplant into the lagoon mesocosm experiments for many years. For each mesocosm simulation run, each individual ramet in the VEM is randomly assigned a value between 12.17 and 25.92 cm in length for its initial canopy height. These values encompass a range of lengths within one standard deviation of the mean leaf length measured in the initial transplants. As explained in Chap. 3, each ramet is assumed to have five leaves and biomass is divided between the LEAF BUNDLE and OLDEST LEAF state variables as standardized against size of the canopy height of the plant, a distribution of leaf material pictured in Fig. 3.6. In this way, the selection of the canopy height, converted to dry weight, allows the individual based model to initialize the above ground leaf biomass compartments. Because the ratio of above and below ground biomass measured in the actual mesocosm experiments was approximately 1:1, the initial biomass held in the LEAF BUNDLE and OLDEST LEAF state variables is used to set an equal biomass contained in the GROWING INTERNODE and ROOTS & RHIZOMES state variables. For the purposes of the simulations, three quarters of this combined biomass was place in the ROOTS & RHIZOMES compartment and the remaining amount was used to initialize the GROWING INTERNODE state variable. The initial biomass of the ROOTS & RHIZOMES is also converted to an internode length so that the visualization of the planted mesocosms in the early timesteps includes the existing length of

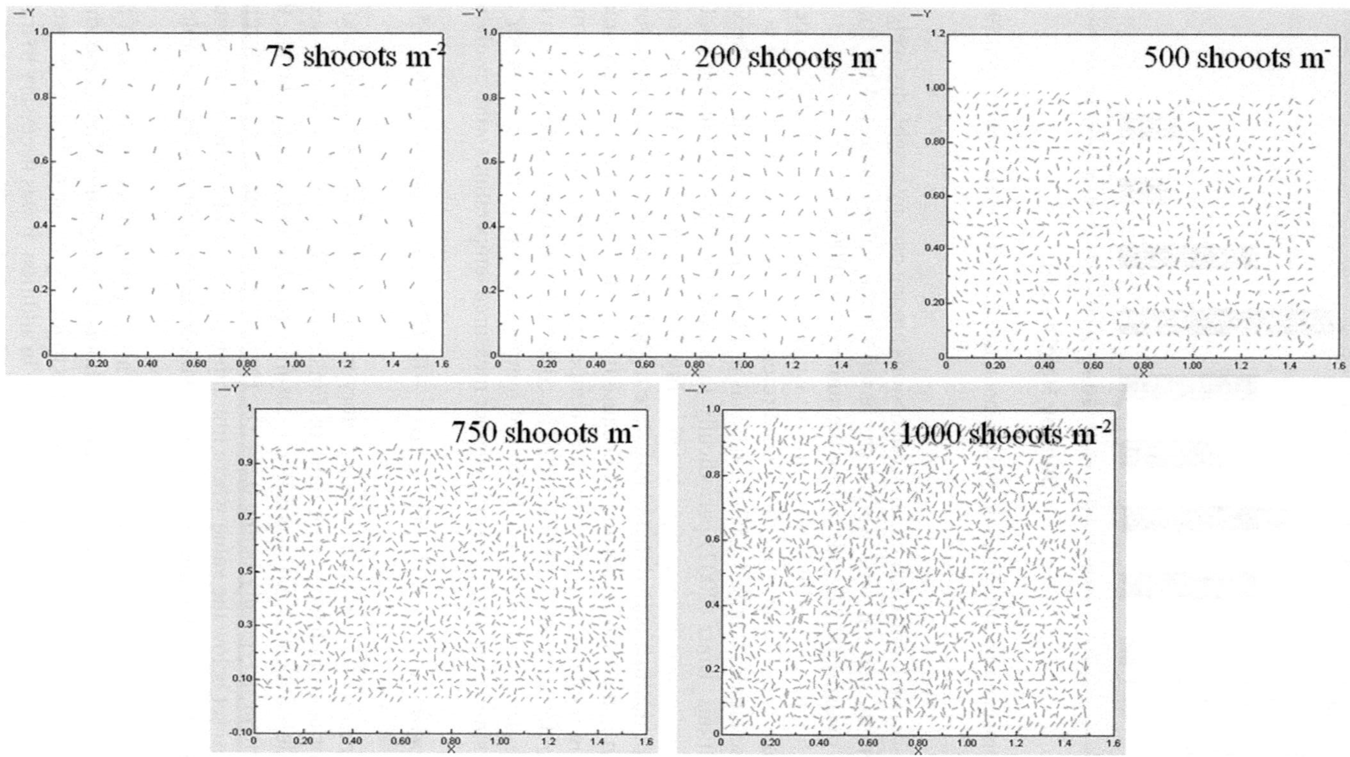

Fig. 5.5 Initial placement of ramets in virtual mesocosms. Locations are regularly spaced but initial direction and size of shoots is randomly selected. All simulations used mesocosm enclosures of 1.6 m by 1.05 m, however the GUI displays vary the scale of the X-Y coordinates without the benefit of user control, so readers will note the varying axes across displays

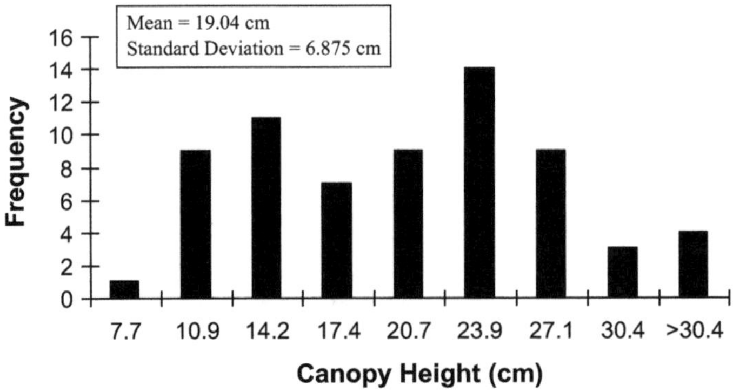

Fig. 5.6 Distribution of initial canopy heights for shoots transplanted to mesocosms in April 1999. (Bintz 2002)

rhizome associated with each ramet. Conversions among canopy height, dry weight, rhizome length, and rhizome weight are based on the values collected by Bintz (2002) and measurements made during the summer of 2000.

Although nutrient loadings were not measured during the actual 2000 experiment, a value is available from the control/reference tanks from 1999 (Bintz et al. 2003). This value of 0.00854 g N m^{-2} d^{-1} was used as a forcing function in the virtual simulations. Bintz (2002) periodically measured the light attenuation coefficient in the reference tanks as reproduced in Fig. 5.7. A mean value of 0.5 m^{-1} over the course of the time period that plants were tagged can be used as a constant forcing function in the VEM experiments because these values varied over a very small range during the tagging period. A daily temperature record is available for most days during the summer of 1999 as reproduced in Fig. 5.8. A quadratic function fitted to these data enabled the prediction of temperature values in the VEM for all days of the simulation, regardless of whether measured temperatures were available.

$$temperature = -0.0015 \times day\,of\ year^2 + 0.6075 \times day\,of\ year - 38.762 \quad (5.1)$$

Light data recorded by the Eppley Laboratory in Newport, RI in 2003 were used to simulate surface irradiance using units of Einsteins PAR m^{-2} d^{-1}. Although sediment sulfide concentrations were not measured in mesocosm experiments, the organic content is typically below 0.5% (B. Buckley pers. comm.), so this forcing function was set below the value where limitation of the specific growth rate would occur. A list of all forcing functions and their values or formulations are available in Table 5.1.

The 2000 experimental data were collected after tagging plants at the start of the manipulations in early May and retrieving shoots in early July. This same time course was followed for the virtual experiments to include a total of 75 days between May 1st and July 11th for each simulation run. In addition, it was necessary to track the appropriate characteristics of the initial population "planted" in the VEM. For a

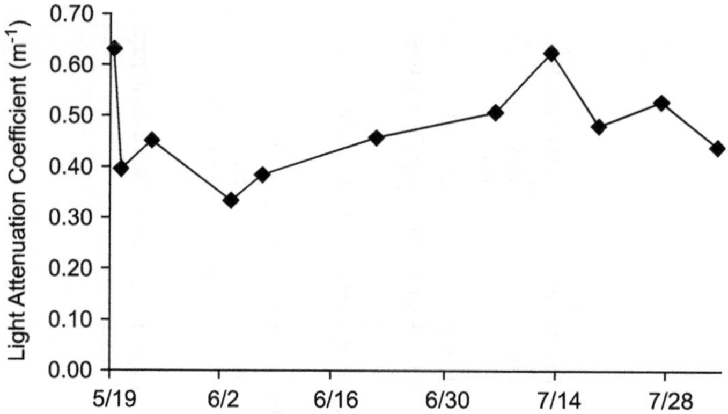

Fig. 5.7 Mean light attenuation coefficients measured between May and July 1999 in control mesocosms. (Bintz 2002)

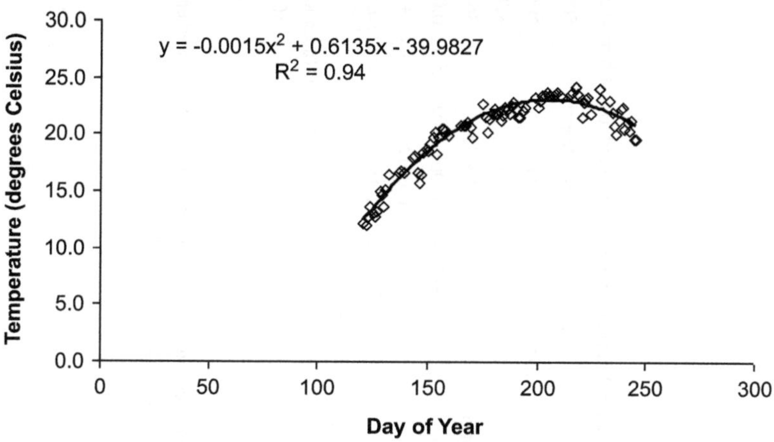

Fig. 5.8 Water temperature measured between May and late July during the summer of 1999 in control mesocosms (Bintz 2002). Quadratic expression used to simulate temperatures in shoot density virtual experiments

typical simulation run, all individuals (including the 2nd or 3rd generation ramets) are tracked using lists holding variables that change at each time step. At this point in time, the Simile software does not allow a user to easily track one individual's traits, instead requiring that an operation limited to the *sum*, *count*, *minimum*, or *maximum* commands be performed on the list holding the entire population. Such commands could be used to calculate a mean and other basic statistics for the entire population, but this would not mimic the tagging that occurred in the actual experiments where only the initial, transplanted shoots were followed.

It is possible to include a conditional submodel that creates a separate list to keep track of an abbreviated selection of variables for the initial "Eve" population of transplanted plants. Using the operators mentioned above, this permits the

Table 5.1 Forcing functions and spatial parameters used in VEM simulations designed to test hypothesis 1

Parameter	75 Ramets	200 Ramets	500 Ramets	750 Ramets	1000 Ramets
Initial Planting Density (ramets m^{-2})	75	200	500	750	1000
Initial Ramet Population	126	330	828	1260	1680
Column & Row Numbers used to define starting location	14 × 9	22 × 15	36 × 23	45 × 28	51 × 33
Space in-between individuals by Column & Row (m)	0.105 × 0.105	0.068 × 0.0625	0.041 × 0.041	0.0333 × 0.0339	0.0291 × 0.0288
Temperature function	$temperature = -0.0015 \times dayofyear^2 + 0.6075 \times dayofyear - 38.762$				
Nutrient Loading	0.00854 g N m^{-2} d *Atmospheric and Narragansett Bay inputs computed by B.Buckley*				
Water Depth	1.1 m				
Light	Solar Photosynthetically Active Radiation measured by Eppley Labs, Newport, RI, 2003				
Sediment Sulfide (μMol/L)	50	50	50	50	50
Initial Canopy Height (cm) *Randomly selected from this range*	12.17–25.92	12.17–25.92	12.17–25.92	12.17–25.92	12.17–25.92

Simulations were performed at the five initial shoot densities indicated by columns below. Simulated environment is a Lagoon Mesocosm. Data used in parameterization from Bintz (2002) and unpublished data from the summer of 2000 calculation of a mean, standard deviation, minimum, and maximum value for several key parameters necessary for a comparison with the actual measurements taken in the summer of 2000, excluding the younger ramets from biasing these calculations. For the virtual mesocosm experiments, these parameters included the number of nodes and leaves produced over the course of the simulation. Similar to the submodel used to allow inheritance of a mother's location by a daughter ramet, an additional submodel was also programmed to determine how many daughter ramets were produced by each "Eve" ramet. The mean and standard deviations calculated from this list could then be used to compare with the actual measured branching rates. Variables virtually "sampled" over the course of a standard mesocosm simulation run using the VEM include branching rates, node production, leaf lengths, leaf-level irradiance, and the total number of shoots in the population. In addition to these simulated statistics, maps of rhizome elongation and branching were produced to provide a visual comparison among density treatments.

Because the initial size of shoots is randomly assigned over the designated canopy height range, and flowering/death events are determined probabilistically, five replicate runs were completed at each of the six simulated densities. Initial debugging simulations indicated that the model runtime was extremely sensitive to search radius values, and this pushed us to vary this parameter to determine if a higher search radius might be a practical solution. The searching radius used by an individual ramet to determine its local density was varied between a distance of 10 cm and 50 cm. With six shoot density levels and five replicate runs at each searching radius, a total of 60 simulations were completed to reproduce the 2000 mesocosm experiment. As an example of the time involved in these simulations, it typically took 28–29 h for one simulation of the 750 shoot density over the 75 timesteps. Technical assistance in debugging the model and cutting down on model run time was provided by Jasper Taylor (Simulistics Ltd.).

5.5.2 *Results*

Examples of final maps of rhizome/ramet locations at the six initial densities used in the virtual experiments are pictured in Fig. 5.9. These maps can be contrasted with the photos reproduced in Fig. 5.10 that were taken in August of 2000 at the mesocosm facility. It is noticeable in Fig. 5.9 that some ramets at the edges of the mesocosm boundary appear to have branched more frequently than other individuals. In fact, these changes in direction are an artifact of a rule that was included to enforce the boundary conditions of the virtual mesocosm walls. If a rhizome grew within 10 cm of a tank "wall" it altered its directional angle by 76°. It does appear that the rhizomes in the lower density simulations are somewhat larger than those produced at the 750 and 1000 shoot density levels. Branching also appears more uniform and less patchy at lower densities.

The light available after attenuation by the water column k value was identical (0.5 m^{-1}) for all ramets, regardless of the starting shoot density. However, the light

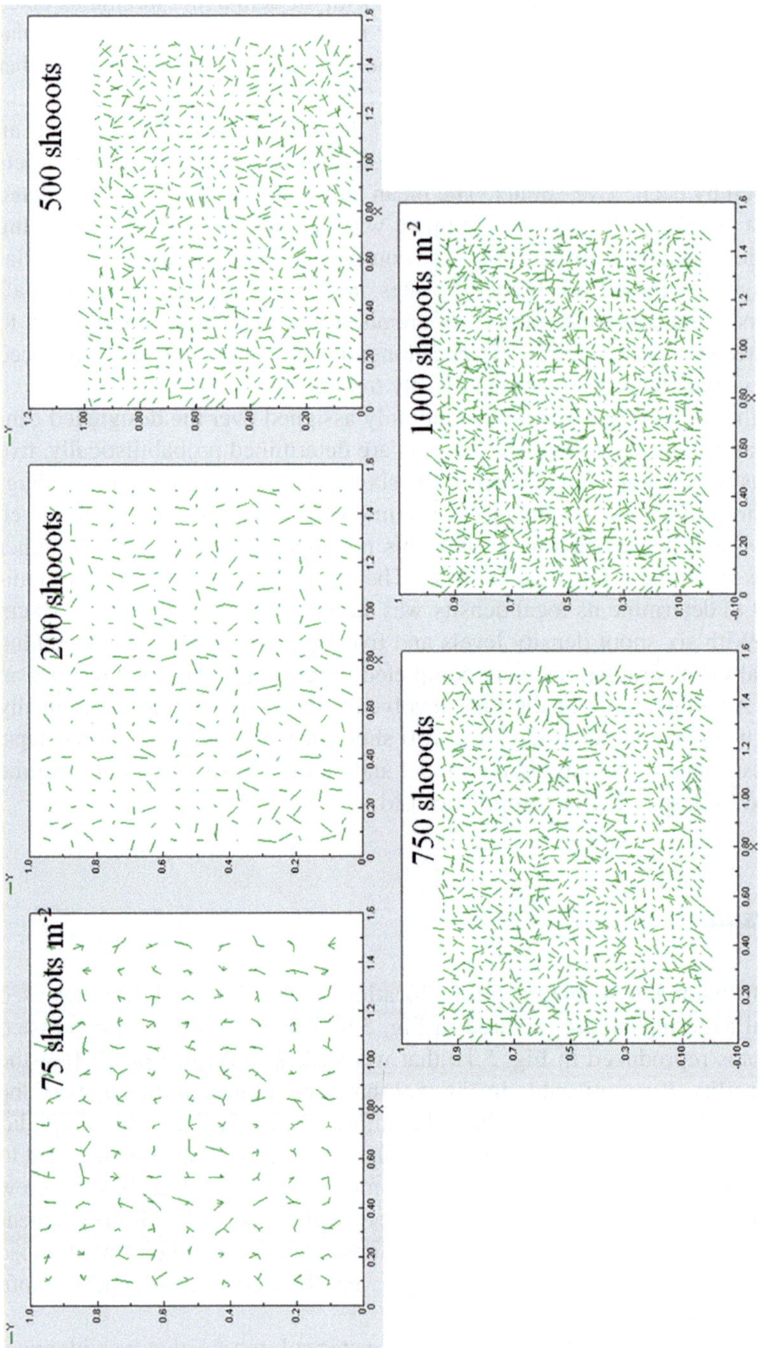

Fig. 5.9 Final maps of rhizome and ramet locations in virtual mesocosms. Shoot densities indicate initial values used to plant virtual tanks as pictured in Fig. 5.5

Fig. 5.10 Photos of mesocosm experiments manipulating shoot densities performed during the summer of 2000

available at the leaf level (Leaf Irradiance) is dependent on leaf length and the local shoot density as detailed in Chaps. 3 and 4. Figure 5.11 displays Irradiance values at the leaf level after attenuation by the water column and neighboring ramets over the time period of each simulation. For many of the timesteps, especially at high solar irradiance values, it appears that more light was available to ramets under the lowest shoot density. Surprisingly, there is little difference among the various densities above 500 shoots m^{-2}. The mean and standard deviation of simulated canopy height is plotted against initial shoot density in Fig. 5.12 for the final timestep of the simulations. It appears that leaves elongated slightly in response to higher shoot densities though leaf lengths were significantly longer in the VEM simulated ramets than those measured during the actual mesocosm experiment.

Finally, it is possible to examine the virtually "sampled" branching rates and node production for the various simulation scenarios. Figure 5.13 compares the mean and standard deviation of the branching rates from the five replicate runs at each searching radius against shoot density. The observed mesocosm data from 2000 are also included on this graph for comparison. Remarkably, not only is there a similar exponential decline in branching with increased shoot density, but the values for these rates are in good agreement with the measurements from the runs using the 10 cm search radius.

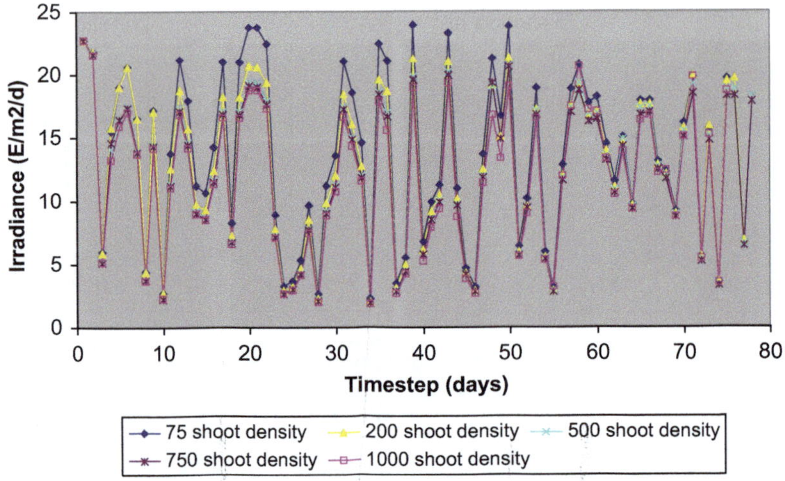

Fig. 5.11 Light available at leaf level of simulated plants after attenuation by water column and surrounding ramets. Results from simulations at five different starting densities are displayed

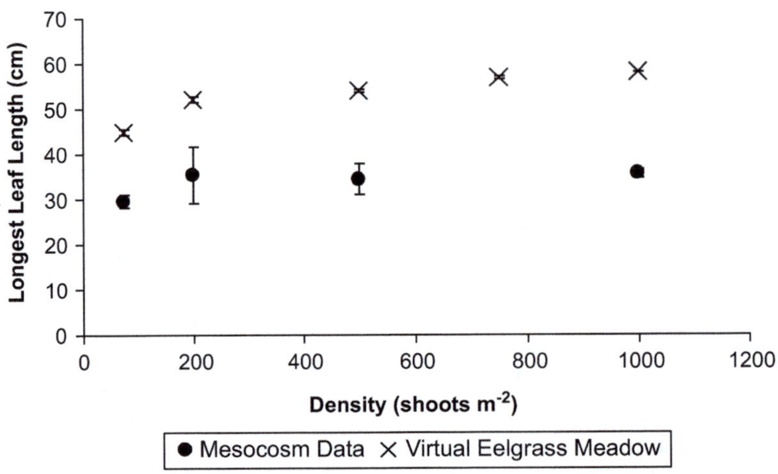

Fig. 5.12 Simulated longest leaf lengths in plants "tagged" for 75 days at six initial shoot densities compared with data measured at five shoot densities in experimental lagoon mesocosms during the summer of 2000. Error bars signify one standard deviation from mean values

The 50 cm searching radius resulted in a branching rate at the 200 shoot density level that is higher than the empirical values and the results of the 10 cm searching radius simulations. The sensitivity of this parameter was the driving rationale for rejecting the linked cell method for computing neighborhood lists with lower memory requirements. It is likely that the boundary conditions of the virtual mesocosm tank walls and the relatively small 1.68 m^2 area they enclose were directly

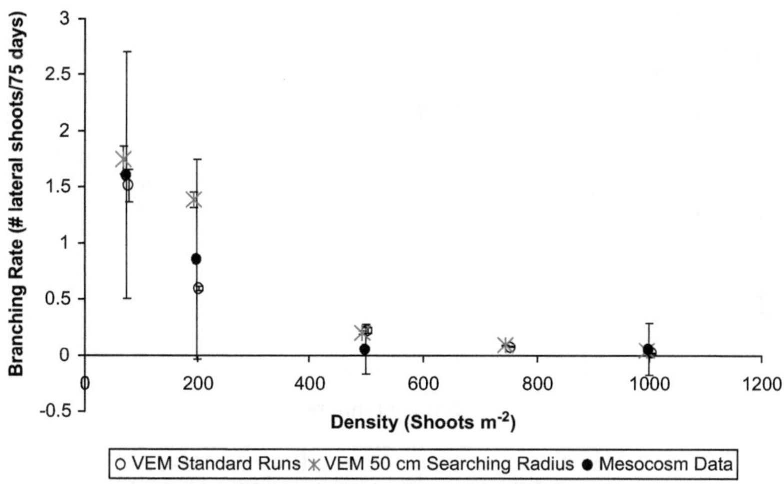

Fig. 5.13 Simulated average branching rates in plants "tagged" for 75 days at five initial shoot densities in comparison with data measured at four shoot densities in experimental lagoon mesocosms during the summer of 2000. Error bars signify one standard deviation from mean values. VEM Standard Runs used a searching radius of 10 cm and were replicated five times to produce mean and standard deviations. Simulated data using a searching radius of 50 cm are also presented. Datapoints are offset for better viewing

responsible for the similar values simulated in the 75 and 200 shoot densities at higher search radius distances. Ramets located at the periphery of the mesocosm tanks will calculate a lower local density simply because the high searching radius accounts for areas beyond the mesocosm walls. A more appropriate searching radius of 10 cm will keep the ramets within the virtual walls and provides a rationale for rejection of the data from the higher searching radius. For this and subsequent mesocosm simulations, the 10 cm radius was used.

Although the agreement between the simulation results and the actual data is encouraging, a further evaluation of node production will help to illuminate whether the mechanisms suspected of creating this pattern are adequately expressed by Hypothesis 1 and the VEM model. Figure 5.14 compares nodes produced over the course of the simulation scenarios with those measured during the summer of 2000. There is a noticeable difference between the simulated values and those measured over the course of the real experiment, with higher node production measured by Bintz (2002) than in the simulations. This discrepancy may be a result of the measurement techniques used during the tagging of the eelgrass shoots. As highlighted by Bintz (2002), cable-tagging of eelgrass rhizomes may not record an emerging, new node during the initial tagging procedure. Upon retrieval of the tagged plants, this "missed" node will be included in the number of new nodes produced during the tagging period, thereby inflating the production estimates by one. This cannot explain all of the differences in our results and likely points to opportunities to further develop the density dependent feedbacks in the model. What is of greater concern than the difference in magnitude of node production between the real and

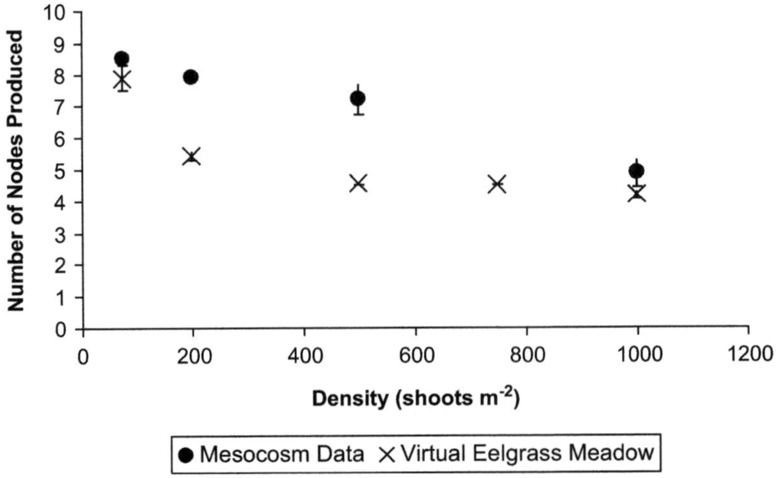

Fig. 5.14 Simulated node production in plants "tagged" for 75 days at five initial shoot densities in comparison with data measured at four shoot densities in experimental lagoon mesocosms during the summer of 2000. Error bars signify one standard deviation from mean values. Five simulations were performed at each of six densities

simulated data is the apparent exponential pattern of node production produced in the VEM, with similar values revealed at the higher shoot densities. This contrasts with the linear pattern of decreased node production with increased shoot density measured during the actual experiment.

5.5.3 *Interpretation*

This formal report of our results in the tradition of the scientific method cannot convey the excitement of realizing an essential goal of the VEM! Encouraging similarities between branching rates in the real and simulated data confirm that a pattern such as density-dependent lateral shoot branching is reproduced using the rules and assumptions of the VEM, most notably the limitation of light availability to individuals under crowded conditions, resulting in comparably low branching rates among the 500, 750, and 1000 shoot density treatments. While some quantitative differences exist among the node and internode production of a virtual ramet versus one tagged and measured in the actual mesocosms, the general pattern of declining node production with increasing shoot density is reproduced by the VEM. This is an encouraging result of our pattern-oriented effort to evaluate this model.

However, several discrepancies do exist between the leaf length and node production output. Because these characteristics are directly linked to the "rules" structure of the VEM it is important to carefully consider the implications of these differences in magnitude and pattern. The Canopy Height relationship with percent surface irradiance (Eq. 3.13, Table 3.1) and the Canopy Elongation Factor were parameterized with the least amount of empirical data and are likely responsible for the difference in predicted leaf lengths. It is still encouraging that the overall pattern of increasing leaf length mimics empirical data, indicating that future studies should attempt to better quantify this relationship between available light and leaf length for improved prediction of this morphological parameter in the VEM.

The node production pattern differences are more troubling and suggest that another mechanism unaccounted for in the VEM may be influencing node production. The most likely candidate for this mechanism is the variable translocation of photosynthate among ramets. Marba et al. (2002) documented extensive translocation in seagrasses and Hutchings (1997) have demonstrated that clonal plants may employ a strategy of "division of labour" to exploit resources in patchy habitats. While the direction of this translocation has not been explicitly studied in seagrasses, it is likely that photosynthate is most commonly translocated toward the rhizome apex from parent ramets. The VEM suggests that diminished branching rates are due to decreased light and growth, but active suppression of branching via hormones as suggested by Sintes et al. (2005) is also possible. Ramets experiencing this type of suppression might have more un-translocated photosynthate available for production of new leaves and nodes. Such a mechanism could explain the higher node production in the mesocosm data, but it is not a feature that can be easily added to the VEM.

The production of lateral shoots in the VEM is triggered by the mother ramet producing 5 nodes to create a space of 4 internodes in-between pairs of lateral branches. Because this feature is tied to node production and leaf shedding, it is constructive to consider how branching rates measured at the various densities were so similar between simulated and empirical data when the underlying node production varied. We propose that the spacing of lateral branches is of paramount importance to a mother ramet and the event-based production of lateral shoots in the VEM is of far greater importance than a slight difference among production rates of nodes. The difference in the number of nodes produced is lower than the 5 node threshold for lateral shoot production, so this also provides a quantitative reason for the difference. However, we may also learn from this relative difference that a minimum spacing exists in-between branches. Such an architectural feature is considered central to the efficient colonization of space by clonal plants (De Kroon and Hutchings 1995; Sintes et al. 2005), enabling connected ramets to use space efficiently without crowding or inhibiting neighbors. Such a programmed (within the VEM and in nature) spacing structure also suggests that "self-thinning" of clonal plants does not occur by mortality as is often assumed, but by a tight control of branching rates and rhizome spacing.

5.6 Hypotheses 2 and 3: Morphological Plasticity

5.6.1 Experimental Design

The predictions that follow from Hypotheses 2 and 3 describe an eelgrass response that depends on the interactive effects of temperature and nutrients. Adjusting the simulation scenarios to evaluate these responses in the VEM can again use the conditions of the lagoon mesocosm facility to satisfy computational limitations, exploit existing programming features already developed to test Hypothesis 1, and follow the pattern of data from actual experiments (Bintz 2002; Bintz et al. 2003). We have retained the structure of the mesocosm area for our simulations to both mimic the conditions experienced by ramets in the validation data and constrain run time of the model. We emphasize that the model can be expanded to a larger area, and offer an example of using this field setting for our next hypotheses.

However, in order to best align pattern-oriented data for model testing, several of the forcing functions and initial conditions must be adjusted to mimic the experimental conditions for the data we have on hand (described by Bintz et al. 2003). Using the ten mesocosm tanks available to them, Bintz et al. (2003) increased the temperature by 4 °C above ambient conditions in four tanks, and decreased the temperature by the same amount in four additional tanks. To examine the interactive effect of temperature and nutrient enrichment, two each of the cooled and warmed treatment tanks were selected to enrich with nitrogen at loading rates of 6.61 mmol N m^{-2} d^{-1}. The remaining two mesocosms were left as control tanks with no manipulation to temperature or nutrients.

Given the 1.6 m^2 encompassed by the mesocosms, an initial population of 580 ramets was used to begin each simulation using the VEM to reproduce the Bintz et al. (2003) starting densities of ~365 shoots m^{-2}. In addition to the ambient temperature curve used to test Hypothesis 1 and described by Fig. 5.8 for the "mean" mesocosm tanks, temperature data recorded over the course of the experiment by Bintz (2002) were used to estimate quadratic equations that predicted temperatures for "warm" and "cool" virtual mesocosm simulations as shown in Fig. 5.15. The nitrogen loading rate was adjusted in the enriched scenarios to the 0.10108 g N m^{-2} d^{-1} added in the actual experiment (enrichment N + ambient N). As for the previous simulations, surface irradiance values measured by the Eppley Laboratory in Newport, RI during the summer of 2003 served as daily light values in the model runs. However, because measurements of light attenuation in the various treatments by Bintz (2002) varied over the tagging periods, weekly measured attenuation values were used to force this variable in the model runs. Figure 5.16 displays these values as measured over the course of the actual experiment, averaged using the two replicate mesocosms for each treatment (Bintz 2002). To avoid gaps in days, a given value was considered representative of the entire week in which it was measured. As with testing of Hypothesis 1, the initial canopy height for each ramet was randomly selected from a range of 12.17 to 25.92 cm, one standard deviation from the mean canopy height measured in transplanted ramets during April of 1999.

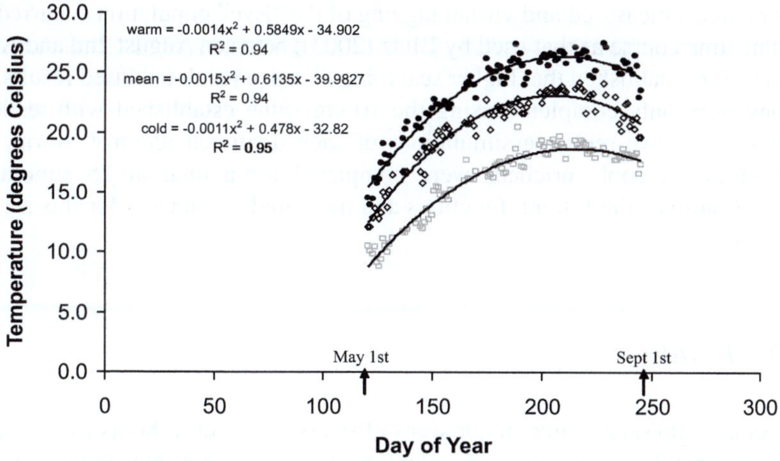

Fig. 5.15 Water temperatures measured in mesocosm experiments designed to manipulate temperature and nutrients in 1999. Quadratic functions listed above were used in the VEM to simulate experimental conditions of warmed, cooled, and mean temperature conditions. (Data from Bintz 2002)

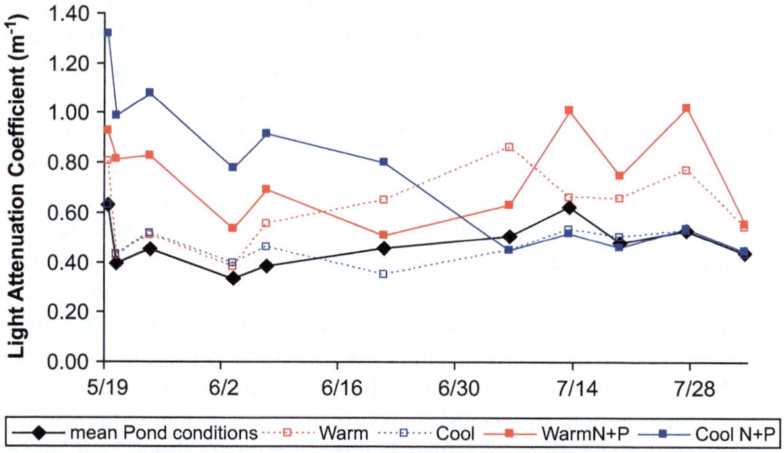

Fig. 5.16 Light attenuation coefficients measured in mesocosm experiments designed to manipulate temperature and nutrients. (Data from Bintz 2002)

Finally, virtual sampling within the VEM simulations was designed to mimic the tagging period used by Bintz et al. (2003) to measure production in the eelgrass shoots during the month of August. This time period documented the most significant response of the plants to experimental manipulations by Bintz et al. (2003). The simulation runs still retained a start date of May 1st, so that initial biomass could be reproduced with virtual ramets exposed to similar conditions. However, the parameters measured and virtual tagging of the "Eve" population occurred over the same time course as that used by Bintz (2003); between August 2nd and August 24th. Having established that higher searching distance result in biased results, simulations were only completed using the 10 cm value established with testing of Hypothesis 1. Five replicate simulations of each treatment (control, warm, cool, warm enriched, cool enriched) were completed for a total of 25 simulations. Table 5.2 outlines the forcing functions and measured parameters for this series of scenarios.

5.6.2 Results

Bintz et al. (2003) cite three major signs of stress in eelgrass shoots in response to the experimental manipulations of water temperature and nutrients in lagoon mesocosms: increased plastochrone intervals, higher above to belowground ratios of plant biomass, and decreased production of lateral shoots. Two of these characteristics of eelgrass growth were documented in the simulations carried out to test Hypotheses 2 and 3. Figure 5.17 displays the number of nodes produced between August 2 and the 24 in the VEM simulations as well as data from Bintz (2002). In general, Bintz et al. (2003) concluded that temperature had a greater effect on branching rates than nutrient enrichment because the cool, enriched mesocosms had comparable rates to those measured in the mean and cool only treatments. Unfortunately, the VEM does not compare favorably with these data. It appears that the VEM creates the opposite conclusion, that nutrient enrichment is more deleterious to branching rates than temperature effects, a result that can be visualized using the final maps of rhizome locations displayed in Fig. 5.18.

A decision was made early in the VEM formulation to limit the effects of temperature on parameters used in Eq. 2.6 to calculate a maximum growth rate (GMAX). Specifically, the loss term is set to a constant value at temperatures above 21 °C, the highest temperature used by Olesen and Sand-Jensen (1993) in the experiments that parameterize the GMAX equation. This assumption limits the effects that temperature may have on ramets experiencing high temperatures. It is clear from Fig. 5.15 that temperatures in both the mean/control treatments and the warm virtual mesocosms exposed to simulations of elevated temperature were above 21 °C for most of the month of August. This artificial control on the specific growth rate is combined with the temperature dependent partitioning coefficient, which continues to increase the percentage of growth devoted to leaves with elevated temperatures as determined by Eq. 3.1 (see Table 3.1). As a consequence, it is understandable that leaves will continue to grow in the model. As the trigger for lateral shoot branching in the VEM, temperatures above the 21 °C threshold do not appear to negatively impact leaf growth in the ramets, especially as over 70% of the total growth determined by the SGR is channeled into the LEAF BUNDLE state variable compartment. This exposes an area for improvement in the VEM, with opportunities to consider

Table 5.2 Forcing functions and spatial parameters used in VEM simulations designed to test hypotheses 2 and 3

Parameter	Mean pond temperature	Cool temperature	Cool temperature + Nutrients	Warm temperature	Warm temperature + Nutrients
Initial planting density (ramets m^{-2})	365	365	365	365	365
Initial ramet population	580	580	580	580	580
Column & Row Numbers used to define starting location	30 × 30	30 × 30	30 × 30	30 × 30	30 × 30
Space in-between individuals by Column & Row (m)	0.05 × 0.05	0.05 × 0.05	0.05 × 0.05	0.05 × 0.05	0.05 × 0.05
Temperature function $temp = a \times dayofyear^2 + b \times dayofyear - c$	$a = -0.0015$ $b = 0.6075$ $c = 38.762$	$a = -0.0011$ $b = 0.4736$ $c = 31.869$	$a = -0.0011$ $b = 0.4736$ $c = 31.869$	$a = -0.0014$ $b = 0.5793$ $c = 33.738$	$a = -0.0014$ $b = 0.5793$ $c = 33.738$
Nutrient Loading (g N m^{-2} d^{-1})	0.00854	0.00854	0.10108	0.00854	0.10108
Water Depth	1.1 m				
Light	Solar Photosynthetically Active Radiation measured by Eppley Labs, Newport, RI, 2003				
Sediment Sulfide (μMol/L)	50	50	50	50	50
Initial canopy height (cm) *Randomly selected from this range*	12.17–25.92	12.17–25.92	12.17–25.92	12.17–25.92	12.17–25.92

Simulations were performed under the temperature and nutrient manipulation conditions listed below. Simulated environment is a Lagoon Mesocosm. Data used in parameterization from Bintz (2002)

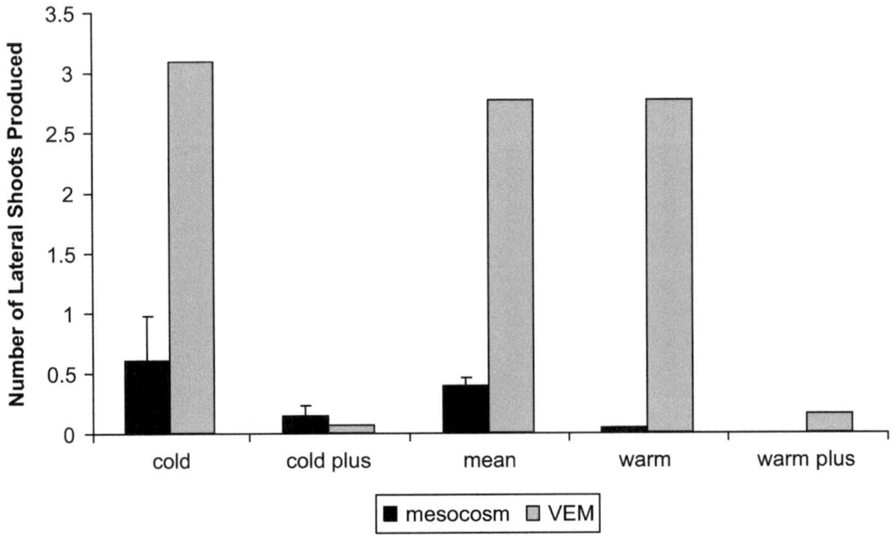

Fig. 5.17 Number of lateral shoots produced between August 2 and August 24 in Lagoon Mesocosm Experiment and VEM simulation manipulating temperature and nutrient conditions. (Data for mesocosms from Bintz 2002)

statistically estimated thresholds reported by Blok et al. (2018) and Berger and Berg (2024) as alternative thresholds.

In contrast, the elongation of leaves due to increased nutrients effectively slows the "clock" used by the VEM to trigger events such as node or lateral shoot production. Figure 5.19 displays the simulated and mesocosm node production rates under the varying temperature and nutrient treatments. Again, the cool and mean mesocosm conditions appear to do an adequate job of reproducing the pattern apparent in the actual dataset when you consider the variability measured in the lagoon mesocosm data, where the number of nodes are highest in the warm treatment and progressively decline in both simulated and observed measurements. The variability of the mesocosm data also overlaps with simulated values. As with results from the testing of Hypothesis 1, the magnitude of the production rates is higher than the actual measurements.

Two other output variables that shed light on the structure of the VEM include the mean internode length of all ramets and the total rhizome length produced by all individuals in the population. Both of these characteristics are reported in Fig. 5.20 and again repeat the pattern of nutrient enrichment having a greater effect on ramets than the manipulation of temperature. For both the cool and warm enriched simulations, the mean internode length of ramets was greater than individuals growing in virtual mesocosms experiencing ambient nutrient loadings. As can be seen in the accompanying graph of total rhizome length produced, this increase in individual internode length did not result in greater overall rhizome elongation of the ramet population. This is likely due to the lower branching rates induced by longer leaf

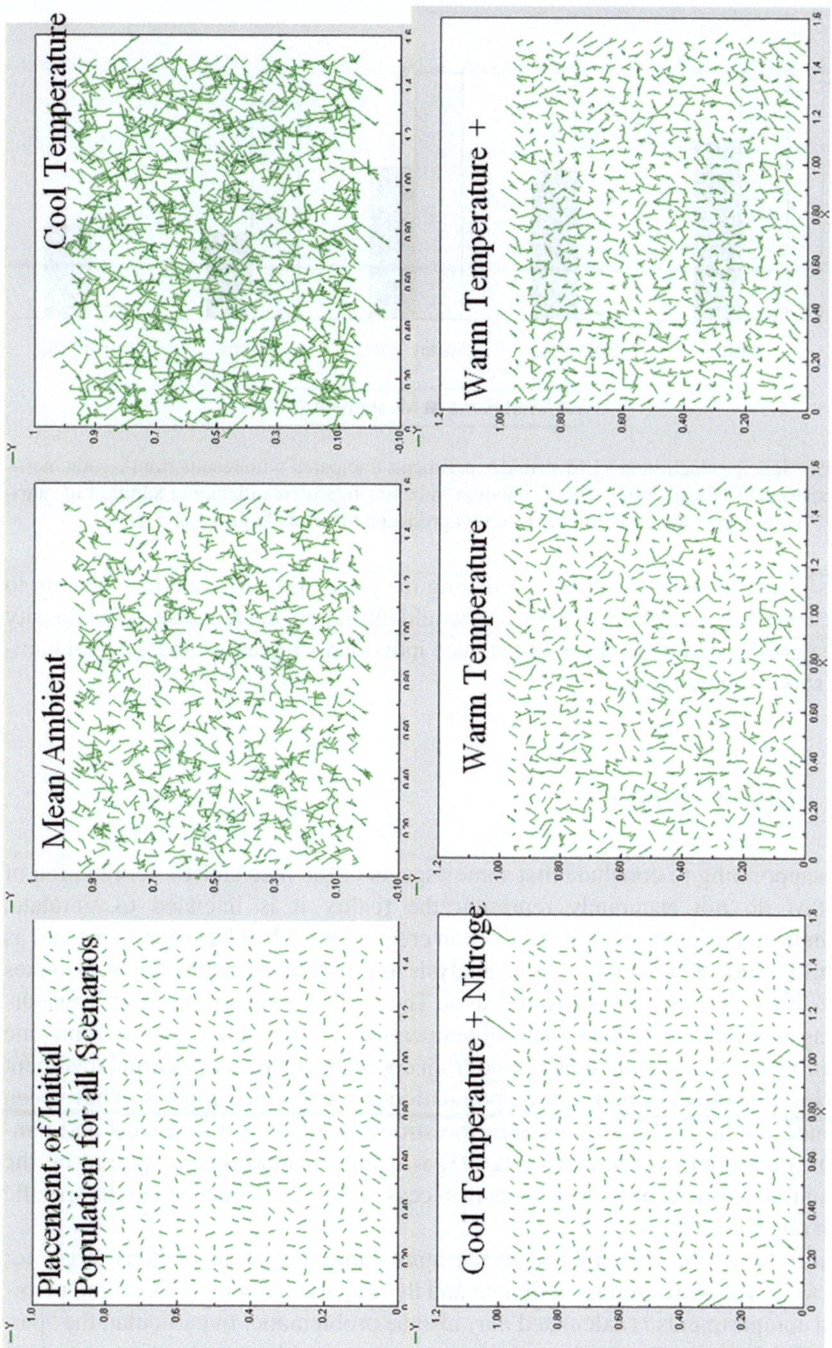

Fig. 5.18 Maps of rhizome locations in virtual mesocosm experiments using the VEM. The first map shows initial placement of population used for all simulations. Other maps display the final location of rhizomes and branching at the final timestep of the simulation (116 days)

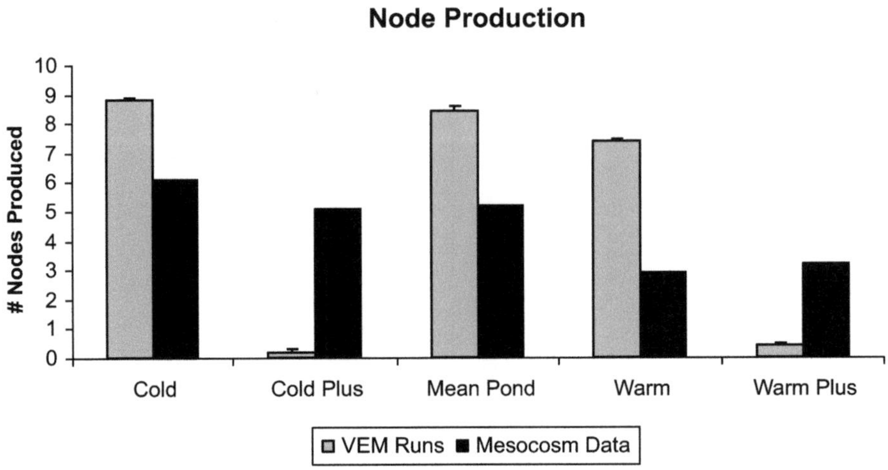

Fig. 5.19 Node production in VEM virtual experiments compared with results from lagoon mesocosm experiment (Bintz 2002). "Plus" notation indicates treatments including addition of nutrients. All values report the total number of nodes produced between August 2 and 24

lengths/internode lengths, thereby reducing the population size and the capacity to produce more rhizomes. Such a process would ultimately decrease the shoot density of an eelgrass meadow as space in-between individuals increases and the total number of shoots remain low.

5.6.3 Interpretation

It is disappointing to conclude that some aspects of the mechanistic formulation of the VEM do not accurately represent the reality it is intended to simulate. Nonetheless, a primary goal of the work in creating the VEM has been to present as straightforward and unambiguous an analysis as possible, including the weaknesses that are inherent to any modeling endeavor. The results of the testing are still encouraging as they indicate that an effect of temperature on branching rates and rhizome elongation can occur; values decreased from cool to mean to warm virtual treatment scenarios. The effect of nutrients on population dynamics also appears to have been accounted for in the VEM. However, the strong interaction of nutrients and temperature measured by Bintz et al. (2003) will not be adequately captured by the VEM until the effects of temperatures in excess of 21 °C are included in the specific growth rate formulation.

While the 21 °C threshold to temperature limitation is an obvious target for future work, the partitioning coefficient and the way that growth in above and below ground compartments is calculated may also be problematic. In particular, the "partitioning" of growth material may be better represented by translocation processes

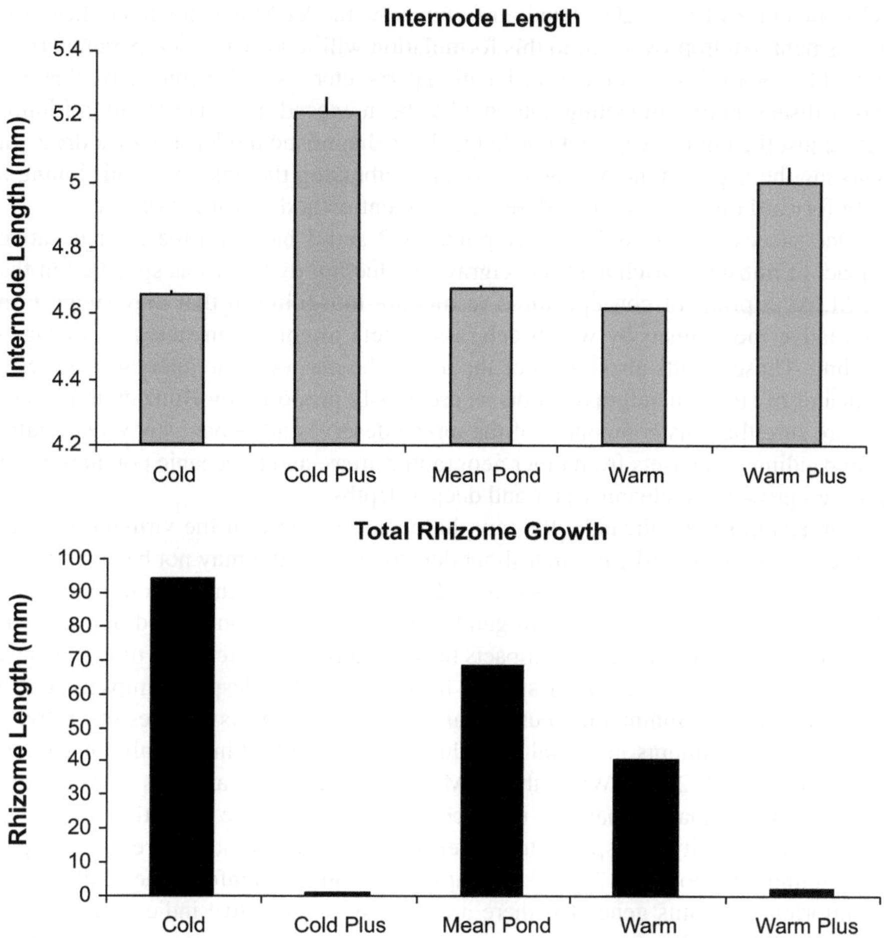

Fig. 5.20 Average internode length and total rhizome growth exhibited by virtual ramets in the VEM under varying temperature and nutrient conditions. "Plus" notation indicates treatments where nutrients were added. Top graph displays mean and standard deviation of internode lengths. Bottom graph displays sum of all internodes produced by the population within a virtual mesocosm

that move materials from below to above ground growth under stressful temperature conditions. Under the current programming structure, a negative specific growth rate is possible but is applied separately to the above and below ground state variables rather than channeling any "negative growth" from the rhizome to the leaf as may occur in the actual plants. As discussed in Chap. 3, economic theory predicts that plants will attempt to minimize structure that represents a "cost" (i.e. respiration of roots and rhizomes), an adaptation which might indicate re-mobilization of sugars from belowground storage into new leaf material until the marginal revenue generated from this storage is equal to the marginal cost (Bloom et al. 1985). Individual based models have frequently been characterized as being "data hungry"

(Grimm and Railsback 2005) and, unfortunately, the VEM appears to confirm this assessment. An improvement to this formulation will require explicit parameterization of below to above ground translocation parameters. We also emphasize that this rather disappointing modeling outcome has been exceedingly successful in illuminating just the kind of gaps in knowledge that a diagnostic model should address. In resisting the urge to tune our model, we are embracing the unknown and shining a light forward on processes that deserve our attention and investigation.

One success of the testing of Hypotheses 2 and 3 has been the clear negative impact of nutrient enrichment on eelgrass production dynamics as specified in the VEM. As a proof of concept, these results are intriguing in that they suggest an alternative mechanism by which eelgrass ramets might be impacted by nitrogen loading. These results also reinforce the use of the plastochrone interval as a useful indicator of stress in eelgrass shoots as previously proposed by Bintz et al. (2003). We are sure that this component of the model deserves additional study, especially in expanding to datasets from other geographic areas, and to oceanic populations of eelgrass growing in clearer water and deeper depths.

Perhaps most significantly, the morphological response of the virtual ramets to nutrient enrichment indicates that shoot density monitoring may not be appropriate for preventative management. A measured decline in shoot density would likely lag the most deleterious effects of nitrogen loading by a significant period of time; leaf growth and rhizome elongation impacts have already occurred by the time a change in density is measurable. Other species have exhibited widespread impacts where shoot density was maintained but overall population impacts as a result of diversions from investments in sexual reproduction still resulted in declining meadows (e.g. Collier et al. 2014). While the VEM doesn't offer clear answers in these contexts, we do emphasize that new research evaluating resource allocation, and morphological plasticity in response to nutrients and high temperatures are a key output of examining Hypotheses 2 and 3. Perhaps these findings reinforce the challenge of monitoring programs generally, there are no easy preventative indicators to apply but these data continue to provide opportunities for post hoc analyses and modeling that can push our understanding forward.

5.7 Hypotheses 4: Climate and Reproductive Phenology

5.7.1 Experimental Design

Model simulations were run in three locations along a latitudinal gradient of the East coast of the United States in support of the masters thesis of co-author Foley (2017). The sites were located at Great Bay, New Hampshire (NH), South Bay, Virginia (VA), and Phillips Island, North Carolina (NC). Frenne et al. (2013) describe using latitudinal gradients as a proxy for climate change: "[latitudinal gradients are] an excellent natural laboratory to investigate the role of temperature and the potential impacts of climate warming". Many studies, including previous eelgrass investigations, have taken this approach as well (Silberhorn et al. 1983; Clausen et al. 2014). Specific simulation sites were selected based on availability of water quality and meteorological data, nearby presence of eelgrass, and location. Model simulations of the VEM were performed to carry out virtual seeding experiments isolating *Z. marina's* response under warming temperatures that would otherwise take years to simulate in field conditions.

Four different temperature simulation scenarios, lasting four years each, were performed at each of the three locations (Foley 2017). The temperature scenarios included one representing ambient water temperatures from 2007 (close in time to data available for pattern comparison) and three under projected water temperatures representative of years 2025, 2050, and 2090. For the total areal biomass simulation results, year 2025 was omitted due to its proximity to year 2007 (ambient conditions). Standard to many simulation models, the VEM benefits from model initiation run up time, and in this context, only 1.5 years of model output is used for interpretive purposes.

The model was forced with data controlling the physical setting (nutrients, water depth, sediment), the light setting (surface PAR, k, Iz) and the temperature setting (Table 5.3) all averaged by day during 2007–2009, with one substitution using 2013 temperature data in South Bay, VA from the Virginia Estuarine and Coastal Observing System (VECOS) due to 2007–2009 missing data. The model simulation sites in NH and NC were forced with water quality and meteorological data from the National Estuarine Research Reserve System (NERRS) System Wide Monitoring Program (SWMP), notably water temperature and surface PAR, which are key model input forcing functions. For Virginia's South Bay site, adjacent NERRS Taskinas Creek surface photosynthetically active radiation (PAR) measurements were used since light data in South Bay were unavailable. Water temperature was recorded in degrees Celsius and averaged by day for model assimilation. For the light setting, 15-min interval PAR measurements were averaged by day using the known daily photoperiod and converted into units of Photosynthetic Photon Flux Density (PPFD) or uMol m^{-2} day^{1}. Light attenuation coefficient (k_d) values were also forced using modeled output from the Lagoon Ecosystem Model (LEM) developed by Brush 2014 and applied in Hog Island Bay, VA.

The projected temperature forcing functions were derived using monthly Chesapeake Bay sea surface temperature (SST) anomalies developed by Victoria Coles as part of the state climate assessment (Boesch 2008). These were then added onto observed temperature data specific to the local sites chosen (Fig. 5.21). The monthly anomalies were averaged over the spatial area of the Chesapeake Bay watershed and reported for years 2025, 2050, and 2090 using the twentieth century data as the baseline. In order to compute the scenario anomalies, Boesch (2008) performed regressions between the IPCC AR4 model surface air temperature and ambient Chesapeake Bay sea surface temperatures. The resulting climate projections were based on 20 of the best performing climate models freely available in the IPCC AR4 archive (Solomon 2007) maintained by the Program for Climate Model Diagnosis and Intercomparison (PCMDI).

Table 5.3 Forcing functions and initial conditions used in hypothesis 4 seeding experiments

	New Hampshire	Virginia	North Carolina
Seeds Initialized in Seed Bank	100	100	100
Seedlings Initialized	0	0	0
Adults Initialized	0	0	0
Initial Density (ramets m^{-2})	24	24	24
Day of Year Initialized	1-Jan	1-Jan	1-Jan
Temperature Forcing Function (°C)	Great Bay, NH NERR	South Bay, VA	Research Creek, NC NERR
Light Forcing Function (source, μMol m^{-2} s^{-1})	Great Bay, NH NERR, Surface PAR	Taskinas Creek, VA, Surface PAR	Research Creek, NC NERR, Surface PAR
K(d) Attenuation Coefficient (m^{-2})	LEM output from Hog Island Bay, VA	LEM output from Hog Island Bay, VA	LEM output from Hog Island Bay, VA
Water Depth (m)	0.8	0.8	0.8
Nutrient Loading (g N m^{-2})	0.00854	0.00854	0.00854
Sediment Sulfide (μMol/L)	50	50	50
Initial Canopy Height (cm)	Seedlings: 4 Adults: 12	Seedlings: 4 Adults: 12	Seedlings: 4 Adults: 12

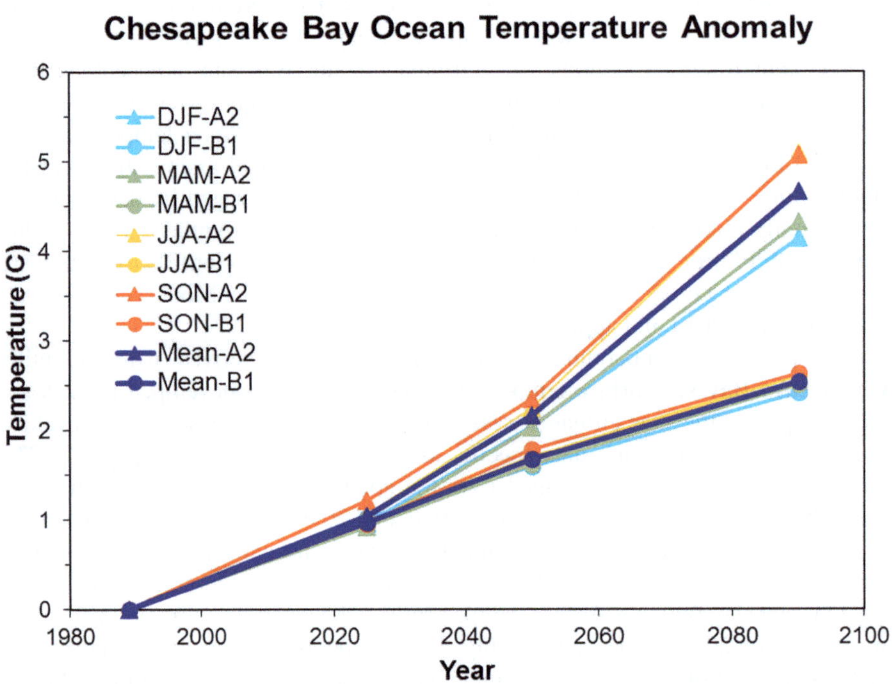

Fig. 5.21 Monthly Chesapeake Bay sea surface temperature (SST) anomalies from 1990 to 2090 (after Boesch 2008)

For application in our model simulation runs, monthly temperature anomalies for 2025, 2050, and 2090 were added to the 2007–2009 ambient water temperature forcing functions to represent the effect that climate change would have on the three simulation sites along the East coast (Boesch 2008) (Fig. 5.22). To maintain consistency across the three sites during the simulations, all other forcing functions and input parameters remained constant. This assumption is open to criticism and improvement.

To carry out the simulations, we chose to set up virtual seeding or restoration experiments by initializing only seeds at the beginning of a four-year period at each of the three locations and over the four temperature regimes (current, 2025, 2050, 2090). with an initial starting seed bank density of 60 seeds m^{-2} (Foley 2017). Seeds, however, were not assigned spatial characteristics in the model. Individuals only obtained spatial coordinates upon successful seed germination, a recruitment process in the model. As one of the model's sexual reproduction rules (Fig. 3.6), 40% of viable seeds in the seed bank germinate. This is within the range of previous restoration projects, namely the work in Virginia's coastal bays (Orth et al. 2006).

Upon germination in the simulations, new seedlings emerged and grew according to the seedling specific growth rate formulation and seedling biomass rules limited and controlled by the model's forcing functions and site parameterization. Once the seedlings amassed four nodes they transitioned to adulthood. The seedlings could also transition to adulthood by flowering when they had amassed 3 nodes and satisfied the conditional flowering probability. Field studies have validated this choice by showing that some seedlings will flower during their first year of growth (Jarvis et al. 2012; Johnson et al. 2017). Once again, the flowering conditional probability is a hybrid mechanistic-stochastic parameter that decides if an individual should flower and is linked to temperature, time of year, number of nodes, and overall probability. As adult individuals, the ramets were then subject to the adult specific growth rate formulation and adult biomass allocation rules. Adulthood also initiated the search radius for determining canopy impacts on light availability.

5.7.2 Results

Reproductive phenology was significantly affected by differing latitudes and changing temperatures across all four climate scenarios, particularly the first flowering day and extent (Fig. 5.23, germination day (Fig. 5.24), seed bank dormancy, and the time when the seedlings transitioned to adulthood (Tables 5.3 and 5.4) (Foley 2017).

In North Carolina, after year 2025, the probability that an individual would flower increased from 50% to 90%. In year 2090 in New Hampshire, plants were flowering 40 days earlier than in 2050. By year 2025 in Virginia an individual's probability of flowering increased from 50% to 90%. By year 2090, flowering was occurring much earlier in the year at all sites, specifically January in North Carolina, April in Virginia, and March in New Hampshire. On average, flowering started 41 days earlier per a 4.5 °C increase in temperature in NH, 2 days earlier per a

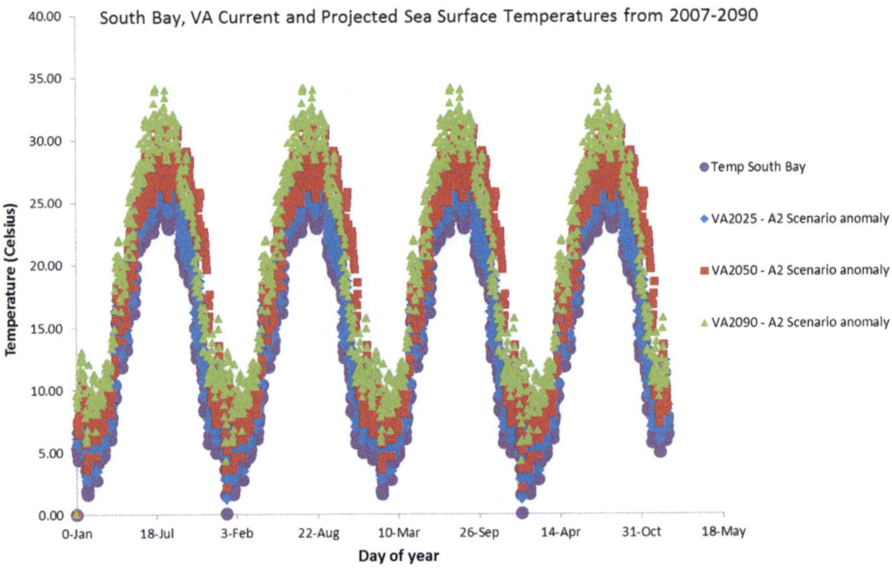

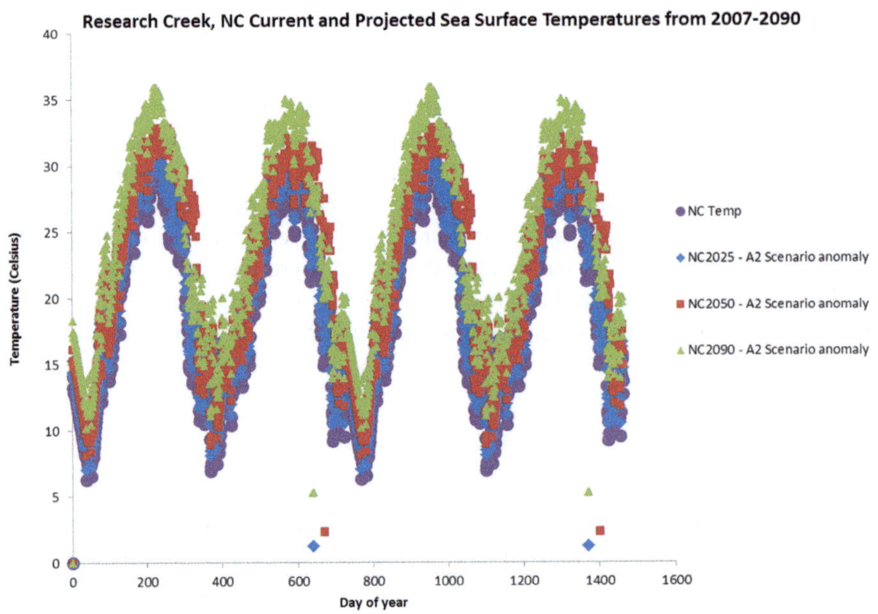

Fig. 5.22 Current and projected temperature forcing functions for use in model climate simulations

4.5 °C increase in temperature in VA, and 71 days earlier per a 4.5 °C increase in temperature in NC.

For seed germination, the largest change at one site was experienced in Virginia between years 2007 and 2050 by occurring 55 days later in the fall with warmer

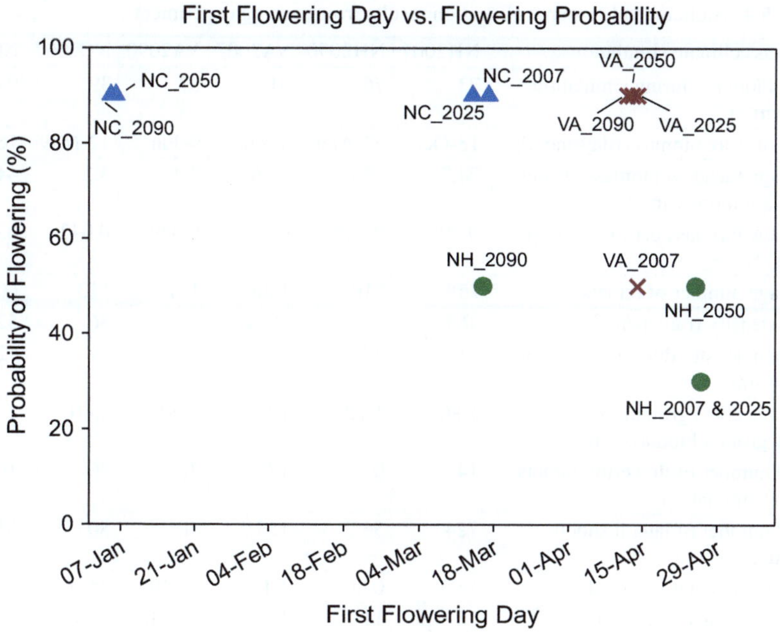

Fig. 5.23 Reproductive phenology results: an individual's probability of flowering versus the first flowering day of the year across the three sites and four temperature scenarios

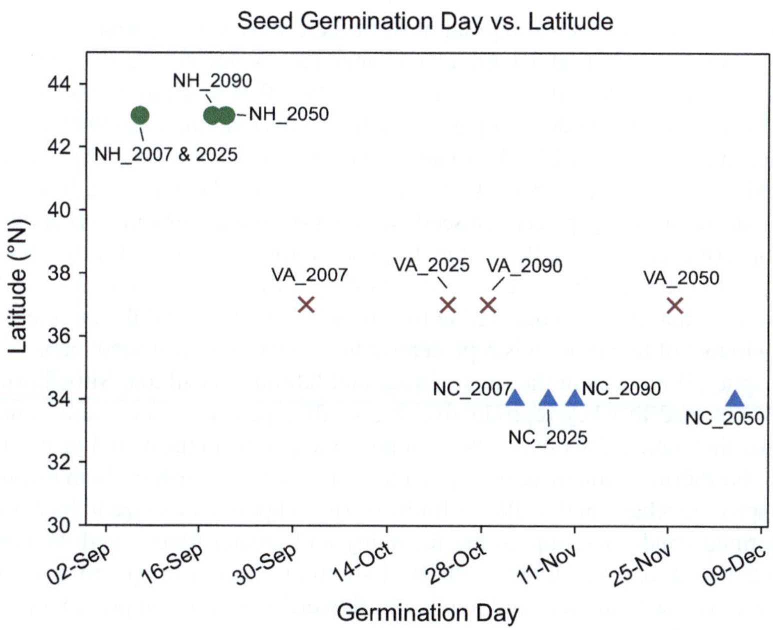

Fig. 5.24 Reproductive phenology results: the effect of latitude on germination day over the model simulations

Table 5.4 Biomass and resource allocation results from seeding experiment

Biomass climate simulations	NH2007	NH2090	VA2007	VA2090	NC2007	NC2090
Peak biomass during simulation (gdw m^{-2})	73	76	316	37	39	94
Date of peak biomass (day-month)	13-Oct	23-Aug	3-Sep	9-Jun	12-May	16-Jun
Average meadow biomass during simulation (gdw/m^{-2})	24.7	15.0	91.6	3.4	5.3	44.4
Average biomass per ramet (gdw $ramet^{-1}$)	0.096	0.048	0.065	0.029	0.047	0.074
Average number of ramets	258	310	1400	117	113	601
Peak density (ramets/m^{-2})	465	358	1854	83	86	523
Median density during simulation (ramets/m^{-2})	71	83	432	83	71	523
Average aboveground to belowground biomass ratio	1.80	1.70	1.80	3.00	2.80	1.10
Total number of flowering ramets during simulation	14	0	17	35	36	108
Total number of lateral shoots produced	724	562	1531	40	80	838
% of ramets that flowered	1.93	0.00	1.11	87.50	45.00	12.89
Date seedlings transitioned to adulthood	16-Apr	11-Apr	13-Feb	17-Mar	19-Feb	15-Feb
Days it took from germination to transition to adulthood	22	207	136	141	111	98

temperatures. It was interesting that most of the differences experienced across the sites, for seed germination in particular, changed across location/latitude then across simulation years within the same site (Fig. 5.24). This was also a case where the year 2050 produced greater changes in model results than the year 2090. For example, germination occurred 76 days later in North Carolina in year 2050 than in New Hampshire in 2050 (Table 5.4). As the seed germination day is pushed further in the year, it decreases the gap between seed germination and the first flowering day. This is a concern because as seeds germinate closer to their flowering day they have less time to grow enough biomass in order to obtain the number of nodes needed to transition to adulthood to be eligible to flower. If the individual then misses out on their window of flowering this represents a loss to the sediment seed bank.

Despite differences in the time of year and latitude, recall that Silberhorn et al. (1983) reported that key reproductive events all appear to occur at the same temperature thresholds. This same phenomenon emerged from the model results (Foley 2017). Furthermore, the results displayed earlier flowering, which is an example of an adaptive mechanism that allows for biomass and population size to increase during optimal conditions, supporting fecundity and greater fitness, and theoretically predicted by Tooke and Battery (2010). Essentially, as flowering shifted earlier in the year, there was an increased number of flowers produced and present during the time of peak flowering.

Another significant finding from the reproductive phenology results was that as temperatures increased across the three sites, the seed bank dormancy time was extended. Seed bank is controlled by the completion of flowering (when the seeds enter the sediment seed bank) and germination (when seeds exit the sediment seed bank). From New Hampshire 2007 and 2090, seed bank dormancy increased by 52 days, for Virginia it increased by 29 days, and in North Carolina it increased by 80 days. This is an important result to consider, especially since *Z. marina* is known to have a short-lived seed viability rate of less than one year. The longer a seed remains in the sediment seed bank, the more at risk it is of losing its viability and being unable to germinate and recruit into the next year's population. The phenomenon of seed mortality is accounted for specifically in Jarvis et al. (2014) sexual reproduction model at a rate of 0.1 d^{-1}. A second concern with an increased seed dormancy period in the sediment is that the seeds are then exposed to predation for a longer period of time. In Jarvis' model, loss of seeds due to predation is captured by a loss rate of 0.33 d^{-1}. However, there has also been work suggesting that the amount of seed predation in eelgrass meadows in the Chesapeake Bay region is not as significant and that seed predation, ultimately, has a limited impact on population recruitment (Manley et al. 2015).

Total areal biomass (gdw m^{-2}) was negatively affected by increasing temperatures in New Hampshire and Virginia with results in North Carolina showing increased total biomass at certain points in the year followed by steep declines (i.e. drastic peaks and valleys) due to stressful temperatures producing negative growth rates and increasing mortality due to flowering (Fig. 5.25 and in Table 5.4).

In the New Hampshire (Fig. 5.25) 2090 simulation, total biomass peaked earlier in the year followed by a steep decline in total biomass and a small recovery due to new germinated seedlings entering the population. By day 800 of the simulation, total biomass in New Hampshire 2090 was 5 times smaller than 2007 levels. After further analyzing the NH 2090 results, it was noted that the individuals should have prematurely died near the end of the run due to sustained negative aboveground biomass values, despite still maintaining positive root biomass. We conclude that mortality of the entire population occurred by late fall.

Results from Virginia (Fig. 5.25) were the most extreme in terms of differences between 2007 and 2090 biomass levels. The 2007 Virginia simulation increased rapidly to nearly 316 gDW m^{-2}. There was a small decline just before the peak in biomass because of mortality due to flowering. Virginia's 2007 total biomass results were the largest and most productive across all simulations. In the Virginia 2090 simulation, all the individuals flowered in the spring and therefore died in early June. No biomass was sustained during the hot summer months in 2090. Eelgrass entered back in the model via seed germination in mid-October where individuals continue to remain seedlings until the end of the simulation.

Results from the simulations of North Carolina conditions (Fig. 5.25) exhibited total average areal biomass that was higher in the 2090 simulation than in the 2007 simulation. In the 2090 scenario, individuals were able to rapidly produce biomass and lateral shoots as the warmer temperatures helped increase the individuals' ability to photosynthesize rapidly. This was followed by a slow decline due to stressful

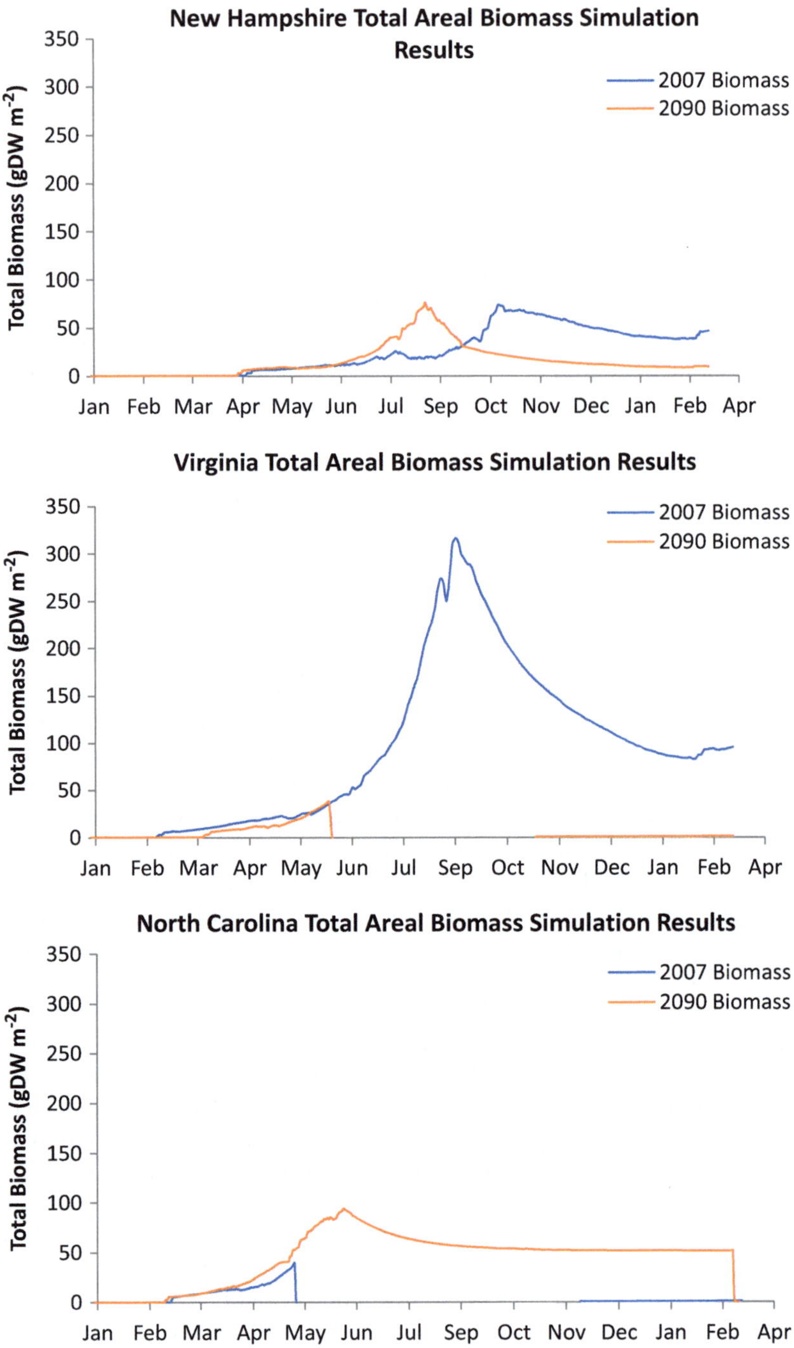

Fig. 5.25 Total areal biomass climate simulation results years 2007 and 2090 (2050 forthcoming)

temperatures, leading to a large meadow die-off as a result of flowering, which occurred very early in the year on January 4.

Looking deeper into the results, the North Carolina 2090 individuals should not have been able to survive to the end of the run due to the very high temperatures reaching 36 °C in the summer and fall months. Additionally, the North Carolina 2090 individuals were not able to flower on their flowering day (January 4) since that day occurred so much earlier in the year and the newly germinated seedlings were not eligible to flower during that earlier time window available. Coupled with mortality due to high temperatures and an inability to supply the sediment seed bank via flowering, the future of eelgrass at the North Carolina site in 2090 seems grim and suggests a narrowing of its biogeographic range. Arnold et al. (2017) suggests equally poor outlooks for temperate seagrasses under warming temperatures.

Other significant biomass characteristics, such as peak densities, number of lateral shoots produced, and average biomass ramet^{-1} were also captured (Table 5.4). The biomass results are within mean reported ranges for observed eelgrass beds (mean 246.2 + −22.6 gdw m^{-2}) and densities (Clausen et al. 2014). The results were also quite similar to those observed and modeled by Jarvis et al. (2014), which included peak total areal biomass results around 100 gdw m^{-2}.

5.7.3 Interpretation

These results imply that with changing and more stressful conditions, we may see *Z. marina* favor sexual reproduction strategies, also known as colonizing characteristics by Kilminister (2015; Fig. 5.26). Colonizing seagrass species are those that invest heavily in sexual reproduction, fluctuate more dramatically and rapidly in year-to-year biomass, and tend to recover from disturbances more quickly (Kilminster et al. 2015). The timing of when seedlings transitioned to adulthood (e.g. length of juvenile development) in the model signifies its overall growing conditions and environment. In North Carolina, all of the seedlings transitioned to adulthood by mid-February while for New Hampshire and Virginia this did not occur until mid-April and March, respectively. In the warming temperatures at lower latitudes individual seedlings transitioned to adulthood in nearly half the time it took individuals in New Hampshire (Table 5.4). Rapid growth and development in the more southern sites was critical in order for the seedlings to develop into adults before passing their earlier flowering window (Foley 2017).

Plant stress signals were evident within the biomass and reproductive results during the four warming temperature experiments throughout the simulations (Foley 2017). These obvious stress signals and characteristics in the results signifying threshold points of death should also prompt improvements in how mortality due to temperature in the model is explicitly represented. At the same time, *Z. marina's* adaptive responses suggests that shifting life history strategies and phenology may allow the species to persist amid some warming, although the stress signals and results as interpreted imply large-scale mortality events by year 2090 and even

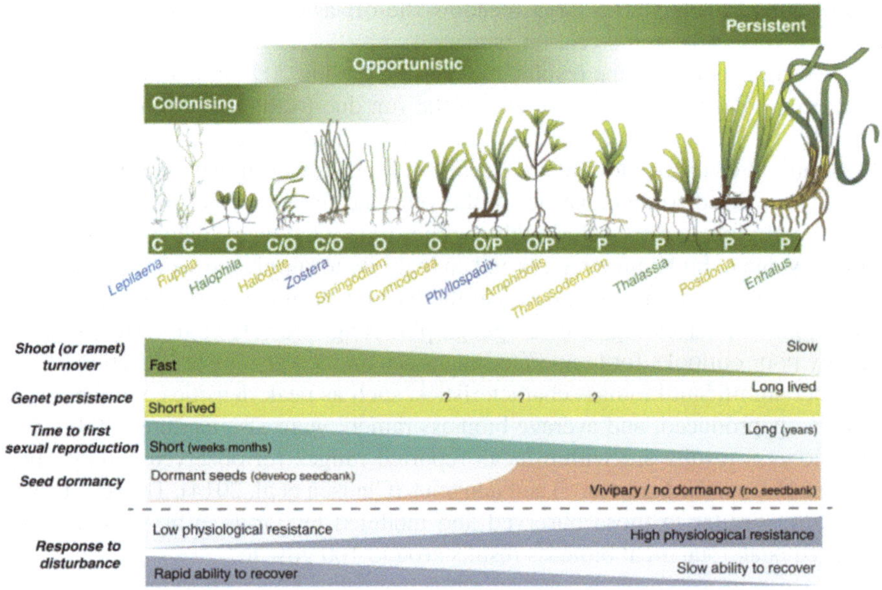

Fig. 5.26 Diagram showing the dominant traits among colonizing (C), opportunistic (O), and persistent seagrass genera with respect to shoot turnover, genet persistence, time to reach sexual maturity and seed dormancy. (Reprinted from Kilminster et al. 2015 with permission from Elsevier)

2050 under the climate forecasts used here. Extremely low levels of ramet biomass are likely indicative of a die-off by year 2090 across all sites. Wilson and Lotze (2019) predict range contraction to New Jersey by 2100, a more optimistic finding than our predictions. However, their statistical models did not consider reproductive phenology which is suggested here as a critical factor contributing to maintenance of meadows as temperatures rise.

5.8 Lessons Learned

An individual based model is by its nature a reductionist exercise that attempts to describe the behavior and "rules" an individual adheres to in its participation within a larger spatial/organizational scale. It is possible that in the Virtual Eelgrass Meadow we have attempted to include too many features of eelgrass growth, physiology, and population dynamics in an attempt to describe the system as fully as possible, a pitfall of IBM's that has been characterized as "naïve realism" by Grimm and Railsback (2013). However, in communicating the efforts and results of this modeling endeavor, the IBM approach seems to demand that the model formulation and programming structure be revealed and exposed to the reader in a frank and straightforward manner, including failures and missteps as well as modeling successes. This openness is not a prerequisite of IBMs or other numerical models, and is often neglected due to limitations of time and space or a modeler's eagerness to report the significant findings of the work. Wyszormirski et al. (1999) proposed that many ecological models result in the "WYWIWYG" effect (What You Want Is What You Get). We are perhaps more hopeful and optimistic. We hope that the ecological modeling community will embrace this diagnostic modeling approach and provide examples to our peer reviewers that do not shy away from the imperfections of these models. Of course, this also asks the community to act openly as reviewers, welcoming in publications that detail the journey of modeling as a powerful tool for identifying promising research areas and gaps (e.g. model weaknesses) to accelerate our knowledge and understanding of species, ecosystems, and ecological processes.

Hopefully, the discussion in Chap. 2 and the results of the hypotheses testing in this chapter have revealed a diverse set of model responses as well as dispelled some of the mystery associated with the modeling process. Even the act of parameterizing model scenarios has been exhaustively described so that readers can see the effort that goes into an attempt to hew as closely as possible to real world conditions. While acknowledging the clear problems in the temperature, nutrient, and mortality formulations and rules of the VEM, we believe there are several lessons learned regarding eelgrass autoecology.

The core of the programming structure of the VEM examines the role of eelgrass ramets in relation to light and space in a subtidal marine environment, and the reproductive phenology results lay out a clear impact of temperature. The clear density-dependent response of branching rates in the testing of Hypothesis 1 is certainly the most exciting result of the VEM model and moves the modeling of self-thinning in plants closer to a mechanistic understanding of this process. The IBM models of mangroves developed by Berger and Hildenbrandt (2000, 2003) overcame significant computational challenges to simply and elegantly model a neighbor-crowding effect among individuals. However, their model did not include forcing functions such as light or mechanistic growth, instead simplifying the neighbor interactions to a series of rules that penalized the chances of survival and reproduction in crowed trees. The success of the VEM in using actual light data and empirically parameterized growth rules, as well as a formulation that explicitly attenuates light in relation to local densities and canopy height, demonstrates that this level of detail can be used in IBMs to permit simulation of plant responses that are comparable in both magnitude and pattern to real data.

The Metabolic Theory of Ecology (MTE) expanded our understanding of how size and metabolic rate are thermodynamically limited. Enquist et al. (1999) demonstrated that the self-thinning law, combined with the relationship between metabolic rate and body size, results in ecosystem metabolism that is independent of plant size as derived below:

$$Density \propto IndividualBodySize^{-3/4}$$
$$IndividualBodySize = b_0 \times e^{-E/KT} \times [R] \times MetabolicRate^{3/4}$$
$$SystemMetabolism = Density \times \overline{IndividualBodySize}$$
$$\therefore SystemMetabolism \propto MetabolicRate^{-3/4} \times MetabolicRate^{3/4} \propto MetabolicRate^{0}$$

$$[\mathrm{R}] = \text{Concentration of Limiting Resources}$$
$$\mathrm{b}_0 = scalingcoefficient$$
$$e^{-E/kT} = BoltzmannCoefficient$$

This finding is in agreement with the thermodynamic perspective of Lotka (1922) who wrote:

> During self organization, system designs develop and prevail which maximize power intake, energy transformation, and those uses that reinforce production…

The Enquist et al. (1999) derivation allows overall ecosystem production rates to be comparable regardless of the size or makeup of the individuals in that system, provided that the same amount of raw materials and resources necessary for metabolism are available. Put another way, the self-thinning law may be a phenomenon in the plant world to maximize the metabolic/production rates permissible under the constraints of limiting resources such as light or nutrients.

While clonal reproduction confers a number of advantages on aquatic plants (Hutchinson 1975; Grace 1993), a self-thinning process that is produced via mortality of connected ramets does not appear to be efficient on an evolutionary time scale. It is much more likely that rhizomatous clonal plants have evolved the capability to calibrate a response to local available resources so that space is occupied effectively with limited crowding and mortality of interconnected neighbors. Oborny et al. (2001) have suggested that rhizome spacing and branching angles are programmed into the architectural constraints of these colonizing plants so that space is occupied efficiently, a concept applied by Sintes et al. (2005, 2006) for seagrasses.

Because the branching angle of seagrasses appears to be such a conservative feature in seagrass species (Marba and Duarte 1998), the VEM proposes that eelgrass ramets exploit the plastic response of leaf length and its impact on internode length to adjust the spacing of ramets, as well as the rate at which new lateral shoots are produced in response to the light resources that are available to an individual. This provides a clear example of how the concentration of limiting resources ([R]) included in the Enquist et al. (1999) model (reproduced above) might work at the individual level in the subtidal environment, while also suggesting that the physical design of eelgrass structures such as leaves and rhizomes are well adapted to respond to a range of environmental conditions. Clearly, with the documented decline of eelgrass habitat worldwide, this range has been exceeded where light availability has declined due to phytoplankton or macroalgae blooms. For the sustainability of an eelgrass population, branching rates and seedling recruitment must balance mortality rates. With the severely depressed branching rates simulated under enriched conditions by the VEM and documented by the work of Bintz et al. (2003), it is reasonable to conclude that eelgrass meadows exposed to these conditions will follow a trajectory that results in loss of habitat.

Our focus on the ramet and its adaptive plasticity in this theoretical context is coupled with the capacity of the VEM to consider population scale processes and use as a practical tool for restoration or predictions of meadow resilience. As the seed and climate simulations from hypothesis 4 testing demonstrated, eelgrass response to increased temperatures will likely lead to a decline in biomass and a shift in the species' reproductive phenology and overall life history strategy as an adaptive mechanism for survival in the face of climate change. Given how increasing water temperatures are expected to play a large role in eelgrass growth and survival (Plaisted et al. 2022), and have already resulted in changes in phenology & life history strategy (Blok et al. 2018), we strongly encourage broader efforts to characterize *both* percent flowering rates and the prevalence of seedlings as a component of monitoring programs.

Certainly, the predictions for eelgrass persistence under 2090 projected water temperatures are grim. However, we also find the results of the virtual seeding experiments encouraging for prospects of restoration using seed in more northern latitudes in the coming several decades. To date, this approach has been largely focused on southern populations, but there may be an opportunity for climate conditions between now and 2050 to capitalize on warming waters to reinforce populations in the mid-Atlantic and New England and even subsidize their losses from climate impacts by increasing seed-derived recruitment. The VEM might offer opportunities to select sites for protection that consider not only water clarity, but ambient temperature conditions.

Finally, the tradition of numerical models in estuarine settings has generally followed an ecosystem approach, where the fluxes of such currencies as carbon or nitrogen are followed through various biogeochemical processes that connect biological states with one another. With the development of the Virtual Eelgrass Meadow, a return to the basics of plant biology and botanical details has been necessary to describe the individual "behavior" of eelgrass ramets. Hopefully, future work with the VEM can overcome some of the computational limits to simulation times as well as problems with the temperature dependence of specific growth rates to allow its use as a valuable tool in our understanding and management of eelgrass resources. In the meantime, we are hopeful that this endeavor has illuminated needed areas of further research and raised the importance of remembering that *Zostera marina* is a clonal plant with complex architecture and life history strategies that have enabled its broad presence around the globe.

5.9 Future Directions and Ramet Rules

When considering next steps for the VEM it is tempting to consider expansion and further detail, or processes to increase the realism of our effort. As in experimental work, modeling is a continuous effort. And, as written in the preface for this book, at some point the perfectionism of our ideals for the work must meet the importance of sharing what progress has occurred! Certainly, the responsible next step is to delve into those areas of the model that did not perform satisfactorily. The question is how to greet that task with motivation and momentum? For those looking to pull the lessons learned of this chapter into your own work, rather than developing a table of failures and successes in the model, we strongly recommend a *table of insights*. We suggest that the impacts of temperature and potential for translocation be prioritized for model improvement, not solely because of poor performance but because the model illuminated these as areas where further information is needed. Additional parameterization efforts in the existing model should include better characterization of the canopy modification rules, the nutrient elongation factor, and optimum temperatures for both seedlings and adults.

With this lens, we can already imagine exciting new prospects for future model development. The work of Berger and Berg (2024) provides tantalizing temperature thresholds from field experiments that can be used to set a separate threshold of 28.6° that might be linked to new rules to shift net growth into negative balance. This might likewise be connected with a separate Growing Degree Days implementation connected with growth that simulates loss under marine heat wave conditions. The phenomenon of translocation via rhizome and resource sharing among mother and daughter ramets has only been briefly investigated in eelgrass (e.g. Marba et al. 2002). However, interest in the rhizosphere has been growing across the plant ecology community, including for seagrasses (Wang et al. 2021; Orth and Heck 2023; Sun et al. 2024). The value of a model like the VEM is that new hypotheses around translocation can be tested and evaluated, and we encourage greater attention to these processes.

Where is the additional potential of this approach? We hope that the community will embrace the VEM alongside other *Zostera marina* individual based models from Sintes (2005) and Salinas and Solana-Arellano (2021). There are certainly the opportunities presented here to use these models diagnostically and in restoration contexts. For those exploring population scale differences in adaptations enabled by our exciting understanding of this species' genome, there is also room to evaluate parameterization of the processes in these models from a genet perspective, perhaps a "Genet Rules" sequel.

Criticism plays an invaluable role in the production of knowledge in our fields. Working across scientific disciplines, which is common to modeling work, can also reveal tensions that may be cultural (Enquist et al. 2024). To an empiricist, models may appear presumptuous and oversimplified. Those focused on large scale patterns may feel frustrated by needed attention to variability and physiological detail. What a lion's den we walk into with this work! Fortunately, there is a joy and intellectual contentment in first charting out a narrative of how we think the world works, followed by the required detail, research, and problem-solving to translate that narrative into a model. What we hope the reader will end with here is an appreciation, recognition, or curiosity for the unique satisfaction of combining creativity with the rigor of mathematical formulations and programmed rules to inform understanding and prediction of our natural world. Onwards!

References

Allen M, Tildesley D (1987) Computer simulation of liquids. Oxford University Press, New York

An L, Grimm V, Sullivan A, Turner II BL, Wang Z, Malleson N, … Tang W (2021) Agent-based complex systems and agent-based modeling

Arnold TM, Zimmerman RC, Engelhardt KA, Stevenson JC (2017) 21st Century climate change and submerged aquatic vegetation in the Chesapeake Bay

Berger AC, Berg P (2024) Eelgrass meadow response to heat stress. I. Temperature threshold for ecosystem production derived from in situ aquatic eddy covariance measurements. Mar Ecol Prog Ser 736:35–46

Berger U, Hildenbrandt H (2000) A new approach to spatially explicit modeling of forest dynamics: spacing, ageing and neighbourhood competition of mangrove trees. Ecol Model 132:287–302

Berger U, Hildenbrandt H (2003) The strength of competition among individual trees and the biomass-density trajectories of the cohort. Plant Ecol 167:89–96

Bintz JC (2002) The ecology and morphology of eelgrass (*Zostera marina* L.) and its associated macrophyte community in relation to environmental variables. Ph.D dissertation. University of Rhode Island

Bintz JC, Nixon SW, Buckley BA, Granger SL (2003) Impacts of temperature and nutrients on coastal lagoon plant communities. Estuaries 26:765–776

Blok SE, Olesen B, Krause-Jensen D (2018) Life history events of eelgrass Zostera marina L. populations across gradients of latitude and temperature. Mar Ecol Prog Ser 590:79–93

Bloom AJ, Chapin FS, Mooney HA (1985) Resource limitation in plants—an economic analogy. Annu Rev Ecol Syst 16:363–392

Bocci M, Coffaro G, Bendoricchio G (1997) Modelling biomass and nutrient dynamics in eelgrass (*Zostera marina* L.): applications to the Lagoon of Venice (Italy) and Oresund (Denmark). Ecol Model 102:67–80

Boesch DF (2008) Comprehensive Assessment of Climate Change Impacts in Maryland. Report to the Maryland Commission on Climate Change. Scientific and Technical Working Group

Canham CD, Cole JJ, Lauenroth WK (2003) Models in ecosystem science. Princeton University Press, Princeton

Casement R (1984) Man suddenly sees to the edge of the universe. Open Court Publishing Company

Cerco CF, Moore K (2001) System-wide submerged aquatic vegetation model for Chesapeake Bay. Estuaries 24:522–534

Clausen KK, Krause-Jensen D, Olesen B, Marba N (2014) Seasonality of eelgrass biomass across gradients in temperature and latitude. Mar Ecol Prog Ser 506:71–85

Collier CJ, Villacorta-Rath C, van Dijk KJ, Takahashi M, Waycott M (2014) Seagrass proliferation precedes mortality during hypo-salinity events: a stress-induced morphometric response. PLoS One 9(4):e94014

de Frenne P, Graae BJ, Rodríguez-Sánchez F, Kolb A, Chabrerie O, Decocq G, De Kort H, De Schrijver A, Diekmann M, Eriksson O, Gruwez R, Hermy M, Lenoir J, Plue J, Coomes DA, Verheyen K (2013) Latitudinal gradients as natural laboratories to infer species' responses to temperature. J Ecol 101:784–795. https://doi.org/10.1111/1365-2745.12074

De Kroon H, Hutchings MJ (1995) Morphological plasticity in clonal plants: the foraging concept reconsidered. J Ecol 83:143–152

Duarte CM, Conley DJ, Carstensen J, Sánchez-Camacho M (2009) Return to Neverland: shifting baselines affect eutrophication restoration targets. Estuar Coasts 32(1):29–36

Duplisea DE (2000) The ecological hierarchy, model complexity, predictive ability and robust management. In: Report on the young scientists conference on marine ecosystem perspectives. ICES Cooperative Research Report No. 240. International Council

Enquist BJ, West GB, Charnov EL, Brown JH (1999) Allometric scaling of production and life-history variation in vascular plants. Nature 401:907–911

Enquist BJ, Kempes CP, West GB (2024) Developing a predictive science of the biosphere requires the integration of scientific cultures. Proc Natl Acad Sci 121(19):e2209196121

Foley JL (2017) Using an individual based model to evaluate the effects of climate change on the reproductive phenology of eelgrass (Zostera marina L.) along a Latitudinal Gradient. Master's thesis, University of Maryland, College Park

Fulton EA, Smith ADM, Johnson CR (2003) Effect of complexity on marine ecosystem models. Mar Ecol Prog Ser 253:1–16

Gallagher CA, Chudzinska M, Larsen-Gray A, Pollock CJ, Sells SN, White PJ, Berger U (2021) From theory to practice in pattern-oriented modelling: Identifying and using empirical patterns in predictive models. Biol Rev 96(5):1868–1888

Ganju NK, Brush MJ, Rashleigh B, Aretxabaleta AL, Del Barrio P, Grear JS, Harris LA, Lake SJ, McCardell G, O'Donnell J, Ralston DK (2016) Progress and challenges in coupled hydrodynamic-ecological estuarine modeling. Estuar Coasts 39(2):311–332

Grace JB (1993) The adaptive significance of clonal reproduction in angiosperms: an aquatic perspective. Aquat Bot 44:159–180

Grimm V (1999) Ten years of individual-based modelling in ecology: what have we learned, and what could we learn in the future? Ecol Model 115:129–148

Grimm V, Railsback SF (2005) Individual-based modeling and ecology. Princeton University Press, Princeton

Grimm V, Railsback SF (2013) Individual-based modeling and ecology. Princeton University Press

Grimm V, Frank, Jeltsch F, Brandl R, Uchmanski J, Wissel C (1996) Pattern-oriented modelling in population ecology. Sci Total Environ 183:151–166

Grimm V, Revilla E, Berger U, Jeltsch F, Mooij WM, Railsback SF, Thulke HH, Weiner J, Wiegand T, DeAngelis DL (2005) Pattern-oriented modeling of agent-based complex systems: lessons from ecology. Science 310:987–991

Hamby DM (1994) A review of techniques for parameter sensitivity analysis of environmental models. Environ Monit Assess 32:135–154

Harris LA, Buckley B, Nixon SW, Allen BT (2004) Experimental studies of predation by bluefish *Pomatomus saltatrix* in varying densities of seagrass and macroalgae. Mar Ecol Prog Ser 281:233–239

Harris LA, Duarte CM, Nixon SW (2006) Allometric laws and prediction in estuarine and coastal ecology. Estuar Coasts 29:340–344

Harte J (2002) Toward a synthesis of the Newtonian and Darwinian worldviews. Phys Today 55:29–35

Hutchings MJ (1997) Resource allocation patterns in clonal herbs and their consequences for growth. In: Grace J, Bazzaz FA (eds) Plant resource allocation. Academic, Oxford

Hutchinson GE (1975) A treatise on limnology volume III: limnological botany. Wiley, New York

Jarvis JC, Moore KA, Kenworthy WJ (2012) Characterization and ecological implication of eelgrass life history strategies near the species' southern limit in the western North Atlantic. Mar Ecol Prog Ser 444:43–56. https://doi.org/10.3354/meps09428

Jarvis JC, Brush MJ, Moore KA (2014) Modeling loss and recovery of Zostera marina beds in the Chesapeake Bay: the role of seedlings and seed-bank viability. Aquat Bot 113:32–45

Johnson AJ, Moore KA, Orth RJ (2017) The influence of resource availability on flowering intensity in Zostera marina (L.). J Exp Mar Biol Ecol 490:13–22

Kilminster K, McMahon K, Waycott M, Kendrick GA, Scanes P, McKenzie L et al (2015) Unravelling complexity in seagrass systems for management: Australia as a microcosm. Sci Total Environ 534:97–109. https://doi.org/10.1016/j.scitotenv.2015.04.061

Kremer JN, Nixon SW (1978) A coastal marine ecosystem: simulation and analysis. Springer, New York

Levin SA (1992) The problem of pattern and scale in ecology. Ecology 73:1943–1967

Lotka AJ (1922) Contribution to the energetics of evolution. Proc Natl Acad Sci 8:147–150

Manley SR, Orth RJ, Ruiz-Montoya L (2015) Roles of dispersal and predation in determining seedling recruitment patterns in a foundational marine angiosperm. Mar Ecol Prog Ser 533:109–120

Marba N, Duarte CM (1998) Rhizome elongation and seagrass clonal growth. Mar Ecol Prog Ser 174:269–280

Marba N, Hemminga MA, Mateo MA, Duarte CM, Mass YEM, Terrados J, Gacia E (2002) Carbon and nitrogen translocation between seagrass ramets. Mar Ecol Prog Ser 226:287–300

Moloney KA (1993) Determining process through pattern: reality or fantasy? In: Levin SA, Powell T, Steele J (eds) Patch dynamics. Lecture notes in biomathematics. Springer, New York

Nixon SW (2009) Eutrophication and the macroscope. Hydrobiologia 629(1):5–19

Oborny B, Czaran T, Kun A (2001) Exploration and exploitation of resource patches by clonal growth: a spatial model on the effect of transport between modules. Ecol Model 141:151–169

Olesen B, Sand-Jensen K (1993) Seasonal acclimatization of eelgrass *Zostera marina* growth to light. Mar Ecol Prog Ser 94:91–99

Orth RJ, Heck KL Jr (2023) The dynamics of seagrass ecosystems: history, past accomplishments, and future prospects. Estuar Coasts 46(7):1653–1676

Orth RJ, Luckenbach ML, Marion SR, Moore KA, Wilcox DJ (2006) Seagrass recovery in the Delmarva coastal bays, USA. Aquat Bot 84(1):26–36

Petty MD (2018) Modeling and validation challenges for complex systems. In: Engineering emergence. CRC Press, pp 199–216

Plaisted HK, Shields EC, Novak AB, Peck CP, Schenck F, Carr J, Duffy PA, Evans NT, Fox SE, Heck SM, Hudson R (2022) Influence of rising water temperature on the temperate seagrass species eelgrass (Zostera marina L.) in the Northeast USA. Front Mar Sci 9:920699

Rademacher C, Neuert C, Grundmann V, Wissel C, Grimm V (2004) Reconstructing spatiotemporal dynamics of Central European natural beech forests: the rule-based forest model BEFORE. For Ecol Manag 194:349–368

Railsback SF, Harvey BC (2002) Comparison of salmonid habitat selection objectives in an individual-based model. Ecology 83:1817–1830

Salinas H, Solana-Arellano E (2021) Importance of elongation and organogenesis on the rhizome length of Zostera marina in an individual-based simulation model. Estuar Coast Shelf Sci 261:107530

Silberhorn GM, Orth RJ, Moore KA (1983) Anthesis and seed production in Zostera marina L. (eelgrass) from the chesepeak by. Aquat Bot 15(2):133–144

Sintes T, Marba N, Duarte CM, Kendrick GA (2005) Nonlinear processes in seagrass colonization explained by simple clonal growth rules. Oikos 108:165–175

Sintes T, Marba N, Duarte CM (2006) Modeling nonlinear seagrass clonal growth: assessing the efficiency of space occupation across the seagrass flora. Estuar Coasts 29:72–80

Solomon S (ed) (2007) Climate change 2007-the physical science basis: working group I contribution to the fourth assessment report of the IPCC, vol 4. Cambridge University Press

Starfield AM, Smith KA, Bleloch AL (1994) How to model it: problem solving for the computer age. Burgess International Group Inc., Edina

Sun H, Liu X, Wang T, Liu S, Zhang R, Guo X, Yu Z, Zhao Y, Shen P, Zhang Y (2024) Rhizosphere microbiomes are closely linked to seagrass species: a comparative study of three coastal seagrasses. Appl Environ Microbiol 90(12):e01754–e01724

Testa JM, Kemp WM, Harris LA, Woodland RJ, Boynton WR (2017) Challenges and directions for the advancement of estuarine ecosystem science. Ecosystems 20(1):14–22

Tooke F, Battey NH (2010) Temperate flowering phenology. J Exp Bot 61(11):2853–2862

Verhagen JHG, Nienhuis NP (1983) A simulation model of production, seasonal changes in biomass and distribution of eelgrass (*Zostera marina*) in Lake Grevelingen. Mar Ecol Prog Ser 10:187–195

Wang L, English MK, Tomas F, Mueller RS (2021) Recovery and community succession of the Zostera marina rhizobiome after transplantation. Appl Environ Microbiol 87(3):e02326–e02320

Wiegand T, Jeltsch F, Hanski I, Grimm V (2003) Using pattern-oriented modeling for revealing hidden information: a key for reconciling ecological theory and application. Oikos 100:209–222

Wilson KL, Lotze HK (2019) Climate change projections reveal range shifts of eelgrass Zostera marina in the Northwest Atlantic. Mar Ecol Prog Ser 620:47–62

Wolfram S (2002) A new kind of science. Wolfram Media Inc., Champaign

Wyszomirski T, Wyszomirska I, Jarzyna I (1999) Simple mechanisms of size distribution dynamics in crowded and uncrowded virtual monocultures. Ecol Model 115:253–273

MIX
Papier aus verantwortungsvollen Quellen
Paper from responsible sources
FSC® C105338

If you have any concerns about our products,
you can contact us on
ProductSafety@springernature.com

In case Publisher is established outside the EU,
the EU authorized representative is:
Springer Nature Customer Service Center GmbH
Europaplatz 3, 69115 Heidelberg, Germany

Printed by Libri Plureos GmbH
in Hamburg, Germany